Law for
Northern Ireland
Social Workers

Edited by

CIARAN WHITE

GILL & MACMILLAN

Published in Ireland by
Gill & Macmillan Ltd
Goldenbridge
Dublin 8
with associated companies throughout the world

© Brian Collins, Brice Dickson, Angela Hegarty, Adrian McCullough,
Dympna Mallon, Patricia Maxwell, Kenny Mullan,
Michael Potter, Ciaran White 1995

0 7171 2239 5

Index compiled by June Stein
Print origination by Carrigboy Typesetting Services
Printed in Ireland by ColourBooks Ltd, Dublin

All rights reserved. No part of this publication may be copied,
reproduced or transmitted in any form or by any means
without permission of the publishers.

1 3 5 4 2

EDITOR'S DEDICATION

For my mother and father.
Do mo mháthair agus m' athair.

ACKNOWLEDGMENT

Crown copyright is reproduced with the permission of the Controller of HMSO.

LIST OF CONTRIBUTORS

Unless otherwise stated the contributors are lecturers in law at the University of Ulster.

BRIAN COLLINS, LL.B., LL.M. (QUB), barrister.

BRICE DICKSON, Professor, B.A., B.C.L. (Oxon), B.L.

ANGELA HEGARTY, LL.B., LL.M. (QUB), solicitor.

DYMPNA MALLON, LL.B. (QUB), is part-time lecturer in law at the East Tyrone College of Further Education and the University of Ulster.

PATRICIA MAXWELL, LL.B. (Bristol), LL.M. (QUB), Cert. Ed.

KENNY MULLAN, B.A. (Dublin), LL.M. (Toronto), solicitor.

ADRIAN MCCULLOUGH, LL.B. (QUB), B.L., is part-time Chairman of the Social Security Appeal Tribunals, the Medical Appeal Tribunals, the Disability Appeal Tribunals and the Industrial Tribunals.

MICHAEL POTTER, LL.B., LL.M. (QUB), is a barrister currently practising with the Law Centre (NI).

CIARAN WHITE, B.C.L. (NUI), LL.M. (QUB).

CONTENTS

Acknowledgment
List of Contributors
Preface   xvii
Table of Cases   xix
Table of Statutes   xxi
Table of Statutory Instruments   xxv

Part 1: The Social Worker and the Legal System   1

1 Introduction to the Legal System   3
Brice Dickson

1.1 Introduction   3
1.2 How Laws Are Made for Northern Ireland   3
    1.2.1 Primary Legislation   4
    1.2.2 How to Consult Primary Legislation   5
    1.2.3 Secondary Legislation   6
    1.2.4 How to Consult Secondary Legislation   8
    1.2.5 Semi-official Documents   8
    1.2.6 Judge-made Law   8
    1.2.7 The Rules of Precedent   9
    1.2.8 The Rules of Statutory Interpretation   10
    1.2.9 International Treaties   10
    1.2.10 European Union Law   11
    1.2.11 The European Convention on Human Rights   12
1.3 How Laws Are Implemented in Northern Ireland   13
    1.3.1 The Court System   13
    1.3.2 Civil and Criminal Courts   16
    1.3.3 Tribunals, Inquiries, and Inquests   17
    1.3.4 Applications for Judicial Review   18
    1.3.5 Important Legal Offices   19
    1.3.6 The Police Service   20
    1.3.7 The Prison Service   21

	1.3.8 Ombudspersons	23
	1.3.9 Watchdogs	23
1.4	**Legal Services in Northern Ireland**	24
	1.4.1 Advice Agencies and Pressure Groups	24
	1.4.2 Solicitors and Barristers	25
	1.4.3 Financial Assistance with Legal Problems	26
1.5	**Further Reading**	30

2 Professional Responsibility
Kenny Mullan

31

2.1	**Introduction**	31
2.2	**Legal Responsibility for Careless Acts or Omissions**	32
	2.2.1 Proving a Duty of Care	33
	2.2.2 Vicarious Liability	35
	2.2.3 Breach of the Duty of Care	36
	2.2.4 Proving Damage in Negligence	37
	2.2.5 Summary	38
2.3	**Keeping Confidences**	39
	2.3.1 The Duty of Confidentiality	39
	2.3.2 Clients' Access to Reports	40
	2.3.3 Confidentiality and Informants	41
	2.3.4 Confidentiality and Children	42
	2.3.5 Confidentiality and Defamation	43
	2.3.6 Summary	44
2.4	**Social Workers and Employment**	45
2.5	**Professional Morality**	47
2.6	**Further Reading**	48

3 The Social Worker in Court
Dympna Mallon and Ciaran White

49

3.1	**Introduction**	49
	3.1.1 Courts and the Truth	50

3.2 Reports 51
    3.2.1 Writing a Report 51
    3.2.2 Preparation of Evidence 54

3.3 Order of Proceedings 55
    3.3.1 Examination, Cross-examination, and Re-examination ... 55
    3.3.2 Standards of Proof 57
    3.3.3 Presumptions 57

3.4 Acting as a Witness 58
    3.4.1 Competence and Compellability 61
    3.4.2 The Barrister's Perspective 62
    3.4.3 What to Say 63
    3.4.4 Refusing to Answer a Question 64
    3.4.5 Referring to Your Notes 65
    3.4.6 Stating Your Opinion 65
    3.4.7 The Rule Against Hearsay 66
    3.4.8 Children's Evidence 69

3.5 Further Reading 70

PART 2: THE LAW RELATING TO SOCIAL WORK PRACTICE   71

4 Criminal Proceedings   73
Ciaran White

4.1 Introduction 73
    4.1.1 Age of Criminal Responsibility 74
    4.1.2 Role of the Appropriate Adult 75

4.2 Arrest and Length of Detention 76
    4.2.1 Arrest Under 'Ordinary' Law 77
    4.2.2 Arrest Under Emergency Law 78

4.3 Treatment in Detention 78
    4.3.1 Custody Records and the Custody Officer 79
    4.3.2 The Right to Inform Someone 80
    4.3.3 Access to a Solicitor 81
    4.3.4 Answering Questions 82
    4.3.5 The Right to an Interpreter 84
    4.3.6 Extending Detention 84
    4.3.7 Searches, Samples, Fingerprints and Photographs ... 85
    4.3.8 Charging the Detainee with an Offence 87

4.4 The Prosecution Process		88
4.4.1 Issuing Cautions		88
4.4.2 In What Court Will the Matter Be Tried?		90
4.4.3 Committal Proceedings		91
4.4.4 Remand on Bail and in Custody		91
4.5 The Trial Process		91
4.6 Sentencing Options		93
4.6.1 Discharge		93
4.6.2 Monetary Penalties		93
4.6.3 Community Disposals		95
4.6.4 Immediate Custody		97
4.6.5 Juvenile Offenders		98
4.6.6 Mentally Disordered Offenders		101
4.7 Further Reading		102

5 Probation Work   103
Ciaran White

5.1 Introduction		103
5.2 The Probation Board for Northern Ireland		104
5.2.1 Scope of Work		105
5.3 Probation Officers		106
5.3.1 General Duty		107
5.3.2 The Courts		107
5.3.3 Community Supervision		111
5.3.4 Prisons		114
5.3.5 Confidentiality		117
5.3.6 Legal Liability for Injury or Damage		117
5.4 Further Reading		118

6 Child Care and Protection   119
Dympna Mallon and *Ciaran White*

6.1 Introduction		119
6.1.1 The Agencies and the Institutional Framework		120
6.1.2 Managing Child Abuse		121
6.1.3 Defining Child Abuse		126

6.2 The 1968 Act	127
6.2.1 Preventing Child Abuse	127
6.2.2 Investigating Child Abuse	127
6.2.3 Emergency Intervention	129
6.2.4 Non-emergency Child Protection Options	130
6.3 The 1995 Order	133
6.3.1 Governing Principles	134
6.3.2 Preventing Child Abuse	138
6.3.3 Investigating Child Abuse	138
6.3.4 Emergency Intervention	139
6.3.5 Non-emergency Intervention	143
6.3.6 Family Proceedings	147
6.4 Employing Children	152
6.4.1 Public Performances	153
6.4.2 Offences and Defences	153
6.5 Further Reading	154
7 Mental Disorder *Michael Potter*	155
7.1 Introduction	155
7.2 The Legal Definition of Mental Disorder	157
7.3 The Role of the Social Worker	158
7.3.1 Legal Liability of the Approved Social Worker	160
7.4 Compulsory Admission to Hospital	160
7.4.1 Admission for Assessment	160
7.4.2 Detention for Treatment	165
7.4.3 Treatment While in Hospital	166
7.5 Guardianship	169
7.6 Powers of the Police	171
7.6.1 Assistance at the Admission of a Patient	171
7.6.2 Assistance in Retaking a Patient Who Is at Large	172
7.6.3 Assistance in Removing a Person to a Place of Safety	172
7.7 Management of Patients' Property and Affairs	172
7.7.1 Boards and Trusts and Residential Patients	175
7.7.2 The Social Security Appointee System	175

7.8	The Mental Health Commission	176
7.9	The Mental Health Review Tribunal	177
7.10	Further Reading	180

8 Vulnerable People — 181
Brian Collins

8.1	Introduction	181
8.2	Statutory Framework for Provision of Services	183
	8.2.1 The Chronically Sick and Disabled	184
	8.2.2 The Elderly	184
	8.2.3 People with Learning Difficulties	185
	8.2.4 Children in Need	185
8.3	Assessment	186
	8.3.1 The Chronically Sick and Disabled	186
	8.3.2 The Elderly	187
	8.3.3 People with Learning Difficulties	188
	8.3.4 Children in Need	190
8.4	Services	191
	8.4.1 The Chronically Sick and Disabled	191
	8.4.2 The Elderly	192
	8.4.3 People with Learning Difficulties	192
	8.4.4 Children in Need	194
8.5	Accommodation	197
	8.5.1 The Chronically Sick and Disabled	197
	8.5.2 The Elderly	201
	8.5.3 Children in Need	201
8.6	Representing Vulnerable People	205
	8.6.1 Presenting their Views and Opinions	205
	8.6.2 Managing Property on their Behalf	206
8.7	Further Reading	207

Contents xiii

PART 3: THE LAW AFFECTING CLIENTS 209

9 Anti-Discrimination Law 211
Patricia Maxwell

9.1 Introduction 211

9.2 Sex Discrimination (Northern Ireland) Order, 1976 212
    9.2.1 The Equal Opportunities Commission 213
    9.2.2 What Constitutes Discrimination? 213
    9.2.3 The Extent of Protection 216
    9.2.4 Sex Discrimination in Employment 217
    9.2.5 Sexual Harassment 218
    9.2.6 Pregnancy Discrimination 219
    9.2.7 Permitted Discrimination 221
    9.2.8 Remedies in Sex Discrimination Cases 221
    9.2.9 Equal Pay 222
    9.2.10 Remedies in Equal Pay Cases 224

9.3 Religious Discrimination 224
    9.3.1 The Fair Employment Commission 226
    9.3.2 The Fair Employment Tribunal 226
    9.3.3 What Constitutes Discrimination? 227
    9.3.4 Permitted Discrimination 229
    9.3.5 Remedies in Fair Employment Cases 229
    9.3.6 The Affirmative Action Provisions 230

9.4 Discrimination Against Ex-offenders 231
    9.4.1 Excluded Occupations 232
    9.4.2 Remedies for Ex-offenders 232
    9.4.3 'Unspent' Convictions 233

9.5 Discrimination on Grounds of Disability 233
    9.5.1 The Legal Framework 234
    9.5.2 The Register of Disabled Persons 234
    9.5.3 The Quota Scheme 236
    9.5.4 Designated Employments Scheme 236
    9.5.5 Other Provisions 236
    9.5.6 Unfair Dismissal 237

9.6 Racial Discrimination 237

9.7 Further Reading 238

10 The Breakdown of Relationships — 240
Ciaran White

10.1 Introduction — 240

10.2 Domestic Violence — 241
    10.2.1 Domestic Violence and the Criminal Law — 241
    10.2.2 Domestic Violence and the Civil Law — 241
    10.2.3 Compensation from the Abuser — 243
    10.2.4 The Right to Remain in the Family Home — 243
    10.2.5 Maintenance and Domestic Violence — 245

10.3 Ending the Relationship: Divorce and Judicial Separation — 246
    10.3.1 Grounds — 248
    10.3.2 Court Procedure — 249

10.4 Property, Finance, and Care of the Children — 251
    10.4.1 Care of the Children — 251
    10.4.2 Financial Arrangements and Divorce — 252
    10.4.3 Maintenance of Children — 253

10.5 Further Reading — 255

11 Social Security Benefits — 256
Adrian McCullough

11.1 Introduction — 256

11.2 Social Security Law — 257
    11.2.1 The Adjudication Structure — 257
    11.2.2 Adjudication Officers — 258
    11.2.3 Appeal Tribunals — 258
    11.2.4 Social Security Commissioners — 260
    11.2.5 The Courts — 260
    11.2.6 Representing Clients Before an Appeal Tribunal — 260
    11.2.7 Time Limits — 262

11.3 The Benefits — 262
    11.3.1 Contributory and Non-contributory Benefits — 262
    11.3.2 Means-tested and Non-means-tested Benefits — 262
    11.3.3 'Passport Benefits' and Overlapping Benefits — 263

11.4 Particular Benefits — 263
    11.4.1 Non-means-tested Benefits — 263
    11.4.2 Means-tested Benefits — 266

	11.4.3 Industrial Injuries Benefits and Industrial Preference	270
	11.4.4 Disability Benefits	271
11.5	Further Reading	273

12 Housing Issues — 275
Angela Hegarty

12.1	Introduction	275
12.2	Some Terms Explained	275
12.3	The Public Rented Sector	276
	12.3.1 The Allocation of NIHE Tenancies	277
	12.3.2 Complaints About Allocation	278
	12.3.3 NIHE Tenancy Agreements	278
	12.3.4 Secure Tenancies	278
	12.3.5 Transferring and Exchanging Tenancies	279
	12.3.6 Non-payment of Rent	280
	12.3.7 Setting NIHE Rents	280
	12.3.8 The Tenant's Right to Buy	280
	12.3.9 The 'Tenants' Charter'	281
12.4	The Private Rented Sector	281
	12.4.1 Setting Rent	282
	12.4.2 Rights of Private Tenants	282
12.5	Repairs	284
	12.5.1 Public Sector Tenants	284
	12.5.2 Private Sector Tenants	285
	12.5.3 Unfit for Habitation	286
12.6	Homelessness	288
	12.6.1 Non-statutory NIHE Administrative Scheme	288
	12.6.2 Statutory Homelessness	289
12.7	Squatting	292
	12.7.1 Squatting in NIHE Property	293
	12.7.2 Squatting in Privately Owned Property	294
	12.7.3 Squatters' Rights	294
12.8	Grants	295
	12.8.1 Renovation Grants	295
	12.8.2 Replacement Grants	296

12.8.3	Disabled Facilities Grants	296
12.8.4	Minor Works Assistance	296
12.8.5	'Common Parts' Grants	296
12.8.6	Repairs Grants	296
12.8.7	Grants for Houses in Multiple Occupation	297
12.9	Further Reading	297

Index 299

PREFACE

The lack of legal materials for those engaged in social work in Northern Ireland has been a considerable disadvantage for lecturers, students and practitioners. This book has developed from the teaching of law to students of social work and attempts to remedy that deficiency.

It is hoped that *Law for Northern Ireland Social Workers* will be a practical, useful and indispensable handbook for the profession. It deals with all the core legal areas that the Central Council for Education and Training in Social Work (CCETSW) requires to be covered in DipSW courses. In compiling this book our objective has been to state the law in as accessible and straightforward a manner as possible, and to address all the major legal topics that social workers are likely to face in contemporary practice. All the contributors to this collection hope that it will encourage debate about particular aspects of social work law and lead to greater interaction between social workers and lawyers which will ultimately be of benefit to their clients.

The ever-changing nature of law and public policy always presents problems when writing books of this sort, and this book was no exception. Two developments presented us with difficulty. The first was the Children (NI) Order 1995 which, though enacted, awaits implementation. It has meant that in some chapters we have had to deal with the present law as well as the law as it will be under the Order. The other development was the continuing transfer of statutory powers and duties from Health Boards to Trusts. This has meant that in some areas it is a Board that has legislative responsibility, whilst in others it is a Trust. Hence we have on many occasions had to refer to 'Boards or Trusts', meaning whichever authority has legal responsibility in a particular area. We have done this even when writing about the Children (NI) Order 1995 despite the fact that no delegation of the powers and duties conferred on Boards in that legislation has yet been made, though it undoubtedly will.

The term 'social worker' is used throughout for convenience sake, as an all-embracing term which best represents the diversity of work engaged in by all those involved in this field. It covers the whole range of occupations concerned with the delivery of health and personal social services, including youth and community workers, residential workers and family centre workers.

There are a number of people who assisted us in the writing of this book and to whom we are very grateful: the staff of Gill & Macmillan, especially Finola O'Sullivan, a patient and understanding editor, and her assistant, Deirdre Greenan; Maurice Leeson (Project Leader, Barnardo's) who acted as an advisor to the contributors, and read and commented quite helpfully on many chapters, distributing others to colleagues and friends for their comments; Kieran McEvoy (NIACRO); Elaine Peel, Jimmy Boyle, Oliver Flanagan and Brian McCaughey (all of PBNI); Brendan Murtagh (Housing Research Centre, Magee); Clare Archbold and Ray Geary (both of the School of Law, QUB); Clodagh McGrory (Child Care NI); Willie Gray (NH & SSB); Stanley Herron; Lorna Montgomery; Paul Ward (Law School, UCD); Les Allamby (Law Centre (NI)); and last, but not least, Edith Ferguson, an eager and efficient typist. Thank you to you all.

I personally wish to thank Úna, Cormac and Liadh for all their love and patience throughout what seemed to them a never-ending project.

The law stated here is correct as at 1 June 1995.

CIARAN WHITE
School of Public Policy, Economics and Law
University of Ulster
June 1995

TABLE OF CASES

Albert v. Lavin (1982) AC 346 163
Alcock v. Chief Constable of South Yorkshire Police [1992] 1 AC 310 38
Argyll v. Argyll [1967] Ch 302 39
Barber v. Guardian Royal Exchange [1990] 2 All ER 660 221
Bolam v. Friern Hospital Management Committee [1957] 1 All ER 118 .. 168, 36
Chuwen v. Debenhams Ltd COIT 655/177 232
Commission for the European Communities v. United Kingdom
 [1982] ICR 578 223
Dekker v. Stichting Vormingscentrum voor Jong Wolvassenen
 (VJV-Centrum) Plus C–177/88 (1990) 220
Department of the Environment v. Fair Employment Agency [1989] NI 149 .. 228
Dornan v. Belfast City Council [1990] IRLR 179 217
Donley v. Gallagher Ltd [1987] Case no. 66/86 220
DPP v. Hawkins 1988 (88) CrAppR 166 77
Duffy v. Eastern Health and Social Services Board [1991] Case no. 38/90 .. 230
Dyson v. Kerrier DC [1980] 3 All ER 313 291
D. v. NSPCC [1978] AC 171 .... 41, 65
English Exporters v. Eldonwall [1973] Ch 415 60
F. v. West Berkshire Health Authority [1989] 2 All ER 545 168
Garlick v. Oldham Metropolitan Borough Council (1933) 2 All ER 65 290
Gillespie and Others v. DHSS and Others [1992] Case no. 309/89 220
Gillick v. West Norfolk and Wisbech AHA and the DHSS
 [1985] 3 All ER 402 .... 42, 164
Gillick v. West Norfolk and Wisbech Area Health Authority
 (1986) AC 112 137
Hayward v. Camell Laird [1988] 2 All ER 257 223
Hedley Byrne v. Heller and Partners Ltd [1963] 2 All ER 575 37
Home Office v. Holmes [1984] 3 All ER 549 216
Horsey v. Dyfed CC [1982] IRLR 395 214
Hurley v. Mustoe [1981] IRLR 208 214
In re D. (infants) [1970] 1 WLR 599 40
In re EOC for Northern Ireland and Others [1988] NI 223 216
James v. Eastleigh Borough Council [1990] 2 AC 751
Jeremiah v. Ministry of Defence [1979] IRLR 436 218
Jordan v. NI Electricity Service [1984] Case no. 28/83 220
M. (a minor) and Another v. Newham London Borough Council ... 32, 33, 34, 38
M. v. Crescent Garage Ltd [1982] Case no. 24/83 218
McCausland v. Dungannon District Council [1992] Case no. 58/90 228
Macarthys Ltd v. Smith [1980] ICR 672 224
McLoughlin v. O'Brien [1982] 2 All ER 278 38

McQuaide v. The Lobster Pot [1989] Case no. 427/89 220
McPhail v. Persons, names unknown (1973) 3 All ER 393 292
Marshall (No. 2) [1993] IRLR 445 (ECJ) 222
Marshall v. Southampton and South-West Hampshire Area Health
  Authority [1986] 2 All ER 584 221
Mulligan v. Eastern Health and Social Services Board (1994)
  Case no. 1258/93 216
Neilly v. Mullaghboy Private Nursing Home [1991] Case no. 31/90 228
New York City Employees' Retirement System v. American Brands Inc.
  [1986] IRLR 239 225
North-Eastern Education and Library Board v. Briggs [1990] IRLR 181 ... 216
Others and X (minors) v. Bedfordshire County Council
  [1994] 2 WLR 554 at 575 .... 32, 33
Pickstone v. Freemans PLC [1988] 2 All ER 803 224
Porcelli v. Strathclyde Regional Council [1986] IRLR 134 218
Property Guards Ltd v. Taylor and Kershaw [1982] IRLR 175 232
Re C. [1994] 1 All ER 819 168
Re Caz (1990) 2 QB 355 69
Re D., a minor (1986) 2 FLR 189 67
Regina v. Mid-Glamorgan Family Health Services and Another,
  ex parte Martin (The Times, 16 August 1994, 34) 41
Re K. (Infants) [1965] AC 201 68
Re M. [1990] 1 All ER 205 43
Re M. (a minor) (Disclosure of Material) [1990] 2 FLR 36 43
R. v. Abadom (1983) 1 WLR 126 60
R. v. Beales [1991] Crim LR 118 83
R. v. Hayes (1977) 64 CrAppR 194 69
R. v. N. (1992) 95 CrAppR 256 (CA) 69
R. v. Northavon DC, ex parte Smith (The Times, 4 August 1993) 290
R. v. Robinson (1970); R. v. Mountford (1971) 293
R. v. Silverlock [1894] 2 QB 766 66
R. v. Somers [1964] 48 CrAppR 11 60
R v. South-Western Hospital Mangers, ex parte M. (1994) 1 All ER 161 .. 161
R. v. West Dorset District Council ex parte Philips (1984) 17 HLR 336 ... 291
T. v. T. [1988] 1 All ER 613 .... 166, 168
The Wagon Mound [1961] AC 388 37
The Wagon Mound (No. 2) [1966] 2 All ER 709 37
Torr v. British Railways Board [1977] IRLR 184 233
W. v. Edgell [1990] 1 All ER 835 39
Wallace v. South-Eastern Education and Library Board [1981] IRLR 193 .. 214
Wallace v. South-Eastern Education and Library Board [1980] IRLR 193 .. 217
Webb v. EMO Cargo (UK) Ltd [1992] 4 All ER 929 219
X v. Y [1988] 2 All ER 648 39

TABLE OF STATUTES

Americans with Disabilities Act 1990 232
Age of Majority Act (Northern Ireland) 1969
                       s.4 164
Children Act 1989 .... 35, 134, 290
Children and Young Persons Act 1933
                       s.38 (1) 69
Children and Young Persons Act (Northern Ireland) 1968 ... 75, 81, 108, 113, 116, 119, 121, 123, 127, 128, 129, 135, 139, 143, 150, 152, 153, 186
                       s.51 91
                       s.52 (2)) 81
                       s.53 (2) 108, 109
                       s.69 75
                       s.72 98
                       s.73 (1) 100
                       s.74(1) 100
                       s.74 (1) (*e*) 100
                       s.76(1) 94
                       s.82 113
                       s.87 99
                       s.90(1) 99
                       s.93 164
                       s.97 113
                       s.103 185
                       s.113 194
                       s.113 (2) 194
                       s.114 202
                       s.124 194
                       s.135 99
Civil Evidence Act (Northern Ireland) 1971 67
Chronically Sick and Disabled Persons (Northern Ireland) Act 1978 ... 182, 184, 185, 186, 187, 191, 192
                       s.1 198
                       s. 1 (2) 182
                       s. 2 182
Criminal Justice Act 1991 70
Criminal Law Act (Northern Ireland) 1967, section 7(5) 94
Data Protection Act 1984 40
Disabled Persons (Employment) Acts (Northern Ireland) 1945 234
                       s.2 235
                       s.15 235

Table of Statutes

    s.9 (1) 236
    s.12 236
Disabled Persons (Employment) Acts (Northern Ireland) 1960 234
Disabled Persons (Northern Ireland) Act 1989 .... 182, 184, 187, 190, 192
    s.1 .... 182, 205
    s.2 .... 182, 205
    s.3 182
    s.4 .... 182, 206
    s.5 .... 182, 190
    s.8 182
Disabled Persons (Services, Consultation and Representation) Act 1986 .. 203
Equal Pay Act (Northern Ireland) 1970 .... 24, 212, 217, 222, 223
European Communities Act 1972 11
Fair Employment (Northern Ireland) Acts 1976 .... 4, 24, 224, 225
    s.26 229
    s.57 229
Fair Employment (Northern Ireland) Act 1989 .. 4, 24, 225, 226, 227, 229, 230
    s.37 229
Housing Executive Act (Northern Ireland) 1971 276
    s.1 276
Government of Ireland Act 1920 13
    s.5 (1) 224
Interpretation Act (Northern Ireland) 1954 10
Interpretation Act 1978 10
Judicature (Northern Ireland) Act 1978 13
Legal Aid and Advice Act (Northern Ireland) 1965 4
Mental Health Act (Northern Ireland) 1961 155
Mental Health Act 1983 155
Mental Health (Scotland) Act 1984 155
Northern Ireland Act 1974 .... 4, 5, 7, 8
Northern Ireland Constitution Act 1973 .... 7, 224
Northern Ireland (Emergency Provisions) Act 1991 ... 4, 7, 73, 74, 75, 78, 84
    s.11 83
    s.44 80
    s.45 81
    s.45(1) 82
    s.61 74
Payments for Debt (Emergency Provisions) Act 1971 280
Police and Criminal Evidence Act 1984
    s.11 40
    s.12 40
    s.14 40
Prevention of Terrorism (Temporary Provisions) Act 1989
    .... 73, 75, 76, 78, 84, 85
    s.14 .... 78, 87
    s.20 78

Table of Statutes xxiii

Probation Act (Northern Ireland) 1950
        s.1 95
        s.1 (4) 112
        s.2A 96, 112
        s.2B 96, 112
        s.2 (4) 112
        s.4 100
        s.5 93
        s.9 108
        s.14 .... 107, 110
        schedule 2, paragraph 4 112
Probation of Offenders Act, 1907 104
Protection of the Person and Property Act (Northern Ireland) 1969 293
Public Health (Control of Diseases) Act 1984 40
Public Health (Ireland) Act 1878, section 110 286
Punishment of Incest Act 1908 128
Race Relations Act 1976 236
Social Security Contributions and Benefits (Northern Ireland) Act 1992
        .... 257, 280
Social Security Administration (Northern Ireland) Act 1992 .... 257, 280
War Crimes Act 1991 5

TABLE OF STATUTORY INSTRUMENTS

Access to Personal Files and Medical Reports (Northern Ireland)
          Order 1991 41
Access to Health Records (Northern Ireland) Order 1993 41
Children Act 1989 119
Children's Evidence (Northern Ireland) Order 1995 62
          – article 3 62
Children (Northern Ireland) Order 1995 ... 16, 68, 69, 98, 119, 120, 121, 123,
          124, 127, 133, 134, 135, 136, 139, 147, 151, 152,153, 184,
          185, 186, 188, 190, 194, 195, 201, 204, 246, 251, 252
          – article 8 251
          – article 15 (2) 198
          – article 25 194
          – article 29 197
          – article 169 (5) 60
          – article 169 (5) 68
          – paragraph 8 (*a*) (ii), schedule 2 73
Child Support (Northern Ireland) Order 1991 .... 253, 254, 255
          – article 7 254
          – article 9 254
Criminal Evidence (Northern Ireland) Order 1988 .... 7, 83, 86
Criminal Justice (Northern Ireland) Order 1980 94
          – article 3(1) 94
Criminal Justice Order (Northern Ireland) 1986
          – article 10 .... 292, 293
Companies (Directors' Report) (Employment of Disabled Persons)
          Regulations (Northern Ireland) 1982 236
Data Protection (Subject Access Modification) (Social Work) Order 1987 .. 40
Domestic Proceedings (Northern Ireland) Order 1980 242
          – article 4 245
          – article 28 (3) 246
Education and Libraries (Northern Ireland) Order 1986 .... 184, 192
          – article 29 .... 185, 188
          – article 36 189
          – schedule 11 188
Enduring Powers of Attorney (Northern Ireland) Order, 1987 174
          – article 10 (4) 174
          – article 116 (1) 175
Equal Pay (Amendment) Regulations (Northern Ireland) 1984 223
European Assembly Elections (Northern Ireland) Regulations 1986 6

Family Law (Northern Ireland) Order 1993
   – article 14 243
Family Law (Miscellaneous Provisions) (Northern Ireland) Order 1984 244
Health and Personal Social Services (Northern Ireland) Order 1972
   ....182, 183, 184, 191, 203
   – article 4 .... 192, 196
   – article 4 (*b*) 187
   – article 15 182
   – article 15 (2) 187
   – article 36 199
   – articles 37 and 38 182
   – article 37 and schedule 6 .... 200, 207
Health and Personal Social Services (Northern Ireland) Order 1991. .182, 183, 184
Health and Personal Social Services (Northern Ireland) Order 1994 ... 155, 182
Housing (Northern Ireland) Order 1981 .... 277, 284
   – article 6 277
   – article 45 284
Housing (Northern Ireland) Order 1983 277
   – article 26 279
   – article 27 278
   – article 29 278
   – article 32 (*a*) (1) 279
   – article 38 (3) 278, 281
Housing (Northern Ireland) Order 1988 .... 288, 289, 290, 292
   – article 13 292
   – article 9 292
Housing (Northern Ireland) Order 1992 282
   – article 96 280
Housing (Northern Ireland) Order 1993 295
   – article 41 295
   – article 52 295
   – article 53 295
   – articles 57–58 295
Industrial Relations (Northern Ireland) Order 1993 220
   – article 52 221
Legal Aid, Advice and Assistance (Northern Ireland) Order 1981 27
Magistrates' Courts (Northern Ireland) Order 1980 94
   – article 127(1) 94
Magistrates' Courts (Northern Ireland) Order 1981
   – article 150 108
Matrimonial Causes (Northern Ireland) Order 1978 245
   – article 3 248
   – article 4 (1) 248
   – article 4 (3) 248
   – article 7 249
   – article 8 250
   – article 20 (2) 247

Table of Statutory Instruments

- article 24 252
- article 25 . . . . 252, 253
- article 26 252
- article 27A 253
- article 29 245
- article 43 250

Matrimonial and Family Proceedings (Northern Ireland) Order 1989 245
- article 3 249
- article 6 253
- article 7 253

Mental Health (Northern Ireland) Order 1986 . . 101, 155, 166, 172, 177, 178, 184
- article 2 (4) (*a*) 161
- article 2 (4) (*b*) 162
- article 3 206
- article 4 (2) 161
- article 6 161
- article 7 (3) 163, 166
- article 8 (1) (*b*) 162
- article 9 (1) 162
- article 9 (4) 163
- article 9 (4–7) 163
- article 9 (8) 163, 166
- article 10 163
- article 10 (2 and 6) 164
- article 12 166
- article 12 (1) 170
- article 13 166
- article 18 (2) 169
- article 18 (3) (*b*) 169
- article 19 169
- article 22 (3) 170
- article 23 (1) 170
- article 24 (3) 170
- article 32 159
- article 32 (3) 159
- article 33 . . . . 160, 185
- article 36 159
- article 36 (1) 160
- article 36 (3) (*c*) 161
- article 40 (2) 158
- article 44 101
- article 45 102
- article 48 101
- article 63 . . . . 166, 167
- article 64 167
- article 64 (3) (*b*) and (5) 167
- article 65 166

– article 68 167
– article 68 (1) (*a*) 167
– article 68 (1) (*b–d*) 167
– article 68 (3) 167
– article 69 167
– article 97 (1) 173
– articles 98 and 99 173
– article 98 173
– article 101 (1) 173
– article 101 (2) 173
– articles 104–5 173
– article 105 (2) 174
– article 105 (3) 174
– article 105 (9) 174
– article 107 173
– article 112 156
– article 115 158
– article 129 166
– article 129 171
– article 129 (1) 172
– article 129 (2) 172
– article 129 (4) 171
– article 129 (5) 172
– article 129 (7) 171
– article 130 166
– article 130 (2) 171
– article 131 (2) 162
Mental Health Review Tribunal (Northern Ireland) Rules 1986 ..... 155, 179
Mental Health (Nurses, Guardianship, Consent to Treatment and Prescribed
       Forms) Regulations (Northern Ireland) 1986 ... 155, 177
Mental Health (Nurses, Guardianship, Consent to Treatment and Prescribed
       Forms) Regulations (Northern Ireland), 1986, no 174 ... 170
       regulation 4 170
       regulation 5 170
Nursing Homes Regulations (Northern Ireland) 1993 200
Police and Criminal Evidence (Northern Ireland)
       Order 1989 .... 8, 24, 70, 73, 74, 75, 76, 85, 130
– article 2 85
– article 26 77
– article 26(2) 77
– article 27 77
– article 30 77
– article 31 77
– article 38 87
– article 38(13) 80
– article 53 86
– article 55 80

Table of Statutory Instruments

- article 57 80
- article 58 80
- article 59 81
- article 65 74
- articles 74 83
- article 75 83
- article 76 83
- article 79 241
- article 81 70

Pollution Control and Local Government (Northern Ireland) Order 1978,
- article 65 (1) 286

Prisons and Young Offender Centre Rules (Northern Ireland) 1995 .... 21, 117
Probation Rules (Northern Ireland) 1950 95
Probation Board (Northern Ireland) Order 1982 .... 104, 107
- article 5 (1) 104
- article 5 105
- article 5 (*a*) 106
- schedule 4, paragraph 2 110
- article 10 118

Registered Homes (Northern Ireland) Order 1992 184
- article 3 199
- article 6 199
- article 16 199

Rehabilitation of Offenders (Northern Ireland) Order 1978 .... 22, 44, 231
Rehabilitation of Offenders (Exceptions) (Northern Ireland)
  Order 1978 232

Rent (Northern Ireland) Order 1978 .... 281, 282
- article 18 284
- article 20 283
- article 27 (2) 282
- article 38 282
- article 41 285
- article 42 285
- articles 43–45 285
- article 54 (1) 283
- articles 54–56 294
- article 62 283

Residential Care Homes Regulations (Northern Ireland) 1993 200
Sex Discrimination (Northern Ireland) Order 1976
  .... 24, 212, 217, 219, 221, 238
- article 3 .... 213, 215
- articles 24–29 216
- articles 17, 48, and 49 218

Social Security (Adjudication) Regulations (Northern Ireland) 1987 7
Social Security (Claims and Payments) Regulations
  (Northern Ireland) 1987 .... 175, 280
- article 71 (4) 178

Table of Statutory Instruments

- articles 72 and 86 (3) (*a*) 178
- article 77 (1) 177
- article 77 (1) (*a*)), or (2) 178
- article 77 (1) (*b*) 178
- article 77 (1) (*c*) 178
- article 77 (2) 178
- article 86 (1) 176
- article 86 (2) 176

Treatment of Offenders (Northern Ireland) Order 1968 97
- section 18 97

Treatment of Offenders (Northern Ireland) Order 1976 .... 96, 108
- article 3 95
- article 7 (4) (*b*) 108

Treatment of Offenders (Northern Ireland) Order 1989 .... 97, 108
- article 3 .... 97, 108, 112
- article 9 97

Will and Administration Proceedings (Northern Ireland) Order 1994 247
- article 13 247

PART 1

The Social Worker and the Legal System

1

INTRODUCTION TO THE LEGAL SYSTEM

BRICE DICKSON

1.1 Introduction

Northern Ireland's social workers, like their counterparts elsewhere, come into contact with the legal system in a variety of ways. If they are to perform their jobs effectively they require a familiarity with the legal system's institutional framework: how laws are made, how they are enforced, and how they can be challenged and changed.

This chapter explains the structures and the most vital processes of the legal system of Northern Ireland. The first section describes how its laws come into being (i.e. the 'sources' of Northern Ireland law). This is followed by an exposition of how existing laws are implemented, the bodies that undertake this task, and the procedures they use. The third section examines the ways in which people can find out more about the law and how they can be helped financially to assert or defend their legal rights.

1.2 How Laws Are Made for Northern Ireland

There are two types of law in Northern Ireland: law made by (or with the authority of) Parliament, which is called legislation, and law made by judges, which is called case law or common law. Usually both types of law have something relevant to say about any matter; but if there is a conflict between a piece of legislation and a judge's ruling, the former must prevail. This is because Northern Ireland's legal system is based on the principle of parliamentary sovereignty, which holds that what Parliament says today can change what any judge or even Parliament itself may have said yesterday. There is no written constitution to set limits on Parliament's powers. The task of judges in such a system is to lay down legal rules for matters that are not clearly covered by legislation, and to interpret legislation when its meaning is in dispute.

Since 1973, however, membership of the European Community (now the European Union) has meant that whenever the law of Northern Ireland, whether parliamentary or judge-made, runs counter to law emanating from Brussels or Luxembourg, the latter must be given priority. To that extent the United Kingdom Parliament is no longer completely sovereign, and the law of the European Union must be considered as part and parcel of the law of Northern Ireland.

1.2.1 *Primary Legislation*

Legislation is either primary or secondary in nature. Primary legislation is enacted directly by Parliament in the form of Acts, also known as statutes. Secondary legislation is made by bodies other than Parliament but under an authority expressly delegated to those bodies by a piece of primary legislation.

Statutes are made by being drafted and then enacted. About sixty are created by the Westminster Parliament each year. Most of them are 'public general Acts', which have passed through Parliament because the government of the day has piloted their passage. But each year one or two Acts start life as private members' Bills, which are proposals for laws introduced by backbench MPs.

Since the abolition of Northern Ireland's own parliament in 1972 and the consequential imposition of 'direct rule' from Westminster, the main method used for legislating for Northern Ireland is the Order in Council procedure (see 1.2.3.2). This is provided for by the Northern Ireland Act 1974. Whenever the Westminster Parliament wishes to make a law concerning an 'excepted' matter (i.e. one that would not be devolved to a local parliament in Northern Ireland if such an institution were to be re-established) it must embody it in an Act. An example is the Northern Ireland (Emergency Provisions) Act 1991, which deals with terrorism. But if the subject of the proposed law is a 'transferred' matter (one that would be made by a devolved parliament) an Act will be employed only if the government wishes to ensure a full parliamentary debate on the topic. This is what was done for religious discrimination when the Fair Employment (Northern Ireland) Acts were passed in 1976 and 1989.

If an Act is silent on its geographical extent it is presumed to apply throughout the United Kingdom. Generally speaking, about half of the United Kingdom statutes passed each year apply wholly or partly in Northern Ireland. Acts confined in operation to Northern Ireland will have the words 'Northern Ireland' or 'Ulster' as key words in their title or within parentheses before the word 'Act'. Acts of the Stormont Parliament of 1921–72 are distinguished from English statutes with similar titles by the addition of the term 'Northern Ireland' *after* the word 'Act', as in the Legal Aid and Advice Act (Northern Ireland) 1965.

As the House of Commons is dominated by the political party that has formed the government, it is in practice the government that decides what legislation should be passed. The government's intentions are outlined in the Queen's Speech when she opens each new parliamentary session. Proposed Acts must be approved by the House of Commons, the House of Lords, and the Monarch, but the power of the House of Lords to delay legislation is limited, and in practice the Queen never refuses her assent.

The granting of Royal Assent does not automatically bring an Act into force. This happens only if the Act itself contains no other indication of when or how it is to start operating. Often an Act says that it is to come into force when a 'commencement order' has been made by a government minister. There is a constitutional convention (i.e. tradition) that legislation should not be retrospective in operation, but occasionally this is ignored, as with the War Crimes Act 1991.

1.2.2 *How to Consult Primary Legislation*

Finding the section of an Act one needs to examine can be very difficult. Part of the trouble is that when new legislation is enacted it is grafted on to existing Acts, sometimes repealing them but more frequently amending them. An amended statute is not re-enacted in its new form: one has to read it in its original form and then read what the amending statute provides. Amendments can be introduced by Acts that have little in common with the original statute. They can even be introduced by secondary legislation (see 1.2.3).

Statutes are published singly at the time they are enacted, as well as collectively in bound or loose-leaf volumes at the end of each year. In Northern Ireland these annual volumes have continued to be produced since 1972, even though they contain not primary legislation but the Orders in Council made under the Northern Ireland Act 1974. Each volume contains tables showing the Acts or Orders repealed or amended during that year and giving a full list of United Kingdom Acts passed that year that are applicable in Northern Ireland. The annual index also lists the amendments made to Acts by secondary legislation (see 1.2.3).

Every three years or so an index is published to all the statutory provisions currently in force in Northern Ireland, arranged under subject headings. At roughly the same interval another table is published of all the statute law affecting Northern Ireland, this time arranged in chronological order and noting amendments and repeals. The *Statutes Revised* (second edition, 1982) is a multi-volume loose-leaf collection setting out in chronological order and in amended form all the statutes affecting Northern Ireland between 1921 and 1981. Unfortunately this collection excludes the relevant United Kingdom statutes enacted since 1920, though four additional volumes (A–D) reprint the amended texts of all pre-1920 legislation still in force in Northern Ireland. A cumulative supplement to *Statutes Revised* is published annually.

All United Kingdom statutes, as well as being published singly and in annual collections, are indexed by the two-volume *Index to the Statutes*, published every two years. Two private publishing companies also produce annotated versions of these statutes: these are *Halsbury's Statutes* and *Current Law Statutes*. There is also an official collection, *Statutes in Force*, which provides the same service for England and Wales that *Statutes Revised* provides for Northern Ireland; it comprises scores of loose-leaf volumes.

1.2.3 Secondary Legislation

All pieces of secondary legislation are ultimately the offspring of an 'enabling' Act, which gives power to a rule-making authority to issue detailed laws on a particular matter. The rule-making authority is usually a department of government but might also be the Privy Council (which makes Orders in Council), a local authority (which makes by-laws), or a committee of judges and lawyers (which makes Rules of Court). Nothing turns on the title of the legislation: Orders, regulations, rules etc. are all equally binding as laws of the land; but some Orders in Council do have special features (see 1.2.3.2).

Secondary legislation is invariably drafted in its final form only after a period of consultation with interested parties. It must usually be laid before both Houses of Parliament and be either positively affirmed or at least not annulled by those Houses. Unfortunately the time allowed for such debates on the floor of the House of Commons is usually just ninety minutes. In addition (or, more usually, instead) the legislation can be discussed for two-and-a-half hours by a standing committee of the House of Commons, and the debate there will obviously influence the way MPs vote on any subsequent resolutions in the House.

1.2.3.1 Statutory Instruments

Most secondary legislation is published in England as consecutively numbered 'statutory instruments' (SIs). Many of these also apply in Northern Ireland. Those that apply *only* in Northern Ireland contain the words 'Northern Ireland' *before* the word 'Rule', 'Regulation', 'Order', etc., an example being the European Assembly Elections (Northern Ireland) Regulations 1986.

1.2.3.2 Orders in Council

Orders in Council are one species of the more general category of statutory instruments just described. The reason for listing them separately is that under the Northern Ireland Act 1974, Orders in Council are used to make laws for Northern Ireland on subjects which, being 'transferred matters' under the Northern Ireland Constitution Act, 1973, would have been legislated for by the Northern Ireland Assembly if it had survived the first few months of 1974. 'Reserved' matters under the Northern Ireland Constitution Act 1973, are also dealt with by Orders in Council. Only 'excepted' matters need to be dealt with by an Act of Parliament at Westminster. 'Law and order' is a reserved matter, but 'terrorism' is an excepted matter: that is why we have the Criminal Evidence (Northern Ireland) Order 1988, which deals with an accused person's 'right to silence', but the Northern Ireland (Emergency Provisions) Act 1991, which deals with 'terrorism' only.

Orders in Council made under the Northern Ireland Act 1974, are published as United Kingdom statutory instruments, a separate number being given to them for publication in annual collections of Northern Ireland 'statutes'. It is not unusual for Orders made under the 1974 Act to sub-delegate law-making powers to other authorities, even though the general rule for secondary legislation is that further delegation of powers is not permitted. These Orders can also amend or repeal primary legislation, again contrary to the normal rule.

Not every item of legislation given the title 'Order' will in fact be an Order in Council. The word is also used for more ordinary pieces of secondary legislation falling within the third type described below. These are not statutory instruments at all. Examples would be the commencement orders mentioned in 1.2.1.

1.2.3.3 Statutory Rules

Statutory rules (SRs) are made by rule-making authorities in Northern Ireland under a power conferred by an Act of the United Kingdom Parliament, by an Act of the Stormont Parliament passed between 1921 and 1972, or by an Order in Council made under the Northern Ireland Act, 1974. They are really the Northern Ireland equivalent of the statutory instruments made for the rest of the United Kingdom (see 1.2.3.1). Sometimes they differ from the corresponding statutory instruments in title only, the content remaining virtually identical. The title will contain the words 'Northern Ireland' in parentheses *after* the word 'Rules', 'Regulations', 'Order', etc. A typical illustration is the Social Security (Adjudication) Regulations (Northern Ireland) 1987.

1.2.4 *How to Consult Secondary Legislation*

As with statutes, in Northern Ireland secondary legislation is published singly as well as collectively in annual bound volumes. The last volume for each year contains a list of that year's United Kingdom statutory instruments that affect the province (other than Orders in Council made under the 1974 Act), and there is an index categorising the statutory rules on the basis of the authorities that made them. Further tables list the changes made by the year's statutory rules, not just to earlier Acts and Orders but also to earlier statutory rules. A large index to all the statutory rules in force, arranged under subject headings, is published every three years.

1.2.5 *Semi-official Documents*

There are various semi-official documents that people often think have the force of law but in fact have not. Even though these documents are sometimes issued pursuant to a power conferred by statute, they can only influence rather than dictate a judge's view on what the law actually is. These publications include the Highway Code, the codes of practice issued by the Labour Relations Agency or agreed to by trade associations, the standing orders issued to the prison service by the Northern Ireland Office, and the codes issued to the police under the Police and Criminal Evidence (Northern Ireland) Order 1989. Statements of practice published by insurance companies, policy statements issued by the Inland Revenue and circulars put out by government departments are also in this category. Similarly, judges and Masters sometimes announce what are called 'practice directions' to provide for better organisation of proceedings within the courts. Strictly speaking, these too are not 'law'.

1.2.6 *Judge-made Law*

In the great majority of court cases the dispute is really about the facts—what was done, by whom, and when—rather than about the law that is applicable to those facts. Only decisions by judges on novel points of law find their way into one or more law reports, although not all cases that do get reported are significant, for they may simply confirm a point that was already fairly well settled. Reported decisions are referred to by lawyers and judges in future cases in order to back up an argument: what has been decided in the past is considered a good guide to what should be decided in the present.

In Northern Ireland there are two main series of law reports, the *Northern Ireland Law Reports* and the *Northern Ireland Judgments Bulletin*. There are also special series of law reports for decisions of the Lands Tribunal, industrial tribunals, and social security appeal tribunals (see 1.3.3). Decisions of courts and tribunals that might not otherwise get reported but might still be of some legal interest are noted in the *Bulletin of Northern Ireland Law*. In England there are several series of reports, with the 'official' law reports being divided into four single series: Appeal Cases (for decisions in the House of Lords and Privy Council: see 1.3.1.1 and 1.2.7), Queen's Bench, Chancery, and Family (see 1.3.1). The last three also contain relevant Court of Appeal decisions (see 1.3.1.2). Also very important are the *Weekly Law Reports* (WLR). The most common of the privately produced series is the *All England Law Reports* (All ER), published by Butterworths.

1.2.7 *The Rules of Precedent*

When law reports need to be consulted, the 'doctrine of precedent' comes into play. This states that a lower court is obliged to follow a higher court's decision in a previous case if the decision is on the same point. A higher court can overrule a lower court's decision, but this just means that the higher court is changing the law from that time onwards, not that the losing party in the earlier decision (which may have been taken years previously) can now have that decision reversed.

As the doctrine of precedent obliges lower courts to follow higher courts only if the earlier decisions are exactly in point, it is essential to deduce from every reported case the precise principle for which it may later be cited as an authority. This nub of the case is called in Latin the *ratio decidendi*, i.e. the 'reason for deciding', or simply the *ratio*. Things said by the judges that are not directly on the main point are called *obiter dicta* ('things said by the way'). Only the *ratio* of a case is binding on later judges. These judges can avoid applying it only if the facts of the case being dealt with can be sufficiently distinguished from those of the earlier case.

As can be seen from fig. 1, the highest court in the Northern Ireland legal system is the House of Lords. Its decisions are binding on all other courts in Northern Ireland. Decisions of the Judicial Committee of the Privy Council, which hears final appeals from some Commonwealth countries, are not absolutely binding on courts in either Northern Ireland or England, but they are very persuasive. Within Northern Ireland, decisions of the Court of Appeal are binding on the High Court and Crown Court, and their decisions are binding in turn on county courts and magistrates' courts. By and large, a court on one level is bound by an earlier decision taken by a court on the same level, although since 1966 the House of Lords has not followed its own previous decisions if it thinks that this is the only way of avoiding injustice. The Court of Appeal in Northern Ireland will usually follow earlier decisions of the Court of Appeal in England.

1.2.8 *The Rules of Statutory Interpretation*

However elaborately it is phrased, no piece of legislation can cater for all the circumstances that may later arise. Today the majority of reported cases involve a point of interpretation, and there are certain approaches to interpretation that judges tend to apply to all statutes. Some questions recur so frequently that Parliament has provided set solutions in the Interpretation Act (Northern Ireland) 1954, and the Interpretation Act 1978. More generally, as far as possible a purely literal approach is shunned. Instead a purposive approach—one that asks, 'What was Parliament really getting at?'—is preferred.

In the first place, judges try to ascertain the intention of Parliament in enacting the particular provision. Until recently, judges were obstructed in their efforts to do this by a rule that the report of proceedings in Parliament ('*Hansard*') could not be looked at. In *Pepper v. Hart* (1992) the House of Lords finally accepted that this rule should be relaxed so as to allow reference to clear statements made by a promoter of the legislation and to other parliamentary material that is necessary to understand these statements. The intention of Parliament can also be deduced from the long title of the Act, the unambiguous effects of other provisions in the Act, the state of the existing law, official reports preceding the enactment of the legislation, the practical consequences of preferring one interpretation over another, and the conventional maxims of interpretation, which it must be assumed the person who drafted the law was aware of.

One of the maxims relating to statutory interpretation is that a statute creating a criminal offence must be interpreted as narrowly as possible so as to preserve a person's freedom. Another is that the express mention of one of a class of things (for example motor vehicles) by implication excludes other items of the same class (for example bicycles), the class here being modes of road transport. Yet another is that a person cannot take advantage of his or her own illegal act to claim a right under a statute: for instance, a murderer cannot claim a widow's pension if the person she killed was her husband.

1.2.9 *International Treaties*

When the United Kingdom government signs international agreements, which may be called treaties, conventions, or covenants, it obviously does so on behalf of the people in Northern Ireland as well as those in Great Britain. But merely signing the treaty does not oblige the United Kingdom to comply with the treaty's provisions vis-à-vis other states. For this to happen the treaty must be 'ratified' by the government, and this normally occurs only after it has been laid before Parliament for twenty-one days.

Moreover, for a treaty to have any effect within the United Kingdom it must be incorporated into national law by an Act of Parliament. Examples of treaties that are binding on the United Kingdom in international law but not in national law are the European Convention on Human Rights of 1950 (see 1.2.11) and the Anglo-Irish Agreement of 1985.

1.2.10 *European Union Law*

When the United Kingdom joined the European Community (now the European Union) in 1973, the treaty establishing that community (the Treaty of Rome 1957) was incorporated into national law by the European Communities Act 1972. According to the most commonly accepted interpretation of that Act, the rules of the common law of the three United Kingdom legal systems (England and Wales, Scotland and Northern Ireland), as well as existing and future United Kingdom legislation, now have effect subject to European Union law. European law is therefore another source of law in Northern Ireland, and judges must interpret Northern Ireland law in a way that is consistent with it. They can even refuse to apply an Act of Parliament if they think the Act conflicts with European legal requirements. The 1972 Act also enables secondary legislation to be made by the relevant minister or government department in order to comply with European Union obligations.

All of European law falls into three categories: (1) provisions of the constitutive treaties, which can be said to be primary law; (2) regulations, directives and decisions of the EU institutions (the Council of Ministers and the European Commission), all of which can be called secondary law; and (3) rulings and decisions of the European Court of Justice, the case law of the EU. At present the European Parliament does not have any law-making powers.

Some of the legislation in the second category (regulations and most decisions) are 'directly applicable' in member-states of the European Union. This means they have the force of law without the need for any further national legislation to be passed. Regulations are binding on all member-states and, if the national parliament has not passed any implementing legislation, people can rely directly upon regulations in any legal dispute. Decisions are binding only on those bodies or persons to whom they are specifically addressed. They do not need any further implementation.

Directives, despite their name, are not directly applicable: each member-state is free to decide how to give them legal and administrative effect. A directive may, however, set a time limit for the implementation of its provisions. If a directive clearly aims to confer rights and duties on individuals, a person who suffers loss as a result of his or her government's failure to change national law within the time specified can sue the government and recover compensation for losses suffered. This is called a *Francovich* action, after the name of the first such case in 1991.

The European Court of Justice, which sits at Luxembourg, can hear many different types of case involving European law, but the most important are those concerned with the validity or interpretation of acts of EU institutions. If such matters arise during the course of a case before any national court or tribunal they can be referred to the Court of Justice under article 177 of the Treaty of Rome. The opinion of that court is then handed back to the local court so that it can be applied to the facts of the particular case. Courts and tribunals against whose decisions there is no further appeal are *obliged* to refer such matters to the Court of Justice unless the correct interpretation of European law is quite clear; the Court of Appeal in Northern Ireland is often in this position.

In 1989 a second court was established at Luxembourg to help take the burden off the Court of Justice. Called the Court of First Instance, it principally hears disputes between the staff of the EU and their employers, and cases involving commercial competition. Appeals lie to the Court of Justice on points of law or serious breaches of procedure.

1.2.11 *The European Convention on Human Rights*

The European Court of Justice should not be confused with the European Court of Human Rights, which sits at Strasbourg in France. This court interprets the European Convention for the Protection of Human Rights and Fundamental Freedoms, a treaty drawn up by the Council of Europe in 1950. The Council of Europe is an international organisation now comprising more than thirty European states. It is quite distinct from the European Union, being more active on the social and cultural fronts than on economic or political matters.

States may be proceeded against for an alleged violation of the Convention either by other states or by their own residents. In the near future the only body enforcing the Convention will be a full-time European Court of Human Rights, but at the moment applications are first considered by the European Commission of Human Rights, which decides whether they are 'admissible' within the terms of the Convention. If they are admissible, the Commission will carry out an inquiry and seek to bring about a friendly settlement. Only if no such settlement is possible will the Commission issue a report on whether there has been a breach of the Convention. The Commission or a state concerned will also decide whether to refer the case to the Court of Human Rights. If no referral occurs within three months of the Commission's report being issued, the Committee of Ministers of the

Council of Europe can look at the case. This Committee is a political rather than a legal body and can reach a decision only if two-thirds of its members agree.

The United Kingdom has not incorporated the European Convention on Human Rights into British law; it is therefore binding only internationally. However, courts in the United Kingdom do occasionally look at the Convention as an aid to the interpretation of national laws. As a result of decisions by the European Court of Human Rights the British government has had to change the national law on, among other things, contempt of court, the closed shop, immigration law, telephone tapping, detention in a mental hospital, prisoners' rights, and corporal punishment in schools. Many cases have originated in Northern Ireland. The court has so far issued judgments in six of these, and at least thirty Northern Ireland cases have been dealt with by the Commission.

1.3 *How Laws are Implemented in Northern Ireland*

The main implementing bodies are courts and tribunals, but the role of the police and prison services must also be borne in mind, as must the work of various watchdog bodies.

1.3.1 *The Court System*

When the Government of Ireland Act 1920 created separate court structures for the two parts of Ireland, the existing court system was closely followed in the North. A Supreme Court of Judicature of Northern Ireland was set up, comprising a High Court and a Court of Appeal. A Court of Criminal Appeal was added in 1930. The position remains much the same today, except that three important changes were made by the Judicature (Northern Ireland) Act 1978: a third division of the High Court—the Family Division—was created, the Crown Court replaced the old system of assizes (which meant High Court judges travelling around the country), and the Court of Criminal Appeal was merged with the Court of Appeal. The Queen's Bench Division of the High Court also contains what is termed a Divisional Court, which is a special court hearing applications for *habeas corpus* (the release of someone from police custody) and some judicial review applications (see 1.3.4). A further appeal lies on many occasions from the Court of Appeal to the House of Lords. The complete hierarchy of courts is set out in fig. 1.

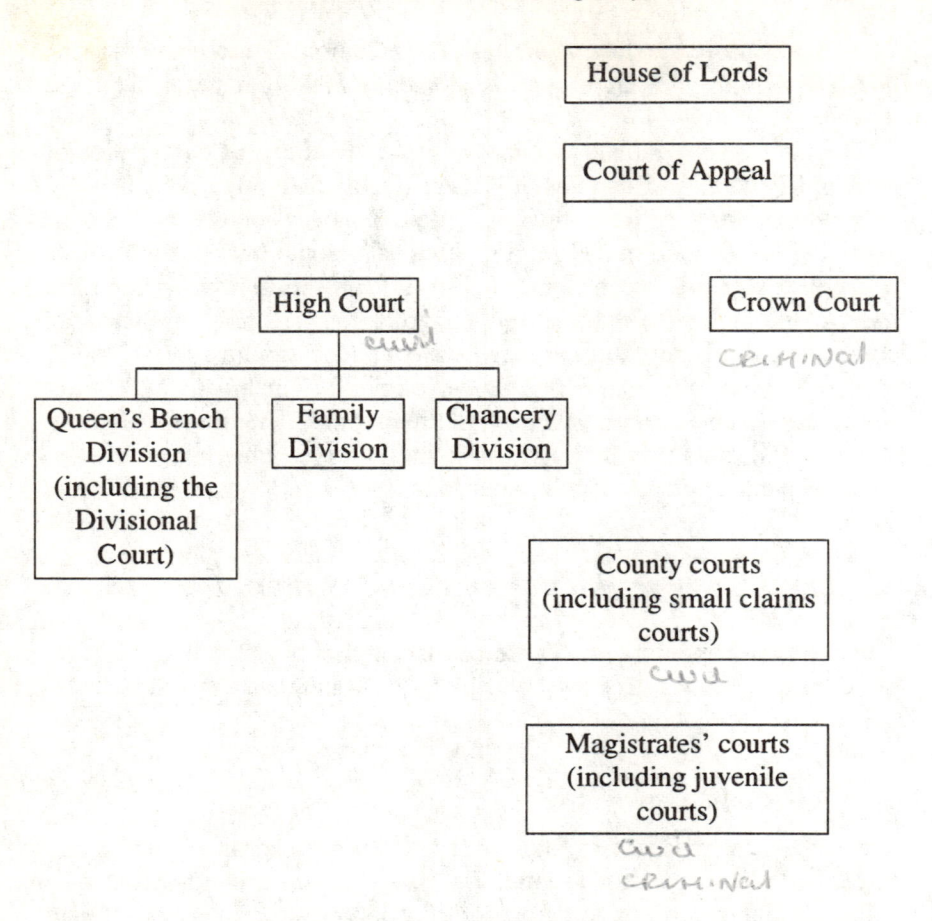

```
                                    ┌─────────────────┐
                                    │  House of Lords │
                                    └─────────────────┘

                                    ┌─────────────────┐
                                    │ Court of Appeal │
                                    └─────────────────┘

          ┌─────────────┐                          ┌─────────────┐
          │  High Court │                          │ Crown Court │
          └─────────────┘                          └─────────────┘
      ┌─────────┼─────────┐
┌──────────┐ ┌────────┐ ┌──────────┐
│Queen's   │ │Family  │ │Chancery  │
│Bench     │ │Division│ │Division  │
│Division  │ └────────┘ └──────────┘
│(including│
│the       │
│Divisional│
│Court)    │
└──────────┘
                           ┌──────────────────────┐
                           │   County courts      │
                           │(including small      │
                           │   claims courts)     │
                           └──────────────────────┘

                           ┌──────────────────────┐
                           │ Magistrates' courts  │
                           │(including juvenile   │
                           │      courts)         │
                           └──────────────────────┘
```

Fig. 1: *The hierarchy of courts in Northern Ireland*

1.3.1.1 The House of Lords

The most senior judges in the United Kingdom are the Lords of Appeal in Ordinary, who hear appeals in the House of Lords whenever that body sits in its judicial capacity. They are appointed, as are all full-time senior judges, by the Queen, but by tradition she acts on the advice of the Prime Minister, who in turn consults the Lord Chancellor (see 1.3.5). They must already have held high judicial office for two years or be barristers of fifteen years' standing, and they must retire at seventy-five. There can be twelve Lords of Appeal at any one time. Usually a couple of incumbents are Scottish lawyers, and from time to time a judge from Northern Ireland is appointed. The House of Lords usually sits as a bench of five judges, and never with a jury. Very important cases are sometimes heard by seven judges.

1.3.1.2 The Court of Appeal and the High Court

The judges in the Court of Appeal and the High Court also sit, as do the county court judges, in Northern Ireland's Crown Court. Since the Court of Appeal, the High Court and the Crown Court form the Supreme Court of Judicature of Northern Ireland, these judges are sometimes referred to as Supreme Court judges. At present there are eleven in office. Only barristers who have practised for at least ten years are eligible for appointment, and again they must retire when they reach the age of seventy-five. They can be removed from office before then if both Houses of Parliament so recommend, but this has never occurred in Northern Ireland.

The most important judge in Northern Ireland is the Lord Chief Justice. He is President of the Court of Appeal, the High Court, and the Crown Court, and in this capacity he assigns cases to other judges and performs a number of administrative duties. The Court of Appeal consists of the Lord Chief Justice and three other judges, called Lords Justices of Appeal. In criminal cases, moreover, all judges of the High Court are eligible to sit as judges of the Court of Appeal. The Lord Chief Justice can also ask a Lord Justice of Appeal to sit in the High Court, or a High Court judge to sit even in civil cases in the Court of Appeal. A case in the Court of Appeal will usually be heard by three judges, always sitting in Belfast, but some matters may be dealt with by two judges or even by one judge sitting alone. A jury is never involved.

The High Court of Justice consists of the Lord Chief Justice and seven other judges. The judges may sit in any of its three divisions but usually acquire an expertise in one of them. Except for hearings in the Divisional Court (see 1.3.1), a High Court case will involve only one judge, always sitting in Belfast. Juries (of seven people, not twelve) are now used only in defamation cases. For a description of the Crown Court see 1.3.2.

1.3.1.3 The Inferior Courts

County court judges, of whom there are now twelve but with thirty-four deputies, sit throughout Northern Ireland. Again, at least ten years' practice as a barrister is required before a person can be considered for appointment, though deputy county court judges, who may after three years be made full county court judges, can be appointed from the ranks of resident magistrates (see below) or from solicitors of ten years' standing. The retirement age is seventy-two. The judges who sit for Belfast and Londonderry are called Recorders. There are also four district judges, who assist the county court judges and exercise an important jurisdiction in the so-called small claims courts, where amounts of up to £1,000 can be sought.

Magistrates' courts are not staffed by judges at all but by resident magistrates (RMs), lay panellists, or (occasionally) justices of the peace (JPs). Less serious criminal offences ('summary' offences) are tried only by RMs, who are full-time and legally qualified. Today only barristers and solicitors of seven years' standing are eligible for appointment. There are at present seventeen RMs in office, with sixteen deputies, and they must retire at the age of seventy. In addition to trying minor criminal cases, RMs conduct 'committal' proceedings in more serious criminal cases to decide whether to commit an accused for trial in the Crown Court. They also deal with some civil law issues, especially matrimonial disputes short of divorce, and are responsible for a number of miscellaneous matters, such as the renewal of licences for public houses.

Lay panellists are people without legal qualifications who sit with RMs when the latter are hearing cases involving juveniles (persons under the age of seventeen). These so-called 'juvenile courts' deal with both 'civil' issues (the care, protection and control of juveniles) and 'criminal' issues (see 1.3.2). For many years there has been pressure to separate these two functions, and when the Children (Northern Ireland) Order 1995 comes into force it will have this effect by creating new 'family proceedings courts' to deal with non-criminal matters. A key principle already applied in all cases involving children is that the welfare of the child concerned must be the court's paramount consideration. (For further details on how the legal system deals with juveniles see chapters 4 and 6.)

JPs remain in office for life. The Lord Chancellor selects people on the basis of recommendations made by local advisory committees in each county court division. In Northern Ireland there are about 1,100 now in office, of whom perhaps 10 per cent are women. They receive no payment for their services, only out-of-pocket expenses. Their main task is to sign summonses, warrants, and various official documents (such as applications for state pensions). JPs retain also the somewhat controversial power to 'bind over' people to keep the peace or be of good behaviour.

1.3.2 Civil and Criminal Courts

Every case that comes to court is either a civil case or a criminal case. A civil case involves a dispute between two or more people, firms, or institutions: one of them is 'suing' the other, usually in order to obtain compensation. A criminal case involves a prosecution of a suspected offender by the state (in the form of the Director of Public Prosecutions or the police: see 1.3.5 and 1.3.6): the object is to punish a person for committing a criminal offence, not to compensate the victim of the crime.

Depending on the amount and size of the claim, civil cases in Northern Ireland will be dealt with by a magistrates' court, a county court, or the High Court. An appeal can then be taken to the next court in the hierarchy, and then to the court beyond that (see fig. 1). This means that cases begun in a magistrates' court or county court can go as far as the Court of Appeal, while cases begun in the High Court can go as far as the House of Lords (but the House of Lords will hear an appeal only if a novel point of law is at issue).

All criminal cases begin life in a magistrates' court. People accused of minor (or 'summary') offences will be tried by the RM, but those accused of major (or 'indictable') offences will undergo 'committal proceedings', in which the RM decides whether to commit the person for trial in the Crown Court. A Crown Court trial involves a jury, except that people accused of 'scheduled' offences (i.e. those with a terrorist connection) are tried by a judge sitting alone in a so-called Diplock court. The Crown Court hears only criminal cases (whereas the High Court hears only civil cases). An appeal against an RM's decision in a summary case can be taken by either side to a county court and then, if a point of law is at issue, to the Court of Appeal. An appeal against a Crown Court decision can be taken only by the defendant and goes straight to the Court of Appeal. All decisions by the Court of Appeal in criminal cases can be appealed to the House of Lords if there is a novel point of law to be resolved.

Cases can be referred directly to the Court of Appeal by a magistrates' court or county court if the RM or judge 'states a case' for the Court of Appeal, i.e. asks for a specific legal question to be answered.

1.3.3 *Tribunals, Inquiries, and Inquests*

In addition to courts, the legal system of Northern Ireland makes heavy use of tribunals in order to implement laws. Tribunals are specialist bodies created by statute to adjudicate on particular kinds of disputes. They are not staffed by judges but by specialists in the field. The two commonest types today are industrial tribunals and social security tribunals. Each of these uses three tribunal members to hear a case, the chairperson usually being a qualified lawyer and the other two members being representatives of groups such as employers, employees, welfare experts and voluntary organisations. There are a large number of other tribunals, but because many of them deal with very specific issues they do not often need to be convened. An example is the Mental Health Review Tribunal.

The legal procedures used at tribunals are not as formal as those used in courts. In fact they are supposed to be sufficiently informal for individuals to be able to represent themselves without having to rely on lawyers. As no state-funded legal aid is made available for tribunal hearings, many people do take their own cases, but an applicant stands a better chance of winning if he or she is legally represented. Sometimes a trade union, an advice centre or a body such as the Equal Opportunities Commission will make legal representation available free of charge.

From the decision of a tribunal there can be an appeal to a higher tribunal or to a court of law, depending on the subject matter in question. Appeals against decisions of industrial tribunals are heard by the Court of Appeal; appeals against the decisions of social security appeal tribunals are heard by a Social Security Commissioner, but sometimes there can be a second appeal to the Court of Appeal.

Tribunals should be distinguished from inquiries, which are set up on an *ad hoc* basis to investigate a particular matter. Inquiries are reasonably common in planning and electoral law but may also be held in the aftermath of a disaster or scandal, for example the Widgery Inquiry into the deaths in Derry on 'Bloody Sunday' in 1972.

Inquests are investigations into unexpected or unexplained deaths. They are conducted by a coroner, who will sit with a jury of between seven and eleven people if the death occurred in an accident. The sole purpose of the inquest is to determine who died, when, where, and by what means. The purpose is not to attribute blame to anyone: that is a function of the civil and criminal courts. Families attending an inquest cannot receive legal aid, and there can be no appeal against the verdict. Procedures at the inquest can, however, be challenged in applications for judicial review (see below).

1.3.4 *Applications for Judicial Review*

Judicial review is the process whereby decisions taken by inferior courts, tribunals or administrative bodies can be challenged in the High Court on the grounds not that they are wrong on the merits but that the correct procedures were not adopted when the decision was being taken. In particular the High Court will look to see whether the principles of 'natural justice' were adhered to. These require decisions to be taken only by a non-prejudiced person or body and only after all sides have had a fair hearing. Likewise, the High Court will strike down a decision if the person or body taking it was acting beyond their powers (*ultra vires*), if it was irrational or perverse, or if relevant considerations were ignored or irrelevant considerations taken into account.

Before an application for judicial review is made, the leave of a High Court judge must be obtained, and the application must be made promptly; usually three months is seen as the longest time it is permissible to wait from the time of the decision being challenged. Judicial review is also the name given to challenges brought against pieces of secondary legislation (see 1.2.3) on the grounds that they are *ultra vires* the body making them.

1.3.5 Important Legal Offices

After consultation with the Lord Chief Justice of Northern Ireland, the Lord Chancellor appoints certain 'statutory officers'. These include the Official Solicitor and eight Masters. The Official Solicitor represents the interests of litigants in cases where they would not otherwise be adequately protected, such as those involving children or people who are in custody for contempt of court. The Masters are former legal practitioners of at least ten years' standing who deal with a variety of procedural and relatively minor substantive issues before a dispute reaches a High Court judge.

The main administrators in county court divisions are called chief clerks, while those in magistrates' courts are called clerks of petty sessions. Process servers and bailiffs are private individuals or firms who are engaged by both public and private bodies to deliver official documents or enforce court orders.

The Lord Chancellor occupies a unique position in the United Kingdom: he or she is not only a minister in the Cabinet (appointed by the Prime Minister) but also the Speaker of the House of Lords in its legislative capacity and the senior judge when the House sits in its judicial capacity. The Lord Chancellor exercises his executive functions in Northern Ireland through the Northern Ireland Court Service, which corresponds to the Lord Chancellor's Department in London. The civil servants in this office help to arrange the business of the courts, service the needs of the judges and magistrates, and advise the Lord Chancellor on legal policy issues.

One of the main responsibilities of the Secretary of State for Northern Ireland, who is a member of the United Kingdom Cabinet, is the content of Northern Ireland law. It is he who must consider introducing into Parliament measures of law reform or updating social and welfare policies. In addition he is generally in charge of the penal system and the treatment of offenders. In this capacity he has the power to refer the convictions of some criminals to the Court of Appeal for reconsideration, to release prisoners on licence or grant them special remission, and to grant pardons. He also has special functions under Northern Ireland's emergency laws.

The Attorney-General is the chief law officer of the government, with responsibility for advising government departments and representing the government's interests in important legal disputes. Like the Lord Chancellor, he is a political appointee (though not a member of the Cabinet), but by tradition he is meant to be non-political when giving legal advice or when acting in his capacity as head of the barristers' profession. Before the abolition of the Stormont Parliament there was a separate Attorney-General for Northern Ireland; now the English Attorney-General acts for Northern Ireland as well, though a senior and junior barrister are appointed to be the Attorney-General's counsel in most cases requiring his involvement in Northern Ireland.

The Attorney-General has power to exercise some important discretions in matters involving the criminal law. His consent is required for the commencement of a wide range of prosecutions, and he can decide that criminal proceedings that are already in progress should be terminated, by entering what is called a *nolle prosequi*. Under Northern Ireland's emergency laws he plays an important role in deciding which offences should be tried in the juryless Diplock courts (see 1.3.2). In civil cases his approval is needed for actions taken by private citizens to protect the public interest (relator actions), and exceptionally he can initiate proceedings himself. Sometimes he or his representative is asked to attend court as *amicus curiae*, i.e. as a general legal adviser on points at issue in a case.

The Attorney-General's deputy is called the Solicitor-General, though he too is a barrister and a political appointee. The Attorney-General appoints a Crown Solicitor for Northern Ireland, whose services are then available to any Northern Ireland executive authority or any United Kingdom government department. The Attorney also appoints the Director of Public Prosecutions (DPP), who must be a barrister or solicitor who has practised in Northern Ireland for not less than ten years. The chief function of the DPP is to decide whether to prosecute people for indictable (i.e. serious) criminal offences and for such less serious offences as he considers should be dealt with by him. To date the DPP in Northern Ireland has considered it right to control the prosecution of all offences arising out of incidents of a political nature as well as offences allegedly committed by police officers. The police continue to be responsible for prosecuting minor cases.

If a prosecution is to be taken by a private individual, or by the police, the consent of the DPP or of the Attorney-General is very often required before the proceedings can officially be begun, and the DPP can step in to take over private prosecutions if this is in the public interest. In addition to conducting prosecutions the Director can require the police to investigate incidents that appear to him to involve an offence. By convention, the DPP's decisions can rarely be judicially reviewed (see 1.3.4).

1.3.6 *The Police Service*

The police service in Northern Ireland is the Royal Ulster Constabulary (RUC). As in other legal systems, the primary role of the RUC is to prevent and detect crime, but because it may have to work in exceptionally dangerous conditions its members are armed. Despite the troubles, the crime rate in Northern Ireland is relatively low, while the detection rate is high compared with that of the other fifty-one United Kingdom police forces. The

RUC has been assisted in its work since 1969 by the British army, though the policy now is that the police have an independent responsibility in all areas and that the soldiers are merely there to give support when needed.

As part of its inter-community work with young people, the RUC runs a football competition, discos, rambles, an inter-school quiz, and sixth-form seminars. Its Police Educational Programme runs in 60 per cent of all schools. The police also try to deal with the problems of juveniles in a sympathetic manner through a Juvenile Liaison Scheme. Every district council has a Community and Police Liaison Committee or a Security Committee (or both), but although police officers sit on these there is not as much contact with community groups in some areas as there could be. The neighbourhood policing scheme, on the other hand, is considered by the RUC to be most satisfactory, as are the support schemes set up to provide assistance to the victims of burglary.

It is not possible to sue the police if you are the victim of a crime which the police negligently failed to forestall, but it is possible to sue them if you are the victim of an unlawful arrest or an assault. The damages awarded by judges in such cases can be quite high ('exemplary' is the legal term), because the courts may wish to mark society's strong disapproval of an abuse of powers.

1.3.7 *The Prison Service*

There are five prison establishments in Northern Ireland: Belfast Prison (Crumlin Road), Maze Prison (formerly Long Kesh, near Lisburn), Magilligan Prison (near Londonderry), and the male and female prisons at Maghaberry (near Lisburn). The service is run by the Northern Ireland Office, which issues an annual report on its work in this field. Unlike the position in many other countries, the prison population in Northern Ireland is not increasing. Since 1989 the average daily population has been about 1,800. Almost 5,000 people are sent to prison each year: a large number of short custodial sentences are still being imposed for minor offences or for non-payment of fines.

The Young Offenders Centre at Hydebank Wood on the outskirts of South Belfast has places for 300 young men, mainly aged between seventeen and twenty-one, who have been sentenced to less than three years in custody. The few females in this category are housed at Maghaberry. Young people aged fifteen or sixteen are sometimes held in the Centre when a court has certified them to be unruly or guilty of serious misconduct, even though they may not have been convicted of any crime (see 4.6.4).

The prison regime is regulated partly by unpublished circulars issued to prison governors by the Northern Ireland Office and partly by the Prisons and Young Offender Centre Rules (Northern Ireland) 1995. These rules require prisoners to engage in useful work, which includes servicing the prisons themselves. Over half of Northern Ireland's prisoners enrol for educational courses.

In Northern Ireland there is no parole system. Instead prisoners can earn up to 50 per cent remission on their sentences, though for prisoners convicted of terrorist offences this is reduced to the one-third rule that also applies in England. People sentenced to life imprisonment and those imprisoned at the Secretary of State's pleasure ('SOSPs') for committing murder when under eighteen have their cases examined after ten and eight years, respectively, by the Life Sentence Review Board (for membership of the LSRB, see 4.6.5.6). This seeks the views of the judiciary and makes recommendations to the Secretary of State. Once released, a life prisoner remains on licence for the rest of his or her life and can be recalled to prison when the Secretary of State considers this necessary to avoid danger to the public (see also 4.6.5.6 and 5.3.4).

Each prison has a Board of Visitors appointed by the Secretary of State and comprising at least two JPs. The prison must be visited by one member of the Board at least once a fortnight. The Board's function is to satisfy itself on behalf of the general public about the state of the prison premises, the administration of the prison and the treatment of the prisoners. For the Young Offenders Centre there is a corresponding Visiting Committee.

Discipline in prisons is primarily the responsibility of the governor, but the most serious punishment a governor can impose is loss of twenty-eight days' remission. Governors have a discretion to allow legal representation at hearings where they preside. Representation should be allowed where the charge is serious or the penalty grave, where points of law are likely to arise, or where a prisoner might be unable to present his or her case properly. The most serious offences are referred to the Secretary of State, who usually passes them to a Board of Visitors. The Board can impose up to 180 days' loss of remission and/or confinement in a prison cell for up to 56 days. At hearings before a Board, prisoners must be allowed to present their own case and to call and cross-examine witnesses. They may also be given financial help under the ABWOR scheme (see 1.4.3.2). Judicial review is available in respect of disciplinary hearings in a prison (see 1.3.4), but otherwise there is no right of appeal.

Under the Rehabilitation of Offenders (Northern Ireland) Order 1978, a person's sentence (whether or not it involved imprisonment) may become 'spent', which means that from then on that person must be treated for most purposes as someone who has not been convicted of, or even charged with, the offence in question. (For more on discrimination against ex-offenders see 9.4.)

1.3.8 Ombudspersons

An ombudsman or ombudswoman is a person appointed to investigate complaints of maladministration by a public body. In Northern Ireland there are at present two such offices, traditionally filled by the same person. One is the Parliamentary Commissioner for Administration, who looks at complaints against central government departments (though if the complaint relates to the work of a United Kingdom department, such as the Inland Revenue, it should be lodged with the Parliamentary Commissioner in London). The other is the Commissioner for Complaints, who deals with complaints against local bodies, such as district councils, the Northern Ireland Housing Executive, the Education and Library Boards, the Health and Social Services Boards, and a host of 'quangos' such as the Sports Council and the Council for Nurses and Midwives.

Complaints to the Parliamentary Commissioner must be channelled through a Member of Parliament and must be made within twelve months of the action complained of. Complaints to the Commissioner for Complaints can be made directly, but the time limit is usually two months. In each case the ombudsman or ombudswoman has extensive powers to investigate the complaint, including the power to examine crucial documents. If the complaint is upheld, the department or public body concerned must rectify the complainant's position in a satisfactory manner, perhaps by paying compensation. A decision by the Commissioner for Complaints can even be used to support a claim for compensation in a county court.

Maladministration covers a multitude of sins. When the Commissioners' posts were first created in Northern Ireland, in 1969, it was felt that they would provide a good mechanism for rooting out religious discrimination. In fact few such complaints are now made through this channel. More common causes for concern are delay, incompetence and high-handedness.

Various organisations in the private sector have adopted the term 'ombudsman' or 'ombudswoman' to describe their own self-appointed watchdogs. This is true, for instance, of insurance companies, banks, building societies and newspapers.

1.3.9 Watchdogs

The legal system of Northern Ireland provides for a number of bodies whose function is to oversee the work of particular organisations or the operation of particular pieces of legislation. The two most prominent of these watchdogs are the Fair Employment Commission and the Equal Opportunities Commission, which deal, respectively, with the Fair Employment (Northern Ireland) Acts 1976–89 (concerning religious and political discrimination), and the Equal Pay Act (Northern Ireland) 1970 and Sex Discrimination (Northern Ireland) Order 1976 (concerning sex discrimination). The Commissions fund cases taken under the legislation and carry out educational work. The Standing Advisory Commission on Human Rights does not give financial support to litigants but issues advice to the government on whether the law of Northern Ireland is properly protecting the human rights of people living here.

An organisation which must be supervised as thoroughly as possible, because of the extensive powers it has been given, is the RUC. It is overseen primarily by the Police Authority for Northern Ireland, though legislation ensures that the responsibility for operational control of the force remains at all times with the Chief Constable. The Authority is essentially the paymaster and quartermaster, though in both capacities it is restricted by what the government will permit. Her Majesty's Inspectorate of Constabulary carries out *ad hoc* inspections of the force. Complaints against the police are investigated by the police themselves, but the investigations are frequently supervised by the Independent Commission for Police Complaints. People detained in police stations can be visited at any time by 'lay visitors', who check on the welfare of detainees and ensure that the police are complying with the codes of practice issued under the Police and Criminal Evidence (Northern Ireland) Order 1989. People detained in holding centres under the anti-terrorism laws may be visited by the Independent Commissioner for the Holding Centres.

Other bodies performing a watchdog role (some based in London) include the Advertising Standards Authority, the Broadcasting Standards Council, the General Consumer Council, the Health and Safety Agency, the Mental Health Commission, the National Audit Office, the Office of Fair Trading, the Press Complaints Commission and the Social Security Advisory Committee. The Lay Observer looks at how the Law Society handles complaints against solicitors, while the Law Reform Advisory Committee is an official body that issues suggestions for law reform.

1.4 *Legal Services in Northern Ireland*

There are a number of sources of legal help in Northern Ireland, but their accessibility depends largely on the financial means of the person needing assistance.

1.4.1 *Advice Agencies and Pressure Groups*

Advice on legal matters is available from various private agencies, such as trade unions and tenants' groups, as well as from public agencies such as

Citizens' Advice Bureaux (CABs) and community advice centres. There are many organisations offering advice on specific issues. Usually these bodies provide their services free of charge, and if the case is one that looks like leading to litigation they will be able to direct the client to a solicitor.

There is one Law Centre in Northern Ireland, based in Belfast but with offices in three other towns. The Centre is permitted to act as a firm of solicitors provided it does not engage in the major areas of work in which private practitioners operate, such as buying and selling houses or dealing with wills, matrimonial disputes and criminal cases. The bulk of the Centre's work therefore concerns social security, housing, debt and employment problems; immigration law is a growing specialism. Generally speaking, the Law Centre deals with cases only if they have been referred to it by another advice agency, and it specialises in test cases.

An especially important part of the Law Centre's work is the provision of training and information to other groups giving advice, mainly in the area of welfare rights. Along with the Northern Ireland Association of CABs the Centre has been instrumental in establishing an Advice Services Working Party, which aims to develop advice services throughout Northern Ireland by, for instance, encouraging liaison between agencies in the voluntary and statutory sectors.

Other bodies in Northern Ireland operate more as pressure groups than as advice agencies. The most prominent in the justice field is the Committee on the Administration of Justice. Some groups based in England also take a keen interest in the Northern Ireland legal system: worthy of mention are British-Irish Rights Watch, the Child Poverty Action Group, the Howard League for Penal Reform, JUSTICE, the Legal Action Group, and Liberty (formerly the National Council for Civil Liberties).

1.4.2 *Solicitors and Barristers*

Practising lawyers in Northern Ireland are either solicitors or barristers. The former are regulated by the Incorporated Law Society of Northern Ireland, with which all solicitors must register every year and from which they receive an annual practising certificate if they are properly insured against loss wrongfully caused to clients. Today there are more than four hundred firms of solicitors in Northern Ireland, many of them consisting of just one person. The Law Society does not permit solicitors to advertise or to attract business through price-cutting or sharing offices with non-solicitors.

Most of a solicitor's work is office-based, though they do have what is called the 'right of audience' in magistrates' courts and county courts (and sometimes even in the Crown Court). Their largest category of work is conveyancing (the legal transfer of land and buildings), other important categories being matrimonial work, wills, the defence of people charged with criminal offences and compensation claims.

The primary duty of solicitors is not to their clients but to the courts. Although they must act for their client to the best of their ability, this does not allow them to conceal evidence or to ignore established procedures. A person may complain about a solicitor to the Law Society, the more serious cases being considered by the Professional Conduct Committee and the Disciplinary Tribunal. An appeal against a decision of the Disciplinary Tribunal can be taken to a judge of the High Court, and in some instances there can be a direct appeal from the Professional Conduct Committee to the Lord Chief Justice. Complaints alleging negligence will be dealt with only if the behaviour amounts to professional misconduct or inadequacy. Other cases of alleged negligence must be processed in the ordinary way through the courts.

In a small proportion of cases handled by solicitors it will be necessary for the services of a barrister (also called counsel) to be used. At the moment barristers cannot take cases directly from clients: they must be 'briefed' by a solicitor. Consequently a barrister cannot sue the client for his or her fees; by legal custom the barrister cannot sue the solicitor either. Barristers are experts in advocacy and have the sole right of audience in the higher courts. They are regulated by the Inn of Court of Northern Ireland, while the Bar Council, elected by practising barristers, oversees standards within the profession and represents it publicly.

Barristers are self-employed and are not permitted to form partnerships. In Northern Ireland they traditionally work out of the Bar Library, which is situated within the Royal Courts of Justice in Belfast. Experienced barristers may apply to the Lord Chief Justice to 'take silk', i.e. to become a Queen's Counsel (QC). After appointment as a QC a barrister will not generally appear in court without a 'junior', as all other barristers are called, and will charge higher fees.

Complaints against barristers should be directed to the Complaints Committee of the Bar's Executive Council. Serious cases of misconduct are dealt with by senior members of the Inn of Court, called 'Benchers'. Again, if a client alleges that a barrister has been negligent, he or she will need to begin a court action. Barristers and solicitors are immune from being sued in respect of their performance as advocates in court (just as judges are immune in respect of their performance as adjudicators), but they can be sued in connection with pre-trial work.

1.4.3 *Financial Assistance with Legal Problems*

There are three quite separate state schemes for the provision of financial assistance in legal matters, and the first has a variant that really constitutes a fourth scheme. They are all governed by the Legal Aid, Advice and Assistance (Northern Ireland) Order 1981, and numerous complex regulations made thereunder or under previous legislation. Some matters are catered for by separate, specially designed schemes, such as the assistance that the Equal Opportunities Commission and Fair Employment Commission can supply in cases of alleged discrimination on the grounds of sex, marital status, religion, or political belief (see 1.3.9).

Probably the most attractive non-state scheme is the fixed-fee interview scheme, which a few solicitors still operate. Under this the client can receive half-an-hour's interview with a solicitor for a nominal flat fee of £5. Anyone can ask for this assistance, though solicitors participating in the scheme have a discretion whether to grant it.

1.4.3.1 The Legal Advice and Assistance Scheme

The value of financial assistance available under this scheme, popularly known as the 'green form scheme', is (in July 1995) £86.50, though in cases where assistance is granted to a detainee in police custody this limit is increased to £150. The decision whether to grant it is made by a solicitor, and the eligibility test applied is a purely financial one, the merits of the applicant's legal position being irrelevant. An applicant will not qualify if he or she has what is termed 'disposable capital' of more than £1,000. This refers to a person's savings and valuables: the value of capital assets such as a privately owned house or furniture is ignored, because these items are considered not to be disposable. Even if the disposable capital is less than £1,000 the applicant will qualify for advice and assistance only if he or she also receives income support or family credit or has a disposable income of less than £156 per week. 'Disposable income' means take-home pay minus regular living expenses (rent, rates, hire-purchase payments and other necessary outgoings).

Adjustments are made to the financial limits if the applicant has dependants (in July 1995 these are £335 for one dependant and £535 for two), and at present the applicant must make a contribution to the value of the help provided if his or her disposable income exceeds £64 per week. The law in Northern Ireland may soon be changed to bring it into line with that in England and Wales, where the contributory part of the green form scheme has been abolished.

If the work that needs to be done for the applicant will be worth more than £86.50, the solicitor can apply to the Law Society for an extension on the upper value of the work he or she can do.

1.4.3.2 The ABWOR Scheme

'Assistance by way of representation' (ABWOR) is possible under the green form scheme only in a very limited range of situations, namely certain civil proceedings in a magistrates' court (domestic cases, debt or land cases and some welfare cases), cases where a person appearing on a criminal charge before a magistrates' court would otherwise be unrepresented and a solicitor is within the precincts of the court, perhaps 'on duty', and cases before the Mental Health Review Tribunal and prison Boards of Visitors (see 1.3.3 and 1.3.7). Representation under legal aid schemes is not possible in any other kind of tribunal (except the Lands Tribunal), but a solicitor can still give advice and assistance (short of representation) on cases that are due to come before a tribunal.

In cases of ABWOR the disposable capital limit for eligibility is £3,000, the same as for legal aid in civil proceedings (see 1.4.3.3). But the rule still applies that only £86.50 worth of assistance is obtainable unless the Law Society grants an extension. The difference between the value of the work done for a client under the advice and assistance scheme and the contributions the client may have to pay is recoverable by the solicitor out of the costs that the other side agrees, or is ordered by the court, to pay to the assisted person, the property that is recovered for the assisted person (unless it is exempted property, such as maintenance payments), or, if all else fails, the Legal Aid Fund (an account established by the Law Society).

1.4.3.3 The Civil Legal Aid Scheme

The decision whether to grant civil legal aid in a particular case is taken not by the applicant's solicitor but by officials of the Law Society, to which the solicitor sends the appropriate forms. When the Law Society has taken a decision on a legal aid application it is not possible to appeal against that decision to the courts. It is possible, however, to apply for judicial review (see 1.3.4).

There is a 'merits' test as well as a financial test to be satisfied. As regards the former, the Law Society's Legal Aid Department must be persuaded that the applicant has reasonable grounds for being a party to the proceedings and that the granting of aid would not be unreasonable in the circumstances. As regards finance, in July 1995 an applicant must have disposable capital that is not more than £6,750 and disposable income not exceeding £7,187 per annum. For cases involving personal injury claims these limits are increased to £8,560 and £7,920. If the disposable capital is more than £6,750, aid may still be granted if the applicant cannot otherwise afford to proceed, but the £7,187 limit on disposable income is absolute. Disposable capital and income are calculated by the Legal Aid Assessment

Office of the Department of Health and Social Services, and in calculating disposable capital no allowances are made for dependants.

Contributions towards the cost of civil legal aid have to be made by applicants whose disposable capital is over £3,000 or whose disposable income is between £2,425 and £7,187, though there are special rules for pensioners. Any part of the excess capital can be requested as a contribution, but only one thirty-sixth of the excess income can be requested each month. The solicitor will be paid for the work, as will any barrister involved in the case, primarily out of the Law Society's Legal Aid Fund. If an unassisted party wins a case against an assisted party, the court may order the former's costs to be paid out of the Legal Aid Fund, provided that this is just and equitable in all the circumstances and (except in appeals) the unassisted party would otherwise suffer severe financial hardship.

Once a civil legal aid certificate has been granted it will cover legal services by a solicitor or barrister both before and during a court hearing. Practically every type of hearing is within the civil aid scheme, with the exception of tribunals (see 1.3.3), arbitrations (including proceedings in a small claims court: see 1.3.1.3), coroners' courts (see 1.3.3), defamation claims, admitted debts and claims relating to elections. In Northern Ireland, 'care' proceedings regarding children and bail applications for Diplock court offences are classified as civil matters for this purpose, as in fact are all appeals in the Court of Appeal on a point of law taken from a magistrates' court (even in what is otherwise a criminal case). The cost of taking proceedings in the Enforcement of Judgments Office or of referring an issue to the European Court of Justice (see 1.2.10) is also covered by the scheme. People who take cases under the European Convention on Human Rights (see 1.2.11) can benefit from a special legal aid scheme administered in Strasbourg.

1.4.3.4 The Criminal Legal Aid Scheme

The two distinguishing features of the present scheme for criminal legal aid in Northern Ireland are that the decision whether or not to grant it is taken by the court itself (not by a solicitor or by the Law Society) and that, if it is granted, the aid is free. The scheme also operates in the juvenile courts, where parents or guardians can apply for aid on behalf of the juvenile. People who bring private prosecutions, however, cannot rely on the scheme, except when defending an appeal. The introduction of ABWOR (see 1.4.3.2) has provided an attractive alternative to criminal legal aid in some situations.

There is no rigid financial eligibility test, but having received an application the court may ask the Department of Health and Social Services to inquire into the applicant's means and report back. For aid to be granted it must simply appear to the court that the applicant's means are insufficient to obtain legal help in preparing and conducting a defence. As a 'merits' test it must also appear to the court that the granting of free aid is desirable in the interests of justice. The court will take into account the gravity of the charge, the ability of the applicant to present his or her own case, and the nature of the defence. The costs payable to the lawyers are assessed if necessary by a Criminal Taxation Committee consisting of one barrister and two solicitors drawn from the Criminal Costs Assessment Panel. In situations where a court intends to sentence the defendant to imprisonment, detention in the Young Offenders Centre, or a period in a training school, criminal legal aid *must* be offered.

If a defendant loses a criminal case it is rare for an order to be made compelling him or her to contribute towards the prosecution's costs as well as paying his or her own costs. On the other hand, if he or she wins the case it is also rare in Northern Ireland for the prosecution to be ordered to pay the defendant's costs. It is only when the prosecution, or the defence, has been totally unsubstantiated that the costs will be ordered 'to follow the event', i.e. paid by the losing side.

1.5 *Further Reading*

Brayne, Hugh, and Martin, Gerry, *Law for Social Workers* (3rd edition), London: Blackstone Press 1993, chaps. 2 and 3.

Dickson, Brice, *The Legal System of Northern Ireland* (3rd edition), Belfast: SLS Legal Publications 1993.

Dickson, Brice, 'Legal Services in Northern Ireland' in Brice Dickson and Deborah McBride (editors), *The Digest of Northern Ireland Law* (2nd edition), Belfast: SLS Legal Publications 1995, chapter 1.

Vernon, Stuart, *Social Work and the Law* (2nd edition), London: Butterworths 1993, chap. 2.

2

PROFESSIONAL RESPONSIBILITY

Kenny Mullan

2.1 *Introduction*

The importance of social workers as integral members of a health and social services team cannot be overstated. To that team the social work profession brings expertise, proficiency and skills that are vital to its efficient and expert effectiveness. As professionals, however, social workers also have duties and obligations that give rise to professional responsibility. It is the nature and form of a social worker's professional responsibility that we wish to analyse in this chapter.

Key questions in such a discussion concern (*a*) the form and source of the duties and obligations that make up professional responsibility and (*b*) the range of people to whom such duties are owed. In relation to the first question we shall see that duties and obligations vary in both their form and their source. Most of the duties and obligations are to be found in and are enforced through various aspects of the law, although that is not always so. In relation to the second question we shall see that as a social worker you may owe obligations to the clients with whom you interact, to your employers, and to the profession within which you work.

Two final introductory remarks should be made about this chapter. Firstly, it is slightly different from the other chapters in that the other authors are often describing a piece of legislation that provides the framework of the area of law in question; often the law in that area is wholly contained within that legislation and can therefore be accurately described in a concise manner. The law relating to professional responsibility cannot be so neatly packaged. The source of the law may be legislation, but it may also be judge-made law, which requires particular and at times lengthy deliberation. Indeed at times the discussion in this chapter will be conjectural to the extent that the judge-made law on a particular point may be vague or open to a number of different interpretations.

Secondly, any discussion of a professional's responsibility within the law will necessarily progress into analysis of professional morality or professional ethics. This means that very often the reader may argue that we are giving a strict legal interpretation to a situation where questions of morality have a more important part to play. We acknowledge that the description of a professional's legal responsibility should include a discussion of the ethical aspects of the duty or obligation, and that social work has a moral as well as a legal reality. While we believe that detailed treatment of this issue is beyond the scope of this book, we have included a brief section on the concept of professional ethics, in the belief that the responsibility social workers have as members of a profession should be discussed.

2.2 *Legal Responsibility for Careless Acts or Omissions*

'Those who engage professionally in social work bring to their task skill and expertise, the product partly of training and partly of experience, which ordinary, uninstructed members of the public are bound to lack. I have no doubt that they should be regarded as members of a skilled profession' (Sir Thomas Bingham in *M. (a minor) and Another v. Newham London Borough Council* and *Others and X (minors) v. Bedfordshire County Council* [1994] 2 WLR 554 at 575.

Negligence has become one of the most important of all civil actions. The main reason for this is that nearly all claims for compensation, for personal injury or for damage to property are based on actions in negligence. Negligence is particularly important for all professionals, including social workers. Should a person, whether a client or not, suffer personal injury, including psychological or mental distress, as a result of the careless conduct of a social worker, they may consider bringing an action in negligence against that social worker.

The onus of proof in a negligence action lies on the plaintiff. To prove that a defendant is liable for the tort of negligence, the plaintiff must establish the following three essential components of the tort:

(1) the defendant owed the plaintiff a duty of care;
(2) there has been a breach of that duty by the defendant;
(3) the plaintiff suffered loss as a result of the defendant's breach.

All three elements of the tort must be proved in turn. Therefore, if a court declares that the defendant did not owe a duty of care to the plaintiff, there will be no need to go any further, even where the plaintiff could have shown a lack of reasonable care on the part of the defendant and resultant damage or loss. Similarly, even if a duty of care is proved, the defendant may escape liability if the plaintiff fails to show that the duty has been broken. A person may act so carelessly that his or her behaviour would provide evidence of breach of a legal duty of care, but in the absence of proof of loss or damage there will again be no liability.

It might even be the case that the plaintiff might prove all three elements of the tort, only to find that the defendant in turn can establish a legally recognised defence to the action, such as 'contributory negligence', where it can be shown that the plaintiff has contributed to the carelessness involved.

2.2.1 *Proving a Duty of Care*

The existence of a duty of care in negligence is a difficult concept for the non-lawyer to understand. This is because the question whether a duty of care exists in a given situation is a question of *law*. It is a commonly held belief that where a person has suffered loss or damage as a result of the obvious carelessness of another, damages will be payable as a matter of course. That an action in negligence is dismissed by a court, without an order to pay damages, because of a failure to establish a legal duty of care is often difficult for the plaintiff to understand. The plaintiff sees that carelessness causing harm has occurred and wonders why those elements alone cannot establish liability.

Even where the careless conduct is not so obvious, the plaintiff often believes that the only element of the action will be measuring the standard of care expected of that person in those particular circumstances against what actually happened. Such considerations are also often to the forefront of the mind of the person being sued. Plaintiffs and defendants concentrate on the facts of their own actual case: for example, ought the social worker to have made more visits to the home of a suspected battered child, or was the diagnosis of child sexual abuse accurate?

The first element of the tort of negligence is in fact concerned with the question whether *every* social worker owes *every* client a duty of care in relation to the work they do. The question is an objective legal one rather than a subjective, particular one.

Do social workers owe a legal duty of care to their clients? Remarkably, the question was decided for the first time by the Court of Appeal in the recent cases *M. (a minor) and Another v. Newham London Borough Council* and *Others and X (minors) v. Bedfordshire County Council* [1994] 2 WLR 554. The court was asked to consider whether an action for negligence could be maintained by a child against a local authority in respect of acts or omissions (i.e. failures) to act for which the local authority, in exercise of its functions as social services authority, was responsible.

The plaintiffs in *M.* were a girl (at the time of the action aged eleven) and her mother. In 1987 the child, then aged four, was interviewed, on the initiative of the local authority, by a consultant psychiatrist and a social worker to determine whether she had been sexually abused and if so by whom, and whether the mother could protect her from further abuse.

It was diagnosed that the child had been sexually abused, but the identity of the abuser was mistakenly interpreted, so that the child was removed from her mother. The two were separated for a year before the error was identified and rectified. Both mother and child alleged that they had suffered psychiatric disorders as a result.

In *X*, the plaintiffs were five children who, it was alleged, had suffered sustained ill-treatment and neglect from their parents between 1987 and 1992. Their claim was that as a result of the local authority's failure to act to remove them from their parents until 1992, despite repeated reports of ill-treatment and neglect, they had suffered illness, their proper development had been neglected, and their health was impaired.

Before beginning to analyse the court's findings on whether a social worker owes a duty of care to their clients, it is important to note a number of other important aspects of the case. First, the plaintiffs in *M*. alleged that they had suffered psychiatric disorders. We shall see below that mental distress is now recognised by the courts as a form of injury or damage. Second, the allegation of negligence was not the only action taken in these cases. The plaintiffs alleged in addition or as an alternative to negligence that the local authority and county council were in breach of a statutory duty. This allegation was that the local authority and county council had been in breach of certain duties imposed on them by various Acts of Parliament. We shall see below how that aspect of the case was concluded. Third, though there were a number of defendants in each of these actions, we shall concentrate solely on the allegations against the social workers.

The case that was put forward on the question of the existence of the duty of care for the plaintiffs was that the social workers, for whom the local authority and county council were liable, were persons exercising a professional skill and the plaintiffs were individuals foreseeably likely to be injured by careless acts or omissions by the social workers. For the defendants it was claimed that there was no precedent for a successful claim such as this and therefore the plaintiffs had to satisfy the current tests on the establishment of a duty of care that had recently been developed by the courts.

The Court of Appeal held, by a majority of 2 to 1, that the local authority and county council, as employers of the social workers, owed no duty of care to the plaintiffs and, with no dissensions, that the local authority was not liable in damages for breach of a statutory duty.

One of the judges, Lord Justice Staughton, thought that social workers no doubt viewed the children as their patients for many purposes. However, the services of the social worker were not engaged by the clients—the children or mother—but rather were thrust upon the client. The social worker, like a doctor, owed a certain duty to the person in their care; however, in the advice the social worker gave to the local authority about the child's needs and problems, the general professional duty was owed to the local authority rather than to the child. Therefore the existing principles on the duty and standard of care owed by professional people such as doctors to their patients need not be considered. Further, it was not practical to extend an established category of negligence to a new situation such as this.

A second judge, Lord Justice Gibson, agreed with Lord Justice Staughton on the question whether a social worker owed a duty of care to his or her clients. The third judge, Sir Thomas Bingham, disagreed, although he was outvoted by his two colleagues. He was prepared to hold that there were no reasons why the children (but not the mother) should not have a right of action against the defendants, including the social workers. His reasoning in reaching this conclusion was based on dismantling the arguments of the defendants' lawyers as to why a duty of care should not be imposed in these, legally novel, circumstances. Those reasons were concerned with the legal issues of foreseeability, proximity, witness immunity, public policy, causation, and damage.

All three judges were agreed that none of the defendants in these actions were liable for breach of statutory duty. As pointed out above, this was a separate action taken by the plaintiffs as an alternative to the action in negligence. The basis of the action lies in the fact that certain pieces of legislation, in this case the Children Act 1989, impose duties on individuals. If those individuals are in breach of those duties, the question arises whether the person injured as a result of that breach may sue. In this case, the court determined that they could not.

2.2.1.1 Probation Officers, Approved Social Workers, and Negligence

It is worth noting that the rules and principles relating to the legal liability of social workers described above are modified in their application to probation officers and approved social workers (see 5.3.6 and 7.3.1, respectively).

2.2.2 *Vicarious Liability*

It can be seen that the main action in each of the cases described above was taken against the local authority, even though the alleged careless acts and omissions were those of the individual members of the care team, i.e. the psychiatrist and social worker. The law states that an employer may be held to be 'vicariously liable' for the wrongful acts of his or her employees if certain conditions are satisfied. The conditions are that the person who actually carries out the wrongful act must work under a contract of service, i.e. be an employee, and that the wrongful act must take place during the course of employment.

The practical reason for suing employers for the wrongs of their employees is that employers are usually in a better position to pay any damages that may be awarded, and indeed may be insured against such circumstances. The fact that an employee is successfully sued under the doctrine of vicarious liability does not absolve him or her from individual liability: the vicarious liability of the employer is in addition to the individual liability of the employee. Liability for damages and actual payment of damages are two separate matters, however. A successful plaintiff may not claim two sets of damages: damages will be awarded against one defendant only. Further, an employer who has to pay damages as a result of the wrongful act of an employee may seek an indemnity from the employee. This may mean that an employee may have to pay back part or all of the damages paid by the employer. It is rare, though, for an employer to seek such an indemnity.

The fact that the plaintiffs failed to show that the social workers owed them a legal duty of care in these cases meant that the court did not have to consider the second and third elements of the tort, namely breach of the duty and resultant damage. It is important, therefore, to consider the issues that normally arise under these headings.

2.2.3 *Breach of the Duty of Care*

If a duty of care is established, the plaintiff must then prove that the defendant was in breach of the duty. This is a question of fact, not law.

The standard of care required is that of the reasonable person. In deciding whether a defendant has been in breach of their duty of care, the law recognises that reasonableness does not mean perfection. While the defendant has to take care, he or she need only take reasonable care; and taking reasonable care can, and does, allow for mistakes.

Although the question of the breach of a duty of care is a question of fact, not law, it is still an objective test that is applied by the courts. A judge will ask whether the defendant came up to the standard that would have been reached by a reasonable person acting in the same situation. For the most part, the defendant will be judged against the standards expected of ordinary members of the public. For example, the standard of a driver will be measured against the standard of a reasonable driver. However, where a person professes to have a particular skill or expertise, the standard of care is measured against the standard of a reasonable person having the same skill or expertise. For example, a social worker will be judged against the standard of a reasonable social worker. The reasonable social worker is not necessarily the best social worker in the world, and need not always work to the standard of perfection (*Bolam v. Friern Hospital Management Committee* [1957] 1 All ER 118).

In a civil case, the usual rule is that the plaintiff must adduce evidence to prove his case on balance of probabilities. In any action, therefore, professional evidence from others with the particular skill or expertise will be adduced to show whether the specific person has reached the appropriate standard or not. Therefore, where social workers are being sued, fellow-professionals in the same field will provide the evidence for what the standard reasonable practice would have been. If the plaintiff cannot show that the defendant did not act reasonably, the claim will fail.

2.2.4 *Proving Damage in Negligence*

The final element in the tort of negligence that a plaintiff must prove is that loss was suffered as a result of the defendant's breach. A non-lawyer may find this difficult to understand, because non-lawyers usually view the issue of damages solely in terms of monetary compensation. Monetary compensation will only be payable where the plaintiff can show that the defendant's breach of the duty of care caused loss. The two main questions that arise in relation to the issue of damage are 'causation' and 'remoteness of damage'.

Causation is concerned with whether the defendant's breach of duty was the direct cause of the plaintiff's loss. The plaintiff will fail in the claim for negligence if the connection between breach and loss cannot be proved. More practically, the plaintiff must show that if it was not for the carelessness of the defendant there would have been no loss.

It is clear, though, that the losses suffered by the plaintiff may be immense, even unlimited. The courts have developed a number of rules that limit the extent of the losses for which the defendant must compensate the plaintiff. These rules are concerned with remoteness of damage or loss. The main rule is that the defendant is only liable to compensate a plaintiff for the type of damage that was reasonably foreseeable as a result of the wrongful act (*The Wagon Mound* [1961] AC 388 and *The Wagon Mound (No. 2)* [1966] 2 All ER 709).

If the plaintiff is in any way to blame for the loss that has occurred, the damages that are payable may be reduced according to the division of liability. This is known as contributory negligence. For example, if the court decides that the plaintiff was responsible for 40 per cent of the loss, the damages will be reduced accordingly.

More often than not, damages are payable for injury to the person, damage to property, economic loss resulting from or as a consequence of physical injury, or economic loss resulting from careless or negligent statements (*Hedley Byrne v. Heller and Partners Ltd* [1963] 2 All ER 575). However, one other type of loss or damage that is of particular concern to social workers is damage for nervous shock.

Nervous shock is the type of damage that is most likely to be claimed in cases involving social workers. This was the basis of the claims in the cases of *X* and *M.* described above. The issue of whether there should be liability for loss of this type has more often than not been discussed in relation to the first element of the tort of negligence, i.e. whether a duty of care is owed in relation to this type of loss.

The courts have not been keen to extend the concept of the duty of care to those who suffer nervous shock rather than physical injury. The usual reasoning for this reticence relates to the question of quantifying loss of this type and a fear of false claims. In recent cases, though, the courts have been prepared to recognise, to a limited extent, the notion of liability for nervous shock. For example, in the case of *McLoughlin v. O'Brien* [1982] 2 All ER 278 the House of Lords was prepared to award damages for nervous shock where the plaintiff had suffered a specific psychiatric illness or physical illness rather than simple mental distress, anguish or grief and where the plaintiff's nervous shock was a foreseeable event.

More recently, the House of Lords has adopted a more restrictive approach to the question of liability for nervous shock. In *Alcock v. Chief Constable of South Yorkshire Police* [1992] 1 AC 310, ten plaintiffs brought claims for damages for psychiatric illnesses suffered after watching the disaster at the Hillsborough Stadium in Sheffield in 1989. The House of Lords held that there must be a close tie of love and affection with the person suffering the nervous shock so that it is reasonably foreseeable that the nervous shock will be suffered and that the plaintiff is close to the accident in time and space for there to be liability for nervous shock. 'Accident' can include the immediate aftermath; and other important factors to be taken into account in establishing whether a duty of care exists include the means by which the shock is suffered, so that damages will not be payable for shock brought about by communication by a third party.

2.2.5 *Summary*

The fact that the Court of Appeal in the cases of *M.* and *X* was not prepared to hold that the local authority and county council, as employers of the social workers, owed a duty of care to the plaintiffs does not mean that you should conclude that you have no professional responsibility to your clients. The issue is likely to come before the courts again, and when the argument about the imposition of the duty of care is put, influential judgments, such as that of Sir Thomas Bingham in *M.*, may persuade a court that it is right to allow claims in negligence. Indeed the House of Lords can and may rule that a duty of care does exist in cases such as those involving *M.* and *X*. (The decision in *M.* and *X*. has recently been affirmed by the House of Lords.)

2.3 Keeping Confidences

In the course of your work you are likely to receive a great deal of information about your clients, much of it personal. That information may come from official sources, such as the police, from other members of the health care team, such as general practitioners, from other agencies, such as the NSPCC, or from anonymous and non-anonymous private sources. It may be oral or in written form, it may be sketchy or detailed. The question is likely to arise whether you can, or indeed have to, impart this information at a later stage. The question of confidentiality and access to information, therefore, is vital for the social worker. The issue was so vital in the *Martin Huston* case that a number of the recommendations of the Social Services Inspectorate related to the development of policies on confidentiality. (See 'An Abuse of Trust: Report of the Social Services Inspectorate in the case of Martin Huston, pp 144–152.) (For the duty of confidentiality in court proceedings see chapter 3.)

2.3.1 *The Duty of Confidentiality*

The law has made it clear that 'where information which is of a confidential nature is entrusted to another in circumstances where that other is relied on to keep the confidence, an obligation of confidentiality will arise' (Brazier, *Street on Torts*, 165).

It is usual for the confidential information to be concerned with a person's commercial interests, but the law will also seek to enforce the obligation of confidence in relation to personal information (*Argyll v. Argyll* [1967] Ch 302).The obligation of confidence in relation to health care matters is most usually discussed under the heading of the doctor-patient relationship. However, the obligation will also extend to others within the health care team, including social workers.

We shall see below that the courts have been prepared to uphold the obligation of confidence even at the expense of the person about whom the information is being held. However, it is important to note that the courts have recognised that it may be justified to disclose confidential information in the public interest. In the case of *X v. Y* [1988] 2 All ER 648 the issue arose whether a newspaper could publish an article allegedly identifying doctors who were continuing to practise in the National Health Service despite having being diagnosed as being HIV-positive. The court held that disclosure of the identity of the doctors could not be justified as being in the public interest. In *W. v. Edgell* [1990] 1 All ER 835 the right of a psychiatrist to send a confidential report, prepared in the interests and at the request of a patient, to the Home Secretary was discussed. The court held that confidence could, in this case, be breached in the public interest.

It is also important to note that Parliament has also indicated that, in certain circumstances, confidences may be breached. For example, the Public Health (Control of Diseases) Act 1984, compels a medical practitioner to provide details concerning a patient suffering from a notifiable disease to the local authority. In addition, the provisions of the Police and Criminal Evidence legislation (Police and Criminal Evidence Act 1984, sections 11, 13, and 14) allow for the obtaining of materials that would normally be excluded on the grounds of confidence, including medical records, by the police on application to a judge.

Obtaining the consent of a person to disclose information about them will be a defence to an action for breach of confidence. The usual remedy sought for a breach of confidence is an injunction.

2.3.2 *Clients' Access to Reports*

Clients may seek or demand access to reports that they know have been compiled about them by social workers. A client may wish to have such reports for a variety of reasons, either from simple curiosity, or perhaps to use as evidence in legal proceedings. The issue of clients' access to records and reports was considered in the case of *In re D. (infants)* [1970] 1 WLR 599. In this case two children had been judicially committed to the care of a county council, which had boarded them out to foster-parents. The mother of the children applied to the court for custody of the children, and in turn the county council sought to make the children wards of court. During the wardship proceedings the mother's lawyer applied to the court for disclosure of the case records kept by the county council.

The Court of Appeal held that the case records that had been compiled and kept by the local authority were private, confidential and privileged records. This meant that there was no legal requirement to produce the notes and records during the wardship proceedings. The privilege attaching to the documents derived from public policy. In particular, Lord Justice Harman was of the view that public policy demanded that those who compiled and kept records of this nature should not have to be continually looking over their shoulders for attacks on their views and opinions.

It is important to note that Parliament has given people certain rights of access to records, whether of a general nature or relating to a person's medical history. The Data Protection Act 1984, allows people access to certain electronic data concerning them. Usually, information kept on a computer must, under this Act, be disclosed. However, an exception exists for electronically held information used in social work. Under the Data

Protection (Subject Access Modification) (Social Work) Order 1987, disclosure of data can be prohibited on two grounds: first, if serious harm to the physical or mental health or emotional condition of the data subject (i.e. the person on whom the file is compiled) or any other person would be likely to be caused; second, if the identity of another person (who has not consented to the disclosure of the information) would be likely to be disclosed.

The Access to Personal Files and Medical Reports (Northern Ireland) Order 1991, establishes a right of access by individuals to information relating to them maintained by certain authorities, such as the Northern Ireland Housing Executive or a Health and Social Services Board, and to reports relating to them provided by medical practitioners for employment or insurance purposes. The order gives an exemption from the provisions concerning access to medical reports where the supply of the data would, among other things, be likely to cause serious harm to the physical or mental health of the person who is seeking access. The meaning of the equivalent provision in the United Kingdom legislation was considered by the Court of Appeal in *Regina v. Mid-Glamorgan Family Health Services and Another, ex parte Martin* (*The Times*, 16 August 1994, 34.)

The Access to Health Records (Northern Ireland) Order 1993, gives a person the right to access to information held, both manually and electronically, by a medical practitioner. Again it is possible for a medical practitioner to refuse access to such information on the grounds that, in the view of the health professional, access would cause serious harm to the physical or mental health of the person concerned or where it would be likely to identify another person to whom the data relates. The term 'medical practitioner' is widely defined but the definition does not include social workers. However, it is clear that social workers will often divulge information to medical practitioners who fall under the provisions of the legislation and that that information will be included as part of the person's medical records.

2.3.3 *Confidentiality and Informants*

Many social workers receive a great deal of confidential information about their clients from private individuals, sometimes in confidence. Indeed you may rely on informers to alert you to situations of actual or potential spouse or child abuse, for example. A further question of confidentiality arises in this context. Can you protect the source of your information against requests to reveal their identity?

This issue arose in the case of *D. v. NSPCC* [1978] AC 171. The National Society for the Prevention of Cruelty to Children had received a complaint from an informant about the treatment of a fourteen-month-old girl and sent an inspector to the child's home to investigate. The child's mother brought an action against the society for damages, alleging negligence in failing to properly investigate the complaint and the manner and circumstances of the inspector's call, which had caused her severe and continuing shock. The society denied that it had been negligent and argued that there should be no disclosure of any documents that revealed, or might reveal, the identity of the informant. The society argued that the proper performance of its duties required that the absolute confidentiality of information given in confidence should be preserved, that if disclosure were ordered its sources of information would dry up, and that disclosure would be contrary to the public interest.

The House of Lords refused to compel the NSPCC to reveal the identity of its informant through disclosure of the documents. It held that the same immunity from disclosure of identity in civil proceedings should be extended to those who gave information about neglect or ill-treatment of children to a local authority or the NSPCC as that which was allowed to police informers. One judge, Lord Edmund-Davies, held that where a confidential relationship exists and disclosure would be in breach of some ethical or social value involving the public interest, the court has a discretion to uphold a refusal to disclose relevant evidence, provided it considers that, on balance, the public interest would be better served by excluding such evidence. The public interest in this case was the effective functioning of a statutory organisation authorised to bring legal proceedings to protect children's welfare (see also chapter 6).

2.3.4 *Confidentiality and Children*

Those social workers whose work brings them into contact with children may find that the children impart confidential information to them. Indeed the child may indicate a willingness to speak only on the understanding that the information will not be divulged elsewhere, particularly to its parents. Obviously this will create particular problems for you, because you will not wish to lose the trust of the child but may feel that the information ought to be passed to others, including perhaps the child's parents.

The approach the law would take on this matter would be based on the child's capacity to form a relationship of confidence with the social worker. The basis for this proposition is the case of *Gillick v. West Norfolk and Wisbech AHA* [1985] 3 All ER 402. Here the House of Lords ruled that a medical practitioner could give contraceptive advice to a girl aged under sixteen without the consent, or even knowledge, of her parents where, essentially, the girl was capable or competent to understand the advice. (Other factors—such as the inability to persuade the girl to inform her parents, the likelihood of sexual intercourse, the effect of a refusal on the girl's physical and mental health, and her best interests—were also to be taken into account: [1985] 3 All ER 402 at 413.

As a result, the law will favour disclosure of information where the child is incompetent to form a relationship of confidentiality, only allowing non-disclosure where there are justifiable reasons for doing so. It has been suggested that this approach is in keeping with the basic principle that the paramount concern of the law is the welfare of the child and that, on the face of it, the welfare of a child is usually best served by others knowing what has been divulged.

The corollary is that a duty of confidentiality will be owed to a child who is competent to form a relationship of confidentiality with the social worker. However, it is clear that the duty of confidentiality may lawfully be broken. In *Re M.* [1990] 1 All ER 205 a child had made an allegation of sexual abuse against a foster-parent but, when removed from the foster-parents' home, asked that the foster-parents not be told of the allegation. The local newspaper wished to publish a story condemning the local authority for removing the children without a valid explanation. The local authority sought an injunction restraining the newspaper from printing a story that revealed the identity of the children and that commented on the case.

The Court of Appeal granted the injunction to prevent the children being identified but allowed the newspaper to comment in relatively general terms on the issue. In so doing, the Court of Appeal discussed the duty of confidentiality and when and how it might be breached. 'A child cannot be sheltered from the consequences of the information disclosed and the person to whom the confidences have been made must give the child a truthful description of the likely outcome. He or she cannot promise what cannot be delivered. Whatever assurances... may be given to a child, he or she has to be told that at some stage... the carers will have to be told' (Lord Justice Butler-Sloss in *Re M.* [1990] 1 All ER 205 at p. 213).

In *Re M. (a minor) (Disclosure of Material)* [1990] 2 FLR 36 a father wished to challenge wardship proceedings based on allegations of sexual abuse by one of his children, and he applied for all records relating to her. The Court of Appeal, in balancing the protection of the child against the father's interests in obtaining justice, allowed for the disclosure of some but not all of the documents.

2.3.5 *Confidentiality and Defamation*

It may be that where someone feels that a statement that has been made about them tarnishes their reputation they will take an action against the maker of that statement in defamation. Defamation consists of publishing a statement that would tend to lower someone in the estimation of right-thinking members of society or that would tend to make them avoid that person.

There are two main types of defamation: libel and slander. Libel is a defamatory statement that is published in a relatively permanent form, for example in a film or newspaper. Slander is a defamatory statement in a transient form, such as speech. Libel is actionable without proof of any damage, whereas slander is only actionable if there has been some damage caused to the plaintiff, or the slander alleges that the plaintiff has committed a criminal offence, or that he or she is unfit for their trade, profession, or office, or, where the plaintiff is a woman, that she is unchaste.

If the plaintiff is to sue successfully for defamation, he or she must prove that the words or other material were defamatory, that they referred to the plaintiff, and that the words were published. If the alleged defamation is only revealed to the plaintiff, there will be no 'publication' in law. However, every time a defamatory statement is repeated there is publication for the purposes of the law.

Certain defences are available to an action for defamation. These include justification, i.e. where the defendant can show that the defamatory statement was true. Where the defamatory statement relates to the criminal conviction of a person who has been 'rehabilitated' under the Rehabilitation of Offenders (Northern Ireland) Order 1978, the defence of justification is negated by proof of malice or spite. A second defence is that of 'fair comment', where the defendant can show that the comment is on a matter of public interest. The comment must amount to an expression of opinion that must be fair and must not be prompted by malice. A final defence is one of privilege. Privilege, of a qualified nature, exists where there is a requirement to make a statement and where there is an interest in receiving it. A good example would be where an employer gives a reference for an employee.

2.3.6 *Summary*

The duty of confidentiality means that as a social worker you must be sure that all information you receive is treated as confidential. It is equally clear that your duty has to be balanced against the rights of your clients and others, arising through legislation and case law, in gaining access to information for specific purposes. Account will also have to be taken of the fact that you may be ordered to produce certain information and that ignoring the order may result in the imposition of penalties. Specific attention will also have to be paid to information relating to children and informants.

2.4 Social Workers and Employment

The employment relationship creates specific rights and duties for both the employer and the employee. An employee's rights in the employment relationship are protected by the law—either through the contract of employment that exists between employer and employee (see below) or through legislation—and employees may seek to enforce these rights through a number of different actions in the courts or tribunals. An employee's rights may arise through the specific duties owed by an employer to him or her, or may not require a corresponding duty. In turn an employee owes an employer certain duties. The non-performance of these duties may allow the employer to take certain action that may involve the termination of the employment relationship.

When an employer makes an offer of employment to an employee, a contract of employment is formed. Employees who work under a contract of employment are to be distinguished from independent contractors, who work under a contract of service. Basically, independent contractors are self-employed and usually do not enjoy the same degree of employment protection under the law as would an employee. All social workers will be employees for the purposes of the law.

Like all other contracts, a contract of employment contains specific terms, and, as we saw above, these terms may determine the distinct rights and duties that employers and employees owe to each other. The terms of an employment contract, like the terms of any contract, may be 'express' or 'implied' or may arise through incorporation.

Express terms are those that are explicitly agreed between the parties, whether in writing or orally, when the contract is made. If an employee receives a written contract of employment, the express terms will be contained in the written document. Employers are obliged, through legislation, to provide full-time employees with a written statement of their main terms and conditions of employment within a certain time of the beginning of the employment. Many employees mistakenly believe that this statement is their contract of employment. The statement may reflect or be evidence of the contract of employment, but it is not the same thing.

Terms may be implied through custom, by the courts, or through legislation. Implied terms often impose important duties on employees and employers. For example, one duty that is implied into each contract of employment is that the employer will take reasonable care for the employee's safety and health. Another duty implied into the contract of employment is that the employee undertakes to obey all lawful and reasonable orders.

Terms may also be incorporated into the contract of employment as a result of a collective bargaining agreement that has been agreed between a trade union and an employer. Such agreements usually cover matters such as wages, time off, and discipline, matters that, incidentally, are also the subject of the written statement of main terms and conditions described above. Whether an individual contract of employment has terms incorporated in this manner will depend on the employer's relationship with a trade union, if any.

In addition to the rights and duties that employees and employers owe to each other under the contract of employment, many types of employees enjoy certain employment rights that have arisen through employment protection legislation. Many of these employment rights find their way into the contract of employment, either through express or implied terms.

Employment rights and duties arise from both judge-made law and legislation, although, as we shall see, it is Parliament that has created most rights and responsibilities in this area. The main duties that have arisen through the implication by judges of terms in the contract of employment are that an employee will obey all lawful and reasonable orders, take reasonable care in his or her work, not wilfully disrupt the employer's business, and be honest. In turn the courts have been prepared to imply terms to the effect that an employer will pay agreed wages, take reasonable care for the employee's safety and health, not require an employee to do illegal acts, not act in a manner likely to destroy the relationship of trust or confidence, and inform an employee of employment benefits available where the benefits have not been negotiated with the individual.

As can be seen, these implied terms create specific duties for employees. In particular, the duty to obey all lawful and reasonable orders is an important one. The courts have indicated that the question of reasonableness is one of fact, to be decided as each case comes before them. To help to determine the issue, principles of good industrial relations may be taken into account. It is important to remember that the fact that an employee does not obey a lawful and reasonable order means that he or she may automatically be dismissed.

The main rights that are enjoyed by employees and that arise through legislation are as follows:

1. Itemised pay statement
2. Notice of termination of employment
3. Guaranteed payment
4. Written statement of employment terms
5. Written reasons for dismissal
6. Redundancy
7. Equal pay (see chapter 9)
8. Maternity rights

9. Time off work for antenatal care, for safety representatives, for public duties, and for trade union activities and duties
10. Sex discrimination (see chapter 9)
11. Religious and political discrimination (see chapter 9)
12. Suspension on medical grounds and remuneration
13. Statutory sick pay
14. Data protection
15. Insolvency
16. Take-overs
17. Deductions from wages

It is important to note that these employment rights do not all accrue naturally to all employees. Many of the rights are dependent on a particular employee having worked continuously for their employer for a qualifying period.

These rights are all equally important to employees. However, it is the area of unfair dismissal that usually receives most attention. A dismissal will be fair where an employer can show that he or she had a substantial reason for dismissing the employee and that the dismissal was handled in a fair way. Employees who feel that they have been unfairly dismissed may make a complaint to an industrial tribunal, which may award one of a number of remedies. In deciding whether an employee was fairly dismissed, a tribunal may ask whether the conduct leading to dismissal was in breach of the employee's professional code of ethics. Industrial tribunals may also deal with a number of the other rights of employees.

It is worth noting that it is often only through an unfair dismissal action that an employee will be able to seek to enforce specific employment rights. The law may recognise that an employee has certain enforceable rights, but in practice those rights may only be enforced when an employee has been dismissed. Undoubtedly this is detrimental to an employee who wishes to continue with their employment but not at a disadvantage. Seeking to legally enforce employment rights at a time when the employment relationship has broken down is of little benefit to an employee.

2.5 *Professional Morality*

It is common for professions to adopt codes of ethics in an attempt to describe their core values. Usually such codes are periodically reviewed and, in consequence, amended to ensure that they are accurate and contemporaneous expressions of the profession's ethics. Many professions regard a breach of their codes of ethics to be a disciplinary matter, which may result in the imposition of a range of sanctions, including the removal of professional status.

Social work is a discipline with a distinct moral reality. Social workers regard themselves as professionals and would assert that they are concerned with ethical principles and values and the duties that are owed by professionals. The British Association of Social Workers has a code of ethics for social work that applies to its members and is generally accepted by all social workers. This code outlines the specific obligations of the social worker as a member of the profession and the particular duties that arise from those obligations. Those obligations and duties are detailed and comprehensive and cover similar ground to codes formulated by other professions. The code also provides a detailed commentary on the meaning and context of the principles of practice that it outlines.

Despite the adoption of such a code by the BASW, the social work profession might still be described as an incomplete profession, in the sense that it has not yet moved towards the formation of a disciplinary body concerned with policing powers over the activities of its members. This is despite the strong pressure that has come from the profession itself for the establishment of such a body.

2.6 *Further Reading*

Almond, Brenda, *The Philosophical Quest*, London: Penguin 1988.

Brazier, M., *Medicine, Patients and the Law* (2nd edition), London: Penguin 1992.

Brazier, M., *Street on Torts* (9th edition), London: Butterworths 1993, parts 4 and 6.

Kennedy, I., and Grubb, A., *Medical Law* (2nd edition), London: Butterworths 1994, chaps. 3–5, 8, and 9.

3

THE SOCIAL WORKER IN COURT

Dympna Mallon and Ciaran White

3.1 *Introduction*

The prospect of a 'day in court' is a daunting one, even to those social workers with some knowledge or understanding of what exactly will happen. This chapter attempts to familiarise you with the terminology and procedure of civil and criminal proceedings and to make preparing for and appearing in court as painless and stress-free as possible. Our hope is that it will remove that feeling of nervousness or trepidation that comes from not knowing what will happen next.

A number of general comments about the relationship of social workers and lawyers need to be made at the outset. There appears to be little contact between the two professions outside situations in which cases are being prepared. (It should, in fairness, be pointed out that there is considerable contact between social workers and lawyers where child care and protection and wardship cases are concerned and where there are child witnesses in a case.) Indeed it seems that even when considering issues with legal implications, social workers do not as a matter of course turn to their agency's lawyers for advice. Greater contact between the two professions might be mutually beneficial.

Also, anecdotal evidence indicates that few social workers are given training regarding the courts, whether that relates to appearing in them, writing reports for them, or being informed about the role of the personnel involved. It appears that social workers learn about the courts, and their role within them, by 'sitting next to Nelly'—by experience, in other words. A social worker is usually only introduced to the legal system when a case arises. Occasionally, on court observational visits, the role of all participants is explained to newly qualified social workers, but this appears to be the exception rather than the rule. A social worker's exposure to the legal process is often, literally as well as metaphorically, on the steps of the courthouse. Greater thought needs to be given to training social work students and practitioners in courtroom procedures.

Let us turn to deal specifically with your role in court. When in court, never feel inadequate or uneasy merely because you are in lawyers' territory, so to speak. You may be a guest actor on the legal stage, but your presence there is important, because you are a specialist in your own field, every bit as important as the lawyers or the judge. This does not mean that you should try to be a lawyer or to outsmart the lawyers: that is not your role. You are there because of your expert training and knowledge, and your task is to present the facts as best you can. You should derive confidence from that training and knowledge. With sufficient preparation and understanding of what is expected of you, a day in court can become a valuable experience rather than an occasion for anxiety and dread.

Your involvement with a court will usually take two forms: report writing, and giving evidence. Both of these activities will involve you closely in the trial process. This chapter is therefore centred on these activities, and our focus is on those aspects of the trial process that will concern you when engaging in these activities.

One last introductory issue: the advice given in this chapter is applicable to all court hearings, whether in civil or criminal courts, or indeed in coroners' courts. (For an explanation of coroners' courts see 1.3.3. Inquests should be treated with the same respect as any other court proceeding, and if required to appear as a witness in an inquest you should make sure that you are legally represented.)

3.1.1 *Courts and the Truth*

Our trial procedure is adversarial, not inquisitorial. This means that the trial process is a competitive argument between two sides, each one presenting the best case for its own side. It is not designed to objectively discover the absolute truth of the matter being tried. The parties are engaged in a struggle with each other, not in a mutual search for the truth. The competitive nature of the process is, in part, an explanation for its reputation as an awesome place for the inexperienced witness under cross-examination.

Social workers occasionally want to use the opportunity of the court hearing to make a clear and concise statement about their clients. You must realise that this will be difficult in the question-and-answer format that the adversarial system is founded on. Indeed your barrister is likely to be reluctant to allow you to make anything but brief responses to his or her questions. This is not because they are denying the importance of the client to the case but because they will fear that if you give unnecessarily long answers you may say something that the opposing side can exploit in cross-examination. Anyway, a good barrister will prefer that the 'clear and concise' statement about the client would be inferred from the replies you make to his or her questions. (For more on the barrister's perspective see 3.4.2.)

3.2 Reports

Our concern here is with the reports you will be asked to prepare in a court context. Therefore, reports prepared for your employer's purposes lie beyond the scope of this book, though the comments made in respect of court reports you may find useful when writing in-house reports.

You should recognise that a report you prepare for court is not just a source of information for all the parties to the case but also a documented reflection of your professionalism as a social worker. An inadequate or incomplete report will not merely damage your case but will create a strong negative impression of you as a professional. Preparing a report for court should be made easier if you understand the use to which that report will be put within the legal process and if you have an understanding of the overall process. You should bear in mind that you may be sued if a report is shoddily prepared and it causes 'damage' or injury to someone. (However, if you are a social worker performing functions under mental health law or a probation officer you may benefit from the modification of the law of negligence as it applies to those specialised types of social worker: see 7.3.1 and 5.3.6, respectively.) The success of such an action depends on the court finding the existence of a duty of care owed by you to the injured party (see chapter 2).

The essential purpose of a report prepared by you is to furnish the court with information about a particular matter, at a particular stage in the proceedings, in order to inform the court in deciding how these proceedings—whether civil or criminal—will progress from that point. Your report will supplement the evidence the court has heard and may be the last item the court considers before arriving at a decision on that case. Written reports play an important role in legal proceedings, if only for the fact that they are easier to assimilate than a mass of oral testimony.

There are a number of different types of report that social workers in Northern Ireland can be required to compile: reports under the mental health legislation (see chapter 7), reports in matrimonial proceedings (see chapter 10), reports in criminal proceedings by probation officers (see chapter 4), and reports relating to the care and protection of children (see chapter 6). In all these circumstances, when compiling a report you are acting as an officer of the court.

3.2.1 *Writing a Report*

It appears that few agencies give training in report-writing, and consequently many social workers end up relying on sample reports, written on previous occasions by colleagues, to guide them. This practice may not be as helpful as it seems, because the quality of past reports may vary and the models you have been given may not be useful for the task ahead of you.

Our first piece of advice regarding the compilation of reports is to reject any notion that there is a definitively correct way in which to compile them. Content, not form, is the most important aspect of any report. Therefore, we set out here a number of principles that apply to the preparation of any report to be used in court. These principles are generated by our perspective as lawyers. In other words, these are the issues that are important to a lawyer, and a report conforming to them or written with them in mind is more likely to win the respect of lawyers and be more easily digested, thus proving more helpful to the court in coming to a decision. These principles are interrelated, and there is a considerable degree of overlap between them. Use them as a check-list when writing your reports.

3.2.1.1 Relevance: 'Does everything in the report need to be there?'

The statutory provision will inform you of the purpose to which the report will be put and should also help you determine what is relevant and what is not. For example, a report into the possibility of reconciling the parties to a matrimonial dispute should not include comments about their wealth, unless financial and property disputes are a bar to their reconciliation.

3.2.1.2 Accuracy: 'Can I defend every word of it?'

The report should, as accurately as words will allow, reflect the factual situation and your views, if required. This means that care should be taken that what you have written is not ambiguous and that the descriptive words chosen should not be too dramatic, for example. The reason for this is simple. If the report is not accurate, the opposing side's barristers will expose those inaccuracies and attempt to discredit it. Doubts about accuracy should be expressed, and you should attempt to check the accuracy of as many facts as possible. It will greatly impress the court if you have cross-checked the evidence of a witness. You should also take care to distinguish matters of fact from matters of opinion.

3.2.1.3 Completeness: 'Have I dealt with all the issues?'

In any problem there will be a number of core issues but also a number of less important ones. The latter should not be ignored: for completeness' sake these less important issues should be dealt with, though obviously not to the same depth as the core issues. Ensuring that your report is complete is commensurate with your role in providing the court with sufficient information for it to act justly. An example might be the failure to consider unlikely, though feasible, arrangements for the care of children in a report made for divorce proceedings.

3.2.1.4 Style and Length: 'Is it easily understood and no longer than it needs to be?'

A report that is short and direct, rather than long and 'waffly', will be more highly valued by the court. Excessive use of jargon should be avoided, though recourse to some jargon is permissible provided that you explain the term on the first occasion it is used and then use that term consistently thereafter. Concentrating on keeping the report to a necessary length should be beneficial, because the report should then be more digestible. This is not an excuse to cut the report short but rather a warning to help prevent it being too long. A simple, concise though precise writing style will often be far more beneficial than a jargon-laden, 'flowery' style that seeks to impress the reader with the author's knowledge of social work principles and of the factual circumstances of the issue.

Just as the document itself will have an overall structure, so too should the sentences and paragraphs within the report. Avoid sentences that are longer than they need to be, remembering that two shorter sentences will be far more comprehensible that one long one. Clarity of expression and of thought should be uppermost in your mind when writing. Confused or awkward writing will often be something you will find difficult to spot yourself, and it is a good idea to ask a colleague to read your report before submitting it. Indeed the 'swapping' of reports between colleagues should form part of everyday practice within your agency.

You should make allowances for the various stages in the completion of a report, and indeed when first instructed to make a report you should plan the time required for each stage, leaving time of course for typing, proof-reading, and any changes that might need to be made.

3.2.1.5 Awareness: 'What is the purpose of this report, and is it clear that I understand that purpose?'

If it is clear from your report that you have an awareness of the relevant facts of the case and of the legal context in which the report arises, your report's value to the court will equally be improved. The clearer you are about the role to which the report is put the better.

3.2.1.6 Diligence: 'Is this report the best it can be?'

What we mean here is that in compiling the report you should leave no stone unturned. You may argue at this point that such an exhortation is unrealistic, given the time constraints within which you work. We fully appreciate those constraints. We are not advocating that you spend an unlimited time on the report: rather, we are saying that what time you have you should spend making it the best it can be. Exercising due diligence in writing the report means that sloppiness should be eliminated. (This could indeed be expressed as the 'sloppiness principle'—i.e. do not be sloppy in compiling the report—but we preferred to frame these principles in the positive rather than in the negative.)

On the form the report should take we make the following suggestions. On the front cover include sufficient details to allow the report to be identified. The court, the case name, date of the hearing and identity of the report writer should appear on the cover, with a clear indication that the contents of the report are confidential. On the first page it is a good idea to inform the reader of your acquaintance with the subject matter of the report and to set out the sources of information used in compiling the report.

Consider beginning the report by stating the obvious, because what is obvious to you may not be obvious to others. Numbering paragraphs is also a good idea and will make reference to the report easier for all concerned—including you, if you have to appear as a witness. Also, if the report involves reference to a considerable number of people, a reader may find it useful to have a list of the people and their titles or occupations and their relationships stated at the beginning of the report. Such a list is particularly important where the people mentioned in the report are family members with the same name.

When you are interviewing people as part of the process of compiling the report, you should ensure that from the outset they are aware of who you are, what your role is, and why they are being interviewed. Be conscious of the danger of suggesting answers to your questions. A barrister in court is not allowed to ask leading questions of his or her witness, and you should exercise a similar restraint on yourself (see 3.3).

Finally, some comments about your conclusions. Make sure that the conclusions you arrive at flow from the information provided in the text. Conclusions suddenly appearing at the end of a document without any apparent foundation are not worth the paper they are written on and will make an easy target for the opposing barrister when he or she seeks to destroy the credibility of your report. When stating a conclusion choose words that adequately describe your *degree of conviction* about the conclusion. Once put down in writing, a person's judgment often acquires greater authority than it might warrant. Words like 'probable', 'possible', 'sufficient' and 'considerable', for example, have different but important meanings, and you should think carefully about the consequences of putting them in your conclusions.

3.2.2 *Preparation of Evidence*

We are concerned here with the preparation of evidence to be presented to the court in written form. You may think this is a report, but in fact it is not. What you are doing is providing evidence to the court by means of a witness statement. (A 'report', on the other hand, would be a document prepared for and requested by the court.)

Documents of this nature are prepared in co-operation with the lawyer representing your agency. The legal procedure involves filing a 'proof of evidence'. This is a legal document that will be used by your agency's lawyer in presenting its case but that is also useful for you in preparing your own testimony. Long before the court case you will have a meeting with your barrister, at which you will be able to refer to your notes and answer fully any questions the barrister may ask. He or she will compile a statement of the relevant evidence, which will then be typed in a particular format and language. Once this is done it will be returned to you, and when you are satisfied that it is accurate you sign and date it, and it is submitted to the court as your statement. Every witness who is to appear will have compiled a similar document.

3.3 Order of Proceedings

It may be helpful for you to understand the order in which the trial will proceed. In a criminal case the party pursuing the case will be the prosecution and the party answering the case will be the defence. In civil cases the parties are known either as the applicant and the respondent (if the case is a matrimonial one, for example) or the plaintiff and the defendant (if the action involves a tort, for example negligence: see chapter 2). (For an explanation of the terms 'criminal' and 'civil' see chapter 1.)

Irrespective of the court in which your case is taking place, the procedure for the introduction of oral evidence is standard. Oral evidence can be introduced at three stages: the examination-in-chief, the cross-examination, and the re-examination.

3.3.1 *Examination, Cross-examination, and Re-examination*

The party bringing the case presents its evidence first. Both sides can, of course, call witnesses. Where a party calls a witness, that party will question him or her first. This is the examination-in-chief. The function of the examination-in-chief is to have the witness tell his or her story and testify to the facts the barrister has called him or her to prove.

'Leading questions' cannot be asked in examination-in-chief, nor indeed at the re-examination stage. It is not easy to define a leading question, but essentially it is one that contains its own answer. For example, it would be a leading question to ask of a witness, 'Were you in Mr Smith's house on the night on which he is alleged to have attacked his wife?' It is acceptable to ask, however, 'Where were you on the night on which this attack is alleged to have taken place?'

You may therefore find yourself a little exasperated at some of the apparently pointless questions your counsel puts to you, feeling that a more direct approach would speed the process considerably; but the reason for this is that counsel cannot ask leading questions.

Once the examination-in-chief is completed, the opposing party has an opportunity to ask questions of the witness. This is known as the cross-examination, and it can be the most trying part of your experience in court. Occasionally you will not be cross-examined, because opposing counsel will feel that there is little or nothing to be gained by doing so. That opposing counsel decides not to cross-examine you does not mean that you have not done well.

Perhaps the two main functions of the cross-examination are (a) to discredit the evidence of a witness and (b) to have a witness confirm, at least partially, the opposing side's version of events. You should remember that the barrister is seeking to discredit your evidence, not you personally, though this can often only be done by robust and searching questioning of you. Obviously a barrister will focus on what he or she considers weak points in your evidence in order to carry out this discrediting. So, for example, if your evidence is that a child faced a significant risk of real harm, the fact that your visits took place at three-week intervals will be the focus of the barrister's questioning. In cross-examination where a party has a number of witnesses, a barrister will often attempt to discredit those witnesses' testimony by highlighting differences between their recollections of events or between their opinions. This can be done by focusing on minor or background details of the case and endeavouring to get them to admit to different recollections of the same events.

We might add that these comments with respect to cross-examination are equally applicable to all witnesses, not just social workers. Accordingly you may find this information valuable in advising those of your clients who are summoned to testify in court.

If the opposing case involves a mutually incompatible version of facts or events, opposing counsel is required to put their side's case to you, even though they are almost certain that you will reject that version. This mandatory requirement that the barrister 'put his case' explains why the barrister will question you in the following way: 'I put it to you, Mr Jones, that you were not in Mr Smith's house on the date in question.' The conclusion of the cross-examination can often appear unnecessary and a little bizarre as the witness denies a number of questions putting forward the opposing view of events. Lastly, we point out that leading questions can be asked in cross-examination.

Once the cross-examination is complete, the first party has an opportunity to re-examine the witness, and so this part of the witness's testimony is known as the re-examination. This is counsel's chance to try to repair the 'damage' done to the witness's evidence in cross-examination. We should remind you that if you are appearing as a witness you will have prepared your evidence, in the form of a sworn statement, well in advance of court proceedings, and this will have been filed with the court and been made available to all the parties involved in the case (see 3.2.2.). However, it is on your oral testimony that the court will base its decisions, not on the statement submitted. In other words, your oral testimony takes precedence over the prepared statement.

3.3.2 *Standards of Proof*

A standard of proof is the level of evidence necessary to win a case. A distinction has to be made between criminal and civil cases, as a different standard of proof exists for each. In a criminal case the standard of proof the prosecution will have to meet is 'proof beyond all reasonable doubt'. In other words, it will have to prove that the accused is guilty beyond all reasonable doubt. In a civil case, however, all that need be proved to the court is that the events were *more likely* to have happened in the manner asserted by the applicant or plaintiff than not to have happened in that way. This lawyers refer to as the 'balance of probabilities'.

These are standards you should be aware of, though you need not necessarily be versed in the details of them. It is these differing standards of proof that explain why a child may be taken into care in a civil law case (because on the balance of probabilities this was needed in his or her interests) and yet the person who you believe abused the child is walking free (because the criminal case against the abuser could not be maintained beyond a reasonable doubt).

3.3.3 *Presumptions*

The law has developed presumptions to simplify the use of material evidence. There are two types of presumption: those that are 'rebuttable' and those that are not. A rebuttable presumption is a presumption that a certain factual situation exists but can be rebutted (i.e. reversed) by adducing evidence to the contrary. An irrebuttable presumption, on the other hand, is one where the basic assumption cannot be reversed. Some examples will illustrate the difference. It is an irrebuttable presumption that if the blood alcohol level of a driver is above the legal limit, he or she is incapable of proper control of a car. It is a rebuttable presumption that someone is innocent until proved guilty.

Presumptions will come into play in a criminal case against a young person, for example, because there is an irrebuttable presumption that a child under the age of ten cannot commit a crime (see chapter 4) and there is a rebuttable presumption that a child between ten and fourteen is incapable of having the necessary intent to commit a criminal offence. So if it is established that a twelve-year-old, for example, did actually carry out the crime, the prosecution will attempt to prove that he or she did have the intent to commit the crime. Other examples of rebuttable presumptions are

- that a man and woman who are cohabiting are married;
- that a child is 'legitimate' at birth;
- that someone intends the natural and probable consequences of his or her actions.

3.4 *Acting as a Witness*

When you are appearing as a witness, preparation can be very helpful. Be familiar with your statement (or statements) and with the facts of the case. You may feel patronised if we remind you to dress neatly, but sloppy dress can be taken by some judges as a lack of respect for the court, and some of them can be quite finicky about the matter.

If the lawyer representing either party regards you as a material witness in his or her case (i.e. essential to the case being argued) you may be asked to be present at the hearing of the case. This may even result in your being called to give evidence against your colleagues, your employer, or your client. In that circumstance you will be known as a 'hostile witness'. As a social worker you have probably been encouraged to think about the case and offer your opinion: social workers often find their opinions not only welcomed but actively solicited at case conferences etc., where there is considerable emphasis on pooling ideas with a view to arriving at the best possible approach after looking at all the alternatives.

The prospect of being called as a hostile witness may arise precisely because of this process of consultation among team members. You should not allow this to constrain your discussion of your active participation. If the other side calls you to give evidence that you favoured a different approach, your obligation is to tell the truth and to be as clear as possible about the evidence you will be giving. You should not feel that you are somehow betraying your colleagues. If the court feels the case demands it it can require you to attend by issuing a *sub-poena* for you to appear at the trial. Refusal to obey a *sub-poena* may result in the imposition of a fine or imprisonment, or both, for contempt of court.

We now turn to discuss what can and cannot be given as evidence. Ultimately this will be an issue for the court to decide, so if you have doubts about whether to introduce any evidence into court, our advice is to attempt to introduce it and let the lawyers argue about its admissibility. Do not take it upon yourself to act as the arbiter of admissibility, in case you wrongly exclude evidence that could have been admitted and was important to the case.

On the question of what can be given as evidence, the main test governing the issue is one of relevance. If the evidence is considered to be relevant to the case at issue, it will be admissible, and vice versa. This is a general test (a rule of thumb, if you like), and there will often be qualifications to it. We might add that the lack of a definition of relevance further confuses the matter. Generally speaking, however, if your evidence goes some way towards tackling the central issue of the case, it will be relevant; if it does not, then it will be irrelevant. For example, if the case deals with a mother who is alleged to have neglected her young children, whom you have found alone in their home, this will be admissible evidence. If, however, you have simply visited the house and found the child with a babysitter, this evidence will be irrelevant and therefore inadmissible, since it doesn't establish neglect on the mother's part.

This example may not be as straightforward as it seems, however. For instance, the age of the babysitter will be relevant if she was only eleven years old, as that fact will have a bearing on whether the mother was neglectful or not. Similarly, if the babysitter is accompanied by a boy-friend, that evidence will also be relevant in deciding whether the mother was neglectful or not. So you can see that the issue of relevance is not an easy one to describe in general terms, as a great deal will depend on the circumstances. You should also be prepared for the inevitable question from the mother's solicitor whether you ever visited the house and found the children alone. If the answer is 'no', that evidence will be relevant to counteract the Board or Trust's case that the mother is negligent. However, it will be up to the judge to assess the evidential significance of the information. Your responsibility (as seen later in 3.4.3) is to answer honestly the questions that are asked of you.

Equally, if you are giving evidence about an allegedly abusive father assaulting his children, it will be relevant that he has a violent temper that you have witnessed, and it will be relevant that the children have injuries consistent with beating that you have seen. However, it will not be relevant that the paternal grandfather was an alcoholic, nor that the alleged abuser was himself abused as a child. This information will not assist the court in establishing the facts of the case.

In the course of their training and practice, social workers regularly encounter research data and statistics relating to their area of work, and you may wonder whether such material can be used as evidence in court. The general rule relating to such information is that it will constitute hearsay (see 3.4.7), since the person relying on it in his or her evidence is unlikely to be its author and cannot therefore verify its accuracy before the court.

One exception to the rule against hearsay evidence is its presentation by an 'expert witness'. In *English Exporters v. Eldonwall* [1973] Ch 415, the court said that while the use of books, journals and the materials of other professionals was acceptable in helping to form an opinion, the use of articles, reports or statistics that are compiled for purposes other than the case at hand will represent hearsay evidence. However, in *R. v. Abadom* (1983) 1 WLR 126 the court permitted a forensic science officer to use Home Office statistics relating to the content of glass to identify an alleged burglar. Although the statistics were unpublished, it was established in this case that an expert may cite and rely on records of data.

This case also established that an expert witness may refer to statistics and other data that are commonly used within a particular profession, even if the expert witness has not been trained in that profession. So in *R. v. Somers* [1964] 48 CrAppR 11 a doctor was allowed to rely on tables listing destruction rates of alcohol, although he was not a trained chemical analyst.

This then will be the general rule, though under article 169 (5) of the Children (Northern Ireland) Order 1995, the judge will have the discretion of admitting into evidence any information that assists the court in reaching a decision that is best for the child (see 3.4.8). Decisions about whether something is relevant or not are made by the court and not by the witness. You may find this irritating or restrictive in practice, since social workers are concerned with extraneous, intangible matters concerning relationships, character assessments, and personal histories, whereas lawyers will often simply want to know if it happened, when it happened, and whether or not you were there. The personalities of the people involved and the surrounding circumstances will be irrelevant (and therefore inadmissible), however much you feel they should be included. (However, in some cases you may get a chance to deal with these issues in a report.)

Having established what will be admissible as evidence, we now turn to deal with the three types of evidence that may come before the court in the course of a hearing.

1. Direct evidence relates to the facts directly at issue, for example evidence of whether or not a parent has been negligent (see chapter 2).
2. Circumstantial evidence is the opposite of direct evidence. It is evidence that points to a certain conclusion or from which inferences can be drawn, for example that someone was last seen at the scene of a crime and therefore it is reasonable to assume that they saw something or indeed that they were involved.

3. A final type of evidence, which you are less likely to be concerned with, is 'real evidence'. This refers to people and things. If you were involved in a murder trial, an alleged murder weapon would be real evidence, which the court would admit. People can also represent real evidence, not just by what they say but also by their demeanour in court. You may often have heard a person described as a 'credible witness'. This refers to how they presented their evidence as being truthful and accurate, and the judge can choose to consider or ignore what they said according to how they came across. Real evidence is of less significance in relation to a child who has suffered physical injuries, because the courts will accept photographic evidence of the injuries rather than put the child through a traumatic courtroom experience. There are two ways in which this evidence can be given. Firstly, testimony is the method you are most likely to be concerned with. This is oral evidence given on oath. The inclusion of the oath is important, since in swearing an oath you are committing yourself to truthful testimony, and failure to tell the truth amounts to perjury, itself a criminal offence. Secondly, it is also possible that you will submit some documentary evidence to the court, for example your case file. Although you will be examined and probably cross-examined on your file if it is evidence in the eyes of the court, it also represents evidence in its own right, and this is another reason why accuracy and diligence are so important in its compilation.

The law of evidence governs what can be presented to the court in support or in defence of a case being heard. The rules of evidence are numerous and complex and tax the ability of lawyers to understand them all! However, there are some basic evidential matters you should be familiar with, even if only superficially. Common sense dictates that without laws governing what could or could not be entered into evidence, irrelevant, prejudicial or unfair evidence could be presented, thus obstructing the court's attempt to do justice to the matter before it. The aspects of the law of evidence on which we will concentrate here include who may and may not appear as witnesses, who may be required by the court to attend, and what may be presented as oral testimony by such witnesses.

3.4.1 *Competence and Compellability*

Not everybody is competent to be a witness. A witness is considered competent if he or she can lawfully give evidence: that is to say, if they satisfy the rules regarding mental capacity, age and understanding and if what they have to say can be admitted into evidence. It is important to be aware that certain people may not be competent to act as witnesses: children and people with learning difficulties are two obvious examples.

The difficulty arises, not with their ability to relate facts to the court but with the question of oath-taking. (However, the Children's Evidence (Northern Ireland) Order 1995, will clear up much of the uncertainty over children's competence. It will abolish the need for a test based on age and require the admission of all children's evidence: see 3.4.8. Under article 3, all children will be competent to give their unsworn evidence to the court, with the court according it the same weight as sworn evidence, except where a child is not capable of giving evidence at all.)

People with a mental illness or impairment are also not considered to have sufficient understanding to give sworn evidence, though this is a rebuttable presumption. (You should be aware that if the fact of illness or impairment is not communicated to the court at the outset, the legality of the hearing may be in doubt. It is not wise, therefore, to attempt to conceal the issue from the court.)

A witness will be compellable if, having refused to give evidence willingly, he or she can be lawfully required to give evidence. Social workers are competent and compellable witnesses in the great majority of circumstances. Thus, if you are invited to attend court proceedings concerning some aspect of the welfare of a family with whom you are working and you decline the invitation, for whatever reason, you may then be summoned before the court to give such evidence, and failure to comply will result in the imposition of either a fine or a prison sentence. Generally speaking, all competent witnesses are compellable, though a person may only be compellable to give evidence against his or her spouse in certain circumstances (see 10.2.1).

3.4.2 *The Barrister's Perspective*

It will be of benefit to you if you understand the barrister's role in court and can assess the proceedings from his or her perspective. A diligent advocate will have planned the questions, or at least the line of questioning, that he or she is going to pursue. The series of questions put to you will not merely have occurred to the barrister as he or she rose to speak. In order to identify such questions or line of questioning, the barrister will first have decided what the objectives are with respect to each witness. Will counsel want to portray a witness as muddled and confused, or thoroughly professional? Will the objective be to undermine the value of a witness's testimony or report findings, for example by impugning the objectivity of that witness? Whatever the objective, the questions asked will be tailored to that end. The examination of witnesses is, or ought to be, concerned with precision, and this explains why questions by barristers are likely to relate to very specific issues, and also why advocates often return to the same points a number of times. These questions will also usually be terse, and very specific, allowing a barrister maximum control over the progress of the witness's testimony. This will be true of your counsel as well as opposing counsel. Keith Evans, in *Advocacy at the Bar: a Beginner's Guide*, takes the view that a good barrister will 'treat all [his or her] own witnesses as being potentially foolish, as being dumbly willing to let [the barrister] down if given the chance and as being in need at all times of [an] obtrusive guiding hand' (p. 118).

3.4.3 *What to Say*

The cardinal rule regarding appearance in court as a witness is the rather obvious one: 'confine yourself to the questions asked of you.' Do not attempt to pass comment or interject during the proceedings; nor should you try to make speeches in answer to questions put to you. Do not be tempted into giving long-winded answers, even if the barrister is nice enough to allow you to do so, because eventually he or she will turn on you and berate you for failing to answer the question. And the judge and jury (if there is one) will view you as the incoherent, 'scatterbrained' one.

Although the questions are directed at you by the lawyers in the court, you should address your answers to the magistrate or judge. In the magistrate's court the correct form of address is 'Your worship,' in the county court 'Your honour,' and in the High Court 'Your lordship' or 'My lord.' It may seem like a point of minute detail to mention the correct form of address for the judge, but it will add considerably to your confidence if you are prepared in that respect, and it will spare you the uncomfortable feeling of being publicly corrected by a judge who may be irritated by what seems to be a lack of respect or a display of ignorance on your part.

Do not come across as dogmatic or unreasonable when giving evidence, whether under examination by your own counsel or under cross-examination by opposing counsel. Such an approach is likely to discredit your testimony. You need to demonstrate that you have arrived at your conclusions having used your professional knowledge and skills and having considered all aspects of the issue at hand.

We would make two other recommendations about responding to questions put to you as a witness. The first is that if you keep your answers short and precise you are unlikely to say anything that will create problems for your 'side'. The other is—and this may appear contradictory—that by keeping your answers too short it may be possible for an opposing lawyer to misrepresent your case by what you do not say rather than by what you do. In essence what we are suggesting is that you are not unduly expansive and confine yourself to what needs to be said. You should be well versed in the contents of your sworn statement, since that is what will be used to formulate the questions that will be put to you by all the lawyers. Your own lawyer will prepare you in advance of the court hearing, but you must be very careful to stay within the confines of your statement and not introduce something new during the trial, since this will create difficulties both for you and your lawyer. But be aware, as mentioned earlier (see 3.3.1), that your oral testimony takes precedence over your sworn statement, and that you can be asked about things not contained in your statement.

Aside from this, you should try to remember that you will be under oath, and therefore everything you say should be the truth. Try to think before you answer the questions put to you, and speak slowly and clearly, so that you will be easily understood. This will give a strong impression of confidence in what you are saying. The more nervous you appear to be, the more likely is it that the opposing lawyers will spend a considerable time cross-examining you in an attempt to 'rattle' you and sow seeds of doubt in your mind about your testimony.

3.4.4 *Refusing to Answer a Question*

The only ground on which a witness can refuse to answer a question is self-incrimination. In other words, if you are asked a question whose answer is likely to implicate you in criminal activity, you may refuse to answer. The frequency with which this occurs, however, is minimal, so generally you will have to answer all questions put to you.

The one argument that you might wish to use to avoid having to answer a question would be the need to protect the confidentiality of your relationship with your client. However, the only confidential or 'privileged' relationship the law recognises is that of a lawyer and his or her client, and what is privileged is any written or oral communications between them made with a view to giving and receiving legal advice on any subject, whether or not a court case was pending.

Many other relationships also involve a degree of confidentiality in order for them to function, and that between the social worker and client is one. Although privilege will not be available, it may be possible to argue that, in certain circumstances, some degree of immunity is required. You—or, more correctly, your agency—may be able to claim 'public interest' immunity, in other words that some particular document or information warrants immunity from general disclosure, in the public interest. This will not be an issue that you will have to decide in the witness-box. Indeed the matter will not be left to you. Pre-trial applications seeking the immunity of particular documents or information will be made that will not involve social workers, except perhaps in having senior staff swear affidavits explaining why particular information should be exempt from disclosure. In the case of *D. v. NSPCC* (1978) the House of Lords refused to require the society to disclose the identity of an informant who (wrongly) alleged that the plaintiff had ill-treated her child. The House allowed the society to benefit from public interest immunity, holding that 'where a confidential relationship exists (other than that of lawyer and client) and disclosure would be in breach of some ethical or social value involving the public interest, the court has a discretion to uphold a refusal to disclose relevant evidence provided it considers that, on balance, the public interest would be better served by excluding such evidence ... If on balance the matter is left in doubt, disclosure should be ordered.' (See also 2.3)

So, to summarise, you may be able to argue that by giving the court particular information, the function of a social worker in the community may be jeopardised and the public confidence in that role eroded, and therefore it would better serve the public interest not to disclose the information in question.

3.4.5 *Referring to Your Notes*

During the trial, all the lawyers will have copies of your sworn statement (see 3.2.2), and they can and will refer to it, quote from it, and of course question you on it. You will not have a copy of it, nor will you be permitted to consult a copy. What you *may* consult are the professional notes made by you as part of the investigation giving rise to the trial.

It is important that you are clear about the contents of your notes. Any notes or records you refer to must have been made at the time of or shortly after the events at issue, otherwise they may actually constitute hearsay (see 3.4.7). Be aware that if you refer to notes during cross-examination, the opposing counsel is also at liberty to refer to your notes, and may find something in them that he or she can use to undermine your side's case.

Furthermore, if your notes constitute part of a file on the case, the whole file will then be open to scrutiny by opposing counsel. You need to be aware of this when preparing the notes or the file for the court hearing. We examine hearsay evidence further on, but it is pertinent to mention here that if someone else has been responsible for compiling part of that file, that part of the file will be considered hearsay evidence (see 3.4.7).

3.4.6 *Stating Your Opinion*

One of the concerns of the law of evidence is with the making of statements of opinion as opposed to those of fact. Generally, opinions are not admissible as evidence when the witness is not describing what he or she saw but is expressing a view about what might have happened or was about to happen. For example, a statement by an observer such as 'I think he was going to hit her' is merely the observer's opinion as an observer and may be based on nothing more than 'gut feeling' and is therefore not admissible.

Only those whom the law accepts as being experts are allowed to have their opinions introduced as evidence. Usually expert witnesses are identified by professional qualifications: psychiatrists, psychologists, etc. However, anyone with considerable knowledge or expertise in the matters at hand may also be regarded by the court as an expert. The decision whether or not you are an expert will be at the discretion of the judge, and in making that decision he or she must be satisfied of two things: first, that the matter before the court is one of expertise, and second, that the witness in question qualifies as an expert.

The legal basis for qualification as an expert witness can be found in *R. v. Silverlock* [1894] 2 QB 766, where the court accepted that a solicitor who had studied handwriting for ten years, mainly in a non-professional capacity, constituted an expert, thereby admitting his opinion as evidence. In stating the test as whether or not the witness was *peritus*, i.e. skilled in his work, the court rejected the requirement of formal qualifications. This means that a social worker who has read extensively, attended training courses or specialised in a particular area of practice for a number of years may be regarded as an expert by the court. If this is the case, the opinion of that social worker will be admissible as evidence. Just be careful that if the question includes the phrase 'in your opinion' you answer in your professional capacity and not as an observer.

You may wonder what happens if your opinion is at odds with that of your agency. You are not compelled to subscribe to the views of the agency merely because it is your employer, even if it is a term of your contract of employment that you do so. Indeed such a term might be unlawful, because it might force you to commit perjury. If, however, you are called upon to *represent* your agency in a professional capacity, whether in court, at a conference, or in the media, the agency is entitled to expect you to support its views and objectives. If you know that you are going to be placed in this sort of situation and there is something in your employer's policy that you disagree with, you should ensure that your employer or your supervisor is aware of your conflicting point of view. If you make them aware of this information and you are still required to represent them in a professional capacity, then you are at liberty to express your own opinion when in the witness-box. Indeed you should do so, because, as pointed out before, failing to tell the truth amounts to perjury.

3.4.7 *The Rule Against Hearsay*

One of the most complex rules governing what evidence can and cannot be presented to the court is the 'rule against hearsay'. Essentially it means that witnesses are only allowed to testify regarding matters of which they have personal knowledge. The rule is designed to exclude 'second-hand' evidence. So, if your testimony that a child has been abused is based on what a neighbour told you, this will be hearsay. It will not be hearsay, however, if your evidence is to the effect that the neighbour did in fact say this. 'Evidence of a statement made to a witness by a person who is not himself called as a witness may or may not be hearsay. It is hearsay and inadmissible when the object of the evidence is to establish the truth of what is contained in the statement. It is not hearsay and admissible when it is proposed to establish by the evidence, not the truth of the statement, but the fact that it was made' (*Cross on Evidence* (6th edition), 454).

Essentially, this means that the court will not accept evidence from a witness who was not present at the scene of an alleged assault, for example. The reason for this is that the court wants the best evidence possible to establish the facts, and the best person to give that evidence will be the one who witnessed the facts. This witness will always be better than one who has been told by someone who saw the events in person. A witness who related what someone else claims to have seen is not completely reliable, and his or her evidence will therefore require corroboration, for example by calling as witness another person who was also told this information. Additionally, one of the virtues of the adversarial system is said to be the opportunity it provides to test, in cross-examination, the truth of a witness's testimony. Allowing hearsay evidence to be admissible would mean that the possibility of cross-examining the witness who, for example, saw the incident take place would not be available.

You will be affected by the rule restricting use of hearsay as evidence. However, as we have already seen, in your professional capacity you may justify the invocation of an exception to the rule against hearsay, i.e. that an expert's opinion is admissible (see 3.4.6). There is one other exception to the rule that may apply to you. If you are the person who compiled the evidence, you may benefit from the statutory exception to the rule found in the Civil Evidence Act (Northern Ireland) 1971, section 4 (3). It provides that a statement in a document is admissible if the document is, or forms part of, a record and that record is compiled by someone acting under a duty. This includes 'a person acting in the course of any trade, business, profession or other occupation in which he is engaged or employed.' However, this statutory test is strictly interpreted, so that the courts have held that notes of an interview conducted by a solicitor were not a record or a document under the Act but an aid to the solicitor in preparing the case (*Re D., a minor* (1986) 2 FLR 189).

So, with reference to the earlier example of using notes from your file in court, you can see that it may be possible for the entire case file to be entered as evidence, even if you do not expect it to be. You should be prepared for such an eventuality.

The subject matter of the case may also affect the application of the rule against hearsay. If you are involved in a dispute relating to an elderly person, or a domestic violence case, most of the rules relating to hearsay will apply. Those involved in cases dealing with children, however, will encounter more exceptions. The *Memorandum of Good Practice* (1992) published for England and Wales sets out guidelines in relation to the videotaping of interviews that are to be submitted as evidence. However, these guidelines apply to any type of hearsay, and so the memorandum is also useful in a Northern Ireland context. It makes two basic points.

1. A child's statement relating to the alleged offences that is made before an interview is conducted will be hearsay and therefore not admissible. This is the equivalent of your reporting to the court that the child informed you of certain facts, rather than the child giving the information to the court. If the interview that is conducted forms the basis of the child's evidence, the statements made beyond the scope of the interview will constitute hearsay.

2. By using a video-recorded interview, only those statements (verbal and non-verbal) made by the child will be admissible. Therefore, anything that the child does or says may have evidential weight; but if the child makes a gesture that is not captured on camera and is instead described by you, this will represent hearsay for the court's purposes. Some of the accuracy may have been lost in being subjected to your interpretation, and as far as possible the court wants to avoid this. In alleged cases of abuse you will find that under the Children (Northern Ireland) Order, much of what was previously considered hearsay will now be admissible (see 3.4.8).

Hearsay evidence contained in statements and reports can be made admissible in family proceedings under the Children (Northern Ireland) Order 1995. Essentially, the scope is unlimited, as article 169 (5) of the Order permits the Lord Chancellor to 'make provision for the admissibility of evidence which would otherwise be inadmissible under any rule of law relating to hearsay.' The Order allows for the making of court rules that will provide guidance for judges and magistrates. It seems that, with respect to children, the balance has shifted away from excessive observance of legal rules in favour of obtaining as much information as possible, to be as fully informed as possible before making a decision that will affect a vulnerable child. (We will look at children's evidence in more detail in the next section.)

We should mention that there has always been the potential to waive the hearsay rule in wardship hearings, and this is due to the fact that wardship falls within the jurisdiction of the High Court (*Re K. (Infants)* [1965] AC 201).

To summarise, what you need to bear in mind is that the court wants the best possible evidence of the facts. If the only evidence of the facts is hearsay, the court will want some corroboration of that evidence, to ensure fairness for all the parties to the case. Relying on information in files compiled by people other than yourself is a good example of hearsay evidence. Can you give evidence on facts that were entered on the file by someone else? Yes, probably, but it will constitute hearsay and thus require some corroboration. Corroboration means that someone else will have to present evidence that leads the court to the same conclusion as the evidence you have presented. Corroborating evidence, then, reinforces the accuracy of your testimony.

3.4.8 Children's Evidence

So far we have concentrated on you, the social worker, as a witness. Here we examine the law relating to children appearing as witnesses. Although you do not need to be specifically concerned with any aspect of children's evidence, those involved in child protection work may nonetheless wish to know the law relating to the admissibility of children's evidence.

We have already said that children involved in court proceedings will be entitled to special treatment, and the Children (Northern Ireland) Order 1995, supports the idea that what the child says is of primary importance and that, where necessary, legal rules can be relaxed to ensure that the best possible evidence will be given. This includes evidence that might otherwise be inadmissible. As has happened in England, it is likely once the Order is in place that court rules will be drafted to indicate to judges when and in what circumstances the rules can be waived, and this discretion will be available to the court in all proceedings.

The current position in relation to the swearing of an oath by children (under the age of fourteen) in civil and criminal proceedings is governed by the Children and Young Persons Act 1933, section 38 (1). This states that a child under fourteen may give unsworn evidence if the court is satisfied that he or she is of sufficient intelligence to justify reception of this evidence and accepts the obligation of telling the truth. There are no fixed age limits at common law. The judge must merely be satisfied of the child's understanding and appreciation of the seriousness of what he or she is doing (*R. v. Hayes* (1977) 64 CrAppR 194; *Re Caz* (1990) 2 QB 355; *R. v. N.* (1992) 95 CrAppR 256 (CA)). However, the Children Order will alter the existing law with regard to children's oath-taking in civil proceedings. Under article 169 the judge will have the discretion to moderate the language of the oath. This means that instead of 'I swear before Almighty God' a child may say 'I promise before Almighty God that . . .' and his or her evidence will still be deemed to be given under oath. A child who does not sufficiently understand the significance of the oath will be allowed to present his or her evidence to the court without taking any oath.

The law regarding children's evidence will shortly be altered by the implementation of Children's Evidence (Northern Ireland) Order 1995. Based on its English counterpart, the Criminal Justice Act 1991, it permits the admission as evidence-in-chief of a videotaped interview, while still requiring the child to submit to cross-examination in person. The current position is that a child in a sexual abuse case may give his or her evidence through a closed-circuit television link (Police and Criminal Evidence (Northern Ireland) Order 1989, article 81). The Order does not seem to have drawn on the experience of the operation of the English legislation over the last four years. It fails to address the need for a child to be taken through his or her evidence, prepared for cross-examination, and where necessary protected from an overzealous defence lawyer.

In addition, the Order provides for the removal of the test relating to the competence of a child as a witness and makes all children's evidence admissible, whether it is sworn on oath or not. In cases involving sexual abuse, violence or cruelty against children the Order will also allow the DPP to bypass the committal stage and transfer a case from the magistrate's court to the Crown Court, in order to protect the child from unnecessary strain or stress. (For an explanation of the criminal process see chapter 4 and in particular 4.4.3).

3.5 *Further Reading*

Brayne, H., and Martin, G., *Law for Social Workers* (3rd edition), London: Blackstone Press 1993, chap. 9.

PART 2

The Law Relating to Social Work Practice

4

CRIMINAL PROCEEDINGS

Ciaran White

4.1 *Introduction*

In this chapter, what we intend to do is familiarise you with the way in which the legal system deals with crime in Northern Ireland. Only those required to act as 'appropriate adults' or those who are probation officers will have a direct interest in the criminal justice system; however, occasionally other social workers may find it useful to have enough knowledge of the process to be able to offer advice and guidance to clients, or their family members, should they become involved in it. (One could argue that a greater number of social workers will need to have a knowledge of the criminal justice system as a result of the duty placed on Boards and Trusts by the Children (Northern Ireland) Order 1995 (paragraph 8 (*a*) (ii), schedule 2), to 'take reasonable steps designed to reduce the need to bring criminal proceedings against children.')

It could be said that there are two criminal processes in Northern Ireland: one for 'scheduled' offences—those listed in the schedule of the Northern Ireland (Emergency Provisions) Act 1991, i.e. terrorist or paramilitary offences—and the other for those that are not scheduled. This statement may be justified by reference to the alterations that have been made to the criminal process to facilitate the prosecution of scheduled offences, principally the arrest and detention powers and altered trial procedures. We look at both, paying particular attention to the role of the appropriate adult (see 4.1.2). All that is attempted here is a broad view of the criminal process, sufficient to allow a social worker, whether acting as an 'appropriate adult' or not, to understand why certain things are happening, what stage of the process has been reached, and what the next step might be. We do not, for example, examine in detail the stop-and-search and questioning powers available to the security forces, as there are other publications that deal more adequately with those (see 4.7).

The legislation we will be concerned with here is chiefly the Police and Criminal Evidence (Northern Ireland) Order 1989 (hereafter referred to as PACE), the Northern Ireland (Emergency Provisions) Act 1991 (hereafter EPA), and the Prevention of Terrorism (Temporary Provisions) Act 1989 (hereafter PTA). The Police and Criminal Evidence legislation relates to arrest and detention under the 'ordinary' law, while the other two statutes relate to what might be termed 'emergency' law, i.e. law introduced as a result of the conflict in Northern Ireland.

Codes of practice have been adopted governing the treatment of people arrested and detained under both the ordinary and the emergency legislation. The codes are not legally binding, and failure to adhere to them is not a criminal offence, nor does it render a detention invalid. However, breach of them may give rise to disciplinary proceedings against the officer in question and may in certain circumstances justify the court in refusing to accept statements as evidence.

Four codes have been made under article 65 of PACE, two of which are of particular relevance to social workers and will therefore be examined here. These are Code C, 'The Detention, Treatment and Questioning by Police Officers', and Code D, 'The Identification of Persons by Police Officers'. Two other codes, made under section 61 of the EPA and relating therefore to people detained under the EPA and PTA, are similar to Codes C and D under PACE; Code I bears the same title as Code C, and Code II bears the same title as Code D. Although these codes are similar, there are some important differences between them. Detainees and appropriate adults have the right to consult these codes, so even if you don't have a copy or cannot remember what is or is not permissible, you can ask to see them. The detainee's right to consult the codes must be explained to them in the appropriate adult's presence, even if it has been explained to them already. This requirement applies equally to other particular rights to which the detainee is entitled, namely the right to have someone informed of their detention and the right to consult a solicitor. Indeed the detainee is entitled to written notice of those three rights and notice explaining the arrangements for obtaining legal advice.

A person detained under ordinary law must also be informed in writing of their right to a copy of the custody record, but because emergency law detainees are not entitled to a copy, except in the event of legal proceedings, the written notice given to them must only state that they are entitled to read the record before release. (The appropriate adult must also be given this opportunity.)

4.1.1 *Age of Criminal Responsibility*

Before embarking on an explanation of the salient features of the criminal justice system, it is necessary to explain how the criminal law categorises one of the vulnerable groups that social workers are likely to be involved with, namely children and young people.

The age of criminal responsibility is the age at which children are deemed by the criminal law to be responsible for their actions. The law in this regard is the same as it is in England and Wales. Children under the age of ten are not criminally responsible for their actions, according to the Children and Young Persons Act (Northern Ireland) 1968 (hereafter CYP68), section 69, while it is a rebuttable presumption that those aged between ten and fourteen are not responsible in criminal law for their actions (see 3.3.3). Those aged fourteen and over are subject to the criminal law in the same way that adults are.

The law relating to the age of criminal responsibility also affects the terms used to describe these groups. Those aged from ten to fourteen are termed 'children', while those aged fourteen to seventeen are known as 'young persons'. Collectively, both categories are known as 'juveniles'. (Naturally, juvenile courts are those courts that try juveniles: see chapter 1.) Offenders aged between seventeen and twenty-one are referred to as 'young offenders'.

4.1.2 *Role of the Appropriate Adult*

The appropriate adult is the description given to those whose function is to protect the interests of juveniles and the 'mentally ill or handicapped' (as the codes of practice describe them) while in police detention if arrested under PACE, the EPA, or the PTA. The role played by the appropriate adult is identical under emergency law and ordinary law, except that under emergency law the appropriate adult will not be informed of the reason the person has been arrested, whereas under ordinary law they must be told this.

Codes C and I (section 11.12) set out, in identical terms, what the role of the appropriate adult is. 'Where the appropriate adult is present at an interview, he should be informed that he is not expected to act simply as an observer, and also that the purposes of his presence are, first, to advise the person being questioned and to observe whether or not the interview is being conducted properly and fairly, and secondly, to facilitate communication with the person being interviewed.'

The appropriate adult must be informed of the detention of the juvenile and the grounds for detention, if detained under ordinary law, and asked to the police station as soon as practicable. In the case of a juvenile who is arrested, such a person can be a social worker but can also be the child's parent or guardian or, if the child is in care, the DHSS or a Health Board or Trust. In the case of a mentally disordered or impaired person, this function can be performed by (*a*) a relative, guardian or other person responsible for their care or custody, (*b*) someone with experience of dealing with mentally ill or impaired people, or (*c*) failing either of these, some other responsible adult aged eighteen or over, though police officers or employees of the Police Authority for Northern Ireland cannot perform this function (Code C and I, 1.8(*b*)). (In respect of mentally disordered or impaired people the codes suggest that it is more satisfactory if the appropriate adult is someone who has experience of the case, rather than a relative lacking such a qualification, though the wishes of the detainee should be respected if practicable (Code C, note 1D, and Code I, note 1C).)

The parent or guardian of a juvenile should be the appropriate adult unless they are suspected of involvement in the offence or are the victim (Code C, note 1B, and Code I, note 1A). Therefore, if asked by the police to act as an appropriate adult you should first inquire whether they have considered asking the detainee's parents or guardians to fulfil the role. However, the codes specifically caution against foisting an estranged parent or guardian on a juvenile to act as the appropriate adult if the juvenile expressly and specifically objects to their presence (Code C, note 1D, and Code I, note 1C). If a child in care admits an offence to a social worker, another social worker should be the appropriate adult, in the interest of fairness (Code C, note 1C, and Code I, note 1B). Only as a last resort should a solicitor act in such a role.

You may wonder what happens where the police doubt that the detainee is a juvenile or is mentally disordered or impaired. The codes state that if the detainee appears to fit either of these categories, the police should presume that they do and act accordingly (Code C and I, 1.5 and 1.7).

An appropriate adult may also be involved when a visually impaired person, or someone who is unable to read, is detained. This involvement would entail the appropriate adult checking documents and perhaps even giving help in signing documents (Code C, 3.8, and Code I, 3.7).

We have decided not to extract for discussion under one heading all the references to the appropriate adult from the codes, as this would not give a view of the role in context. Instead we take you through the arrest and detention process, referring to the circumstances in which an appropriate adult becomes involved as we encounter them.

4.2 *Arrest and Length of Detention*

Anyone arrested in Northern Ireland is likely to be arrested under either PACE or the PTA. We will consider later some of the main arrest provisions in the legislation mentioned above, but first we want to make a few general points about arrest.

If a police officer (or a soldier) asks someone to 'accompany them to the police station,' that does not amount to an arrest, and that person is free to leave whenever they desire. There is no 'half-way house' between being arrested and not being arrested within which the police may detain and question you: one is either arrested or not. (PACE, article 31, confirms that a person voluntarily attending at a police station shall be entitled to leave at will, unless placed under arrest.) The arrested person must be told why they are being arrested, though it should be said that some of the offences created by 'emergency' legislation are so broad that this requirement may be easily fulfilled by the police.

The purpose of arrest is to question someone in order to ascertain whether there is enough evidence to charge or prosecute them for the offence. It is not, or at least it should not be, a 'fishing expedition' whereby the police trawl for general information about people or places rather than specific information about a crime that the detained person is suspected of committing.

The police are entitled to use such force as is reasonably necessary to effect the arrest.

4.2.1 *Arrest Under 'Ordinary' Law*

PACE powers of arrest allow detention for a maximum of ninety-six hours (see 4.3.6) and relate to two types of offence. The first is an 'arrestable offence' (article 26): this is an offence carrying penalties set in law or any other offence for which the term of imprisonment is at least five years or which is specifically outlined in article 26(2) of PACE. This will include, of course, a broad range of serious offences, for example murder, arson, rape, and theft. The second type may be described as a 'non-arrestable offence' and is outlined by article 27. A police officer may arrest, without warrant, a person on reasonable suspicion of having committed a non-arrestable offence if it appears that the serving of a summons would be 'impracticable and inappropriate' because of doubts about the identity of the suspect, or because the police officer believes it necessary for the protection of persons, property, a child or other vulnerable person.

Someone must be told that they are being arrested as soon as practicable after arrest, if not otherwise informed (PACE, article 30). The detainee must be told of the reason for the arrest, and a caution must also be administered (see 4.3.8). Failure to give reasons may not invalidate the arrest, but it may allow the detainee to sue for damages for false imprisonment (*DPP v. Hawkins* 1988 (88) CrAppR 166). The arrested person must be brought to a designated police station—the larger stations are designated—if arrested outside such a station and if the detention appears likely to last longer than six hours (article 32). An arrested person can be searched 'on the spot', (i.e. at the time of arrest), for evidence of concealed or dangerous items, as can premises they have just come from, provided there are reasonable grounds for believing that such a search is necessary. Such searches cannot involve the removal of outer clothing (article 34).

4.2.2 *Arrest Under Emergency Law*

The main emergency arrest power is section 14 of the PTA, and the maximum period of detention is seven days. Although there are a range of other arrest powers in that Act and in the EPA, the great majority of people arrested in Northern Ireland in recent years in connection with terrorist or paramilitary crime have been arrested under section 14.

The power of arrest arises where the police officer has a reasonable suspicion that the person is or has been concerned in the commission, preparation or instigation of acts of 'terrorism', defined as 'the use of violence for political ends' (PTA, section 20). Such acts must be connected solely with the affairs of Northern Ireland, or must relate to 'international terrorism'.

4.3 *Treatment in Detention*

It is during the detention period that the appropriate adult plays his or her greatest role (see 4.1.2). There are a range of rights accorded to arrested people relating to the conditions under which they are detained (Code C and I, 8). Detainees should, as far as practicable, be detained in cells on their own; cells must be adequately heated, cleaned, and ventilated; the only additional restraints that are allowed are handcuffs; blankets, mattresses, pillows and other bedding should be of a reasonable standard and of a clean and sanitary condition; access to toilet and washing facilities must be provided; two light meals and one main meal must be provided every twenty-four hours, including meals necessary to meet special dietary needs or religious beliefs; and brief outdoor exercise must be provided daily, if practicable. The fact that these rights are applicable only as far as 'practicable' is a considerable limitation on the utility of some of them.

Paragraph 9 of Codes C and I governs improper treatment, particularly improper treatment requiring medical intervention. A complaint made about ill-treatment must be communicated as soon as practicable to an officer not below the rank of inspector and not connected with the investigation. If the complaint involves possible assault or the possibility of unnecessary or unreasonable force, a medical officer must be called. Additionally, an onus is placed on the custody officer to call a medical officer if the detainee is injured or appears to be suffering from a physical or mental illness. This must be done irrespective of whether the treatment is requested or whether the detainee has recently had medical treatment (save for the situation where the detainee comes to the police station from hospital). The detainee can be examined by a medical officer on request, and indeed can be examined by a medical practitioner of his or her own choosing at his or her own expense. In this respect there is a difference between emergency law detainees and those detained under ordinary law. The emergency law detainee can also be examined by a medical practitioner of his or her choice (though the choice is limited to the health centre at which the detainee is registered), but the examination must take place in the presence of the medical officer, whereas this is not the case with the ordinary law detainee. The other key difference between the two categories is that a request by an emergency law detainee to be medically examined can be delayed if the custody officer believes (*a*) that an unnecessary delay to the investigation or the administration of justice would be caused, (*b*) that the request is designed to delay or disrupt the course of an interview or prevent or delay further arrests, or (*c*) that in the case of an examination by a medical practitioner of the detainee's choosing such an examination would 'prejudice the investigation'. Complaints under paragraph 9 and matters relating to the medical examination of detainees must be recorded on the custody record (see 4.3.1).

(You should note that Codes C and I both state that a juvenile is not normally to be put in a cell with adults. This should only be done if no other secure accommodation is available and the custody officer considers that it is not practicable to supervise him or her if not placed in a cell. A record should be kept of the reason the juvenile was placed in a cell (Codes C and I, 8.8).)

4.3.1 *Custody Records and the Custody Officer*

We have already referred to a 'custody officer' and a 'custody record', and you may wonder what these are. There are custody officers for each designated police station, who are police officers not below the rank of sergeant whose job it is to monitor an arrested person when in custody and in particular to record matters relating to that custody on the custody record, a document intended to provide a detailed record of detention. The legislation and the codes stipulate when it is to be used and what is to be recorded on it.

In this chapter we will refer to some of the more important matters that are to be recorded on the custody record. All ordinary law detainees or their legal representatives can request a copy, and the police must allow detainees, their legal representatives or the appropriate adult to inspect the original record (Code C, 2.5). As stated earlier, emergency law detainees only have the right to inspect the original custody record (Code I, 2.4).

If the custody officer is not available, any police officer can perform that function, though the custody officer should not be one of the officers investigating the crime. One of the other important functions of the custody officer is to decide whether the detainee should be charged (see 4.4). In particular, where a juvenile is arrested the custody officer must ascertain the identity of a person responsible for the welfare of the arrested person and inform them, if practicable, of the fact of the juvenile's detention and the offence for which he or she is being detained. The custody officer is also under a duty to inform the supervisor of a juvenile who is subject to a supervision or probation order of the fact that he or she has been arrested (PACE, article 38(13)).

The custody record must be opened as soon as practicable after the arrested person is brought to the police station. One of the first matters to be included in the record will be details of everything the arrested person had when arriving at the station (PACE, article 55, and Code I, 2.1). The custody officer can require the detainee to hand over items of clothing or personal effects if in his or her opinion they might cause harm to the detainee, be used to interfere with evidence, damage property, effect an escape, or are needed as evidence, though the custody officer must explain why they are being retained, and this reason must be recorded on the custody record. The custody officer is responsible for the safekeeping of any belongings taken from the detainee (Codes C and I, 4(1)(b)).

At this point intimate searches can only be carried out as described in 4.3.7, though non-intimate searches can be made on the authority of the custody officer. Strip-searching (i.e. a search involving the removal of more than the outer layer of clothing) is allowable on the authority of the custody officer if he or she considers it necessary to remove an article that the detainee might use to harm him or herself, interfere with evidence or property, or effect an escape, or because it is needed as evidence. The results of and the reasons for the strip-search must be recorded.

4.3.2 *The Right to Inform Someone*

It is not permissible to hold someone in detention incommunicado. However, although PACE (article 57) and the EPA (section 44) create the right to have someone informed when a person is arrested, this right can be delayed—for up to thirty-six hours in the case of ordinary detainees and for forty-eight hours in the case of emergency law detainees—on the authorisation of a superintendent.

The grounds for exercising this power with respect to an ordinary law detainee are that informing the named person (*a*) will result in interference to evidence or interference or serious physical injury to others, (*b*) will lead to other co-offenders being 'tipped off', or (*c*) will hinder the recovery of any property obtained as a result of such an offence. Two further grounds for delaying the exercise of the right in the case of emergency law detainees are that its exercise (*a*) would lead to interference with the gathering of information about the commission, preparation or instigation of acts of terrorism or (*b*), by alerting any person, would make it more difficult to prevent an act of terrorism or secure the apprehension, prosecution or conviction of any person in connection with the commission, preparation or instigation of acts of terrorism. The fact that the notification of the right has been delayed must be recorded on the custody record, and the detainee must be informed of the reasons the right is being delayed.

If the detainee's first choice cannot be contacted, he or she can nominate two others. If they are also not contactable, the custody officer has a discretion whether to allow further attempts (Codes C and I, 5.1). If the detainee is not aware of anyone who can help, Codes C and I direct the custody officer to 'bear in mind' any local voluntary bodies or other organisation that might be able to offer help in such cases (Code C, 5C, and Code I, 5A). The ability to delay the exercise of the right to inform someone also applies to juveniles and to those with a mental illness or impairment, but the notification of the appropriate adult cannot be delayed (annex B, note B1).

In the case of juveniles, an extra duty is placed on the police by CYP68 (section 52 (2)), as amended by PACE (article 58), to ascertain the identity of a person responsible for their welfare and inform him or her that the juvenile has been arrested, why he or she has been arrested and where he or she is being detained. This duty is owed to parents or guardians or to anyone who has responsibility for the juvenile.

An ordinary law detainee is allowed writing materials and has the right to make a telephone call of a reasonable length, though any communications can be listened to or read (Code C, 5.6–8). The right to be provided with writing materials seems to be given in the context of drafting a letter or message: it is unclear whether a detainee can use materials to record, for example, their thoughts regarding treatment during detention. Code I is silent on this point, and therefore no similar right appears to exist for emergency law detainees.

4.3.3 *Access to a Solicitor*

A detainee's right to legal advice while in custody is found in article 59 of PACE and in section 45 of the EPA. Emergency law detainees must be told of this right (EPA, section 45(1)), while ordinary law detainees have no absolute right to be told, though annex B, 3, suggests that they should be. As with the right to have someone informed of one's arrest, this right can also be delayed for a maximum of thirty-six hours in the case of ordinary law detainees and forty-eight hours for emergency law detainees. This delay must be authorised by a police officer not below the rank of superintendent. The grounds for refusing immediate access to a solicitor are the same as for delaying the notification to someone the arrested person wants informed (see 4.3.2).

The detainee can be interviewed if access to a solicitor is denied in this way. Ordinarily, if there is delay between the request for a solicitor and his or her arrival, the detainee cannot be interviewed unless an officer has reasonable grounds for believing that (*a*) the delay will involve an immediate risk of harm to people or property, (*b*) there would be an unreasonable delay before the solicitor arrives, or (*c*) the solicitor cannot be contacted or will not attend (Code C, 6.3, and Code I, 6.4). The fact of the delay and the reason for it must be noted on the custody record when a person is detained under ordinary law (Code C, 6.10, and Code I, 6.9). A request for a solicitor must be recorded in the custody record. The appropriate adult can call the solicitor on behalf of the detainee.

In the absence of the appropriate adult, unless annex D applies where a superintendent considers that harm will come to people or property if the interview is delayed (Code C, 11.10, and Code I, 11.12) a juvenile or a person suffering from mental disorder or impairment must not be interviewed or asked to sign a written statement. The effect of this should be that if the police are anxious to secure a conviction that will withstand an appeal they will be less likely to proceed without the appropriate adult. This means that the appropriate adult is even more important because there may be times when he or she is the detainee's only source of independent advice.

When the solicitor arrives, he or she may wish to conduct an interview with the detainee in private. This is not because the solicitor considers those of you who act as appropriate adults untrustworthy or anything of the sort. The reason is that only lawyers can refuse to disclose to a court what their client has said: in other words, the only category of information that a court considers privileged is that obtained within the lawyer-client relationship. Social workers cannot plead such privilege and therefore could be required to divulge such information in the witness-box. (On confidentiality in general see chapter 2.)

4.3.4 *Answering Questions*

The main task of the police when interviewing a suspect is to obtain a confession. The admissibility of confessions obtained in interview rooms is governed by PACE (articles 74–76) in the case of ordinary law and by the EPA (section 11) in the case of emergency law. We deal first with confessions under ordinary law.

A court will not allow the admission into evidence of a confession that was or may have been obtained by 'oppression' or in consequence of anything said or done that was likely to render unreliable any confession that might be made as a result. Continual hectoring and bullying of a detainee may well amount to oppression (*R. v. Beales* [1991] Crim LR 118). Article 76 also gives the courts a wide discretion to exclude evidence that, having regard to all the circumstances, would affect the fairness of the case.

Additionally, if the confession of a 'mentally handicapped person' is made without an 'independent person' (which can of course include an appropriate adult) being present, then at a trial on indictment the judge must warn the jury that there is a special need for caution before convicting in reliance on such a confession (article 75). This does not mean that the confession is not admissible or that the detainee will be automatically acquitted, only that the jury should take special care before deciding to convict.

The threshold governing the acceptance of confessions in the trial of emergency law offences (i.e. scheduled offences) is even lower than that under PACE. Under section 11 of the EPA a confession may only be excluded if it was induced by torture, inhuman or degrading treatment, or any violence or threat of violence (whether or not amounting to torture). The appropriate adult should observe the interview with these standards in mind and intervene if it is felt that they are being breached.

Although the arrested person's right to remain silent still exists, it has been significantly affected by the Criminal Evidence (Northern Ireland) Order 1988. The effect of this legislation is difficult to state succinctly, but should a suspect remain silent throughout detention, the court is entitled to draw adverse inferences from this silence if the suspect (*a*) fails to account for his or her presence at a particular place when an offence was committed, (*b*) fails to account for objects, substances or marks on his or her person that the police reasonably believe to be attributed to his or her participation in an offence, or (*c*) fails to mention a fact when questioned in detention but subsequently relies on that fact in his or her defence. This curtailment of the right relates to both emergency and ordinary law and is the reason why the caution administered to people who are about to be arrested or charged is as follows: 'You are charged with [offence]. You do not have to say anything unless you wish to do so but I must warn you that if you fail to mention any fact which you rely on in your defence in court your failure to take this opportunity to mention it may be treated in court as supporting any relevant evidence against you. If you do so wish to say anything, what you say may be given in evidence.'

A record of the interviews of detainees must, of course, be made in respect of both emergency and ordinary law detainees. If an appropriate adult has been present during the interview, he or she should be given an opportunity to read and sign that interview record (Codes C and I, 11.8).

4.3.5 *The Right to an Interpreter*

An arrested person has the right to have an interpreter present if he or she has hearing difficulties or has difficulties understanding English (Code C, 3.5, and Code I, 3.4). Indeed a parent or guardian who is acting as an appropriate adult and who is deaf also has the right to have an interpreter called. An interview cannot be conducted with someone who has 'genuine difficulty' understanding English and who wishes an interpreter to be present if the police officer does not speak the detainee's language, unless annex D of Codes C and I apply (i.e. if an urgent interview is needed to protect lives or property). A police officer may only act as interpreter with the written agreement of the appropriate adult and cannot do so if the matter to be interpreted relates to the imparting of legal advice. An interpreter may make a telephone call or write a letter on a person's behalf (Code C, note 5A). However, an interpreter cannot do this for an emergency law detainee, because such a detainee has no right to make a telephone call or write a letter.

The interviewing officer is to make sure that the interpreter makes a note of the interview in the detainee's language. The accuracy of this note must be certified by the interpreter. Codes C and I (13.8) place the onus on the police to communicate the right to have an interpreter to those who are deaf or who have 'genuine difficulty' in understanding English by requesting that 'all reasonable attempts' should be made to make it clear to the detainee that 'interpreters will be provided at public expense.' It is the custody officer's responsibility to call the interpreter. Allegedly unlawful immigrants, however, have none of the above rights, because their detention is not covered by the PACE Codes.

4.3.6 *Extending Detention*

As we have seen, under both ordinary and emergency law the initial periods for which an arrested person may be detained can be extended (see 4.2). A 'review officer' has the function of deciding whether a detainee should continue to be detained. The review officer in PTA or EPA detentions must be of at least the rank of inspector in the case of reviews carried out within twenty-four hours of the beginning of detention and the rank of superintendent thereafter. A written record must be made of the outcome of the review in the presence of the detainee, and the detainee must be informed of the reason for his or her continued detention.

In the case of detentions under PACE the review officer is the custody officer if the arrested person has been charged, and if not then a police officer not below the rank of inspector who has not been involved in the investigation.

The first review during PACE detentions takes place after six hours and subsequent reviews at nine-hour intervals, while under the PTA the first review takes place as soon as practicable after detention and before questioning can begin, with subsequent reviews at twelve-hour intervals. For those arrested under PACE the initial period for which they may be detained is twenty-four hours, extendable to a maximum of ninety-six hours. An extension of twelve hours, after the initial twenty-four hours, is permissible on the authorisation of a police officer not below the rank of superintendent. A further extension of up to thirty-six hours can only be made by a magistrate. The final extension is for twenty-four hours and must be authorised by the magistrate's court (article 42), though the court can extend detention for a maximum of thirty-six hours provided that the overall periods of extension do not exceed ninety-six hours. Detention under the PTA (section 14) is initially for forty-eight hours, but this may be extended by the Secretary of State to a maximum of five days. (There may be more than one extension, for example two days, then one day.)

Reviews and extensions of detention also call for the involvement of the appropriate adult. When deciding whether to extend the detention of a juvenile or person with a mental disorder or impairment, the appropriate adult is among those who must be consulted, if available at the time (Code C, 15.1, and Code I, 15.6).

4.3.7 *Searches, Sample, Fingerprints and Photographs*

This area of detention is governed by Codes D and II (see 4.1). The appropriate adult plays an important role. The consent of mentally disordered or impaired detainees is only valid if given in the presence of the appropriate adult. In the case of a young person, the consent of a parent or guardian is also required, whereas if the detainee is a child the parent or guardian's consent is sufficient.

Searches are classified by the legislation as 'intimate' and 'non-intimate'. An intimate search is one 'which consists of the physical examination of a person's body orifices' (PACE, article 2). It must be authorised by a police officer of at least the rank of superintendent and can only be carried out if the officer believes (*a*) that the detainee has concealed something that he or she might use to injure him or herself or others while in police detention or (*b*) that he or she have a 'Class A' drug concealed on their person and that, in either case, an intimate search is the only way of removing it.

Intimate searches may only be conducted by a medical officer or registered nurse, unless a superintendent considers that this is not practicable. Searches for concealed items that may pose a threat to the detainee or others in police custody may be carried out in a police station, hospital, medical surgery, or other medical facility, while those for Class A drugs can only be carried out by a medical officer or nurse in a hospital, medical surgery, or medical facility. The custody record must show which parts of the detainee's body were searched, who carried out the search, who was present, the reasons for the search, and its result (Code C, annex A). Non-intimate searches should have been conducted according to the procedures discussed in 4.3.1 when the detainee was first brought to the police station.

An appropriate adult of the same sex as the detainee must be present when an intimate search of a juvenile or mentally disordered or impaired person is carried out at a police station. However, in the case of a juvenile, if he or she objects to the presence of the appropriate adult while being searched (which objection must be made in the presence of the appropriate adult) and the appropriate adult agrees, the appropriate adult will not be allowed to be present (Codes C and I, annex A, 4).

Intimate samples are samples of blood, semen, tissue, urine, or pubic hair, or a swab taken from any body orifices except the mouth. Non-intimate samples are mouth swabs, nail samples or samples taken from under a nail, hair (other than pubic hair), a swab from any part of the body other than a body orifice, or a footprint or impression of any part of the body other than a hand (PACE, article 53, and Code II, section 5). The taking of intimate samples requires the authorisation of a police officer of the rank of superintendent or above and the consent of the detainee. (Before consent is sought the detainee must be warned that a refusal to give a sample might be treated as corroborating prosecution evidence by virtue of the Criminal Evidence (Northern Ireland) Order 1988 (Codes D and II, 5.2) (see 4.3.4).) The taking of such samples is only justified if there are reasonable grounds for suspecting the detainee's involvement in a 'serious arrestable offence' and that that sample would tend to prove or disprove that suspicion (article 62). A note must be made on the custody record that the sample was taken, what the grounds for doing so were, whether any force was used, and giving the names of those present (Code D, 5.9, and Code II, 5.8).

Non-intimate samples can be taken, on a superintendent's authorisation, without the consent of the detainee. The authorising officer is required, however, to have reasonable grounds for suspecting the involvement of the person in a serious arrestable offence and for believing that the sample would tend to confirm or disprove this involvement. The fact of the taking of the non-intimate sample, the authorisation by which it was taken and the grounds for giving authorisation must be recorded in the custody record. No consent is necessary for procuring non-intimate samples from emergency law detainees, provided there is reasonable suspicion that the detainee has committed, prepared or instigated terrorist offences.

A person's fingerprints can be taken without his or her consent on the authorisation of a superintendent or above if they have been charged with a recordable offence (i.e. serious offences that the police are required to record for statistical purposes) or informed that they will be reported for such an offence. The reason for taking fingerprints without consent must be communicated to the detainee and recorded in the custody record (article 61 (7) and Code II, 3.4). Fingerprints and samples taken during detention under ordinary law are to be destroyed if the person is not prosecuted or cautioned or is ultimately cleared of that offence, but this does not apply to emergency law detention.

Photographs of people arrested under the PTA (section 14) can be taken without their consent (Code II, 4.2), and reasonable force may be used. Those arrested under PACE can have their photographs taken without their consent if (*a*) they have been arrested with others and a photograph is necessary to establish who was arrested, at what place, and at what time, (*b*) they have been charged, or (*c*) they are to be reported for a recordable offence. No force can be used. Once again photographs taken of ordinary law detainees must be destroyed if they are not convicted or cautioned, but those of emergency law detainees need not be destroyed.

4.3.8 *Charging the Detainee with an Offence*

At the end of the permitted detention period (see 4.2) the arrested person must either be charged or released without charge. (It is at this stage that the cautioning of the detainee as a form of 'resolving' the offence can take place (see 4.4.1).) Charging someone with an offence is one way of commencing the prosecution process and takes place when there is sufficient evidence to justify it. The charging procedure for ordinary and emergency law detainees is the same and is found in PACE, article 38, and Code C, section 16.

The custody officer determines whether there is sufficient evidence to charge. A detainee who is charged is cautioned in the same way as when first arrested (see 4.3.4). The caution is administered orally, but the detainee is also given written notice of the caution and the particulars of the offence, including the name, station and reference number of the police officer in the case. The charging of a juvenile or mentally ill or impaired person should take place in the presence of the appropriate adult. Both the appropriate adult and the vulnerable person represented are given the written notice showing particulars of the offence charged, including the name and station address of the officer.

A detainee who is charged must be released, either on bail or without bail, unless (*a*) the detainee's name or address cannot be ascertained or there is doubt about those matters, (*b*) the custody officer has reasonable grounds for believing that the detention is necessary for the protection of the detainee or of others, or (*c*) the custody officer has reasonable grounds for believing that the detainee will fail to appear in court or will interfere with the investigation if released.

An additional ground exists for retaining juveniles in detention if the custody officer believes that they should be detained in their own interests. A juvenile who is kept in police custody must be taken to a 'place of safety' (see chapter 6).

Those who are charged and not released on police bail must be brought before a magistrate's court as soon as practicable but usually not later than the day after they are charged.

The fact that a detainee is released without charge does not mean that a prosecution cannot, or will not, take place. The prosecution can be initiated by the issuing of a summons—a document issued by a justice of the peace or clerk of petty sessions requiring the accused to answer in court the charges made out—after the police investigation has been completed and the DPP's office has examined the police file on the matter.

4.4 *The Prosecution Process*

A detailed breakdown of the prosecution process is shown in fig. 2. What we will do here is provide a commentary on particular aspects of this diagram that we feel are of most interest. As the diagram shows, the great majority of criminal prosecutions are brought by the police, because they relate to minor criminal matters. Only those of a more serious nature are turned over to the Director of Public Prosecutions for prosecution by that office.

4.4.1 *Issuing Cautions*

The police can elect to caution an offender rather than prosecute him or her. Cautions are of two types: informal and formal. Cautioning schemes exist both for adults and juveniles and are administered according to Home Office guidelines and thus are conducted in the same manner as in the remainder of the UK. (Cautions are used quite regularly as a way of dealing with juveniles under the Juvenile Liaison Scheme.)

Criminal Proceedings 89

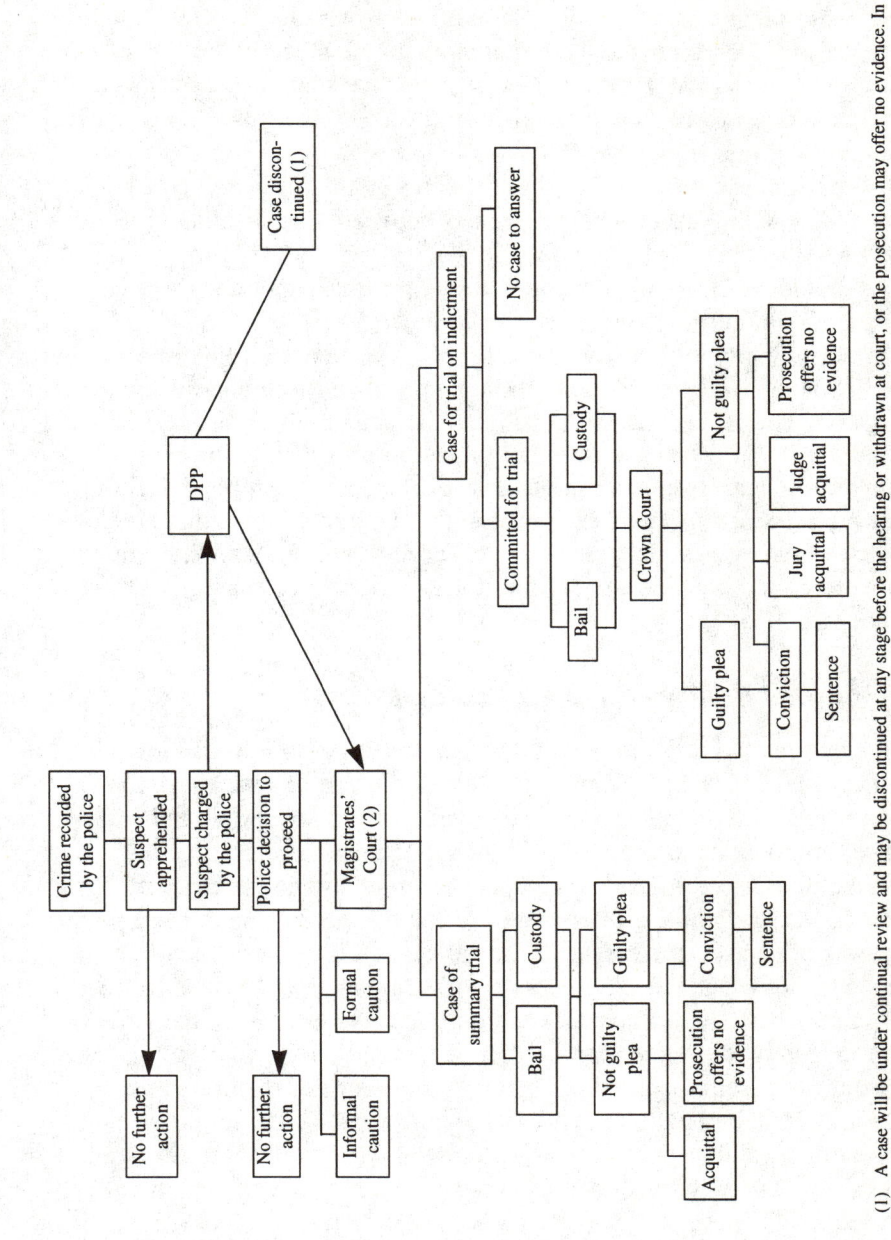

Fig. 2 The prosecution process

(1) A case will be under continual review and may be discontinued at any stage before the hearing or withdrawn at court, or the prosecution may offer no evidence. In addition, the charge may be altered up to the final decision of the court.
(2) Although the majority of prosecutions are handled by the police, certain offences are prosecuted by the DPP, while some are prosecuted by private organisations (including government agencies such as the Inland Revenue). © HMSO

A formal caution is one given by the police in circumstances where they consider that sufficient evidence exists to prosecute the offender and where the offender admits to having committed the crime and consents to the issuing of a caution. Usually given in the police station by an inspector or higher officer, formal cautions are recorded by means of a 'certificate of caution'. This is signed by the cautioned person.

An informal caution usually takes the form of an oral warning or letter in less formal language. The difference between formal and informal cautions lies in the fact that not only are the former recorded but they may also be cited in court if at some future time the cautioned person is accused of committing another criminal offence.

Cautions cannot initially be issued for offences that must be referred to the DPP, though if the DPP decides that no prosecution should take place, it is open to the police to make a caution. Adult cautioning was introduced in 1990, and 778 cautions were administered in 1991. Cautioning is a much more usual option for juveniles: 68 per cent of juveniles found guilty or cautioned in 1990 were cautioned. (Do not confuse this type of caution, which is essentially a substitute for prosecution, with the caution administered to someone who is about to be arrested or charged with an offence: see 4.3.4.)

4.4.2 *In What Court Will the Matter Be Tried?*

For the purposes of trying offences there are two types of criminal offence: summary and indictable. Summary offences are tried in the magistrate's court (officially called the court of summary jurisdiction), while indictable offences are tried in the Crown Court, though there is a preliminary stage in the trial of indictable offences, called the 'committal stage', that takes place in the magistrate's court. (For more on court structures see chapter 1.) Summary offences are usually less serious ones, while indictable offences are more serious. The key differences between the two types is that (*a*) trials in the magistrate's court are not before a jury, while those in the Crown Court are, with the exception of 'scheduled' offences, and (*b*) in the magistrate's court the accused has no prior knowledge of the strength of the case against him or her. Statutes usually prescribe which offences are triable on indictment and which are triable summarily, though there are some offences that are triable either on summary or on indictment, sometimes at the election of the accused, sometimes at the election of the prosecution.

4.4.3 *Committal Proceedings*

Committal proceedings take place in the magistrate's court and are the preliminary stage in the trial of an offence on indictment. The purpose of such proceedings is to discover whether there is sufficient evidence to commit the accused to the Crown Court for trial. If in the opinion of the magistrate there is not enough evidence to do so, the accused must be discharged; but, because he or she was not formally acquitted, retrial at a later date is a possibility.

4.4.4 *Remand on Bail and in Custody*

Where a case is adjourned, as often happens, the judge or magistrate has to decide whether to remand the accused in custody or on bail. Thus the accused is kept in detention or released, but required to return to court for the hearing or forfeit a sum of money. Our consideration of bail and remand will be confined to vulnerable groups with which a social worker is concerned.

Accused people with a mental disorder can be remanded either for a report on their mental condition or to hospital for treatment. The former type of remand can be for twenty-eight days, renewable for a total of twelve weeks. The latter type is not available if the penalty for the offence is fixed in law. An order making such a remand requires the oral evidence of a part II doctor (see chapter 7) and the written or oral evidence of one other medical practitioner that the person is suffering from mental illness or severe mental impairment of a nature or degree that warrants their detention in hospital for treatment. A further remand can be made on the written or oral evidence of a medical practitioner. Before either of these remand options is used, the DHSS must be given an opportunity to make representations.

Juveniles must be remanded in custody to any one of the four training schools (see chapter 6), all of which are designated as remand homes (CYP68, section 51). The only exception to this is where a young person is so unruly or depraved that they should be remanded to prison or a remand centre.

4.5 *The Trial Process*

We propose to say very little about the trial itself, because social workers have very little direct involvement in it, save perhaps when they act as witnesses. (Chapter 2 gives guidance in this regard.)

92 *The Law Relating to Social Work Practice*

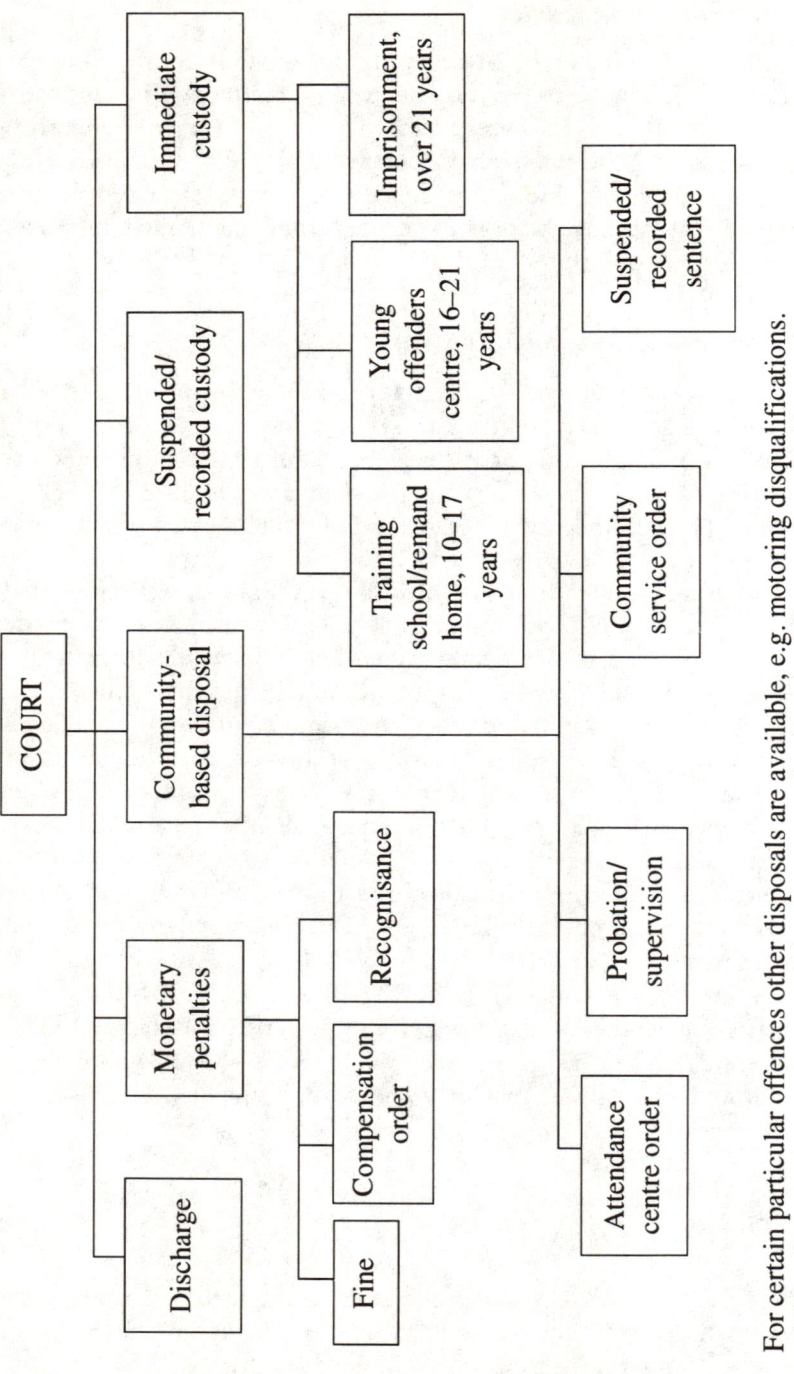

```
                                              ┌── Imprisonment, over 21 years
                          ┌── Immediate custody ┤
                          │                    └── Young offenders centre, 16–21 years
                          │
                          ├── Suspended/recorded custody
                          │
                          │                    ┌── Training school/remand home, 10–17 years
                          │                    ├── Young offenders centre, 16–21 years
COURT ──┬── Community-based disposal ──────────┤── Suspended/recorded sentence
        │                                      ├── Community service order
        │                                      ├── Probation/supervision
        │                                      └── Attendance centre order
        │
        │                    ┌── Discharge
        │                    ├── Fine
        └── Monetary penalties┤── Compensation order
                             └── Recognisance
```

For certain particular offences other disposals are available, e.g. motoring disqualifications.
© *HMSO*

Fig. 3: The options open to a court when a person is convicted

4.6 Sentencing Options

The options open to a court when a person is convicted are illustrated in fig. 3. What we do here is provide a description and explanation of each option and make some comments on their use. The specialised options that relate to juveniles and mentally disordered offenders are discussed separately (see 4.6.4 and 4.6.5). (For an explanation of the role of probation officers in sentencing, see chapter 5.)

4.6.1 Discharge

'Discharges'—governed by the Probation Act (Northern Ireland) 1950 (section 5)—allow a court, having had regard to the circumstances of the offence, including the nature of the offence and the character of the offender, to decide that it is 'inexpedient to inflict punishment' and that a probation order is 'not appropriate' and thus to absolutely or conditionally discharge the offender.

4.6.1.1 Absolute Discharge

An absolute discharge means that, although convicted, the offender is not subject to any punishment. This option is used when the offence committed is a trivial one or when the court believes there is little likelihood of the person re-offending. The offender is not left with a criminal record, though if he or she should be prosecuted for a criminal offence in the future then the discharged conviction can be revealed at the trial.

4.6.1.2 Conditional Discharge

One might class this sentencing option as a probation order without the requirement for supervision. The court can impose a condition that the offender commit no further offence for a specified period (up to a maximum of three years): if he or she does commit a further offence they may be sentenced for the original offence as well as the new (i.e. subsequent) one. Conditional discharges are more common than absolute ones. The court is obliged to explain to the offender in simple language the effect of choosing such a disposal. A conditional discharge differs from a suspended sentence in that with the former no specific sentence has been set that will be activated by the commission of the subsequent offence (see 4.6.3.4).

4.6.2 Monetary Penalties

These sentencing options involve the offender (or his or her parent or guardian in the case of a juvenile) paying out a sum of money as a punishment, as compensation to the victim, or as surety for the offender's future good behaviour.

4.6.2.1 Fines

Fines are the most usual form of punishment, with 74 per cent of all offenders in magistrates' courts in 1993 being fined. Imprisonment can of course follow should the offender default in the payment of the fine.

A fine imposed on a child must be paid by his or her parents, and the courts can require the parents of a young person to pay if it so wishes (section 76(1)).

4.6.2.2 Compensation Order

Available for adults and juveniles, these orders enable courts to order the offender to make direct monetary reparation to the victim. The Criminal Justice (Northern Ireland) Order 1980, allows a court to require the offender to pay compensation for any personal injury, loss or damage resulting from an offence (article 3(1)). Such an order can be combined with other disposals and can be made both by Crown Courts and magistrates' courts, though the latter cannot make an award over £2,000. One of their advantages is that they avoid the expense and the need for civil litigation between the victim and the offender for the former to be compensated.

As with fines, compensation ordered to be paid in the case of a child must be paid by a parent, and in the case of a young person the court has a discretion to order the parent to pay the compensation (CYP68, section 76(1)).

4.6.2.3 Recognisance

A recognisance is an undertaking to behave in a certain way or to perform some particular obligation in the context of the criminal justice system, usually to 'be of good behaviour' and involving a surety (i.e. a sum of money). The practical effect of breaking a recognisance is that the surety will be forfeited. Those who make recognisances are usually described as being bound over.

The Criminal Law Act (Northern Ireland) 1967, section 7(5), gives the courts the power to bind over offenders to keep the peace or be of good behaviour. The specific power for magistrates' courts and justices of the peace is contained in the Magistrates' Courts (Northern Ireland) Order 1980 (article 127(1)). In respect of juveniles the relevant provision is CYP68, section 76. Where a juvenile is charged with an offence a court can, in addition to or in lieu of any other order, order his or her parents or guardian to enter into a recognisance as security for the juvenile's good behaviour. Such an order cannot be made without giving the parent an opportunity to be heard, but if they have been requested to attend and fail to do so, then they can be bound over in their absence.

4.6.3 *Community Disposals*

Though community disposals—i.e. sentencing options that are non-custodial and deal with the offender in the community—may appear to be 'soft' options, they are in many respects more effective than imprisoning someone, as prison tends to have little effect on the probability of the person re-offending, They are certainly cheaper options: it costs £6,000 a month to imprison someone, while the administration of a probation order costs approximately £1,300 and community service of average length about £600 (HMSO, *Crime in the Community*, 51).

4.6.3.1 Probation Order

A probation order means that an offender is put under the supervision of a probation officer for a period of six months to three years with a view to encouraging him or her to avoid re-offending and come to terms with the consequence of the offence. A court can make a probation order if it is of the opinion that having regard to the circumstances, including the nature of the offence and the character of the offender, it is expedient to do so. Thus the legislative implication of this formulation is that a probation order is not a punishment but an alternative to punishment.

The power to make probation orders, deriving from the Probation Act (Northern Ireland) 1950 (section 1), as amended by the Treatment of Offenders (Northern Ireland) Order 1976 (article 3), allows courts to attach such conditions to the orders as it thinks necessary in order to 'secure the good conduct of the offender'. There are three conditions outlined in the Probation Rules (Northern Ireland) 1950, usually attached to probation orders: (*a*) that the offender lead an honest and industrious life, (*b*) that he or she keep the probation officer notified of any change of address or employment, and (*c*) that he or she remain in contact with the probation officer in accordance with the probation officer's instructions and in particular receives visits from the probation officer in his or her home.

There are, however, a number of specific conditions or requirements that a court can attach to a probation order. These are set out in the legislation and relate to (*a*) residence, (*b*) attendance at specific places, to participate in specific activities, and (*c*) attendance at a day centre.

The first of these, governed by the Probation Act 1950 (section 1(4)), requires the offender (or probationer, as the legislation describes him or her) to reside in a specific place, for example a probation hostel, if it is thought that the offender's usual environment is unsuited to him or her leading an 'honest and industrious life'. The second condition allows a court to direct that the offender attend at a specified place to engage in specified activities. It is found in the Probation Act 1950 (section 2A), as amended by the Treatment of Offenders (Northern Ireland) Order 1989 (article 3), and is therefore referred to by probation officers as a '2A order'. The last of the three conditions allows the court to order an offender to attend a designated day centre. This originates in the Probation Act 1950 (section 2B), as amended by the Treatment of Offenders (Northern Ireland) Order 1989 (article 3), and is therefore commonly referred to by probation service staff as a '2B order'.

The court is required to give copies of the order to the probation officer assigned to the court, who then gives copies to the offender and the supervising probation officer. It must also explain to the offender, in simple language, the consequences of the order and that failure to comply may lead to sentencing for the original offence. (For an explanation of the role of probation officers in the making and supervising of probation orders see 5.3.3.1.)

Probation is available for all offenders, i.e. from the age of ten upwards, although if the offender is under fourteen the courts cannot make the order without his or her consent. This contrasts with the position in England and Wales, where probation is only available for offenders aged sixteen and over.

A range of alternative consequences flows from the breach of a probation order. If the order was originally made by a magistrate's court, (*a*) a fine can be imposed without prejudice to the continuance of the order, (*b*) if the offender is under seventeen an attendance centre order can be made, (*c*) if the offender is over seventeen it can make a community service order, or (*d*) the court can deal with the offender in any manner open to the court that made the original order. This last option terminates the probation order. If the original order was made by a Crown Court then a magistrate's court can commit him or her to custody or on bail to that court. The Crown Court can treat the offender as the magistrate's court could have without terminating the order, or it can treat him or her in the manner open to the Crown Court, thus terminating the order.

4.6.3.2 Community Service Order

Community service orders, which are made under the Treatment of Offenders (Northern Ireland) Order 1976, as amended, are available for offenders aged sixteen and over, except where the penalty for the offence committed is fixed by law. The idea is that the offender performs a number of unpaid hours of work in the community. A sixteen-year-old can be sentenced to a maximum of 120 hours' community service, while the maximum for those aged seventeen and over is 240 hours.

The consent of the offender is needed before an order can be made, as is a report by a probation officer (see chapter 5), and the court must be satisfied that arrangements can be made for the offender to carry out the work. The court must explain to the offender in simple language the purpose and effect of the order and the consequences of failing to comply with it, and it must give him or her a copy of the order. The offender is required to report to his or her probation officer and to notify the officer of any change in address. (For more on the role of the probation officer, see chapter 5.) A community service order may be made in respect of an offender who breaches his or her probation order.

Breach of a community service order renders the offender liable to a fine of £50 or (following the revocation of the order) to be dealt with for the original offence in any manner open to the court that originally made the order.

4.6.3.3 Suspended Sentence

A court may impose a term of imprisonment on an offender but it may feel that, because of exceptional circumstances, it should not be served and thus may be suspended. However, should the offender commit an imprisonable offence—as opposed to an offence for which she or he may not be imprisoned, for example some road traffic offences—the suspended sentence may be reactivated.

Sentences of up to seven years can be suspended for between one and five years, and sentences of up to two years can be suspended for between one and three years (Treatment of Offenders (Northern Ireland) Act 1968, section 18, as amended by Treatment of Offenders (Northern Ireland) Order 1989, article 9). On making the suspended sentence the court has to explain to the offender in simple language their liability should they commit an imprisonable offence. A suspended sentence is treated as a sentence of imprisonment for all legislative purposes, except legislation that provides for disqualification from or loss of office for those sentenced to imprisonment. Suspended sentences are available for juvenile offenders, in contrast to the position in England and Wales.

4.6.4 *Immediate Custody*

A court may feel that a community disposal is not appropriate and decide to send an offender to a penal establishment immediately on conviction. Young offenders serve custodial sentences in the Young Offenders Centre, whereas prison is for those offenders aged over twenty-one. (For a list of the penal establishments in Northern Ireland see 1.3.7.)

4.6.5 *Juvenile Offenders*

Children may not be imprisoned or sent to a young offenders centre for an offence or for defaulting on a fine, though a young person may be if the court certifies that he or she is 'of so unruly or depraved a character that no other method of dealing with him or her is appropriate' (CYP68, section 72). However, where a juvenile commits certain serious offences—offences that in the case of an adult would carry a term of imprisonment of fourteen years or more in the case of non-scheduled offences or five years or more in the case of scheduled offences—other than an offence carrying a penalty fixed by law, and the court is of the opinion that no other method of dealing with the case is suitable, it may sentence the offender to be detained for such a period as it specifies in the sentence (CYP68, section 73 (2)). Thus the juvenile can be detained in such place as the Secretary of State decides—at a young offenders centre, a training school, or a prison. Juveniles detained in this way can be released on the licence of the Secretary of State, though licences may be revoked and the offender recalled on the same basis as an SOSP (see 4.6.5.6).

The options described above at 4.6 apply equally to juveniles. However, there are some options that are available to juveniles only, and it is these that we well deal with here. The overlap between the care and justice aspects of child law means that until the Children (Northern Ireland) Order 1995, is implemented, some of these options are available for use with juveniles who commit criminal offences and also with those requiring 'care, protection or control' (see chapter 6).

For an offence punishable in the case of an adult by imprisonment (with the exception of murder, which is dealt with separately: see 4.6.4.6), the options open to the court, apart from those we have looked at, are to make a training school order, a fit person order, or an attendance order, or to commit the offender to a remand home. In the case of child offenders only, a supervision order can be made. When considering which of these options to use, the court must have regard to the welfare of the juvenile and take steps to remove him or her from undesirable surroundings and ensure that proper provision is made for his or her education and training (CYP68, section 48).

4.6.5.1 Training School Order

This is one of the most commonly chosen custodial options for juvenile offenders. It is not intended to be purely a custodial option but an opportunity to help the juvenile, through training and guidance, not to re-offend on release. Therefore, training school orders also provide for post-release supervision.

Available for those aged ten to seventeen-year-olds at the time of committal, this order allows a court to send the offender to a training school for up to two years or until the expiry of four months after the offender reaches the maximum compulsory school age (sixteen), whichever is later (CYP68, section 87). The order must come to an end when the offender reaches nineteen. (However, where a juvenile is due to be released from training school and the school managers are satisfied that further care or training is needed they may, with the consent of the Secretary of State, detain him or her for a further period or periods not exceeding six months (CYP68, section 90(1).) The exact length of the detention is not decided by the court but is a government decision. After six months the child may be released on licence or, before that, with the approval of the Secretary of State for Northern Ireland. (The government intends to change this situation in future criminal justice legislation so that the courts will set determinate sentences for those sentenced to training schools.) Supervision in the community continues after the offender is released for three years or until he or she reaches the age of twenty-one, whichever comes first (CYP68, section 89(1)). (For the use of training school orders in care proceedings, see also chapter 6.)

4.6.5.2 Supervision Order

This option involves the offender being put under the supervision of a social worker or a probation officer. Only available for those aged ten to thirteen, these orders are made for a specified period, for a maximum of three years. (For the role of the supervising officer, see 5.3.3). Supervision orders are also available for use in care proceedings or for persistent truancy, although in those cases this option is available for ten to sixteen-year-olds inclusive. (See chapter 6.)

4.6.5.3 Attendance Centre Orders

These are orders, available for offenders aged ten to sixteen, requiring the offender to attend at a centre for instruction and training given by teachers. They are usually restricted to those living within a reasonable distance of Belfast, because there is at present only one attendance centre in Northern Ireland, at Millfield, Belfast, and because the governing legislative provision, CYP68, section 135, requires the court to consider the accessibility of the centre to the offender.

The order specifies the total number of hours of attendance by an offender. This should be twelve hours, unless the offender is a child and the court is of the opinion that twelve hours would be excessive or, in the case of an offender aged over fourteen, that twelve hours is not enough. In the latter case the court may order the offender to attend for up to twenty-four hours. The court will also set the date for the first attendance, with subsequent attendance dates and times being set by the centre manager.

Attendance at the centre should be organised so as not to interfere with any educational or work commitments the offender has. Offenders can only be required to attend once in any one day and then only for a maximum of three hours (section 135(5)). An attendance centre order is also used where an offender is in breach of a probation order (Probation Act (Northern Ireland) 1950, section 4, as amended).

4.6.5.4 Committal to a Remand Home

Provided for by CYP68 (section 74 (1) (*e*)), this is a sentence that is rarely used that commits the juvenile to a remand home (i.e. training school). The difference between it and a training school order is that it is a determinate sentence. It is used where an imprisonable offence has been committed (i.e. an offence for which an adult offender might be imprisoned) and no other method of dealing with the offender is suitable. Committal to a remand home must not exceed one month or the term of imprisonment that would have been available for an adult, whichever is shorter (section 74(3)). This option is also available for juvenile fine-defaulters in situations where an adult would be liable for imprisonment and no other method of dealing with the juvenile is suitable (section 75(1)).

4.6.5.5 Fit Person Order

This is an order, made under CYP68, section 74(1), placing a juvenile offender in the care of a 'fit person'—someone *in loco parentis* with respect to the maintenance of the child—because the circumstances of the child are such that long-term supervision at home is not possible or perhaps conducive to the child's best welfare. The fit person is usually a Health Board or Trust, although in reality juveniles are boarded out to foster-parents or children's homes. A relative or other person willing to undertake care of the child can also be named as a fit person. A fit person order lasts until the child is eighteen.

4.6.5.6 Detention at the Secretary of State's Pleasure

Juveniles found guilty of murder must be ordered to be detained at the pleasure of the Secretary of State (CYP68, section 73(1)). This is the juvenile equivalent of the life sentence, and 'SOSPs' (as they are commonly called) can be released on licence of the Secretary of State, after he has consulted the Lord Chief Justice for Northern Ireland and the trial judge, if available, as life prisoners can. In practice the Life Sentence Review Board (LSRB) (see 1.3.7 and 5.3.4) recommends to the Secretary of State that a prisoner be released having carried out reviews of the prisoner's case. The LSRB is chaired by the permanent under-secretary of the NIO, and its other members are the chief probation officer, senior NIO officials, a principal medical officer of the DHSS, and a consultant forensic psychiatrist. Such conditions as the Secretary of State thinks fit can be contained in the licence, and, perhaps most importantly, the licence can be revoked and the juvenile recalled for breaches of the condition of the licence or for committing another offence.

4.6.6 *Mentally Disordered Offenders*

Mentally disordered offenders convicted in either the Crown Court or a magistrate's court can be subject to hospital orders and guardianship orders, except for offences with penalties fixed by law (Mental Health Order 1986, article 44). A hospital order can be made on the oral evidence of a 'part II doctor' (see chapter 7) and the written or oral evidence of one other medical practitioner that the offender is suffering from mental illness or severe mental impairment of a nature or degree that warrants their detention in hospital for medical treatment and the court is of the opinion that having regard to all the circumstances, including the nature of the offence and the character and the antecedents of the offence, this is the most suitable means of dealing with the case.

A guardianship order is available for use with offenders aged sixteen and over but can only be made on the evidence of the following three people: (*a*) a 'part II doctor', (*b*) another medical practitioner, and (*c*) an approved social worker (see chapter 7). The medical personnel give evidence that the offender is suffering from mental illness or severe mental handicap of a nature or degree that warrants reception into guardianship, and the approved social worker gives written or oral evidence that it is necessary in the interests of the welfare of the patient that he or she should be received into guardianship. If the court is then of the opinion that, having regard to all circumstances, a guardianship order is the most suitable way of dealing with him or her, it can issue such an order. Patients admitted to hospital under a hospital or guardianship order are treated under part II of the Mental Health Order, 1986 (see chapter 7).

Where a hospital order has been made, the court may make a restriction order if it appears to the court that it is necessary to do so, having regard to the nature of the offence, the antecedents of the person, and the risk of their committing further offences if set at large. This order attaches special restrictions to a hospital order, including the stipulation that none of the provisions relating to duration, renewal and expiry of authority contained in part II will apply, nor does a right to make an application to the Mental Health Review Tribunal exist (see chapter 7), nor can powers of transfer or granting leave of absence be given other than by the Secretary of State.

The Secretary of State can bring a restriction order to an end if satisfied that it is no longer required for the protection of the public (Mental Health Order, 1986, article 48).

A residential medical officer (see chapter 7) has the responsibility of making reports on a person subject to a restriction order. These reports are made at the direction of the Secretary of State, and the legislation provides that there must be at least one a year, though in practice they are more frequent than that.

An interim hospital order is also available, allowing the court to place the offender in the care of the DHSS for admission and detention in a hospital. It can be made on the oral evidence of a part II doctor and the written or oral evidence of another medical practitioner that the offender is suffering from mental illness or severe mental impairment and that there is reason to suppose that the mental disorder may warrant a hospital order (MHO86, article 45). Such an order can be made into a hospital order at a later hearing, or indeed renewed, without the need for the accused to be present, provided the accused has the opportunity of being represented at that hearing. Interim hospital orders can be made for a maximum of twelve weeks but are renewable for periods of twenty-eight days on the written or oral evidence of a residential medical officer that continuation of the order is warranted, for a maximum limit of six months.

In respect of all of the orders outlined here, the DHSS must be given an opportunity by the court to make representations before the orders can be made.

4.7 *Further Reading*

Boyle, and Allen, *Sentencing Law and Practice in Northern Ireland* (2nd edition), SLS, Belfast: Legal Publications 1989.

Crime and the Community: a Discussion Paper on Criminal Justice Policy in Northern Ireland, London: HMSO 1993.

Dickson, Brice, 'The powers of the police' in *Civil Liberties in Northern Ireland: the CAJ Handbook* (2nd edition), Belfast: Committee on the Administration of Justice 1993.

Dickson, Brice, *The Legal System of Northern Ireland*, Belfast: SLS Legal Publications 1994, chap. 4.

Digest of Information on the Northern Ireland Criminal Justice System, 1992, London: HMSO 1993.

Jackson, J., 'Questioning suspects' in *Civil Liberties in Northern Ireland: the CAJ Handbook* (2nd edition), Belfast: Committee on the Administration of Justice 1993.

5

PROBATION WORK

Ciaran White

5.1 *Introduction*

The focus of this chapter is on the work of the probation service, and though much of this could be included in chapter 4, it is dealt with here, firstly, because the Probation Board for Northern Ireland is an autonomous statutory body and, secondly, because of the specialised nature of the service provided by probation officers.

Placing this chapter immediately after that relating to the criminal justice system in general has been a deliberate decision. According to statute, probation officers become involved at the later stages of the criminal process (i.e. after conviction but before sentencing), though in practice they do intervene before conviction in some instances by preparing pre-trial reports on an accused juvenile who it is known will plead guilty for example; and they remain involved with offenders long after the trial has concluded. Because of the scope of this book the primary focus of this chapter must be on the statutory work of probation officers, though reference is frequently made to the non-statutory work they engage in and to non-statutory standards of practice, particularly those contained in the probation service manual.

The *National Standards for the Supervision of Offenders in the Community* (London: HMSO 1992), the standards that govern the probation services in Great Britain, do not formally apply in Northern Ireland. However, standards specific to Northern Ireland, governing the work of probation officers when supervising people subject to probation or community service orders, are included in the manual compiled by the service. It outlines the legal framework within which the service operates and provides practical guidance for probation officers. We will refer to the manual at various points in this chapter.

There are a number of differences between the organisation and provision of probation services in Northern Ireland and the remainder of the UK. Structurally the probation service differs from others in the UK in that it has no link with local authorities, while operationally the key differences are that (*a*) the service in Northern Ireland is community-based and therefore does not include members of the judiciary or magistracy (though lay panellists are included: see chapter 1) and (*b*) it does not undertake any civil work. (The probation service in Great Britain has responsibilities in matrimonial proceedings.)

Other important differences are that probation is available in Northern Ireland for those aged ten and over, whereas in England it is available only for those over the age of sixteen, and that no system of parole exists in Northern Ireland, though remission is available and there are 'home leave' and pre-release schemes (see 5.3.4). Those serving fixed-term sentences qualify for 50 per cent remission. However, since 1989 those serving five years or more for scheduled offences qualify for 33 per cent remission only.

5.2 *The Probation Board for Northern Ireland*

Although the possibility of making probation orders with respect to offenders has been available since the Probation of Offenders Act 1907, and an organised probation service was in existence for some time, the Probation Board for Northern Ireland (PBNI) was put on a statutory footing only as recently as 1982, by the Probation Board (Northern Ireland) Order (hereafter referred to as PBO82). The PBNI's powers and duties are outlined in articles 4 and 5 of the Order, as amended. As well as being responsible for 'the maintenance of an adequate and efficient probation service,' it must also ensure that 'arrangements are made for persons to perform work under community service orders' (for more on these see chapter 4, and 5.3.3.2 below) and 'provide such probation officers and other staff as the Secretary of State considers necessary to perform social welfare duties in prisons and young offenders' centres.' It is open to the Secretary of State for Northern Ireland to prescribe other duties for the PBNI to undertake. (It is the PBNI that has the statutory duty—under PBO82, article 5 (1)—to select and appoint probation officers for each petty sessions, i.e. magistrate's court district.)

The Board comprises a maximum of eighteen members (at present there are fourteen), appointed by the Secretary of State for three-year terms, served by a full-time secretary. The PBNI has an annual budget of approximately £10 million. The work of the service is headed by a Chief Probation Officer (CPO) and staffed by approximately 150 probation officers, supported by eighty administrators, working in thirty-four offices throughout the region. The CPO is aided in his or her task by a Deputy CPO, a senior management team of eight people, and a middle management team of twenty-nine. The service operates through thirteen field teams, five prison-based teams, and a specialist court team in Belfast, with each team supervised by an area manager. Two training officers and a research and information officer provide support services.

The PBNI is supervising approximately 1,400 people at any time as well as providing a service to 400–500 clients in a non-statutory capacity. (Incidentally, the Chief Probation Officer is a member of the Life Sentence Review Board, which examines the cases of those sentenced to life imprisonment or detained at the Secretary of State's pleasure: see 1.3.7 and 4.6.5.6.) We consider in more detail later other aspects of the work engaged in, including the compilation of court reports.

5.2.1 *Scope of Work*

The PBNI avails of the powers conferred on it by article 5 of PBO82 to provide or finance a range of services related to dealing effectively with offenders and helping to prevent re-offending.

5.2.1.1 Work with Voluntary Organisations

The PBNI can give effect to schemes for the supervision and assistance of offenders and the prevention of crime, whether made by voluntary organisations or by the PBNI, and to enter into arrangements with those organisations and people to organise these schemes. A wide range of organisations and activities is financed. For example, in 1993/94 the PBNI spent almost £2 million on schemes run by voluntary organisations. These included once-off grants to small community-based schemes as well as continuing grants to large charitable and voluntary organisations. Given the range of projects supported, all we can do here is provide a flavour of these.

The PBNI part-finances voluntary organisations operating in the criminal justice field, for example the Northern Ireland Association for the Care and Resettlement of Offenders (NIACRO) and 'Extern'. In particular it works closely with both these organisations in establishing schemes to provide employment opportunities to ex-offenders. In 1987 the PBNI jointly with the NIACRO established 'Prison Link' to give higher priority to the families of released and serving prisoners. It also provides financial support for the Dismas House project (a hostel for ex-prisoners) and Runkerry outdoor pursuits centre.

5.2.1.2 Prisons

A probation unit is found at each of Northern Ireland's six prisons (for a list of these see 1.3.7). The PBNI also helps finance the child-minding facilities and family centre at Belfast, Maze and Maghaberry prisons, though these are in fact run by voluntary organisations.

5.2.1.3 Probation Hostels and Bail Hostels

PBO82 (article 5 (*a*)) allows the PBNI to 'provide and maintain probation and bail hostels.' Probation hostels 'provide residential facilities for offenders who require enhanced supervision to live in the community. Such hostels are provided for, among others, high-risk offenders who have been released from custody, or offenders on a probation order with an additional residence requirement order' (Vernon, *Social Work Law*, 165). The PBNI's Ramoan House in Country Antrim is an example of a probation hostel. Indeed probation officers refer to probation orders with a residence requirement (i.e. a requirement that the offender live in a specific place: see 4.6.3.1) as 'Ramoan orders'.

Bail hostels, on the other hand, are residential facilities to which people awaiting trial are sent if the courts believe they require a substantial measure of supervision as well as support during the remand period, thus making it possible for bail to be considered. Only those over the age of seventeen are sent to them. Residents usually live at the hostel until the next court appearance. These orders are usually used where the alleged offence is one against property rather than one involving violence.

Although at present there is no specialist bail hostel provision in Northern Ireland, it is probable, following the review of the criminal justice system undertaken in *Crime in the Community* (London: HMSO 1993), that such provision will be made in the future. Consequently the PBNI is likely to be involved in the provision of these services in time, either by directly providing the hostels or by entering into arrangements with voluntary organisations and others to allow them to provide hostels.

5.3 *Probation Officers*

Probation officers might be perceived as playing a dual role: on the one hand they operate as officers of the court, yet on the other hand, because of their involvement in the provision of welfare service to prisoners, prisoners' families, and people recently released from prison, they could be described as specialised social workers endeavouring to assist their clients. Indeed this latter perspective of probation officers is reinforced by the view that possession of either a Certificate of Qualification in Social Work (CQSW) or a Diploma in Social Work (DipSW) is a necessary qualification for appointment as a probation officer and by the fact that in its present corporate plan the PBNI states that one of the values that underpins its work is the view that the 'core professional base in probation work is social work' (*PBNI Corporate Plan, 1993–97*, 7).

Not surprisingly probation officers are employees of the PBNI but they do not appear to have an independent legal status in the way that police officers do. The post of probation officer is not created or defined by statute, though, as we shall see, there are statutory references to probation officers.

There are four main areas of work that a probation officer is likely to be engaged in: (*a*) the courts, (*b*) community supervision, (*c*) prisons, and (*d*) offenders' families. There are statutory provisions relating directly to the first two only; the latter two are non-statutory areas of work or areas in respect of which statutory provisions are enabling rather than directive. For that reason we deal principally with the first two categories, though we also consider work done within the prisons. We do not consider the work done with offenders' families.

5.3.1 *General Duty*

There is a general statutory duty on probation officers that governs all the work engaged in by them. It is outlined by the Probation Act (Northern Ireland) 1950 (hereafter PA50), section 14, as amended by PBO82, and requires probation officers '(*a*) to supervise persons placed under their supervision and to advise, assist and befriend those persons, (*b*) to enquire in accordance with any direction of the court into circumstances or home surroundings of any persons with a view to assisting the court in determining the most suitable method of dealing with him,' and generally '(*c*) to perform any other duties the Board may from time to time direct.'

5.3.2 *The Courts*

The role of the probation officer in criminal proceedings is the focus of our attention here. The production of social enquiry reports (SERs) on offenders, to aid the courts in deciding what sentence to impose, is one of the main functions of the service. ('Social enquiry report' is the term by which such reports are commonly known, though in fact it is not used anywhere in the legislation. For an explanation of sentencing options, see 4.6). Broadly speaking, these reports are compiled as a result of inquiries made by the probation officer into the offender's home and family circumstances. The PBNI's annual report for 1993/94 (p. 9) describes these reports thus: 'A SER is an objective, constructive document which contains (i) a summary of the defendant's background; (ii) an evaluation of the effectiveness of previous sentences; (iii) an assessment of the defendant's motivation to stay out of trouble; (iv) an assessment of the community options which could help the individual lead a law abiding life.'

The newly drafted guidelines on preparing SERs require the probation officer to consider (among other issues) the offending behaviour (including previous offending behaviour, if applicable) and personal circumstances of the offender (which include his or her employment status or prospects and family relationships, for example) and to offer guidance on making recommendations for an appropriate mode of disposal. These new guidelines also detail the principles underpinning the content of an SER. These include objectivity, accuracy, and confidentiality.

Probation staff are acting as officers of the court in this instance, and therefore their role is to present information to the court regarding the offender, assess the utility of the various disposal options available to the court, and then make a recommendation. It is not the role of a probation officer when preparing SERs to act as an advocate for the offender.

Indeed the report is the property of the court. A copy of the report is to be given by the court to the offender or to his or her legal advisers (or, if the offender is a juvenile and is not represented by a legal adviser, to his or her parents or guardian) (PA50, section 9). Approximately four thousand SERs are prepared in a year. In the twelve months to 31 March 1994, for example, 4,148 SERs were produced by PBNI staff. (For advice on how to compile reports generally, see chapter 2.)

SERs are required in only a limited number of cases. Where the offender is a juvenile, an SER must be compiled. The Children and Young Persons Act (Northern Ireland) 1968 (hereafter CYP68), section 53 (2), requires SERs to be made for alleged juvenile offenders, except where the offence is a trivial one. These reports are to provide information relating to the 'home surroundings, school record and physical and mental health and character of the child and in proper cases, the availability of training schools.' If a court is minded to make a community service order, it must also request an SER. With regard to the making of a community service order, the court must satisfy itself that the offender is a 'suitable person to perform work' under such an order by considering a report of a probation officer (Treatment of Offenders (Northern Ireland) Order 1976 (article 7 (4) (*b*)).

In relation to probation orders, a court is only required to request a report if it intends to make an order with a residence requirement, or a requirement to engage in specific activities, or to attend a day centre (PA50, sections 1 (4), 2A, and 2B, as amended by the Treatment of Offenders (Northern Ireland) Order 1989, article 3). In all other cases it is at the court's discretion whether to seek an SER.

Magistrates' and juvenile courts have the power to adjourn proceedings to decide the 'most suitable method of dealing with the case' (Magistrates' Courts (Northern Ireland) Order 1981, article 150), and this also allows for the preparation of an SER.

The service only compiles an SER if the offender agrees to this. (Where an offender is aged fourteen or over, the probation order can only be made with his or her consent in any case: see 4.6.3.1.) If the offender does not agree, then no report is prepared. The service's manual requires officers to obtain consent from the parents of children (i.e. those under the age of fourteen) and from the parents or guardian and the young person him or herself in the case of juveniles (defendants aged between fourteen and seventeen). This requirement of consent does not apply to those already subject to a probation or community service order who are charged with committing an imprisonable offence (see chapter 4) while subject to supervision. The rationale is that these people have already undertaken certain obligations, and if they have failed to adhere to these then this should be a matter for the court. These reports are referred to by the PBNI as 'progress or response to supervision reports' and are, strictly speaking, not SERs.

Because many young offenders are dealt with by the issue of a caution (see 4.4.1), most cases in the juvenile courts will involve the preparation of an SER. This is because those offences that remain to be dealt with by the courts are more serious. However, some juveniles do not have the opportunity of having an SER prepared for them. SERs on juveniles are to be made by a 'welfare authority', unless arrangements have been made for the report to be made by a probation officer (CYP68, section 53 (2)). Thus those juveniles who do not have reports prepared by probation officers have reports prepared for them by an officer of a Board or Trust if they are in care or by an officer of a training school if they are already there as a result of a training school order made for their care, protection, and control (see chapter 6).

A significant number of people who perhaps should have SERs prepared on them at present have not. In 1991, for example, 86 per cent of those receiving immediate custody and 87 per cent of those receiving suspended custody in magistrates' courts did not have reports prepared (*PBNI Corporate Plan*, 13). (For an explanation of 'immediate' and 'suspended' custody see chapter 4.) One of the reasons for the failure of the courts to seek as many SERs as they might may be the length of time involved in their preparation. The service is keen to reduce the preparation time for SERs (*PBNI Corporate Plan*, 15). Another reason may be that judges or magistrates do not consider that probation officers are sufficiently objective when compiling reports. As the PBNI's corporate plan puts it (p. 13), 'Clearly one obstacle to the increased use of SERs is sentencers' perception of an unreasonable bias on the part of probation officers towards community disposals for offences the seriousness of which clearly warrants imprisonment.'

Statistics illustrate the importance to an offender of having a SER prepared and presented to the court. Where a report is presented, a community supervision disposal is likely, and, conversely, where there is no report, custody is likely. For example in 1991, where reports were presented in magistrates' courts, 71 per cent of offenders received community supervision, while the remainder were sentenced to custody. However, where a report was not presented, 17 per cent of offenders received community supervision and 83 per cent were sentenced to custody (*PBNI Corporate Plan*, appendix 1A).

The acceptance of recommendations made in SERs also varies considerably from court to court. In the juvenile court the rate of acceptance in 1991 was 60 per cent, while for the magistrates' courts and the Crown Court it was 69 and 33 per cent, respectively (*PBNI Corporate Plan*, 13). The considerable divergence in these statistics between magistrates' courts and the Crown Court may be partly explained by the serious nature of offences heard in the latter courts and their restricted scope for making a non-custodial disposal.

The preparation of SERs for use in the Crown Court is not governed by legislation, though it is established PBNI practice to prepare reports for use in the Crown Court, but only in the trial of non-scheduled (i.e. non-terrorist) offences. Pre-trial reports are prepared on those who it is known will plead guilty, and post-trial reports may be requested by the judge following conviction. SERs are prepared for trials of non-scheduled offences in two exceptional circumstances (for a full explanation of 'scheduled' and 'non-scheduled' see 4.1): firstly, where the trial judge, having found the accused guilty, requests it; this circumstance is governed by the Chief Probation Officer's 'Circular on Scheduled Offences'; and, secondly, where the person charged is subject to 'statutory supervision', i.e. to a probation order or a community service order. The report in this instance will inform the court of the response to supervision and will be prepared after the trial.

Nor are SERs normally prepared where the sentence for the crime the person is charged with is a mandatory one, as is the case with murder, for example. An exception to this policy is made if the trial judge requests a report.

There is a statutory requirement on probation officers to send documents and information relating to a young offender to the principal or governor of a training school or a young offenders centre to which he or she is sent (PA50, section 14, as amended by PBO82, schedule 4, paragraph 2), though it is the practice of the service to send copies of SERs of all offenders given custodial sentences to the senior probation officer attached to the penal institution to which an offender is sent, as well as to the director of an attendance centre if an attendance centre order is made.

SERs for use in the appeal courts are also prepared, though where a report has been prepared for the trial court it is that report, along with any supplementary information, that will be presented. It is only in situations where reports are not prepared for the trial that they are freshly prepared for the appeal court.

Should the probation officer who prepared the report be unable to attend in court, the Crown Court liaison officer or the court duty officer in the magistrate's or juvenile court will present the corporate report. The service manual requires probation officers to attend if the judge or magistrate specifically requests that officer to attend or if the defendant is subject to statutory supervision. A written explanation of why the probation officer cannot attend should be given to the duty officer so that he or she has this available at the court hearing.

5.3.3 *Community Supervision*

Not surprisingly, the PBNI advocates community supervision as a method of helping to reduce re-offending. However, at present a smaller proportion of offenders in Northern Ireland, in both the magistrate's court and the Crown Court, are made subject to community service orders and probation orders than is the case in England (*PBNI Corporate Plan*, 19).

Probation officers can find themselves assigned to work with offenders who are subject to different types of court orders. The circumstances in which these orders can be made by the court are discussed in 4.6.3; our concern here is with the probation officer's role in relation to the making of these orders and to the offenders made subject to them. We remind you of probation officers' general duty towards people placed under their supervision (see 5.3.1).

Occasionally probation officers may find themselves involved in the supervision of people released on statutory licence from English or Welsh penal institutions and people subject to community service orders made in Great Britain. These include people released under statutory supervision from young offenders institutions in Britain. They will not, however, be required to engage in the supervision of probation orders made in Britain, as no system exists allowing the transfer to Northern Ireland of probation orders from England and Wales or from Scotland.

5.3.3.1 Probation Order

As we have seen (4.6.3.1), although a court can attach requirements or conditions to a probation order, before it does so it must be satisfied about certain matters, and so the probation officer will be asked to make a report. Before attaching a residence requirement to a probation order the court is required to 'consider the home surroundings of the offender,' while a court cannot make a '2A order' (specific activities order) unless it has first consulted a probation officer about '(*a*) the offender's circumstances and (*b*) the feasibility of securing compliance with the requirements.' Before making a '2B order' (day centre order) the court must first consult a probation officer and then be satisfied that 'arrangements can be made for the probationer's attendance at a centre and that the person in charge of the centre consents to the inclusion of the requirement.'

Attendance at a day centre and participation in specified activities is in accordance with instructions given by the supervising probation officer. These instructions must, as far as is practicable, be such as to avoid any interference with the times at which the offender normally works or attends an educational institution (PA50, section 2A and B, as amended by the Treatment of Offenders (Northern Ireland) Order 1989, article 3).

Where one of the conditions attached to the order is that the offender be medically treated, the probation officer's duty to supervise him or her is only to such an extent as may be necessary for the discharge or amendment of the order (PA50, section 2 (4)). Discharge or amendment of the order will include involvement with doctors and the offender. Where the doctor wishes to vary or cancel the treatment being given, he or she must first furnish the probation officer with a written report, whereupon the probation officer applies to the supervising court (i.e. magistrate's court) for an order to make the appropriate variation or cancellation (PA50, schedule 2, paragraph 4).

A supervising probation officer is closely involved when the offender breaches the conditions of the probation order. The officer is responsible for initiating the court procedure and prosecuting it, though if the offender pleads not guilty then the PBNI will obtain legal support (i.e. counsel) for the supervising officer. Where the officer has the task of prosecuting the breach, he or she will be responsible for preparing an SER, drafting witness statements and the 'statement of facts' (i.e. outlining the nature of the breach), and notifying other agencies that might have an interest in the matter. Once again the manual provides detailed guidance for supervising officers faced with this task.

5.3.3.2 Community Service Order

Before making a community service order the court must be satisfied, after considering a report by a probation officer about the offender and his or her circumstances and, if the court thinks it necessary, hearing a probation officer, that the offender is a suitable person to perform work under such an order and that arrangements exist to allow him or her to perform that work. The court must give copies of the order to a probation officer assigned to the court, and he or she must then give a copy to the offender and to the supervising officer.

As with probation orders, the probation officer may issue instructions to the offender when performing work under a community service order, and those instructions must not, as far as is practicable, conflict with educational or work commitments the offender might have, nor should they conflict with his or her religious beliefs.

If the offender breaches the order, the supervising officer will be involved in any proceedings that are initiated. The manual requires every application to the court for such proceedings to be accompanied by a written report, which will probably be prepared by the supervising officer. It will provide information and express a view about '(i) the setting and nature of the work and the time when it had to be done, (ii) the tasks undertaken and the worker's response to the demands made of him, (iii) the extent of the worker's overall compliance with the order and (iv) action taken to enable the worker to complete the order.'

5.3.3.3 Supervision Order

While CYP68 allows probation officers to be supervisors (see 4.6.5.2), in practice supervision is usually carried out by social workers or welfare officers employed by the Health and Social Service Boards or Education and Library Boards, respectively. The service manual provides that should a probation officer make an SER on a child charged with a criminal offence and a supervision order appear a suitable option, the officer should consult local social services before including a recommendation of that nature in the report.

Where a probation officer is appointed to supervise a child or young person subject to a supervision order, he or she is required 'to visit, advise and befriend' that person and 'when necessary, endeavour to find him suitable employment' (CYP68, section 82). While this duty closely resembles that placed on officers when supervising offenders on probation, there are two differences. The duty to find the supervised person employment is one, and the other is the requirement to visit the person, which suggests that the officer must meet the juvenile in his or her home environment.

A probation officer does have the power, though it is rarely used, to bring the supervised person before a juvenile court if it 'appears to the officer to be necessary in his interests to do so.' The court may then (*a*) make a training school order, (*b*) make a fit person order, or (*c*) order the juvenile's parents or guardian to exercise proper care and guardianship (CYP68, section 97). (For more on these options see chapters 4 and 6.) Note that it is not necessary for the juvenile to have broken the terms of the order before he or she can be brought before a court: it is enough if the supervising officer considers it 'necessary in [the juvenile's] interests to do so.'

Where the young person is subject to medical treatment as part of the supervision order and the medical practitioner treating him or her wishes to alter that treatment, the medical practitioner must make a full report to the supervisor, and the supervisor must then apply to the juvenile court to make the necessary amendment or variation in the medical treatment.

Before leaving our consideration of the work done by probation officers working in the community, we might mention the role of probation officers in child protection cases. Though neither the PBNI nor probation officers themselves have a specific statutory role with regard to child abuse, the Board has child protection procedures that govern the role officers should play if they encounter child abuse or suspected abuse in the course of their work. Pro-formas exist allowing the probation officer to inform social services of any suspected, confirmed or potential abuse of a child. It is then the function of social services to contact the police; PBNI procedures do not put any obligation on staff to contact the police directly. These procedures are detailed, dealing with suspected abusers released on bail as well as those actually convicted. They are designed to ensure that relevant information flows from PBNI staff to social services. (For an explanation of the role of PBNI staff when 'schedule 1' offenders are about to be released from prison see below.)

5.3.4 *Prisons*

The range of functions and activities engaged in by probation officers working in penal establishments is broad. The service is attempting to direct its work in prisons towards the provision of a range of services to enhance prisoners' social progress and to prepare them for release, rather than to expend a great deal of energy on day-to-day matters relating to prisoners' welfare. However, as admitted in the PBNI corporate plan (p. 39), this has only met with limited success in the past, because '(i) the welfare mode is hard to break; (ii) the expectation is that probation will carry out routine tasks, some of which in effect could be more efficiently undertaken by prison personnel or the prisoner him/herself; (iii) some paramilitary prisoners have seen the Probation Service as an arm of Government and therefore unsuitable to provide a service to them.'

Examples of the work engaged in by such staff include preparation for 'home leave' (a scheme whereby prisoners are allowed home for short periods, usually at Christmas and summer) or release (though such release work is carried out by prison-based staff in conjunction with field probation staff, i.e. probation officers based in the community rather than in the prisons); interviewing prisoners at their request; and maintaining case records on all prisoners. These interviews usually deal with prisoners' problems or with difficulties associated with their imprisonment. The requirement to maintain case records extends to all prisoners, even those on remand. The rationale for this, obviously, is to aid future work with the prisoner.

Prison-based probation officers are operationally responsible to the governor of the prison, though they remain professionally responsible to the Chief Probation Officer, with whom a channel of communication always remains open.

As well as maintaining contact with and providing counselling services for prisoners throughout their detention, officers are frequently asked to prepare reports regarding prisoners in a wide variety of situations, often at the request of prison governors. These can include applications for compassionate home leave, requests for transfer, and requests for travel warrants. (It should be pointed out that occasionally field probation staff will find themselves preparing these reports.)

Home circumstances reports are designed to establish the nature and extent of a prisoner's home and family circumstances. They are used, for example, in relation to prisoners seeking transfer to the region from Great Britain or for discovering why a particular prisoner is receiving few or no visits from his or her family and appears to be isolated.

Post-sentence assessments are prepared on those given life sentences and are designed to aid the management of the prisoner. The issues to be included in this report are listed in the manual and deal with such matters as relationships with other prisoners, chances of sustaining such relationships, home circumstances, and the level of family support. The purpose of these reports is to draw together relevant information about the prisoner for use in working with him or her. The reason for preparing them is that, given PBNI policy regarding working with those charged with scheduled offences or offences carrying mandatory sentences (see 5.3.2), it is likely that no SER will have been prepared and therefore no source of information will exist with which to begin working with the prisoner.

Reports are also prepared by prison-based PBNI staff for hearings before the Life Sentence Review Board (LSRB). (For an explanation of the LSRB see 1.3.7 and 4.6.5.6.) New guidelines have recently been issued governing the compilation of these reports and include a list of headings governing the arrangement of the report's content. These headings relate to the prisoner's personal history (both before and during custody), the nature of the offence, including an assessment of the risk posed by the offender in the future (though this is only done for non-scheduled offenders), current circumstances, and future plans. It is not intended that the probation officer make a recommendation about the appropriateness of releasing the prisoner where the offence committed was a 'scheduled' one (see 4.1). These reports are prepared as a matter of course for non-scheduled offenders but only at the written request of scheduled prisoners, though the latter are invited to make such a request. Pursuant to general PBNI policy, the prisoner is consulted about the writing of the report, and, in particular, the nature of his or her consent will be confirmed when the report is completed, before its delivery to the LSRB.

It is also PBNI practice to inform social services if a 'schedule 1 offender' (i.e. a prisoner convicted of an offence under schedule 1 of CYP68—essentially abusing children) is released, either on licence or on the expiry of his or her sentence. These reports are made one month before the release date and contain information relating to the prisoner, including medical reports, if appropriate, and a report of the prison-based probation officer. Policy guidelines in the manual govern the role of various grades of probation officer in relation to child abuse. These guidelines are to be strictly observed, departure from them requiring consultation with the probation officer's line manager.

The supervision of licensees also forms part of the duties of probation officers. A licensee is someone released from prison on the licence (i.e. permission) of the Secretary of State for Northern Ireland. This means that should they engage in any criminal activity they can be recalled at any time by the Secretary of State: it is not necessary for them to have been convicted of a further offence. Those convicted of murder or otherwise sentenced to life imprisonment, and their juvenile equivalent, 'SOSPs' (see 4.6.5.6), are always released on licence.

Supervision of licensees after release is a feature of the PBNI's work, though it only supervises those convicted of non-scheduled offences. It is possible that one of the conditions the Secretary of State attaches to the licence is that the licensee be subject to the supervision of a probation officer. Licensees are required to meet their supervising officer regularly, and a change of employment or residence requires the permission of the supervising officer. Other restrictions may be included in the licence according to the circumstances of the crime. After a substantial period, normally several years, if the licensee has shown that he or she has settled in the community and his or her behaviour has not given rise to any cause for concern, the supervising conditions are usually cancelled. Otherwise they are retained for as long as is thought necessary. They can, of course, be retained for the duration of the licensee's life. The liability of the licensee to be recalled at any time does continue, however, despite the revocation of the supervising conditions.

Periodic reports to the NIO are made on the licensee in the post-release stage. These reports are sent to the Life Sentence Unit (LSU) of the NIO through the Chief Probation Officer, who may add his or her comments, if appropriate.

Obviously the supervising officer will be involved in recommending to the Secretary of State that a licensee be recalled, though such a recommendation would also be endorsed by the Assistant Chief Probation Officer (Prisons) and the Senior Probation Officer.

As stated earlier, no system of parole operates in Northern Ireland, though there are schemes designed to reintroduce the life-sentence prisoner into society. Perhaps the most important of these is the pre-release or 'working out' scheme, in which probation officers are involved. It is a scheme that lasts for approximately nine months in which a prisoner is found paid or voluntary work in the community before his or her sentence expires. Initially the prisoner returns to prison each night but eventually will live and work in the community, reporting to prison at fortnightly intervals. When a prisoner becomes involved in the pre-release scheme, field probation staff take over. The field probation officer designated to supervise a licensee on his or her release is expected to provide reports during the 'working-out' stage to the LSU. The manual prescribes the manner in which these should be organised. Such reports are to consider negative as well as positive aspects of the prisoner's behaviour and detail prospects for a resumption of domestic relationships and employment. These reports aid the authorities in deciding whether to release a prisoner on licence.

Prisoners' rights are outlined in the Prisons and Young Offender Centre Rules (Northern Ireland) 1995. These govern such matters as visiting rights and correspondence rights, and the PBNI produces a pamphlet summarising these.

5.3.5 *Confidentiality*

Confidentiality outside the court context is governed by PBNI guidelines. (On the issue of confidentiality and social workers in general see chapter 2; on confidentiality in relation to court proceedings see chapter 3.) Essentially the guidelines state that the probation officer should attempt to respect the client's confidentiality in all circumstances, except where to do so would (*a*) endanger the client's life, (*b*) represent a serious danger to others, (*c*) represent a serious threat to the client him or herself, (*d*) threaten the reputation of the PBNI in such a way that there would be loss of confidence in the service offered, or (*e*) involve the probation officer in a breach of statutory duty to release, for example in cases of child abuse.

The contents of any report are unlikely to be kept from the client. It is the probation service's practice 'to share with their clients as much as possible both of information and thinking. Probation practice rests on the assumption that individuals have a responsibility for their own lives and behaviour and that the purposes of our intervention is to help them exercise that responsibility more constructively whether through material or personal support, the provision of advice and counselling or through structured supervision' (*Probation Service Manual*, 169).

5.3.6 *Legal Liability for Injury or Damage*

The rules and principles relating to the legal liability of social workers for injury or damage caused by them in the course of their employment (dealt with in chapter 2) are modified in their application to probation officers

(PBO82, article 10). PBNI staff are exempted from personal liability for acts done on the basis of a statutory provision if they acted (*a*) reasonably and (*b*) in the honest belief that their statutory duty required or allowed them to do the act. However, the PBNI remains liable for acts of its staff members. The practical effect of this is that individual officers will not have to pay out of their own pockets if injury or damage is caused as a result of their actions, provided, of course, the PBNI thinks that officer's actions reasonable and that the officer honestly believed the statute allowed him or her to do what was done. The PBNI itself will remain liable to pay compensation to the injured party by virtue of the doctrine of vicarious liability (see chapter 2).

Additionally, should the officer engage in activity not within the scope of his or her employment—thus not rendering the PBNI vicariously liable—the PBNI is entitled to indemnify the officer for damages he or she may have to pay as a result of any legal action, provided it is satisfied that (*a*) he or she honestly believed that the act complained of was within the scope of their employment and that (*b*) they honestly believed that their duty under the statutory provisions required, or empowered, them to do it.

Not surprisingly, where an employee does something outside the scope of his or her employment, the law will not ordinarily hold the employer liable. The employee is considered to be doing something he or she is not entitled to do—'off on a frolic of his own,' as some of the older cases put it—and therefore fully liable for the consequences. It will be a matter of fact (and a very difficult matter of fact at that) whether a probation officer was acting outside the scope of his or her employment. This provision does not relieve staff members of liability but does mean that if they do incur liability personally, the PBNI can reimburse them, provided it is satisfied that these conditions are complied with.

Lastly, disciplinary proceedings may be brought against an officer who strays beyond what is permissible, but those proceedings will not result in compensation for injured parties and therefore will provide little satisfaction for them.

5.4 *Further Reading*

Caul B. and Herron S., 'A Service for People—Origins and Development of the Personal Social Services of Northern Ireland', December Publications, Belfast, 1992, pp 150–159.

See chapter 4.

6

CHILD CARE AND PROTECTION

DYMPNA MALLON and CIARAN WHITE

6.1 *Introduction*

The subject of this chapter is the civil law (as opposed to the criminal law) relating to the protection of children from abuse. We therefore do not consider how a child abuser may be punished, for example, nor do we consider the law relating to the provision of services to children (and their families). The law relating to services for children in care is set out in chapter 8—though it has to be admitted that it is difficult to draw a neat dividing line between the law governing child protection and that requiring or allowing support services to be provided to children and their families.

The law relating to child care and protection work in Northern Ireland is about to undergo considerable change. The existing legislation governing this area of social work, chiefly the Children and Young Persons Act (Northern Ireland) 1968, is to be replaced by the Children (Northern Ireland) Order 1995, Northern Ireland's equivalent of the Children Act 1989, which has been in operation in England and Wales for a number of years now. (The 1968 Act will not be repealed entirely, but its role in protecting children in civil law cases will cease.)

Though the Order has been enacted by Parliament, it is not likely to be brought into force until at least the autumn of 1996, and the 1968 Act remains for the time being the operative legislation. However, because this Act will eventually be overtaken by the Order, we saw little value in confining ourselves to it. We have therefore set out the law relating to child care and protection as it is and as it will be. We deal first with the law under the 1968 Act and then with the law under the 1995 Order. (References in this chapter to 'sections' relate to the 1968 Act, while those to 'articles' relate to the 1995 Order.)

Before turning to deal with the substance of the 1968 Act and the 1995 Order, we think it appropriate to make one general comment. The reform of child care law to be brought about by the 1995 Order comes at a time when children's rights seem to be accorded their correct place on governments' agendas, as shown by the adoption of the UN Convention on the Rights of the Child by the General Assembly in 1989. (The UK has, since 1991, been a party to the convention and indeed has already been subject to examination by the committee that oversees the convention.)

Unless otherwise stated, any reference here to a child is to a person under the age of eighteen.

6.1.1 *The Agencies and the Institutional Framework*

You should realise from the outset that the law in this area acts to facilitate the management of child abuse cases by social services authorities rather than setting out in detail what can and cannot be done. Child care law, therefore, sets out the range of court orders that can be applied for, or the services that can be supplied to children and their families, leaving the agencies to organise the institutional framework for investigating child abuse. It is appropriate therefore to consider at this point those agencies and the institutional framework within which they operate.

The present framework for managing child abuse is set out in the Department of Health and Social Services' guide for Health and Social Service Boards on the management of child abuse, *Co-operating to Protect Children* (1989). It is based on the 1988 version of the policy document used in Great Britain, *Working Together*, and has been amended to take into account the development of Trusts and 'directly managed units' (DMUs), the term by which local units of management are now known, and the delegation to Trusts of statutory functions conferred originally on Boards. (For an explanation of the institutional structure for the delivery of health and personal social services see 8.1, and also the preface.)

Each Health and Social Services Board produces its own child protection handbook, which is written to conform with the structure and guidelines contained in the department's Guide but is more detailed. Each Trust is in turn entitled to develop and issue its own handbook, but again these must not depart from the guidelines set out in the Board's handbook. The Guide is for the use of social workers when they become involved in this area, and we will refer to it throughout the chapter. (The Guide is at present being amended to ensure that it is relevant to the Children (Northern Ireland) Order 1995.)

One further point: inter-agency co-operation is undoubtedly the key to the successful management of child abuse cases and to developing the best possible strategies for combating and preventing child abuse in general. However, only a limited number of agencies have legal responsibilities in this area.

Aside from the Health Boards and Trusts, which obviously have statutory functions under the old and new legislation, the police also have a statutory involvement in child care and protection (see 6.2.3 and

6.3.4.4). Until recently, responsibility within the RUC for child protection issues was invested in liaison inspectors based in each of the nine subdivisions, who would then designate officers to become involved in child proceedings. However, since September 1994 the RUC has restructured its work in this area. It now operates throughout the force a system of Child Abuse and Rape Enquiry (CARE) units, providing a 24-hour service and dealing exclusively with sexual offences.

The officers who staff the CARE units have joint-protocol (i.e. inter-agency) training, and work exclusively in child protection. They are responsible not just for the criminal investigation and prosecution of offenders but also for helping Boards and Trusts find counselling for the victim. There are nine CARE units, corresponding to the administrative divisions of the RUC rather than with the Area Child Protection Committee boundaries, and consultation between the agencies is at detective-superintendent level. The RUC has thus moved beyond the concept of 'designated officers' to the designation of teams of permanent child protection officers. The role of the liaison inspector is at present under review, in line with the development of the CARE units, with a view to exploiting their potential as fully as possible.

The other agency with statutory functions is the National Society for the Prevention of Cruelty to Children (NSPCC). Unusually for a voluntary organisation, it is authorised to bring care proceedings in its own right (Children and Young Persons Act 1968—hereafter referred to as CYP68 —section 94; Children Order 1995—hereafter CO95—article 49 (2)). Obviously there are other voluntary and charitable agencies or government entities that may be involved in child care and protection matters, but because these have not got statutory functions we do not deal with them. (The Guide provides detail on all the agencies involved in child protection work, including those with no statutory responsibilities (Guide, parts 3 and 4).)

As you will appreciate, while the legislation refers to Boards, Trusts, and the NSPCC, in reality it is social workers and related staff employed by those authorities who will often find themselves implementing the legislation.

6.1.2 *Managing Child Abuse*

We have constructed the diagram below, based on the information contained in the Guide, to set out the various stages in the investigation and management of child abuse cases. As we have pointed out, the guidance is under review, and the child protection system that will be used in conjunction with the 1995 Order may differ from the one set out here— though we suspect that those changes will not be significant.

MANAGING CHILD ABUSE

Stage I
Recognition & Investigation

- Suspicion
  - Emergency → Court Order
  - Non-Emergency
- Case Conference

Stage II
Assessment & Planning

- Short-Term Plan
- Long-Term Plan
- Assessment Report
- Case Conference
- Child Protection Plan

Stage III
Implementation & Review

- Child Protection Register
- Review Registration (Case Conference(s))
- De-Registration (Case Conference)

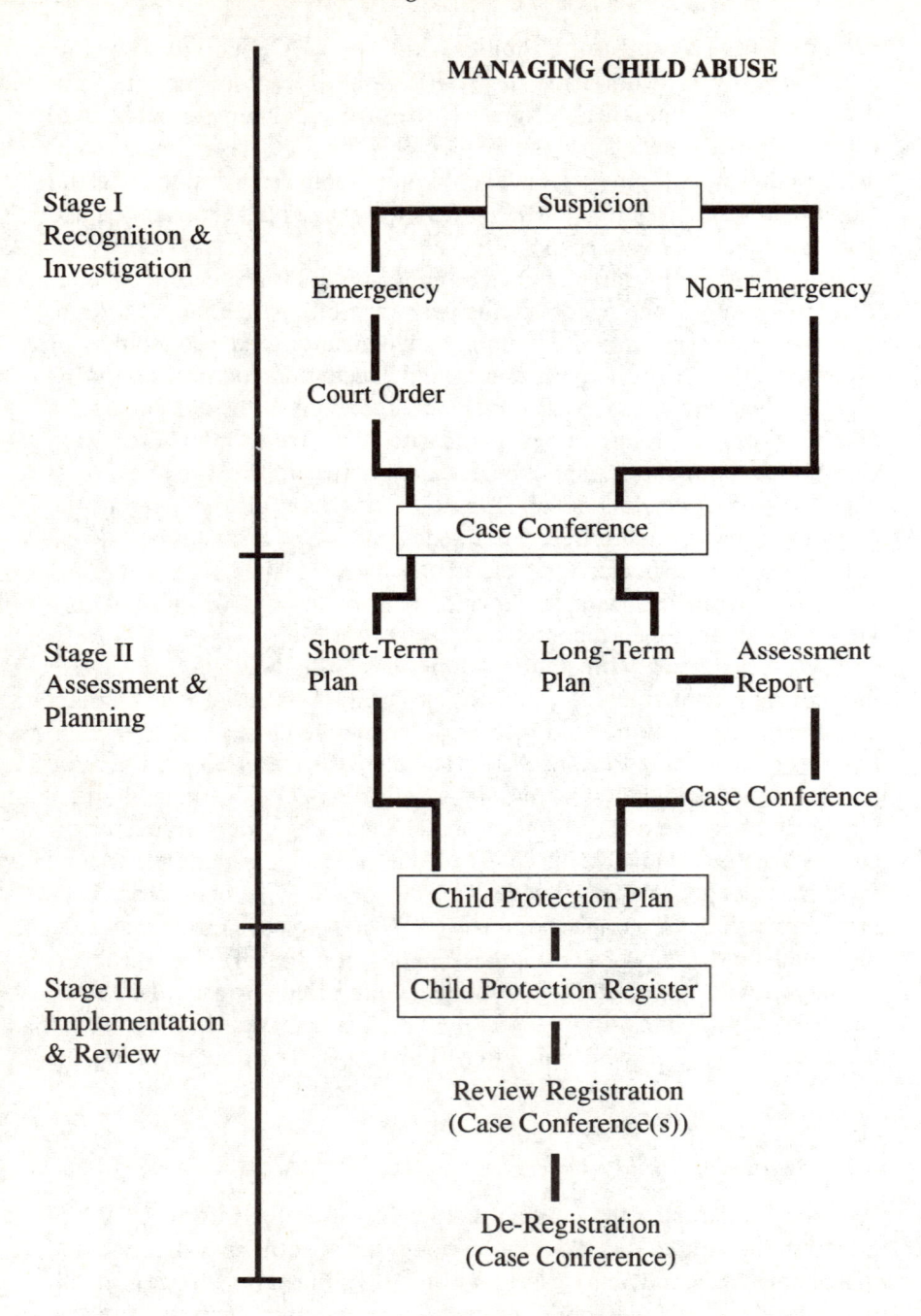

Area Child Protection Committees, Child Protection Panels, Case Management Reviews

6.1.2.1 Stage 1: Recognition and Investigation

This is the first stage in a child abuse case, and it is at this point that the statutory agency will investigate any suspicions it might have that a child has been or is at risk of abuse. (For the legal requirements to investigate under the 1968 Act and the 1995 Order see 6.2.2 and 6.3.3, respectively.) This suspicion may have developed from the authority's own dealings with the family or from information received from other sources, such as the police or other non-statutory agencies.

One of the first issues to be considered is whether the child's situation is so grave as to require emergency legal intervention. If so, the appropriate order is sought (see 6.2.3 for the options available under the 1968 Act and 6.3.4 for the options under the 1995 Order), sometimes before a case conference is convened. Conversely, if it is felt that the child's situation is not an emergency one, no court order need be sought before the case conference is convened. (In case we cause confusion we had better point out that emergency orders are available at any time in the management of the case: their availability is not confined to the earlier stages of an investigation.)

A case conference is an interdisciplinary meeting convened by the statutory agency with responsibility for the case (i.e. either a Board, a Trust, or the NSPCC) at which information is exchanged between professionals. In particular it involves the participants considering if and how a child protection plan would be to the child's benefit. If it is decided to draw up a child protection plan, the child must be added to the child protection register (see below).

At later stages in the process, case conferences will be convened, in particular to review the implementation of the child protection plan but also to assess the general management of the case. One particular function of the case conference is to assess whether care proceedings are necessary, and the Guide advises that 'the chairman of the conference should have access to legal advice where necessary to assist in the evaluation of evidence indicative of care proceedings' (the Guide, paragraph 7.2).

Although ordinarily composed of professionals who can make a contribution to dealing with or who need to know about the child's situation, on occasion non-professionals working with the child or his or her family, for example volunteer workers or foster-parents, can be invited to attend.

Parental involvement is also of course encouraged. The Guide advocates the participation of the parents if this is practicable. Parents may be accompanied by a friend or relative or even a representative, including a legal adviser. The Guide places a general requirement on responsible staff to keep parents informed of developments and to have explained to them 'the reasons for professional concern, the statutory powers, duties and roles of the agencies, their own legal rights and the changes in the family's situation which the agencies consider necessary or desirable in the interests of the child' (Guide, paragraph 4.37). Indeed parents should be informed in writing of the outcome of the case conference.

At the case conference not only may a child protection plan be conceived and arrangements made for reviewing the plan drawn up but if it is agreed that a plan be drawn up, the conference will also decide who should be informed that the child is to be included on the child protection register. Usually the child and his or her parents or guardian and school should be informed, though much will depend on the child's capacity to understand the fact of registration before he or she will be informed.

The entry on the register will contain details identifying the child, including the names and addresses of the child's parents and/or carers and details of the children in the household and whether they are also on the register; the nature of the abuse; and details of the child protection plan, including the name and contact point of the case co-ordinator (see below).

6.1.2.2 Stage 2: Assessment and Planning

The main task during the second stage is to formulate the child protection plan. This is a proposed interdisciplinary programme of action that attempts to protect the child and perhaps provide treatment or other services for the child and/or other family members. A case co-ordinator is appointed to oversee each child protection plan; he or she will be an employee of the agency with responsibility for the case. It is this person that all other agencies must deal with regarding the child.

If the case conference decides that a short-term plan is needed, there is likely to be no great difficulty in drawing it up. However, where it is agreed that a long-term plan is needed, the Guide requires that an 'assessment report' be prepared. This is a comprehensive assessment, co-ordinated by the agency with responsibility for the case, 'of the child's family needs, including an assessment of the levels of risk of future abuse to the child' (the Guide, paragraph 4.27) and drawn from the information provided by a range of agencies. It is considered at a later case conference, following which a child protection plan should be adopted.

The plan can include provision for securing court orders in care proceedings. Indeed under the present legislation, if it appears to the agency that the child is in need of 'care, protection and control', he or she must be brought before a juvenile court, which can then make one of the four orders outlined in 6.2.4.1–4. Under the 1995 Order an agency will not be required to bring a child before a court, but if it discovers a child who is subject to or likely to be subject to significant harm it will have the option of doing so (6.3.5 and 6.3.6).

6.1.2.3 Stage 3: Implementation and Review

In this third and last stage the intention is to ensure that the child protection plan is implemented as envisaged and that it is having the desired effect. Reviews of plans should be conducted regularly but in any event at six-monthly intervals. As noted above, the child must be registered if the decision is taken to draw up a child protection plan. The case conferences convened during this final stage will examine not only whether the child's plan is being implemented but also whether the child needs to remain on the register. If it is felt that he or she need no longer be registered, deregistration takes place and the child's name is removed from the register. 'When the professionals who are working with the child and the family decide that the risk to the child has been eliminated or reduced to an acceptable, minimal level, the child's name should be removed from the child protection register' (Guide, paragraph 4.35).

There are three other elements of the framework for managing child abuse that require explanation. These are (*a*) area child protection committees (ACPCs), (*b*) child protection panels, and (*c*) case management reviews.

The first of these exist at Area Board level and are responsible for overseeing policy in this area, including suggesting developments, if necessary. The Guide sets out their functions (paragraph 8.7). These include:

(*a*) establishing, maintaining and reviewing local inter-agency guidelines on procedures to be followed in individual cases,
(*b*) reviewing significant issues arising from the general handling of cases, as well as reports from inquiries, to ensure that appropriate attention is focused on preventive work along with reporting on the investigation of allegations of child abuse,
(*c*) ensuring that appropriate arrangements for providing expert advice and inter-agency liaison exist with each Trust or DMU, and
(*d*) monitoring the volume of investigation and the proportion that are proved or unproved and examining the implications for work with families.

ACPCs are required in particular to review every year the work done with regard to child care and protection work and to draw up plans for the following year.

As stated above, each ACPC also provides a child protection procedural handbook for the use of staff within its area. This lists those who should be represented on ACPCs: Health Board social work, nursing, medical and psychiatric services personnel, general medical practitioner services, educational services (i.e. the appropriate Education and Library Board and teachers), police, forensic medical service, the Probation Board for Northern Ireland, the magistracy, and, where appropriate, the armed services. Trusts and DMUs should also be represented.

Child protection panels are bodies whose function is to liaise effectively with ACPCs, providing them with information and commentary from the staff working directly with children and their families. Each Trust and DMU is expected to have one of these panels 'where practice-based experience complements and stimulates policy and development' (circular HSS CC 4/89, supplement no. 1).

Case management reviews are assessments of the manner in which a case has been dealt with if a child who is the subject of a child protection plan is seriously harmed or killed. The action taken in a case management review should have five objectives: (1) to establish the facts; (2) to assess whether decisions and actions taken in the case were reasonable and responsible; (3) to check that established procedures were followed; (4) to consider whether the services provided matched the needs of the case, bearing in mind the resources available; and (5) to recommend any appropriate action in the light of the review's findings.

The responsibility for initiating case management reviews lies with the Board or Trust. Where a Trust is involved, the review should be begun by agreement with the Board. The Trust will instigate and manage the review in that instance and then report the findings to the Board and the DHSS. There should be at least one representative of a Board on any review group set up by a Trust.

These review teams are composed of representatives of a range of disciplines, and all are appointed by the Board or Trust carrying out the review. The Guide directs that the team should include a representative of an agency that is not involved. Copies of the report should be sent to the general manager or chief executive of the responsible agency, to the ACPC, and to the DHSS. If the review is conducted by a Trust, a copy must also be given to the Board.

The Board or Trust must inform the DHSS of a case that it intends to examine in a case management review. This gives the department an opportunity to consider the need for a statutory inquiry under section 167 of the 1968 Act.

6.1.3 *Defining Child Abuse*

Thus far we have referred to child abuse without explaining the term. There is no legislative definition of the term (simply because it is not a legislative term of art), but the Guide does provide a catalogue of some of the forms abuse may take, thus providing a working definition for practitioners. These categories are:

Neglect: The actual or likely persistent or severe neglect of a child, the failure to protect a child from exposure to any kind of danger, including

cold or starvation, or extreme failure to carry out important aspects of care, resulting in the significant impairment of the child's health or development, including non-organic failure to thrive.
Physical abuse: Actual or likely physical injury to a child, or failure to prevent physical injury (or suffering) to a child.
Sexual abuse: Actual or likely sexual exploitation of a child or adolescent.
Emotional abuse: Actual or likely persistent or severe emotional ill-treatment or rejection resulting in severe adverse effects on the emotional and behavioural development of a child. All abuse involves some emotional ill-treatment: this category should be used where it is the main, or sole, form of abuse.

Each category is further divided into three sub-categories: 'potential', 'suspected', and 'confirmed' (where 'potential' and 'suspected' equate with 'likely' and 'confirmed' equates with 'actual'). This categorisation of abuse is used when registering a child on the child protection register.

6.2 *The 1968 Act*

The 1968 Act is the main piece of legislation governing the care and protection of children and young people and will remain so until the Children (Northern Ireland) Order 1995 comes into force.

6.2.1 *Preventing Child Abuse*

Aside from the particular duties placed on Boards and Trusts to investigate in cases of suspected abuse (see 6.2.2), there are generalised duties placed on them to protect children from abuse. For example, there is a general duty on Boards to promote the welfare of children with a view to 'diminishing the need to receive children into care under this Act or to bring them before a court' (section 164). The legislation requires that a Board 'make available such advice, guidance and assistance' as will achieve this goal. In practice the services provided under this section will be made available by a Trust on a contractual basis.

6.2.2 *Investigating Child Abuse*

A duty to investigate arises from three different provisions of the Act: sections 94 (2), 103, and 163. If a Board or Trust receives information suggesting that a child may be in need of 'care, protection or control', it is required to 'cause inquiries to be made into the case,' unless it is satisfied that such inquiries are unnecessary (section 94 (2)). This condition is defined in section 93: 'A child or young person is in need of care, protection or control . . . if any of a range of conditions is satisfied with respect to him, and he is not receiving such care, protection and guidance as a good parent may be reasonably expected to give.' These conditions are that (*a*) he or she is falling into bad associations or is exposed to moral danger; (*b*) the lack of care, protection or guidance is likely to cause him or her unnecessary suffering or seriously affect his or her health or proper development; (*c*) any of the offences mentioned in schedule 1 of the 1968 Act (see 5.3.4) has been committed in respect of him or her or in respect of a child or young person who is a member of the same household; (*d*) he or she is a member of the same household as a person who has been convicted of such an offence in respect of a child or young person; or (*e*) the child or young person is a female member of a household of which a member has committed or attempted to commit an offence under section 1 of the Punishment of Incest Act 1908. Alternatively a child will be 'in need of care, protection and control' if he or she is beyond the control of his or her parents or guardian.

If a Board or Trust finds that the child appears to satisfy this condition, it must bring the child before a juvenile court (see 6.2.4), unless it is satisfied that the taking of proceedings is undesirable in the child's interest, or that proceedings are about to be taken by some other person.

The second provision relating to the investigation of child abuse is section 163. It requires a police officer to report to a Board or Trust any circumstances in which a child or young person in need of 'advice, guidance or assistance' comes to his or her attention during the investigation of a crime. So, for example, as a result of an investigation into a drugs ring or the production of pornographic videos the RUC might become aware of a child or young person whose health or welfare is at risk, and it must involve the Board or Trust. In appropriate circumstances a police officer might wish to use one of the emergency options outlined in 6.2.3. On receiving such information, the Board or Trust has a duty to investigate the report. (In legal terms, what happens is that the Board or Trust's duty, under section 94 (2), to investigate and—if the child appears to be in need of care, protection, or control—to take a child before a juvenile court becomes operable.)

If as a result of such investigation a social worker is satisfied that some support or services are necessary, these must be provided in order to fulfil the duty in section 164 (see 6.2.1). Often this will be adequate to guarantee the child's well-being. However, the reality is that there will be situations where further action will be required because of the gravity of the case, and it may be necessary to resort to care proceedings.

Finally, a duty to investigate also arises from section 103. Where it appears to a Board or Trust that a child under the age of seventeen (*a*) has neither parent nor guardian, or (*b*) has been and remains abandoned by his or her parents or guardian, or (*c*) is lost, or whose parents or guardian are, for the time being or permanently, prevented by reason of mental or bodily disease or infirmity or other incapacity or any other circumstances from providing accommodation, maintenance and upbringing and that its intervention is necessary in the interests of the welfare of the child, then it must take the child into care, provided that the parents or guardian consent. This duty will obviously require Board or Trust staff to investigate the circumstances of certain children. (For more on section 103 see 6.2.4.5.)

6.2.3 *Emergency Intervention*

There may be circumstances where emergency intervention to protect the child is necessary because any delay in proceedings to secure the child's removal may result in serious detriment to him or her, 'causing him unnecessary suffering or injury to health' (section 32). Such situations are likely to arise where the suspected abuser has easy access to the child and the opportunity to abuse him or her. In such an emergency there are two legislative options. Both options authorise removal for five weeks—though the courts can stipulate a shorter period—at the end of which time the child must be brought before a juvenile court.

Firstly, under section 32 anyone 'acting in the interests of a child or young person' may make an application to a justice of the peace for a warrant, and this can be granted if there is reasonable cause to suspect (*a*) that the juvenile has been or is being assaulted, ill-treated or neglected in a manner likely to cause the child unnecessary suffering or injury to health or (*b*) that a 'schedule 1' offence (see 5.3.4) has been, is being or is about to be committed against the juvenile. This warrant authorises a police officer to enter any premises, by force if necessary, and to search for the juvenile and/or to take him or her to a place of safety. A place of safety is defined in the legislation, and the list includes Board homes, police stations, hospitals, and doctors' surgeries (CYP68, section 180). Any child taken to a place of safety in this way must remain there until he or she can be brought before a juvenile court to allow the court to decide whether to choose any of the options outlined in 6.2.4.

The alternative action is to seek a place of safety order (section 99). This allows any person to apply to a court, or to a Justice of the Peace, for the authority to remove a child to a place of safety on the grounds that a 'schedule 1' offence has been or is likely to be committed against the child and that he or she needs to be given refuge. In practice, however, it is usually a police officer or a Board or Trust employee who makes this application. At the end of the period stated in the warrant the child must be brought before a juvenile court.

The distinction between the place of safety order and the power we have just looked at under section 32 is that there is no power to enter any premises by force, whereas under the section 32 power the police have such a right. With a place of safety order, the consent of the householder must be obtained before entering; where this consent is withheld, an application for a section 32 warrant can be made.

When the child is taken to a place of safety without a warrant, or goes to a place of safety of his or her own volition, the child must be brought before the juvenile court within eight days. This is to ensure that an order securing the child in the place of safety can be made; and such an order can also be for a maximum period of five weeks.

The only circumstance in which an appearance before the juvenile court will not be necessary is where the child has been put into the care of the Board or Trust on a 'voluntary' basis (see 6.2.4.5). There is one other residual option that can be used if it would take too long to obtain a warrant and where prompt action is necessary to save a person from death or injury: the Police and Criminal Evidence (Northern Ireland) Order 1989 (article 19(1) (c)), allows a police officer to enter premises in such a situation.

6.2.4 *Non-emergency Child Protection Options*

A child who appears to the relevant statutory agency to be in need of 'care, protection or control' must be brought before a juvenile court (section 94), and so too must a child in respect of whom an emergency option is adopted, as outlined above. The juvenile court has a range of options open to it. If it is satisfied that the child is indeed in need of care, protection and control (6.2.2) then it can choose one of these; and it is these we now examine. (For more on the juvenile court see chapter 1.) As noted earlier, the child protection plan can direct that one of these orders be sought (see 6.1.2).

6.2.4.1 Training School Order

A training school order places the child in a recognised training school, to try to positively influence the child's attitude. There are four training schools in Northern Ireland: (1) Rathgael, Bangor, Co. Down; (2) St Patrick's, Belfast; (3) Lisnevin, Millisle, Co. Down; and (4) St Joseph's, Middletown, Co. Armagh. The purpose of a training school is to educate and train the child to be positive about his or her role in society and to expose him or her to a habit-forming pattern of school attendance or work to prepare him or her for a return to society.

The court does not fix the period for which the juvenile can be kept in care, but an order can last for three years if the subject is under sixteen, or until the age of nineteen if he or she is already sixteen. A child under ten cannot be made the subject of a training school order unless the court is satisfied that there is no suitable alternative way to deal with the child.

After the period of detention has expired, the young person is subject to supervision by the school's managers for three years or until he or she is twenty-one, whichever occurs first. Children placed in training schools should be placed in one that accords with their religious persuasion.

Training school orders are also an option for dealing with juvenile offenders (see 4.6.5) and also for dealing with persistent truants.

6.2.4.2 Supervision Order

A supervision order (section 81) will be made by the court in respect of a child whose domestic situation is not so bad as to require placing him or her in the care of a Board or Trust. Such an order places the juvenile, for a period of not more than three years, under the supervision of a social worker or probation officer—although it is usually education officers (Education and Library Boards) or welfare officers (Health and Social Services Boards) that are appointed to act as supervisors. They are required to visit, advise and befriend the child and, when necessary, endeavour to find him or her suitable employment.

The supervising officer has the power to return a young person before the juvenile court if he or she considers it necessary in the child's interests; and the court can make a training school order, a fit person order, or an order requiring his or her parents to make a recognisance (see 5.3.3). Supervision orders are also available for youngsters who offend, but only for those aged between ten and thirteen.

6.2.4.3 Fit Person Order

A court may make an order putting a child into the care of a 'fit person'. A 'fit person' can be, and usually is, a Board or Trust, which by virtue of such an order will have the same rights and duties as the parent of the child, though the fit person is prohibited from changing the child's religion or freeing or placing the child for adoption. Such an order lasts until the child reaches the age of eighteen (section 91).

Even if the child's place of residence changes or is altered while the fit person order is in effect, so that the child is no longer in Board or Trust accommodation, the rights given when the order was made remain with the Board or Trust until the order comes to an end. In other words, the Board or Trust can, during the life of the order, let the child live at home without affecting the order.

6.2.4.4 Recognisance

A recognisance resembles an undertaking given by someone on bail. The child's parents give an undertaking to the court to exercise due care and guardianship in relation to the child in the future; if they fail to fulfil that undertaking they are required to reappear before the court. A report would be made to the court by the social worker involved, and the court would request the parents to answer the charges made in the report.

6.2.4.5 Voluntary Reception into Care

Even if a child is not in need of 'care, protection, and control,' he or she may still come into care by a different route. As we have seen (6.2.2), a Board or Trust must intervene and take into care a child who appears to it to have neither parent nor guardian, or is lost or abandoned, or whose parents, by reason of their mental or physical state, cannot provide the child with appropriate care (section 103). Such a child can be kept in care until he or she is eighteen. No reference to a court is necessary, though a Board or Trust cannot take a child into its care if a parent or guardian 'desires to take over the care of the child.' In other words, the parent or guardian must agree, and therefore this method of taking a child into care is referred to by the Guide as 'voluntary reception'. In any case there is a general duty on Boards and Trusts to ensure that a parent or guardian does indeed take over the care of the child or family, or that a relative or friend does so, where that is in the best interests of the child.

A Board or Trust may seek a 'parental rights order' from a juvenile court in respect of some of the children that come into its care under section 103. If it appears to it that (*a*) a child's parents are dead and that he or she has no guardian, or (*b*) that the whereabouts of any parent or guardian have remained unknown for a year or more, or (*c*) that the parent or guardian who has abandoned the child suffers from a physical or mental disability rendering them incapable of caring for the child, or is of such habits or mode of life as to be unfit to have the care of the child, or (*d*) that a parent or guardian has so persistently and unreasonably failed to carry out the duties of a parent as to be unfit to have the care of the child, then the Board or Trust may seek such an order (section 104).

Parents, guardians, relatives or friends may object in court to the making of the order, though the court can override that objection if persuaded that these conditions are satisfied.

A parental rights order vests in the Board or Trust all the rights and powers that a parent or guardian has in respect of the child, and therefore it can take decisions affecting the child.

Even if subject to a parental rights order, a child can be allowed to live with a parent or guardian or a relative for such period as the Board or

Trust determines if it appears to be for the child's benefit. An order remains in force until the child attains the age of eighteen and does not lapse by virtue of the fact that the child ceases to be in the care of the Board or Trust. In fact if a parental rights order is in force in respect of a child who was taken into care but is no longer in care, the Board or Trust has the power to receive the child back into care in any circumstances in which it appears to it that its intervention is necessary for the welfare of the child.

A parental rights order can be discharged on the application of the Board or Trust or of the parent, guardian, relative or friend, as appropriate, if the court is satisfied that its discharge would be for the benefit of the child.

One last point regarding a child taken into care under section 103. The Board or Trust can make an application to court, and such children can be made subject to a training school order or a fit person order (and the latter can include a supervision order), if the juvenile court is convinced that they are 'refractory' (section 108).

6.3 *The 1995 Order*

The Children (Northern Ireland) Order 1995, involves the codification of the public and private law with respect to children into one piece of legislation. (Public law is that law relating to the child's care and protection and the circumstances in which the state can and should become involved. Private law is the law relating to the child's care and upbringing by its parents or guardian.) As the Explanatory Document that accompanied the proposal for a draft order in 1993 puts it (p. 2), the Order is a 'single coherent modernised code in order to provide a simpler, clearer and fairer system for children and their families.'

This new legal regime is to be administered by a unified court system. This is 'a concurrent system of jurisdiction covering magistrates' courts, county courts and the High Court within which all proceedings relating to the child and his or her family can be consolidated and heard together, and within which the complexity or weight of the case can be matched to the right level of court and judge' (Explanatory Document, 3). This is to avoid the problems experienced in the past of different legal issues affecting the same family being heard in different courts at different times because of the fragmented and piecemeal nature of the courts' jurisdiction in respect of child care and family law issues.

This unified court structure means that the same range of orders is available in each court and that the criteria applied in each are the same; and, quite importantly, 'where aspects of a case affecting the same child come before more than one court, the proceedings can be brought together in one venue.' Thus the possibility will exist of consolidating a variety of proceedings involving the same child. Cases will be allocated to what is considered the appropriate level of court, and therefore not all cases will begin in the magistrates' court. Provision will also be available for transferring cases from one level to another. The Lord Chancellor will draw up court rules at a later stage governing the transfer of cases, as well as where they may begin. The main principles governing the allocation of courts in England and Wales are (*a*) the complexity of the case, (*b*) its likely duration, (*c*) the availability of court time, and (*d*) the number of expert witnesses who may be involved.

When the legislation is fully implemented, the juvenile court (see 1.3) will become the Family Proceedings Court when hearing cases dealing with child care and protection matters. This will bring about a division between the 'care' and 'justice' functions of the courts with respect to children that is much overdue, having been made originally in the Black Report. (Criminal matters relating to children and young people will, of course, continue to be heard by the juvenile court.)

While the exact nature of the changes that will be made is unclear, we may derive some benefit from looking at the changes that have been made in England and Wales under the Children Act 1989. There the magistrates' court has also become the family proceedings court, but the county court now has two 'divisions' within it: the care centre and the family hearing centre. The former deals with both private and public cases, the latter exclusively with private cases. The Family Division of the High Court continues to exercise its jurisdiction in family matters. It is reasonable to assume that a similar restructuring of the courts will be carried out in Northern Ireland, once the appropriate court rules have been drafted.

6.3.1 *Governing Principles*

There are a number of principles that underpin the legislation and need to be discussed at the outset before we explain the substance of the Order. These are outlined in article 3 (and are examined below) and are considerations that the courts must bear in mind when acting under the Order.

Some broader ideas that are not explicitly stated in the legislation have nonetheless helped to shape it. Chief among these is the policy that children are best looked after by their parents and consequently should only be received into care if the circumstances really warrant it; and such intervention should be open to challenge.

6.3.1.1 The Welfare Principle

The most important element of the new legislation is what is known as the welfare principle. This means that the welfare of the child is the 'paramount consideration' in any court proceedings that relate to the upbringing of the child or the administration of a child's property or the application of any income arising from it (article 3 (1)), thus overriding all other considerations. On the face of it this is no innovation. Section 48 of the 1968 Act states: 'Every court in dealing with a child or young person who is brought before it . . . shall have regard to the welfare of the child or young person.' What is new is the emphasis given to the welfare principle in the 1995 Order. It is the most important factor that any court must take into account in its decision-making, overriding all others, and will therefore be instrumental in shaping judicial decisions.

In particular cases the courts are directed by the legislation to come to a conclusion that reflects the welfare principle. When considering an application for an article 8 order that is opposed, or for a care or supervision order, there is a range of matters, referred to as the welfare check-list. to which the court must have regard. These are (*a*) the ascertainable wishes and feelings of the child concerned (considered in the light of his or her age and understanding), (*b*) his or her physical, emotional and educational needs, (*c*) the likely effect on him or her of any change in circumstances, (*d*) the age, sex, background and any other characteristics of the child that the court considers relevant, (*e*) any harm he or she has suffered or is at risk of suffering, (*f*) how capable each of his or her parents (and any other person in relation to whom the court considers the question to be relevant) are of meeting his or her needs, and (*g*) the range of powers available to the court in the proceedings in question.

6.3.1.2 The Principle of No Delay

There is a general duty on the court to avoid unnecessary delay in court proceedings, or, to put it more accurately, 'the court shall have regard to the general principle that any delay in determining the question [before it] is likely to prejudice the welfare of the child' (article 3 (2)).

To ensure that no unnecessary delay is involved in applications for article 8 orders (and almost by way of emphasising the point) the legislation requires the court to draw up a timetable with a view to determining the question before it without delay and to give such directions as it considers appropriate for the purpose of ensuring, as far as is reasonable practicable, that that timetable is adhered to. The rules of court may specify periods within which specified stages must be taken in relation to such proceedings.

6.3.1.3 No Order to be Issued

This principle is that a court should not issue an order unless failure to do so would be to the child's detriment. Article 3 (5) states: 'No order is to be made unless [the court] considers that doing so would be better for the child than making no order at all.' The principle of no order means that even if the grounds are satisfied, the order will not be made automatically.

One of the reasons for including this principle was that it was felt that in the past courts had tended to make orders relating to children without giving a lot of thought to why the order was being issued. In other words, the courts tended to issue orders too freely, without due regard to whether this improved the situation of the parties. This meant that when faced with a decision about the child's future, a court was inclined to make an order, feeling it to be a solution of sorts, in preference to not making an order, which appeared to leave the issue unresolved. Under the 1995 Order, however, the courts are under an obligation to avoid making an order unless the failure to make one would be of some detriment to the child. The purpose behind this principle is clear: the courts should only intervene if their intervention would be of benefit to the child.

6.3.1.4 Parental Responsibility

Parental responsibility is a concept created by the Order and that, though not a specific principle in itself, pervades the legislation, and so it is better to deal with it at this point. Parental responsibility is defined by article 6 as 'all the rights, duties, powers, responsibilities and authority which by law a parent of a child has in relation to the child and his or her property.'

You may feel that this is not a very helpful definition. It has indeed been left deliberately vague, because the Law Commission did not consider it practicable to provide a statutory list of all these 'rights, duties, powers, responsibilities and authority'. However, a leading commentator has suggested that it includes the following: (*a*) the power to control education; (*b*) the power to discipline the child; (*c*) the power to determine the child's religious education; (*d*) the power to administer the child's property; and (*e*) the right to represent the child in legal proceedings (Cretney, *Principles of Family Law* (5th ed.), London: Sweet and Maxwell, 486–93). The term 'parental responsibility' was chosen because it was felt that it more accurately reflected the nature of parental rights, because these in fact were often expressed as powers to carry out certain duties, and because it serves as a unifying umbrella term for the range of powers, duties and rights that parents have with respect to their children.

Parents who are married to each other automatically acquire parental responsibility for their children. Where they are not, only the mother automatically acquires parental responsibility; the father in such circumstances can acquire it by making a 'parental responsibility agreement' with the mother or by making an application to the court (article 7). Parental responsibility is not affected by the separation or even the divorce of the parents but continues to exist: the intention is that both parents continue to play a full part in the child's upbringing (Explanatory Document, 1). Each person having parental responsibility may act alone on meeting that responsibility, unless, of course, statute requires them to consult others having parental responsibility. This does not authorise those with parental responsibility to behave in any way they wish, however: they must behave in a way that is compatible with that responsibility.

Parental responsibility, in line with the reasoning in *Gillick v. West Norfolk and Wisbech Area Health Authority* (1986) AC 112 (see 2.3.4), decreases as the child grows older and advances in maturity and understanding.

The issuing of a residence order, a care order, an emergency protection order or an order appointing a guardian gives parental responsibility to those in whose favour such orders are made.

It is worth noting that the fact that someone has parental responsibility does not make him or her a relative of the child in law.

To summarise, the core of the concept is that parental responsibility remains with the parents, even in the event of divorce or separation or the reception of the child into care, so that, short of adoption, parental responsibility cannot be relinquished.

6.3.1.5 Consistent Decision-Making

Once again this is not a principle but rather a desired policy goal that it is hoped the legislation will help in attaining. The legislation attempts to aid practitioners by incorporating clearer standards and duties. For example, article 18 imposes a general duty on Boards and Trusts to provide services and support to children and their families, and this is supplemented by detail in schedule 2 (see chapter 8). This is not just an attempt to make more information available to the public but is a recognition of the shortcomings in earlier child care legislation, which failed to indicate clearly to the various bodies involved precisely what was expected of them.

Similarly, the welfare check-list in article 3 attempts to promote consistent decision-making. By providing such a check-list as part of the statutory guidelines, the potential for misinterpretation should be reduced.

The promotion of consistent decision-making is intended not only to benefit those passing through the system but also to help those working with the legislation. The idea is that if there are well-known and established principles that govern the way decisions are made, there should be more confidence both in those making the decisions and in the system of which they are a part. If a client knows what decision you have reached and understands why the court has reached a particular decision, he or she should be less likely to feel alienated.

6.3.2 Preventing Child Abuse

Aside from the duty to investigate child abuse, broad duties are often imposed on social services authorities to promote and safeguard children's welfare. Thus every Board and Trust is required to take reasonable steps to reduce the need to bring (*a*) proceedings for care or supervision orders with respect to children within its area, (*b*) any family or other proceedings with respect to such children that might lead to their being placed in the authority's care, or (*c*) wardship proceedings (paragraph 8, schedule 2 (*a*)).

In addition, every Board or Trust must take reasonable steps, by providing services, to prevent children within its area suffering ill-treatment or neglect (paragraph 5, schedule 2).

6.3.3 Investigating Child Abuse

Investigations into child abuse may arise from two provisions of the Order: articles 56 and 66. We deal with each of these in turn.

If, in any family proceedings (see 6.3.6) in which a question is raised about the welfare of a child, it appears to a court that a care or supervision order (see 6.3.5) might be appropriate, it may direct the Board or Trust to undertake an investigation of the child's circumstances (article 56). When undertaking an article 56 investigation, a Board or Trust is specifically required to consider whether it should (*a*) apply for a care or supervision order, (*b*) provide services or assistance for the child or his or her family, or (*c*) take any other action with respect to the child (article 56 (2)).

If a Board or Trust decides not to apply for a care or supervision order, it must inform the court of (*a*) the reasons for so deciding and (*b*) any service or assistance that the Board or Trust has provided to the child or his or her family, or any other action it proposes to take with respect to the child. This information must be relayed to the court within eight weeks, though the court may, when directing that the investigation be undertaken, extend that time limit.

Interim care or supervision orders (see 6.3.5.1 and 2) may be made pending the outcome of an article 56 investigation but can only be made if the court is satisfied that there are reasonable grounds for believing that the conditions in article 50 (2) are satisfied (i.e. that the child is suffering, or likely to suffer, significant harm). These last until the care or supervision order application is dealt with, or until the report of the article 56 investigation is completed, or on the expiry of eight weeks from the making of the order, whichever occurs first.

Article 66 requires a Board or Trust to investigate if it receives information about a child subject to an emergency protection order (see 6.3.4.1), or who is in police protection (see 6.3.4.4), or who it has reasonable cause to suspect is suffering or is likely to suffer significant harm. (This duty to investigate is the closest counterpart in the 1995 Order of section 94 (2) of CYP68.) The Board or Trust is required to consider certain matters in an article 66 investigation:

(1) Should an application be made to the court?
(2) If the child is subject to an EPO and is not in Board or Trust accommodation, would it be in the child's best interest to be in such accommodation?
(3) It must obtain access to the child, unless it is satisfied that it already has sufficient information about the child.
(4) If issues concerned with the child's education arise, the Board or Trust must consult the appropriate Education and Library Board.

Where the Board or Trust at first decides not to apply for a court order, it must consider whether or not it would be appropriate to review that decision later, setting a date for such a review if it does not so consider.

6.3.4 *Emergency Intervention*

As with emergency interventions under the 1968 Act, what we are focusing on here are situations in which it is necessary to intervene quickly to protect a child from an abuser. Emergency intervention may or may not be as a consequence of an investigation carried out under either article 56 or 66 (see 6.3.3).

The two legislative options available in emergency cases are the child assessment order (CAO) and the emergency protection order (EPO). Although they are available in different circumstances, there is a degree of overlap between them. A court is not allowed to make a CAO if it is satisfied that there are grounds for making an EPO and that an EPO should be made instead of a CAO.

Application for either of these orders can be made by a Board or Trust or the NSPCC.

6.3.4.1 Emergency Protection Order

Of the new orders, it is the emergency protection order (provided for in article 63) that most closely resembles the place of safety order, but then only to a limited degree. The emergency protection order is designed to be a short-term measure to deal with cases where a child is in severe and immediate danger, and gives the applicant parental responsibility for the child (article 63 (4) (*c*)).

The grounds for an EPO vary according to who the applicant is. Where the applicant is not a Board or Trust or the NSPCC, an EPO can be made if the court is satisfied that there is reasonable cause to believe that the child is likely to suffer significant harm if not removed from his or her usual residence or kept in accommodation provided by the applicant. If the applicant is a Board or Trust, it must satisfy the court that inquiries are being made with respect to the child and that these inquiries are being frustrated by someone unreasonably refusing access to the child in circumstances where the Board or Trust feels that access is required as a matter of urgency.

Should the NSPCC make the application, it must also satisfy the court that it is making inquiries, that the child is one who it has reasonable cause to believe is suffering or likely to suffer significant harm, and that those inquiries are being frustrated by access to the child being unreasonably denied where it believes that access is required as a matter of urgency.

Because the requirements for securing an EPO are simpler where the applicant is a Board or Trust, it is likely that they will be tempted to use this method, rather than a CAO, to bring children into care.

'Significant harm' is not defined in the legislation except for a provision that 'where the question of whether harm suffered by a child is significant turns on the child's health or development, his or her health or development shall be compared with that which could reasonably be expected of a similar child' (article 50 (3)).

Once granted, an emergency protection order can be made for a maximum of eight days. It may be extended by the court in a special application for that purpose for a further period of up to seven days. The court must have reasonable cause to believe that the child concerned is likely to suffer significant harm if the order is not extended.

In making an EPO, a court may give directions, firstly, about appropriate contact between the child and any other person and, secondly, the medical or psychiatric examination or other assessment of the child. However, the child may refuse to submit to the examination or assessment, notwithstanding the court's directions, provided he or she is 'of sufficient understanding to make an informed decision.' (It is open to the court to order that no assessment or examination be made.) In any event, irrespective of whether the court issues any directions, reasonable contact must be allowed between the child and his or her parents or carers or anyone with parental responsibility, among others.

An important feature of EPOs is that once the immediate urgency of the situation abates, the child will have to be returned to his or her home. When it is safe for the child to be returned home this must be done (article 63 (10)), though the person or agency in whose favour the EPO is made may exercise the power of the EPO again while it remains in force (i.e. without having to return to court) if a change in the child's circumstances makes it necessary to do so.

As with social workers' reports under the Order (see 6.3.6.7), the court is given a discretion to accept any relevant evidence when considering an application for an EPO, regardless of any statutory provision or rule of law that would otherwise prevent it from doing so; and therefore the rule against hearsay does not apply (see 3.4.7).

The child, his or her parents, anyone with parental responsibility or a carer may apply for the order to be discharged, but not within the first seventy-two hours of the life of the order. However, no discharge can be given if the applicant was given notice of the hearing at which the order was made and was present at the hearing. Neither can an application to discharge be made in respect of an extended EPO. No appeal can be made against the making of, or refusal to make or to discharge, an order.

6.3.4.2 Child Assessment Order

The aim of this order is to permit an investigation to resolve concerns about the welfare and safety of the child while at the same time causing the minimum disruption to the domestic environment of the child. It is designed for situations where the concerns are not of sufficient gravity to justify applying for an emergency protection order but where the risk of significant harm is nonetheless present and you feel that an assessment is required. Therefore it does not automatically authorise removal from the home (see below).

A court can make a child assessment order in favour of a Board, a Trust or the NSPCC if it is satisfied (*a*) that the applicant has reasonable cause to suspect that the child is suffering, or is likely to suffer, significant harm, (*b*) that an assessment of the state of the child's health or development or of the treatment of the child is required to enable the applicant to determine whether or not the child is suffering, or is likely to suffer, significant harm and it is likely to suffer significant harm, and (*c*) that it is likely that such an assessment will not be made or be satisfactory in the absence of such an order.

The order lasts for a maximum of seven days, though it can be made for a shorter period. As with an EPO, the child can refuse to submit to a medical or psychiatric examination or other assessment if he or she is of sufficient understanding. The child can be kept from home but only in accordance with the directions in the order and if necessary for assessment and for such period or periods specified in the CAO. If the child is to be removed from his or her home surroundings, the order must specify what contact the child is to be allowed to have with other people. Such steps as are reasonably practicable to give notice of the application must be taken to give notice to the child's parents or carers or those with parental responsibility, and to the child.

The Board or Trust is also required to inform the child, the child's parents, anyone with parental responsibility and anyone who has a contact order in respect of the child (see 6.3.6) or anyone allowed to have contact with the child by virtue of an order under article 53 of its intention to apply to the court for an order.

6.3.4.3 Recovery Order

This is an order ancillary to emergency protection and child assessment orders. It requires anyone with information about a missing or abducted child to disclose that information if asked to do so by the police, allows the child to be removed, allows a police officer to search for the child, using reasonable force if necessary, and requires someone in a position to do so to produce the child if asked (article 69).

An application for a recovery order can only be made by someone with parental responsibility for the child by virtue of a care or emergency protection order, or by a 'designated police officer' if the child was in police protection (article 69 (4)) (see 6.3.4.4).

The raison d'être of this order is that a child who is subject to an emergency protection order or in the care of a Board or Trust, or in police protection, may run away, go missing, or be abducted.

6.3.4.4 Police Powers and Children at Risk

It is necessary to look in a little detail at the powers the police have in an emergency where a child is at risk. The police will be permitted by law to act in ways that would not be appropriate or lawful for the social worker, and often their back-up is very necessary (see also 6.3.4.3).

In an emergency a child can be brought into 'police protection' for a maximum of seventy-two hours if the police believe that the child would otherwise be likely to suffer significant harm. As soon as is reasonably practicable after the child is taken into police protection by a 'designated officer' (i.e. a police officer appointed for this purpose), that officer must inform the Board or Trust in whose area the child was found and the Board or Trust of the area the child is normally resident in of the steps that have been and are about to be taken. The child (provided that he or she is capable of understanding) must also be informed about what has happened and is likely to happen.

The designated officer must also take such steps as are reasonably practicable to discover the wishes and feelings of the child. As soon as is reasonably practicable after the child is taken into police protection, the child's parents must also be informed of the steps that have been taken, the reason for taking them, and what further steps may be taken.

Once the designated officer completes the inquiry into the child's case, the child must then be released, unless the officer considers that there is still reasonable cause for believing that he or she would be likely to suffer significant harm if released.

The designated officer does not acquire parental responsibility for the child but must do what is reasonable in all the circumstances for the purpose of safeguarding or promoting his or her welfare.

The fact that the child is taken into police protection does not mean that he or she cannot have contact with others. The designated officer is to allow (*a*) the child's parents, (*b*) carers, (*c*) those with parental responsibility, (*d*) someone in whose favour a contact order is made or (*e*) someone allowed to have contact by virtue of article 53, or anyone acting on behalf of those persons, to have such contact as is in the opinion of the designated officer both 'reasonable' and in the child's best interests.

6.3.5 *Non-emergency Intervention*

Just as with the 1968 Act, what we examine here are the legislative mechanisms available to protect a child outside of emergency situations. Again no definition or category of 'non-emergency' exists. Three orders are created by the new legislation: the care order, the supervision order, and the education supervision order.

The threshold criteria for securing the first two of these orders are identical. A care or supervision order may be granted (*a*) if the child is suffering, or is likely to suffer, significant harm and (*b*) if the harm, or likelihood of harm, is attributable to the fact that the care given to the child, or likely to be given, if the order was not made is not what it would be reasonable to expect a parent to give to him or her, or (*c*) if the child is beyond parental control (article 50).

The complementary relationship between care and supervision orders is seen in the fact that on an application for one of the orders, a court may make the other order instead.

Where an application for a care or supervision order is made, the court is obliged to draw up a timetable to dispose of the application without delay (article 51); and this requirement is of course consistent with the principle of no delay (see 6.3.1.2). Once again an application for a care or supervision order can be made by a Board or Trust or the NSPCC. Education supervision orders are sought by Education and Library Boards. We will now look at each of these orders in turn.

6.3.5.1 Care Order

Care orders are available for children under the age of seventeen and give a Board or Trust parental responsibility for the child and the power to decide the extent to which a parent or guardian may meet their parental responsibility (article 52). It does not give the Board or Trust power to interfere with the child's religious beliefs, nor does it allow any decision to be taken with regard to the adoption of the child.

The child must be allowed reasonable contact with his or her parents or guardian, or the person in whose favour a residence order is made, or a person looking after the child in the exercise of the High Court's inherent jurisdiction (essentially wardship) (see 6.3.5.4.).

6.3.5.2 Supervision Order

A supervision order requires the supervisor to 'advise, assist and befriend' the supervised child and to do what is 'reasonably necessary' to give effect to the order. Where the order is not being complied with or perhaps is no longer necessary, it is the supervisor's duty to apply to court to have it varied or discharged.

The supervision order will be issued for one year, and although it may be extended on application to the court, it cannot last any longer than three years in total. If an application for a care order is already pending, an application for a supervision order will not be considered.

A supervisor can require the child to reside at a particular place for a particular time, to present him or herself at a particular location and on a particular day, or to engage in activities on a specified day. In addition, the child can be required by the order to undergo a medical or psychiatric examination, or indeed any examination directed by the supervisor, though such a requirement cannot be included unless the child has sufficient understanding to make an informed decision and he or she consents (schedule 3).

A supervision order is not intended to be as formal or as far-reaching as a care order, as can be seen from the fact that a Board or Trust does not acquire any parental responsibility over the child.

In a situation where the court may be considering the welfare of the child and there is concern about the child should he or she return home pending a final decision, it is possible to apply for an interim care or supervision order. Interim orders may also be made if the court has directed the Board or Trust to undertake an investigation into the child's circumstances under article 56 (see 6.3.3). Interim orders last for up to eight weeks, although it is possible to apply to have a subsequent interim order made after the expiry of the first. In practice this will only be done in the most exceptional circumstances.

6.3.5.3 Education Supervision Order

This order is applied for by Education and Library Boards but after consultation with the appropriate Health Board or Trust (article 55) and is granted if the court is satisfied that the child is not being properly educated (i.e. that he or she is not 'receiving efficient full-time education suitable to his age, ability and aptitude and to any special educational needs he may have') (article 55 (3)). An education supervision order cannot be made where the child is already in the care of a Health Board or Trust.

The order will require the supervising officer to assist, advise and befriend the child and his or her parents, along the same lines as the supervision order (see 6.3.5.2) but, obviously, with specific reference to the child's education. The supervisor may issue directions to the child, his or her parents, or anyone with parental responsibility for the child. Before giving directions to anyone as a result of the order, the supervisor must ascertain the wishes and feelings of that person, in particular with regard to where the child is to be educated.

The order can also be made for one year but may be extended, though not for more than three years at a time. It also ceases to have effect when the child reaches compulsory school age—sixteen years—or on the making of a care order.

Failure to comply with an education supervision order is an offence that can be committed by the parent or the child. Persistent failure to comply means that the Education and Library Board must notify the appropriate Health Board or Trust.

6.3.5.4 Maintaining Contact with the Child in Care

There is a general additional duty on a Board or Trust when a care or supervision order is made to encourage and support reasonable contact between a child in care and any of his or her parents and someone in whose favour a residence order is made (article 53).

If there is a dispute about the level of contact allowed, the courts can resolve the matter. Application can be made to the court by a Board or Trust, a child or any of those with whom the child is to have reasonable contact to have it decide what is reasonable contact (article 52 (1)). If the application is made by the Board or Trust or the child, the court can prohibit any contact between the child and the parent. Such an order can be made in conjunction with the application for a care order (i.e. it need not be a separate application for a separate order: article 53 (5)).

A court may refuse to allow the contact between the child and parent if (*a*) the Board or Trust is satisfied that it is necessary to do so in order to safeguard or promote the child's welfare and (*b*) the refusal (i) is decided upon as a matter of urgency and (ii) does not last for more than seven days.

Once the child is no longer in care, the order permitting contact will cease to have effect. (While this would be a court order permitting contact between the person named in the order and the child, it should not be confused with a contact order available under article 8: see 6.3.6.2).

A similar duty is imposed with respect to other children looked after by the Board (i.e. not brought into care for their protection but because, for example, they are in need: see chapter 8). Boards and Trusts must—unless it is not reasonably practicable or consistent with the child's welfare—endeavour to promote contact between the child and his or her parents, those with parental responsibility, and any other person connected with him or her. In particular the Board or Trust must, as far as reasonably practicable, keep the child's parents or those with parental responsibility for the child informed of where he or she is being accommodated, and they in turn must keep the Board or Trust informed of their address (article 29).

The Board or Trust is required to appoint a visitor—someone with the duty of visiting, advising and befriending the child—for children looked after by it if it appears to it that communication between the child and his or her parents has been infrequent and that he or she has not been visited by any such person within the preceding twelve months. A child can, however, object to the appointment of a visitor or have the appointment of an existing visitor rescinded; and if he or she has sufficient understanding to make an informed decision, the Board or Trust cannot make the appointment or must rescind the appointment, as appropriate (article 30 (5) and (6)).

6.3.5.5 Secure Accommodation

While the use of training school orders for children in need of care, protection and control (see 6.2.4.1) will be abolished by the 1995 Order, it will still be possible in exceptional circumstances for a child in care to be accommodated in a training school. Children 'looked after' by a Board or Trust can be placed in 'secure accommodation' (i.e. accommodation provided for the purpose of restricting liberty); Lisnevin training school would qualify as secure accommodation. (For a list of training schools see 6.2.4.1.) However, this can only be done (*a*) if the child has a history of absconding and is likely to abscond from other types of accommodation and, if he or she absconds, is likely to suffer harm or, (*b*) if he or she is kept in any other type of accommodation, if he or she is likely to injure him or herself or others (article 44). Detention in secure accommodation pending resolution of the application is also possible.

Regulations governing the exercise of this power may be made by the DHSS. These will specify the maximum period of detention in secure accommodation with and without the authority of the court.

6.3.6 *Family Proceedings*

The 1995 Order introduces a whole new range of (private law) court orders for use in 'family proceedings', thus overhauling the way in which the courts will exercise their jurisdiction with regard to the care of children within their families.

What are 'family proceedings'? you may ask. Family proceedings are given a very wide definition by the legislation. Included in the definition are not only applications for care or supervision orders and for article 8 orders relating to parental responsibility and to the appointment of guardians but also separation and divorce cases, actions under adoption legislation, applications for exclusion orders or personal protection orders (see 10.2.2), and applications regarding maintenance of a spouse and children (see 10.2.5) (article 8 (3)).

Article 8 of the Order sets out the new range of orders that can be made in any family proceedings, and these orders are therefore commonly referred to as 'article 8 orders'. The types of orders available are:

(1) Residence order—dealing with the arrangements about where the child is to live and with whom.
(2) Contact order—requiring the person with whom the child is living or going to live to permit contact between the child and the person named in the order, e.g. estranged spouse, grandparent.
(3) Specific issues order—resolving specific issues of parental responsibility that are in dispute.
(4) Prohibited steps order—requiring permission of the court to take certain steps that the court has already prohibited.

We will look at each type of order individually below, but a few general comments about article 8 orders are appropriate

These remedies are intended to be practical and not legalistic. 'The orders themselves are much more flexible [than those previously available], allowing the court to make whatever arrangements seem best in the particular case but dealing with practical questions rather than abstract rights' (p. 5).

Article 8 orders are also available in public law actions (i.e. applications for care or supervision orders), though public law orders are not available in an application for an article 8 order. One of the significant aspects of article 8 orders is that the court can make an order, of its own volition, that has not been sought by the applicant (article 10).

Those who can apply for an article 8 order include (*a*) the parents or guardian of the child and (*b*) anyone in whose favour a residence order in respect of the child has been made. However, Boards and Trusts are specifically prohibited from applying for these orders.

6.3.6.1 Residence Order

A residence order will resolve issues about where the child lives and with whom, not only when the parents are living apart but also when there are other interested parties, e.g. grandparents or other relatives. Residence orders carry with them the potential for 'shared care' arrangements. So, for example, if the parents of a child are estranged, separated, or divorced, either or both may apply for a residence order, which will determine if the child resides with one or other of them, or between the two. If a residence order is made in favour of two or more people who do not live together, the order may specify the periods during which the child is to live in the different households (article 11 (4)). Therefore in the future the care of children when their parents divorce is unlikely to be simply a matter of one parent getting custody and the other acquiring access.

A residence order can be made in relation to a child who is subject to a care order (see 6.3.5.1), but only a residence order can be made, and once it is granted the care order is discharged (article 9).

Someone who is not the child's parent but who makes an application with leave of the court and has a residence order made in his or her favour acquires parental responsibility for the child (see 6.3.1.5), and this allows him or her to apply for any of the other article 8 orders.

If a residence order is in force, the child cannot be removed from the United Kingdom nor can its surname be changed without the written permission of all those with parental responsibility or with leave of the court.

6.3.6.2 Contact Order

If a person has been granted a contact order, the child can visit or stay with that person as well as exchange telephone calls and letters. While the child is in his or her care that person will be expected, so far as is reasonable, to safeguard and promote the child's welfare at all times, even if he or she has not got parental responsibility. If a parent does not exercise his/her right to contact the child there is nothing that can be done to force him/her to maintain contact, notwithstanding that it is generally recognized that continued contact with a divorced parent is beneficial to the child. One of the features of the 'custody and access' regime of the past was that the degree of contact between the non-custodial parent and the child tended to diminish rapidly. It will remain to be seen whether the new regime will improve matters in this regard.

6.3.6.3 Prohibited Steps Order

This order will be issued when the court feels that one or more of those with parental responsibility must be prohibited from doing particular things or taking particular steps with respect to the child where to do so would not be in the best interests of the child. An example might be an order preventing a child being taken on an extended trip abroad in the middle of the school year.

Neither this order nor a specific issues order can be made to achieve an outcome that could be achieved by making a contact or residence order (article 9(5)(*a*)).

6.3.6.4 Specific Issues Order

A specific issues order will involve the court making a decision relating to some dispute about the care or upbringing of the child that has arisen between the parties exercising parental responsibility. That decision will naturally reflect what the court feels is best for the child. This could concern a decision about the child's education, for example, or an issue about the medical treatment the child should undergo.

6.3.6.5 Family Assistance Order

In any family proceedings in which an article 8 order is available, the court also has power to make a family assistance order, irrespective of whether an article 8 order had in fact been made (article 16). This order requires the Board or Trust to make a suitably qualified person available to advise, assist and, where appropriate, befriend any person named in the order, which can be the parent or guardian of the child or anyone with whom the child is living. The 'major purpose [of a family assistance order] is to provide help to the family in the immediate aftermath of family breakdown, in particular where [there] are difficulties about matters such as contact between children and estranged parents' (Explanatory Document, p. 5).

While there is a strong parallel between the legislative language used in the provisions describing the family assistance order and the supervision order (see 6.3.5.2), there are distinctions between the two. The family assistance order is made by the court of its own accord and has the Board or Trust acting merely as a facilitator to the family. On the other hand it is the Board or Trust that applies for a supervision order, and it relates to the child alone. A court cannot make such a family assistance order unless it is satisfied that the circumstances of the case are 'exceptional'. The consent of each of the people named in the order (other than the child) is the second prerequisite for making a family assistance order (FAO).

A family assistance order lasts for six months, unless the court specifies that it last for a shorter period. The suitably qualified person has a further role to play where an article 8 order is also in force: he or she can apply to the court in cases where any article 8 order in force should be varied or discharged.

You can see that the FAO attempts to ensure that as far as possible the child is cared for at home by his or her own parents. The type of situation where a family assistance order might be appropriate would be where the child was not being wilfully neglected or ill-treated but was not being cared for in a satisfactory way as a result of inadequate parenting skills.

The intention in making this order is to assist the family, with a minimum of intervention; but the introduction of a social worker means that if the situation deteriorates the Board or Trust can then become involved, because it is aware of the circumstances and is in a position to exercise its statutory powers. So, for example, if a specific issues or order that gave rise to a family assistance order had been made to decide the question of schooling and one parent was not abiding by its terms, the social worker for the parent with whom the child lives may bring the matter to the court.

Where a family assistance order has not been made and one party refuses to comply with an article 8 order, it is up to the party whose court order is being ignored to bring the matter back to the attention of the court.

6.3.6.6 Guardians *Ad Litem*

Although guardians *ad litem* have no equivalent in the 1968 Act, they are not a legal innovation, having been around for a long time, and have been used previously in adoption and wardship cases. They are, however, new to this jurisdiction and to this field of social work. This extension of the role and functions of a guardian *ad litem* is designed to further strengthen the position of the child as a party to the proceedings and to accord him or her the same status as any other party to the action.

A guardian *ad litem* is someone who will represent the child's interests and only the child's interests. He or she is 'under a duty to safeguard the interests of the child in the manner prescribed by [court] rules' (article 60).

GALs are appointed by the court in accordance with rules of court yet to be drawn up. They must be appointed (*a*) in applications for a care or supervision order, (*b*) in any proceedings in which the court has given an article 56 direction or has made, or is considering, an interim order, (*c*) in any application for discharge or variation of a care or supervision order (or a CAO, EPO and recovery order), and (*d*) in cases where the court is considering whether to make a residence order with respect to a child who is subject to a care order, or an appeal from any of these, unless the court is satisfied that it is not necessary to do so in order to safeguard the child's interests. As you can see, there is a wide range of circumstances in which the appointment of a guardian is recommended, and the Explanatory Document promises that a GAL 'will be appointed in nearly all public law cases under the Order' (p. 8).

The Department of Health and Social Services will draft regulations providing for the compiling of panels of people to act as GALs, from which people will be chosen in particular cases. These regulations will also outline any training they should receive and set out the qualifications before a person is chosen as a GAL. Rules of court will govern such matters as the assistance any GAL may be required by the court to give and the participation of the GAL in reviews, of a kind specified in the court rules, conducted by the court. The court rules in England set out the duties of the GAL, and these include investigating all the circumstances of the case, representing the child, providing a report to the court, and considering whether an appeal should be made.

To facilitate the performance of his or her role, the guardian is entitled to examine and take copies of records relating to the child in connection with any court action or contemplated court action under the Order or in connection with the delivery of any personal and social service relating to the child, or any record held by authorised people. The copies of such records are admissible in evidence given by the GAL, whether made orally or in writing, in any report he or she gives to the court, regardless of any statutory provision or rule of law that would ordinarily prevent the admission of such evidence. This means that the rule against hearsay, for example, does not apply to the GAL's evidence (article 61 (4)).

It is not clear who will fulfil this function under the Children (Northern Ireland) Order. Some social workers have acted as guardians in the past in wardship and adoption proceedings. Yet it might seem that solicitors are the obvious choice, given their legal training. One option under consideration is that Boards and Trusts would employ a panel of social workers to act exclusively as guardians *ad litem*.

6.3.6.7 Social Workers' Reports

Reports from any 'suitably qualified person', which category will of course include social workers, can be ordered by any court when considering any question with respect to a child in any proceedings under the Order. Such reports will relate to matters regarding the welfare of the child (article 4). The report can be made orally or in writing, though in practice it is likely to be in writing.

These reports will not be bound by the hearsay rule (see 3.4.7). Article 4 (4) allows a court to take account of any statement contained in such a report and any evidence given in respect of matters referred to in the report, regardless of any statutory provision or rules of law that would otherwise prevent the court from doing so, once the statement or evidence is, in the opinion of the court, relevant to the question it is considering.

6.3.6.8 Receiving 'children in need' Into Care

Article 21 obliges Boards or Trusts to provide accommodation for any 'child in need' (see 8.2.4) who appears to need accommodation because (a) there is no-one with parental responsibility for him or her, (b) he or she is lost or abandoned, or (c) the person caring for the child is prevented from providing him or her with suitable accommodation or care. Accommodation must also be provided for vulnerable adolescent children in need. Those who have reached the age of sixteen and whose welfare the Board or Trust considers likely to be seriously prejudiced if it does not provide accommodation must be accommodated. There is no court involvement in this process, unlike the other mechanisms we have examined. This provision then is somewhat similar to the voluntary reception of children into care under section 103 of the 1968 Act (6.2.4.5).

Boards or Trusts have the power to provide accommodation for any child, or any person aged between sixteen and twenty-one, if it would safeguard or promote his or her welfare, provided that anyone having parental responsibility does not object. Indeed such a person can remove the child at any time from Board or Trust accommodation.

6.4 Employing Children

Although not normally considered part of child care and protection law, we have included here the law relating to the employment of children because in its own way it attempts to prevent the abuse and exploitation of children and therefore is relevant to those working in this area.

The present law on employing children is found in part III of the 1968 Act, but it will be replaced by part XII of the 1995 Order—though few substantive changes will be made: this is largely a consolidation, with only minor amendments being made to the law. There is no duty on the authorities to intervene when children are being illegally employed, for example, to parallel the duty to intervene when a physically abused or neglected child is encountered.

Both pieces of legislation set out what is and is not permitted, as well as making provision for a licensing scheme, leaving it to the responsible authorities—the Education and Library Boards—to make by-laws or regulations filling in some of the details.

The employment of children is prohibited in all of the following circumstances:

(a) if the child is under the age of fourteen (thirteen in the Children (Northern Ireland) Order);

(b) during school hours on a school day;
(c) before 7 a.m. and after 7 p.m.;
(d) for two hours or more on a school day;
(e) in street trading;
(f) in any occupation likely to be injurious to the child's life, health, or education, regard being had to his or her physical condition. (The 1968 Act also places a prohibition on the employment of children for more than two hours on a Sunday.)

6.4.1 *Public Performances*

Children under the age of sixteen can only take part in public performances if a licence has been granted to them by an Education and Library Board; this is regardless of whether the performance is for remuneration or not. A public performance includes performances on licensed premises or a performance shown or recorded for broadcasting.

A licence is not to be given unless the Education and Library Board is satisfied (a) that the child is fit to do so, (b) that proper provision has been made to secure his or her health, and (c) that having regard to any provision made in regard to his or her education, that education will not suffer. However, a licence is not required (a) if the performance is by a school and the child is not paid for performing or (b) if the child has only performed for three days or less in the preceding three months.

Children under the age of fourteen will only be given a licence if the performance (a) involves a part that can only be played by a child of that age or (b) involves dancing in a ballet and, once again, a child of that age needs to play that part or (c) is one that is wholly or mainly musical or consists only of an opera or ballet, or if the nature of the child's part in it is wholly or mainly musical.

A blanket prohibition applies to performances in which there is danger to 'life or limb'. Indeed causing a child to engage in such a performance is a criminal offence. Furthermore, no child under twelve may be trained to take part in dangerous performances. Those aged between twelve and sixteen may do so, but only in accordance with a licence granted for this purpose, and such a licence will only be granted if the person is fit and willing to be trained and where proper provision has been made to secure his or her health.

6.4.2 *Offences and Defences*

The employment of a child in contravention of the legislation is an offence for which the employer may be punished. (Perhaps the main difference between the 1968 Act and the 1995 Order is that the latter makes it explicit that a parent can also be guilty of an offence for allowing the child to be employed: article 147 (2) (*b*).) The child is not guilty of an offence, except when he or she engages in street trading.

However, it is a defence if the accused can show (*a*) that the commission of the offence was due to an act or default of some other person and (*b*) that he or she took all reasonable precautions and exercised due diligence to avoid the commission of the offence by anyone under his or her control.

Social workers have no duty to act in this area, and their powers are limited; and although it might be possible to act on the need to protect the child's welfare and to use one of the emergency options outlined in 6.2.3 and 6.3.4, that might not seem appropriate. However, a police officer or an officer of the Education and Library Board can, within forty-eight hours of the issue of a warrant, enter premises where a child is known or believed to be employed, trained or performing and make inquiries about the nature of the work being undertaken (section 45; article 146).

6.5 *Further Reading*

Department of Health and Social Services, *Co-operating to Protect Children: a Guide for Health and Social Services Boards on the Management of Child Abuse*, Belfast: DHSS 1989.

Department of Health and Social Services, Circular HSS (CC) 4/89 (supplement no. 1).

Kerr, G., *Family Breakdown, Children and the Law*, Belfast: SLS Legal Publications 1985.

Lavery, Ruth, *Children and the Law: Digest of Northern Ireland Law*, Belfast: SLS Legal Publications 1995.

O'Halloran, K., *Wardship in Northern Ireland*, Belfast: SLS Legal Publications 1988.

O'Halloran, K., *Adoption Law in Northern Ireland*, Belfast: SLS Legal Publications 1994.

7

MENTAL DISORDER

Michael Potter

7.1 Introduction

In Northern Ireland the care of people suffering from a mental disorder is governed primarily by the Mental Health (Northern Ireland) Order 1986. The Order is divided into parts, each governing a particular aspect of the law. In this chapter, references to parts and to articles are to those of the 1986 Order.

The Mental Health (Northern Ireland) Order replaced the Mental Health Act (Northern Ireland) 1961. The Northern Ireland Review Committee on Mental Health Legislation, appointed to review the 1961 Act and chaired by Lord Justice McDermott (and hence known as the McDermott Committee), published its report in 1981. Many of its recommendations were implemented in the Order. While the Order is similar to the English Mental Health Act 1983, and the Mental Health (Scotland) Act 1984, there are a number of significant differences. You should bear this in mind when consulting books and articles outlining the position in other parts of the United Kingdom.

There are some other sources of mental health law that you should be familiar with. Order 109 of the Rules of the Supreme Court (Northern Ireland) lays down rules and procedures for the management of the property and affairs of patients by the Office of Care and Protection under the jurisdiction of the High Court. The Mental Health Review Tribunal (Northern Ireland) Rules 1986, prescribe the rules of procedure for hearings of the Mental Health Review Tribunal. The Mental Health (Nurses, Guardianship, Consent to Treatment and Prescribed Forms) Regulations (Northern Ireland) 1986, contain important regulations relating to guardianship and medical treatment. The Health and Personal Social Services (Northern Ireland) Order 1994, has amended the Order where a Health and Social Services Trust is exercising those functions formerly exercised by a Health and Social Services Board (see chapter 8). The Department of Health and Social Services issued a Code of Practice, in accordance with article 111 of the Order, which provides guidance for medical practitioners, Boards and Trusts, hospital staff and approved social workers in relation to their duties and responsibilities under the legislation. While the Order does not impose a legal duty to comply with the code, failure to comply can be referred to in evidence in legal proceedings. Finally, the DHSS has published a guide to the Order.

The Order governs the care and treatment of people with a mental disorder. Part II prescribes when a person can be compulsorily admitted to hospital for assessment and treatment on the grounds of mental disorder, and the duration of detention (see 7.4). Part II also governs the reception into guardianship of people suffering from mental illness or severe mental handicap (see 7.5). (In mental health law, guardianship refers to a supervisory arrangement for people aged sixteen or over who suffer from a mental disorder and require supervision in the interests of their welfare.) Part IV sets out the statutory framework regulating consent to psychiatric treatment. Part VIII provides for the management of the property and affairs of those people who, because of mental incapacity, are no longer able to manage them (see 7.7).

The majority of patients in psychiatric hospitals are voluntary patients: in March 1992 fewer than 10 per cent of psychiatric patients were involuntarily detained. As a general rule, voluntary patients can discharge themselves at any time and cannot be forcibly treated under part IV. However, doctors and nurses can in certain circumstances detain voluntary in-patients where they are minded to leave (see 7.4.1 below), and urgent treatment can be administered to voluntary patients without their consent (see 7.4.3).

The Order provides for the continuing monitoring of mental health care and review of individual cases. It does this through the Northern Ireland Mental Health Commission and the Mental Health Review Tribunal. The former is a statutory watchdog whose role is to monitor the detention and treatment of people under the Order, with a specific brief to monitor ill-treatment, deficiency in care and treatment, improper detention, or loss or damage to the property of a patient, while the tribunal exercises a judicial role. Patients can appeal to the tribunal if they believe they are being detained unjustifiably, either in hospital or under guardianship, and the tribunal, if it finds that an applicant is unlawfully detained or subject to guardianship, can discharge that person (see 7.8 and 7.9).

While the Secretary of State has ultimate responsibility for the care and treatment of mentally disordered people, this responsibility is in practice delegated to and carried out by the responsible authority, whether a Board or a Trust. Authorities are under a statutory duty 'to make arrangements designed to promote mental health, to secure the prevention of mental disorder and to promote the treatment, welfare and care of persons suffering from mental disorder' (article 112). These functions are carried out by doctors, nurses, and social workers, among others. In relation to patients in the community, the general practitioner, the social worker and the community psychiatric nurse will take primary responsibility for their care and welfare. In hospitals controlled by an authority, psychiatrists and psychiatric nurses will take primary responsibility. Psychiatrists performing certain statutory functions are classified as either (*a*) 'responsible medical officers' (RMOs), i.e. psychiatrists responsible for the care of a patient, appointed by the Mental Health Commission for the purpose of performing functions under part II and therefore known as 'part II doctors', or (*b*) psychiatrists with considerable experience appointed to exercise certain functions under part IV and who hence have become known as 'part IV doctors'.

7.2 *The Legal Definition of Mental Disorder*

The legal definition of mental disorder is set out in article 3. The term 'mental disorder' encompasses 'mental illness, mental handicap and any other disorder or disability of mind.' Detailed definitions of mental illness and of mental handicap, i.e. 'arrested or incomplete development of mind,' are set out in the article. Mental illness is accorded a general and somewhat equivocal definition as 'a state of mind which affects a person's thinking, perceiving, emotion or judgment to the extent that he requires care or medical treatment in his own interests or the interests of other persons.' Focusing on the effect of the disorder rather than the cause, the legal definition of mental illness embraces the variegation of psychiatric disorders.

Three separate categories of 'arrested or incomplete development of mind' are set out in article 3:

(1) 'mental handicap', where the handicap significantly impairs intelligence and social functioning;
(2) 'severe mental handicap', where the handicap severely impairs intelligence and social functioning;
(3) 'severe mental impairment', where there is severe impairment of intelligence and social functioning and which additionally 'is associated with abnormally aggressive or seriously irresponsible conduct.'

The categories are graduated in severity of condition. Not all people with a mental handicap will fall into these categories, for example those people whose disability does not significantly impair social functioning. The legal significance of these categories will become clear as we examine the criteria governing who can be admitted for assessment, detained for treatment, or received into guardianship.

The definition of 'mental disorder' does not include people who suffer from a mental disorder '*by reason only* of personality disorder, promiscuity or other immoral conduct, sexual deviancy or dependence on alcohol or drugs' (article 3 (2); emphasis added). Such persons can of course obtain treatment on a voluntary basis. Article 3(2) enshrines and re-enforces the requirement in article 5(1)(e) of the European Convention on Human Rights that compulsory detention be free from arbitrariness: no person should be compulsorily detained solely because his/her view or behaviour deviates from the norms prevailing in a particular society.

7.3 *The Role of the Social Worker*

The Order contains a number of powers which social workers may exercise in respect of the admission of patients to hospital, the reception of patients into guardianship, the continued applicability of guardianship, and the removal of patients to a place of safety. They must be performed by social workers who have been 'approved by the Board as having appropriate competence in dealing with persons who are suffering from mental disorder' (article 115). 'Approved social workers (ASWs) are social workers specially trained in dealing with persons who are suffering from mental disorder and appointed by a Board to act as an ASW for the purposes of the Order' (Code, paragraph 1.18). To become approved, a social worker must have two years' postqualification experience and have attended an additional training course.

If you are an approved social worker you are under a specific duty of care regarding the admission of patients to hospital and their reception into guardianship. Article 40 requires you to make an application for admission to hospital for assessment or an application for reception into guardianship where you are 'satisfied that such an application ought to be made' and, 'having regard to the wishes expressed by relatives or any other relevant circumstances you are of the opinion that it is necessary or proper for the application to be made.' Therefore you must be satisfied that an application must be made, and it should be made by you. It will be appropriate when considering whether an application should be made to consult other professionals who have been involved with the patient's care (paragraph 2.19). While the Code (paragraph 2.18) suggests that the views of close friends can in certain circumstances be taken into account, this should not conflict with your duty of confidentiality to the patient (see chapter 2).

When considering whether an application for admission to hospital or reception into guardianship should be made, you must interview the patient in a suitable manner. Before making an application you must be satisfied that admission to hospital or reception into guardianship 'is in all the circumstances of the case the most appropriate way of providing the care and medical treatment of which the patient stands in need' (article 40 (2)). The Code sets out some practical guidance for the interview. You should begin by identifying yourself to the patient, the family, and other professionals present, and explain in clear terms the nature of your role and the purpose of the interview. (It is a good idea to carry your identification at all times on occasions such as these.) You should check that the other professionals have explained their roles. Good communication with the patient is essential, particularly where he or she has difficulty in hearing or speaking or is not fluent in English (paragraph 2.6). The services of an interpreter may be required.

While both professionals (doctor and social worker) should be present at the time of admission, the patient should, if possible, be interviewed separately, to allow the professionals to form independent opinions. However, this is not always practicable, as the patient is often distressed and the holding of prolonged interviews can make matters worse. It may be more appropriate for the doctor and social worker to interview the patient together. This will ultimately be a matter for your judgment.

You should attempt to identify the 'nearest relative', as defined by the Order, and make sure that your responsibilities to the relative are fulfilled. Wherever possible you should ascertain the views of the nearest relative, inform that person that you are considering making an application for admission, and explain the implications of an application. The criteria for ascertaining the nearest relative are found in article 32. There is an established hierarchy, as follows: spouse, child, parent, sibling, grandparent, grandchild, uncle or aunt, nephew or niece. The hierarchy is operated in conjunction with a test of relational proximity: the nearest relative is the 'person first listed . . . who is caring for the patient or was so caring immeiately before the admission of the patient to hospital' (article 32 (3)). People under the age of eighteen are disregarded, unless they are either the spouse or parent of the patient. Moreover, guidance is provided for more complex situations: half blood relationships are treated as full blood (though full blood takes precedence), and an 'illegitimate' person is regarded as a legitimate child of the mother. Where two people appear in the same category, the determining factor will be seniority. A person cohabiting with the patient as husband or wife (and not being of the same sex) for at least six months will be treated as the spouse. However, such a person will not be treated as the spouse if the patient was married and there has been neither permanent separation nor continuing desertion. The decision is a matter, in practice, for the approved social worker.

Where there is a difficulty filling the position of nearest relative, the approved social worker or a relative or other person with whom the patient is residing may apply to the county court to have himself or herself or another specified person appointed to act as the nearest relative (article 36). Such an application may be made if the nearest relative cannot be ascertained, does not exist, is incapable of acting because of mental disorder or other illness, unreasonably objects to the making of an application for assessment or guardianship, or exercises his or her powers to discharge the patient, or is likely to do so, without due regard to the welfare of the patient or the interests of the public. The court may accede to the application if it finds that the proposed person is 'a proper person to act as the patient's nearest relative and is willing to do so' (article 36 (1)). The procedure is straightforward and can be expedited by the lawyers acting for the authority.

7.3.1 *Legal Liability of the Approved Social Worker*

Social workers are required by law to perform their duties to the standard of the reasonably skilled professional (see chapter 2). An indemnity clause (article 133) absolves social workers from criminal and civil liability when exercising their statutory functions under the Order, though this does not cover actions carried out in bad faith (i.e. intentional misconduct, such as sexual impropriety) or without reasonable care (e.g. disregarding the Code of Practice). An approved social worker is personally liable for such actions while carrying out his or her functions—for example failing to make an application for assessment where the nearest relative was not making such an application and where the social worker was of the opinion that such an application ought to be made. The social worker 'should exercise his own judgment and not act at the behest of his employers, doctors or other persons involved in the patient's welfare' (Jones, *Mental Health Act Manual*, 47). Thus the law allows for a social worker to make his or her own decision, providing that the decision can be explained and the explanation is one that a skilled professional might reasonably have arrived at.

7.4 *Compulsory Admission to Hospital*

It is always preferable if a person in need of psychiatric in-patient care and treatment consents to being admitted and treated in hospital. However, where such a person is unwilling to consent in accordance with the advice of his or her doctor and social worker they can, by law, be admitted to hospital and treated without their consent. This is known as compulsory or involuntary admission. Such people deemed to require in-patient care are initially admitted to hospital for assessment for a period of either forty-eight hours or seven days; this assessment period can be extended for up to fourteen days. Thereafter, a patient who requires further in-patient care can be detained for treatment.

7.4.1 *Admission for Assessment*

An application for admission to hospital can be made either by the nearest relative or by an approved social worker. The applicant must make the application not more than two days after seeing the patient. The application is made to the hospital to which the patient is to be admitted. Where the approved social worker makes the application, he or she should consult the nearest relative. The consultation should be full and effective, to ensure that the relative has the opportunity to play his or her full part in the process (see *R. v. South-Western Hospital Managers, ex parte M.* (1994) 1 All ER 161).

If consultation is not reasonably practicable or would involve unreasonable delay, the application can be made without consultation, but in such a case the nearest relative must be consulted as soon as practicable after the admission. Where an approved social worker consults the nearest relative and the relative objects to the application, the social worker must consult another approved social worker, and the second social worker should interview the patient and record his or her conclusions. If the social worker decides to proceed, the objection of the nearest relative should be recorded on the application. An alternative is to apply to the county court to have an 'acting' nearest relative appointed, on the grounds that the nearest relative has objected to the making of an application (article 36 (3) (*c*)). Where a patient is admitted to hospital on the application of the nearest relative, the patient should be interviewed by a social worker as soon as possible thereafter to provide the responsible medical officer with a report on the patient's social circumstances. This social worker does not have to be approved.

The application is founded on the medical recommendation of a doctor, preferably the patient's general practitioner or some other doctor who already knows the patient. A doctor on the staff of the hospital to which the patient is to be admitted cannot provide the recommendation except in a case of urgent necessity (article 6; Code, paragraph 2.21). In the recommendation the doctor should state that in his or her opinion the patient 'is suffering from mental disorder of a nature or degree which warrants his detention in a hospital for assessment ... and failure to so detain him would create a substantial likelihood of serious physical harm to himself or to other persons' (article 4 (2)). For these grounds to be fulfilled the patient must be suffering from a mental disorder as set out in article 3, and his or her condition must be so serious that detention in hospital is warranted.

When deciding whether a patient presents a substantial likelihood of serious physical harm to himself or herself, regard should be had only to evidence 'that the patient has inflicted or threatened or attempted to inflict serious physical harm on himself' or that 'his judgment is so affected that he is or would soon be unable to protect himself against physical harm and that reasonable provision for his protection is not available in the community' (article 2 (4) (*a*)). When making the recommendation the doctor should specify the nature of the mental disorder and give details of evidence of any likelihood of serious physical harm. Examples of serious physical harm include gross neglect of hygiene and personal safety that would create a hazard to the patient or others, serious and protracted neglect of diet that would lead to malnutrition, and uncontrolled over-activity likely to lead to exhaustion (Code, paragraph 2.22).

In determining whether the failure to detain a patient would create a substantial likelihood of serious physical harm to other people, regard should only be had to evidence 'that the patient has behaved violently towards other persons or has so behaved himself that other persons were placed in reasonable fear of serious physical harm to themselves' (article 2 (4) (*b*)). The assessment of a patient may legitimately involve consideration of the known history of his or her mental disorder and any prognosis of future deterioration of the patient's mental health.

A lawfully completed application gives authority to the applicant (or a person authorised by the applicant) to detain the patient and convey him or her to the hospital specified in the application. The approved social worker will be responsible for the conveyance of the patient to hospital either if he or she is the applicant or if the nearest relative requests the assistance of a social worker. The nearest relative should be informed that the advice and assistance of a social worker is available on request. The patient must be conveyed within two days of the date of application. In exceptional circumstances this period can be extended for up to fourteen days if a part II doctor certifies that such an extension is necessary (article 8 (1) (*b*)).

Where you have responsibility for the conveyance you should seek to transport the patient in the most humane and least threatening way consistent with the needs and safety of the patient and his or her escort (Code, paragraph 2.40 and sequel). You are ultimately responsible for the patient being conveyed lawfully and humanely. It is normal practice to use an ambulance (Code, paragraph 2.41). The Code also advises (paragraph 2.44) that the police should be asked to help if the patient is likely to be violent or dangerous, and in practice few compulsory admissions take place without police assistance. Where a patient is being conveyed by private car there should always be an escort in addition to the driver (article 9 (1)).

While being conveyed to hospital the patient is in legal custody, and a patient who escapes can be retaken under article 131 (2) by the person who was conveying him or her or by any police constable or approved social worker. You should inform the receiving hospital of the likely time of arrival and should ensure that the admission documents arrive at the hospital at the same time as the patient. On arrival, pass the documents to the appropriate personnel in the hospital and remain in the hospital until the patient has been medically examined. A person admitted for assessment must be examined immediately on admittance. The examining doctor must be a part II doctor or a psychiatrist on the staff of the hospital. The psychiatrist should furnish a report of the medical examination as quickly as possible, preferably within a few hours. The patient can only be further detained if the psychiatrist recommends detention for assessment (article 9 (4)).

A person admitted for assessment may be detained for seven days if the RMO or a part II doctor so certifies. If the initial examination and report are not undertaken by the RMO or a part II doctor, the patient may only be detained for up to forty-eight hours to allow the RMO to examine him or her, whereupon detention may be extended to the seven-day period (article 9 (4–7)). Before the expiry of the initial seven-day period the RMO or a part II doctor will again examine the patient. The patient may be detained for a further period not exceeding seven days if the examining doctor recommends further detention (article 9 (8)).

7.4.1.1 *Detaining Voluntary Patients for Assessment*

Voluntary in-patients can, under article 7, be prevented from leaving hospital. An in-patient can be detained by a psychiatrist or a nurse to enable an application for assessment to be made. A psychiatrist can detain a patient if 'it appears... that an application for assessment ought to be made in respect of the patient.' The patient can be detained for up to forty-eight hours to enable an application for assessment to be completed. If there is no psychiatrist available, a mental health nurse can hold a patient for up to six hours or until a psychiatrist arrives if it appears to the nurse that an application for assessment ought to be made and it is not practicable to secure the immediate attendance of a hospital doctor (article 7 (3)).

Article 7 does not apply to out-patients, and such people can only be detained once the application forms are completed in the normal way. Although out-patients cannot be held against their will by nursing staff under the Order, this does not preclude their detention in an 'emergency'. In *Albert v. Lavin* (1982) AC 346 the House of Lords confirmed that 'every citizen in whose presence a breach of the peace is being, or reasonably appears about to be, committed has the right to take reasonable steps to make the person who is breaking or threatening to break the peace refrain from doing so; and these reasonable steps in an appropriate case include detaining him against his will.'

7.4.1.2 Discrimination and Assessment for Treatment

An innovation, not found elsewhere in mental health legislation in the United Kingdom, is the anti-discrimination provision found at article 10. The McDermott Committee observed that 'a stigma continues to attach to an individual who has been detained as a formal patient' (paragraph 17, p. 4).

The stigma of being labelled a psychiatric patient has practical disadvantages, for instance in matters of insurance, employment, and emigration. The committee therefore envisaged an interim period of assessment before a patient is formally labelled a psychiatric patient in law, and recommended a 'careful and thorough assessment of each patient . . . before [he or she] can be designated as formal.'

These recommendations were enacted in the legislation and embodied in the initial fourteen-day assessment period. If during, or at the expiry of, the assessment period a patient is regarded as voluntary, i.e. not detained for treatment, he or she is not obliged to disclose that they were compulsorily admitted to a psychiatric hospital, except in judicial proceedings (article 10 (2 and 6)). Failure to disclose this fact cannot be grounds for dismissal or exclusion from any occupation or employment. The importance of this article is highlighted by the fact that during the year 1991/92, 646 patients were admitted for assessment but only 86 were detained for treatment.

7.4.1.3 Admitting Minors for Treatment

Although there is no age limit for the admission of people to hospital under part II, the Order is rarely used for the compulsory admission of children under sixteen. A statutory alternative is the institution of care proceedings. Under section 93 of the Children and Young Persons Act (Northern Ireland) 1968, a child can be committed to the care of a local authority where 'his health is being avoidably impaired or neglected' (see chapter 6 for more and the options under the Children (NI) Order 1995).

Any person aged sixteen or over can voluntarily enter a hospital for psychiatric care and treatment (Age of Majority Act (Northern Ireland) 1969, section 4). The position is more complex where a child under sixteen wants to enter a hospital of his or her own volition. A child under sixteen can consent to medical treatment despite the views or wishes of their parent or parents if they have sufficient maturity and intelligence to fully understand the nature and purpose of the treatment and make a considered decision whether it is in their best interests. Until a child is regarded in law as having capacity to consent, the decision will normally be for the parent or parents, although in exceptional circumstances it may be reasonable for a doctor to proceed without a parent's knowledge or consent, for example in cases of emergency, parental neglect, and other special circumstances (*Gillick v. West Norfolk and Wisbech AHA and the DHSS* [1985] 3 All ER 402). While in the *Gillick* case the proposed treatment was contraception, the logic of *Gillick* should apply equally to voluntary admission to hospital for psychiatric care and treatment, 'provided there is good evidence that the decision is in his or her best interests' (Gostin, *Mental Health Services*, 10.2.2).These questions are matters of medical judgment, the lawfulness of which can be reviewed and adjudicated on by the courts.

7.4.2 *Detention for Treatment*

Article 12 provides for detention for treatment (note that social workers are not involved at this stage). If at the end of the fourteen-day assessment period a part II doctor, having examined the patient, submits a report stating that the grounds in that article are satisfied, the patient may be detained for treatment for up to six months from the date of admission. The criteria allowing detention for treatment are narrower than for admission for assessment: these are that (1) the patient must be suffering from 'mental illness or severe mental impairment of a nature or degree which warrants his detention in hospital for medical treatment' and that (2) 'failure to so detain the patient would create a substantial likelihood of serious physical harm to himself or to other persons.'

The category 'severe mental impairment' is designed 'to limit the application of the long-term powers of compulsory detention on persons with a mental handicap to those whose handicap is severe and who exhibit abnormally aggressive or seriously irresponsible behaviour' (see the DHSS Guide). Its introduction ensures that mental handicap can never by itself be sufficient ground for long-term detention in hospital, and distinguishes 'that small group of people with a mental handicap who need to be detained from the majority who do not' (Guide, paragraph 12). As with mental disorder, the doctor must give particulars of the mental condition and evidence for his or her opinion regarding the likelihood of physical harm. Only at this point is a patient 'detained for treatment' for the purposes of the legislation.

Detention can be renewed for a further period of six months, and thereafter annually. The first renewal can be, and usually is, founded on a report by the RMO. However, after the first year of detention the patient must be examined by two doctors appointed by the commission, one of whom must be a doctor from a different hospital who has not previously examined the patient and was not involved in the patient's admission. This 'independent' opinion acts as a safeguard to ensure that the clinical judgment of the RMO (or part II doctor) is accurate, proper, and lawful. The doctors must furnish a joint report setting out their recommendations.

The RMO can discharge the patient at any time if he or she is satisfied that one or other of the conditions in article 12 is no longer fulfilled. A nearest relative must give the Board or Trust seventy-two hours' notice of their intention to apply for a patient's discharge, whereupon the RMO will furnish a report to it. The proposed discharge will not have effect if the RMO states that the criteria are fulfilled or (if one or both of the criteria are no longer fulfilled) the RMO 'is not satisfied that the patient if discharged would receive proper care' (article 14 (4)). This is a crucial provision, as it authorises the continued detention of a patient who no longer satisfies the criteria in article 12 (1).

7.4.3 *Treatment While in Hospital*

The law on consent to treatment is governed by common law and by part IV. (For an explanation of common law see chapter 1.) The application of the Order is confined to psychiatric treatment (see *T. v. T.* [1988] 1 All ER 613), and consequently the lawfulness of treatment for other conditions is governed by common law.

The provisions of part IV apply to patients 'liable to be detained' only, with the exception of articles 63 and 68, which apply to those detained under articles 9, 12, and 13 (i.e. those detained for assessment or treatment). This includes people liable to be detained under a court order made under part III; it does not, however, include patients held under article 7 by a nurse or doctor, those detained on the basis of a warrant under articles 129 and 130 (see below), patients under guardianship, or voluntary patients.

Article 63 applies to psychosurgery, i.e. 'any surgical operation for destroying brain tissue or for destroying the functioning of brain tissue,' and sex hormone implant treatment (see article 63 and the Mental Health Regulations (Northern Ireland) 1986, SRO no. 174, regulation 6). This can comprise a course of treatment under a treatment plan (article 65). Treatment under article 63 requires both the patient's consent and a second medical opinion. The medical opinion must state that the patient understands the nature, purpose and likely effects of the treatment and that his or her consent is genuine. This must be the unanimous opinion of three independent people appointed by the Mental Health Commission, one of whom is a psychiatrist. The psychiatrist must also certify that the treatment is likely to alleviate or prevent a deterioration in the patient's condition. This provision applies equally to all patients, detained and voluntary.

More frequently used treatments are the multifarious forms of medication and electroconvulsive therapy. These treatments can be administered under article 64 without consent. A patient can be treated under article 64 in two circumstances: (1) where he or she consents to the treatment and a part IV doctor has certified that the patient understands the nature, purpose and likely effects of the treatment (i.e. what he or she is consenting to) (article 65), or (2) where the patient does not consent to treatment but the following conditions are fulfilled: (*a*) a part IV (or part II) doctor (not being the RMO) certifies in the prescribed form that the patient is not capable of consenting or, having such capacity, is not prepared to consent, (*b*) the doctor certifies that 'having regard to the likelihood of its alleviating or preventing a deterioration of his condition the treatment should be given,' and (c) the doctor consults those people 'principally concerned with the patient's medical treatment' (article 64 (3) (b) and (5)).

Article 64 can only be brought into effect if three months have elapsed since the patient received any form of medication for disorder: in other words, the article cannot be used as a means of administering to a patient his or her first treatment for mental disorder. The article also applies to treatment plans and a course of treatment under a treatment plan.

Article 69 permits the RMO to treat a patient 'liable to be detained' with those forms of treatment for mental disorder, medication etc. to which articles 63 and 64 do not apply, without the patient's consent.

Only in an emergency does the Order authorise the forcible treatment of voluntary patients. Where any patient urgently requires psychiatric treatment, he or she can be treated without his or her consent (article 68). Urgent treatment can be administered in four situations:

(1) where treatment is immediately necessary to save the patient's life (article 68 (1) (a)) (this sub-article applies to any treatment, including irreversible treatment, i.e. treatment that has 'unfavourable or irreversible physical or psychological consequences,' or hazardous treatment (article 68 (3))—psychosurgery, for example);
(2) where the treatment is immediately necessary to prevent a serious deterioration of the patient's condition;
(3) where treatment is immediately necessary to alleviate serious suffering;
(4) where treatment is immediately necessary 'and represents the minimum interference necessary to prevent the patient from behaving violently or being a danger to himself or to others' (article 68 (1) (b–d).

In none of the last three circumstances can irreversible treatment be administered to a patient.

As stated above, where part IV does not apply it is the common law that governs the treatment of patients with a mental disorder. It is a principle of common law that no person can touch or treat any other person without that person's consent. Treatment without consent can be trespass to the person, which is both a civil wrong and a breach of the criminal law. Where a patient consents to treatment, that consent can be withdrawn by the patient at any time before or during treatment. If a patient is unable to give consent, the doctor can lawfully operate or give treatment providing that it is in the best interests of the patient. The treatment must be accepted at the given time as proper by a responsible body of medical opinion skilled in the particular form of treatment.

A patient can only lawfully consent to a proposed treatment if he or she is informed of the nature, purpose and likely effects of such treatment and has sufficient mental capacity to comprehend the information and arrive at a decision. The doctor is obliged to provide the information necessary to enable the patient to make a balanced judgment in deciding whether to submit to treatment. This obligation is, however, subject to the doctor's overriding duty to have regard to the best interests of the patient.

The doctor is generally required to make the patient aware of certain side-effects or risks associated with a treatment. Whether a given risk should be disclosed depends on its seriousness and the likelihood of it occurring. While foreseeable risks should be disclosed, it might be reasonable for a doctor to choose not to disclose a remote risk if he or she believes it is in the best interests of the patient (see *Bolam v. Friern Hospital Management Committee* [1957] 2 All ER 118). However, the more serious the potential side-effect, the stronger will be the patient's right to know.

The patient must have the mental capacity to sufficiently understand the nature, purpose and likely effects of the proffered medical treatment, to retain the information, to believe it, and to arrive at a clear choice about his or her willingness to be so treated. These are matters for clinical judgment, but the lawfulness of doctors' decisions or proposed decisions can be adjudicated upon by the courts. The courts generally uphold the clinical judgment of the doctor unless there is real doubt about it. However, in a recent case the courts upheld a patient's right to refuse consent, flying in the face of medical opinion. In *Re C*. [1994] 1 All ER 819, the patient, a paranoid schizophrenic, had gangrene in his foot. The hospital doctors had formed the opinion that if the condition further deteriorated his leg might have to be amputated in order to save his life. The patient refused to consent and sought an injunction to prevent the operation. Despite the hospital's contention that the patient's capacity to give a definitive decision had been impaired by his mental illness and that he was unable to appreciate the risk of death if the operation was not performed, the court granted the injunction, holding that, despite his mental illness, the patient had sufficient capacity to make the decision.

It seems accepted good practice for doctors who are considering treatment in the form of sterilisation and abortion for women who are unable to consent because of mental disorder to obtain court approval before the operation (see *F. v. West Berkshire Health Authority* [1989] 2 All ER 545). In the case of *T. v. T.* (1988) 1 All ER 613, a nineteen-year-old woman with a mental handicap became pregnant. The doctors formed the opinion that abortion and sterilisation were in the best interests of the patient, and the court declared that the doctors could proceed with their recommended course.

7.5. Guardianship

Guardianship refers to a supervisory arrangement for people aged sixteen and over who suffer from a mental disorder and require supervision in the interests of their welfare. 'The purpose of guardianship is primarily to ensure the welfare (rather than the medical treatment) of a patient in a community setting where this cannot be achieved without the use of some or all of the powers vested by guardianship' (Code, paragraph 3.1). If appointed, a guardian assumes certain powers and responsibilities, the exercise of which is monitored by the relevant authority and the Mental Health Commission.

To be received into guardianship a person must meet two criteria: (1) he or she must be suffering from 'mental illness or severe mental handicap of a nature or degree which warrants his reception into guardianship,' and (2) reception into guardianship must be 'necessary in the interests of the welfare of the patient' (article 18 (2)). These grounds are known as the medical and welfare grounds, respectively. An application for a person to be received into guardianship must be accompanied by two medical recommendations stating that the medical criteria are fulfilled and one welfare recommendation stating that the welfare ground is fulfilled.

An approved social worker must make the welfare recommendation. If you are making the recommendation you should state that it is necessary in the interests of the patient that he or she be received into guardianship, giving reasons for this opinion. Moreover, you must provide a statement about any personal interest you might have in the case, for example if you are related to the patient or if you have any pecuniary interest in the patient's reception into guardianship (article 18 (3) (*b*)). An approved social worker should not be pressured into making this recommendation by a doctor, relative, or other person. The recommendation should only be made if you are completely satisfied that the statutory criterion is fulfilled, i.e. that reception into guardianship is necessary for the welfare of the patient.

An application to have a person received into guardianship can be made either by the nearest relative or by an approved social worker (article 19). The application must be made within fourteen days of the applicant last seeing the patient. If an approved social worker makes the application, the welfare recommendation must be made by a different approved social worker. As with an application for admission, the social worker should consult the nearest relative, unless such consultation is not reasonably practicable or would involve unreasonable delay. If a patient is admitted into guardianship without the knowledge of the nearest relative, the social worker should inform the nearest relative as soon as may be practicable. If the nearest relative objects to the making of an application, a third approved social worker must be called on to interview the patient and form an opinion regarding the proposed application (article 19 (5)). The objection of the nearest relative must be recorded on any application subsequently made. The application must be forwarded to the relevant authority within seven days of the date of the last medical examination.

The purpose of appointing a guardian is to enable the 'establishment of an authoritative framework for working with a patient with a minimum of constraint to help him to achieve as independent a life as possible within the community' (Code, paragraph 3.1). A guardian has three 'essential' powers: (1) to require the patient to reside at a certain place, (2) to require the patient to attend for medical treatment, occupation, education or training at specific times and places, and (3) to require access to be given at any place where the patient is residing to a doctor, approved social worker or other person so specified by the Board (article 22 (1)).

The law places a number of duties on guardians, whether the guardian is a private individual or a Board or Trust. Private guardians are required to notify the relevant authority of the patient's GP, if the patient changes address, if the patient dies, or if the patient goes absent without leave, and on the return of a patient who has been absent without leave (Mental Health (Nurses, Guardianship, Consent to Treatment and Prescribed Forms) Regulations (Northern Ireland) 1986, no. 174, regulation 4). They must also obey any directives the responsible authority might give. If a Board or Trust itself is the guardian it must arrange for the patient to be visited at least four times a year by a representative of the authority, and one of these visits must be by a part II doctor. The Board or Trust must notify the Mental Health Commission of all developments and changes in the custody, care and control of the patient (including all changes of which a private guardian must notify the authority) and any other circumstance that results in the termination of the guardianship arrangement (Mental Health (Nurses, Guardianship, Consent to Treatment and Prescribed Forms) Regulations (Northern Ireland), 1986, no. 174, regulation 5).

Guardianship initially lasts for six months (article 22 (3)). It may be renewed for a further six months, and thereafter annually (article 23 (1)). A patient can be discharged from guardianship either if the RMO states that the medical ground no longer applies or if an authorised social worker states that the welfare ground no longer applies. An authorised social worker is a senior social worker authorised by the authority to perform this function under the Order (article 24 (3)). A patient can also be discharged from guardianship by the application of the nearest relative if the relative gives the authority seventy-two hours' notice and neither the RMO nor the authorised social worker objects to discharge. Finally, a patient can be discharged by a Mental Health Review Tribunal (see 7.9). Guardianship automatically ends if a patient is detained for treatment under article 12 (1).

7.6 Powers of the Police

Two important functions are conferred on the police by mental health legislation: the power to remove a mentally disordered person found in a public place, and, where a warrant has been issued, the provision of assistance with the retaking of patients and the removal of patients to a place of safety.

If a police officer finds in a public place a person who appears to him or her to be suffering from mental disorder and 'in immediate need of care or control,' they may remove that person to a place of safety (article 130). A person so removed may be detained for forty-eight hours to allow him or her to be examined by a doctor and interviewed by an approved social worker so that 'any necessary arrangements for his care or treatment' can be made (article 130 (2)). The police officer is obliged to inform both a responsible person residing with the person and (if not the same person) the nearest relative of the person's removal to a place of safety. A 'place of safety' means any hospital that receives such people, or a police station, or 'any other suitable place the occupier of which is willing temporarily to receive such persons' (article 129 (7)). Each authority provides a list of hospitals that can be used as places of safety.

Article 129 provides authority for a justice of the peace on complaint by an officer of the authority (usually an approved social worker) or a police officer to issue a search warrant authorising an officer accompanied by a doctor to enter premises (if need be by force) and remove a patient. Assistance is contemplated in three main situations: (1) assistance at the initial admission of a patient to hospital; (2) assistance in retaking a patient liable to be detained who is at large; and (3) assistance in removing a person at risk to a place of safety.

7.6.1 *Assistance at the Admission of a Patient*

Where an application for admission to hospital for assessment has been completed under the Order, the applicant is authorised to take the patient and convey him or her to hospital. If the applicant finds that it is not reasonably practicable for him or her, or a person authorised by him or her, to fulfil this duty, and the responsible authority, having been requested to assist, has failed so to do, the applicant may apply for a warrant if there is reasonable cause to believe that the patient is to be found on any premises. The warrant authorises a police officer accompanied by a doctor to 'enter, if need be by force, the premises and to take and convey the patient to the hospital specified in the application' (article 129 (4)).

7.6.2 Assistance in Retaking a Patient Who Is at Large

Where an officer of the relevant authority (including a social worker) or a police officer has reasonable cause to believe that a patient who is liable to be held under the Order but who is at large is to be found in any premises, a complaint on oath may be made to a justice of the peace and a warrant issued authorising a police officer accompanied by a doctor to enter the premises and remove the patient, if need be by force (article 129 (2)).

7.6.3 Assistance in Removing a Person to a Place of Safety

If an officer of the relevant authority (including a social worker) or police officer has reasonable cause to believe that a person suffering from mental disorder 'has been or is being ill-treated neglected or kept otherwise than under proper control or being unable to care for himself is living alone,' he or she may make a complaint on oath to a justice of the peace (article 129 (1)). A warrant may then be issued authorising a police officer accompanied by a doctor to enter the premises and remove the person to a place of safety. The person removed may be detained in the place of safety for up to forty-eight hours (article 129 (5)).

7.7 Management of Patients' Property and Affairs

Where a person becomes unable to look after his or her property and affairs by reason of a mental disorder, the law contains a number of mechanisms to provide protection. Part VIII of the Order provides for the management of the property (which includes land, money, and possessions) and affairs of a patient by the Master and Office of Care and Protection (see chapter 1) under the jurisdiction of the High Court, usually through the appointment of a 'controller'. Authorities have jurisdiction to look after property up to a specified limit for people in accommodation for which they are responsible. The Department of Health and Social Services can appoint a person to receive and administer social security benefits payable to someone who is 'unable to act'. Alternatively, patients themselves can create an enduring power of attorney.

Part VIII operates as follows. The Order places a duty on Boards and Trusts, the Mental Health Commission and 'any person carrying on a nursing home, a home for persons in need or a private hospital' to notify the Office if they are satisfied (*a*) that a person for whom they have responsibility (or, in the case of the Mental Health Commission, of whom they have knowledge) is incapable of managing his or her property or affairs, (*b*) that part VIII is appropriate, and (*c*) that no other procedures are in place (article 107). Such notification must be made within fourteen days of the body or person becoming so aware.

An application must be made in writing to the Office of Care and Protection for the appointment of a controller to deal with the day-to-day management of the patient's financial affairs. Where there is no-one suitable to make the application, the Office can direct an officer of the court or the Official Solicitor (see chapter 1) to make the application. In urgent cases the requirement to apply in writing can be waived. The application can specify a person suitable and willing to act as controller, for example a relative, friend, or professional adviser. Where there is no-one suitable and willing to act as controller, an officer of the court or the Official Solicitor can be appointed. Once an application for the appointment of a controller has been lodged, a date will be fixed for a hearing and all interested parties notified.

The jurisdiction of the court is set out in article 97 (1). 'The powers in part VIII shall be exercisable where, after considering medical evidence, the court is satisfied that a person is incapable by reason of a mental disorder of managing and administering his property and affairs.' Where the court finds that a person is so incapable, it will normally appoint a controller (article 101 (1)). Articles 98 and 99 set out a wide range of powers that can be exercised by the court once it has found a person to be incapable. The court can delegate some or all of its powers to a controller. The breadth of a controller's powers will be set out in the order of appointment (article 101 (2)). (A useful booklet entitled *Handbook for Controllers* can be obtained from the Office of Care and Protection.) A controller can be discharged by court order if the patient dies, or if the court becomes satisfied that the patient is no longer incapable, or if discharge is regarded as otherwise expedient. There are two main mechanisms designed to ensure propriety on the part of the controller: the lodgment of security (such as a sum of money) with the court, and the regular inspection of the patient's accounts (RSC, Order 109, parts 12 and 13).

An emergency procedure is provided for cases where urgent measures must be taken in respect of a person's property and affairs. Where the court believes that a person may be incapable and is of the opinion that it is necessary to make immediate provision for the maintenance or other benefit of the patient, of his or her family, or of other people whom the patient might be expected to provide for, or otherwise for administering the patient's affairs, it can invoke the powers under part VIII pending the determination of the person's mental capacity (article 98). The court can appoint an interim controller.

'Visitors' are appointed by the Lord Chief Justice to ensure the proper administration of part VIII of the Order (articles 104–5). There are three panels of visitors: medical visitors, being doctors who have a special knowledge and experience of mental disorder; legal visitors, being lawyers of at least ten years' standing; and general visitors. If it appears to the court that a visit is necessary 'for the purpose of investigating any particular matter or matters relating to the capacity of the patient to manage and administer his property and affairs, or otherwise relating to the exercise in relation to him of the functions of the court under [part VIII],' a patient will receive a visit (article 105 (2)). A general visitor will be sent unless 'it is in the circumstances essential for the visit to be made by a Visitor with medical or legal qualifications' (article 105 (3)). The visitor may interview the patient in private and will make a report for the court. The information in such a report may be disclosed only to the court and to people to whom disclosure has been authorised by the court (article 105 (9)). The Master himself may make the visit.

There is an aptly named 'short procedure' that bypasses the normal procedures and is less costly than appointing a controller (RSC, Order 109, rule 5). The procedure may be used if it appears to the court that the property of the patient does not exceed £5,000 or if it is otherwise appropriate to proceed under this rule and it is not necessary to appoint a controller for the patient. In such a case the court can direct an officer of the court or some other suitable person to deal with the patient's property and affairs.

Finally, we will consider the creation of an enduring power of attorney. Any person can authorise another to manage his or her property and affairs on his or her behalf. This relationship is known as agency, and the power of attorney is an example of agency. However, if the donor becomes mentally incapable the donee no longer has authority to so act. The Enduring Powers of Attorney (Northern Ireland) Order 1987, makes provision for the continuation of a power of attorney if the donor becomes mentally incapable. (See also RSC, Order 109A.) The purpose of the Order is to enable a person to give a power of attorney (which endures despite a supervening incapacity) to a person of his or her choice and empowers the attorney to deal with their property in the way the attorney thinks fit, subject to any restrictions in the power of attorney.

The High Court regulates enduring powers of attorney under a system of registration. Every enduring power of attorney must be validly registered, and the court can cancel registration if it is satisfied that the donor is likely to remain mentally capable, that the attorney is unsuitable, that the power was not a valid and subsisting enduring power when registration was effected, that fraud or undue pressure was used to induce the donor to create the power, or that the power has expired or has been revoked, inter alia (see Enduring Powers of Attorney (Northern Ireland) Order, 1987, article 10 (4)).

The Master and Office of Care and Protection regulate the appointment through a system of registration. An enduring power of attorney must be validly registered with the Office, and the court can cancel registration if, among other reasons, it is satisfied that the donor is likely to remain mentally capable, that the attorney is unsuitable, or that there was no valid enduring power of attorney.

7.7.1 Boards and Trusts and Residential Patients

Authorities enjoy some powers in relation to the property of people in accommodation for which they are responsible. Under article 116 (1) these powers apply to patients 'incapable by reason of mental disorder of managing and administering [their] property and affairs' who reside in accommodation for which a given Board is responsible. An authority may receive and hold money and valuables on behalf of such a patient up to a total value of £5,000, unless the Mental Health Commission authorises a higher figure. (This figure is determined by the DHSS.) A receipt for the money or valuables must be given to the patient. The authority has the power to spend money and dispose of valuables, although it must have regard for items that may have a sentimental value for a patient or would have but for his or her mental disorder. This power does not apply if a controller has already been appointed in the jurisdiction.

7.7.2 The Social Security Appointee System

The Department of Health and Social Services can authorise an appointee to act on behalf of someone who cannot claim for themselves because of mental incapacity, for example if they are mentally ill or suffering from senility (Social Security (Claims and Payments) Regulations 1987, regulation 33). This provision does not apply to people who, despite a physical disability, understand and control their own affairs. In such a case an agent can be appointed, either by the claimant personally or, under regulation 34 of the Claims and Payments Regulations, by the DHSS. For an appointee to be authorised, an application must first be made in writing to the claimant's social security office. A social security officer should visit the claimant to check that the appointment is needed. Medical evidence may be sought if the officer has doubts about incapacity or where the claimant is not in hospital. An appointment will not be made if someone has already been formally appointed to act legally on behalf of a person temporarily or permanently unable to manage their affairs, for example if there is an enduring power of attorney or if a controller has already been appointed.

An appointee must be aged eighteen or over and will normally be a close relative or friend, or a residential or nursing home or hospital. The social security officer is instructed to ensure that the appointee will act in the best interests of the claimant. Where a person has been acting in this capacity before an official appointment, his or her actions can be retrospectively validated by an appointment. The appointee exercises any right to which the claimant may be entitled, and deals with any money payable to the claimant on his or her behalf.

The duties of an appointee include claiming and receiving benefit and using the benefit in the interests of the claimant. Where the claimant is in hospital, the appointee must ensure that the weekly allowance provided to meet personal needs is used to the best advantage of the patient and the patient's dependants. The appointee must notify the relevant social security office of any change in circumstances that may affect the payment of benefit. (See Ruth Lavery and Laura Lundy, 'The Social Security Appointee System' in *Journal of Social Welfare and Family Law*, 1994, 313.)

7.8 *The Mental Health Commission*

The Mental Health Commission for Northern Ireland was established by part VI and was charged to 'review the care and treatment of patients, including the exercise of the powers and the discharge of the duties conferred or imposed by the Order' (article 86 (1)). The commission is chaired by a lawyer and is composed of members with a range of relevant professional expertise, including psychiatrists, psychologists, social workers, and lawyers. The commission has a secretariat at Elizabeth House, Holywood Road, Belfast 4. Members of the commission serve for a maximum of four years. The Department has directed that the commission report once every two years on its activities; the commission has published four reports since it came into existence in 1986.

The Mental Health Commission is essentially an independent monitoring and investigative mechanism designed to safeguard the rights of patients. Its main duty is to make inquiry where it appears to the commission that any patient is or may be suffering ill-treatment, deficiency in care or treatment, improper detention in hospital or reception into guardianship, or loss or damage to property (article 86 (2)). Where the commission finds evidence of such practices, or indeed any matter concerning the welfare of patients that the commission considers sufficiently important for the body responsible to be made aware of it, it must inform the hospital or home responsible for the care of that patient. To make possible the fulfilment of this duty, the commission can at any reasonable time visit and interview patients, medically examine patients in private, and inspect the medical records of any patient, whether they be in hospital, a private hospital, a residential care home, a voluntary home, or a nursing home, or in respect of a patient who is or has been subject to guardianship under the Order (article 86 (3)). The commission has codified its hospital visiting policies and procedures in a Visiting Manual to provide a reference guide for commissioners and the secretariat (see *Third Report of the Mental Health Commission for Northern Ireland*).

The powers in the Order permitting compulsory admission to hospital, detention in hospital and treatment and reception into guardianship are, in law, activated through the completion of prescribed forms (see Mental Health (Nurses, Guardianship, Consent to Treatment and Prescribed Forms) Regulations (Northern Ireland) 1986). These forms are contained in the DHSS Guide. The commission receives and inspects all prescribed forms to ensure procedural propriety. Other functions performed by the commission include the appointment of part II and part IV doctors, the reviewing of hospital decisions to withhold postal packets from patients (article 17), and the monitoring of treatment given under part IV (in particular of urgent and irreversible treatment). The commission may, if it thinks fit, refer the case of any patient who is liable to be detained in hospital, or is subject to guardianship, to the Mental Health Review Tribunal.

7.9 *The Mental Health Review Tribunal*

The purpose of the Mental Health Review Tribunal is to provide a safeguard against unjustified detention, or control under guardianship, by means of an independent review of cases from the medical and non-medical points of view. Following the report of the Royal Commission on the Law Relating to Mental Illness and Mental Deficiency (the Percy Commission), 1954–57 (Cmnd 169), Mental Health Review Tribunals were introduced in Northern Ireland in 1961 to provide an independent tribunal to which patients could appeal. The current chairman of the Mental Health Review Tribunal is Mr Fraser Elliot QC. The responsibility for appointing tribunal members rests with the chairman. Tribunals are normally composed of three members: a legally qualified president, a psychiatrist, and a third member, who is neither a lawyer nor a psychiatrist. The tribunal sits locally, usually in the hospital where the patient is being treated.

The role of the tribunal is to adjudicate on the lawfulness of the detention or guardianship of patients. It has the power to discharge any patient (article 77 (1)). It must discharge a patient from hospital if it is satisfied that (1) his or her mental condition does not come within the criteria under which he or she is detained, i.e. he or she is not suffering from a prescribed mental condition that warrants his or her detention (article 77 (1) (*a*)), or (2) if discharged he or she would not create a substantial likelihood of serious physical harm to himself or to other people (article 77 (1) (*b*)). Where the nearest relative has applied to have the patient released but the RMO has certified that if discharged he or she would not receive proper care, the patient can be discharged on the application of the nearest relative if the tribunal is satisfied he or she would receive proper care (article 77 (1) (*c*)).

The tribunal must release an applicant from guardianship if it is satisfied that the medical or welfare criteria are not fulfilled (see above). It can also direct the discharge of the patient on a future date, recommend that he or she be granted leave of absence or transferred to another hospital or into guardianship, or order that the tribunal be reconvened to further consider the case if the directive is not complied with (article 77 (2)). (For a more detailed discussion see Gostin and Fennell, *Mental Health Tribunal Procedure*.)

Cases come before the tribunal by way of application and referral. Patients admitted to hospital or received into guardianship under part II may apply to the tribunal within the first six months of being admitted and once during each renewal period, i.e. during the second six months, and thereafter annually. Where a nearest relative has requested the discharge of a patient and this request has been turned down, he or she may apply to the tribunal within twenty-eight days of being informed of that decision and within twelve months of the date of the order, and in any subsequent period of twelve months (article 71 (4)).

There is a mandatory referral system under which the responsible authorities must ensure that the tribunal considers the case of every person detained or subject to guardianship once every two years. (This period is only one year if the patient is under sixteen.) Finally, the Attorney-General, the Department of Health and Social Services, the Master of Care and Protection (on the direction of the High Court) and the Mental Health Commission may refer the case of any person detained in hospital or subject to guardianship (articles 72 and 86 (3) (*a*)).

Where a patient wishes to appeal to a tribunal, application should be made in writing to the Mental Health Review Tribunal, Room 112B, Dundonald House, Belfast 4. The application should include the name and address of the applicant. Where the nearest relative makes the application it should contain the name and address of the applicant and the patient and indicate the nature of the relationship between the two. The application should refer to the provision of the Order under which the patient is detained or subject to guardianship and should contain the name of any representative who may be acting for the applicant. On receiving the application the tribunal sends notification of the application to the relevant authority. If the applicant is legally entitled to a hearing, the tribunal will arrange a hearing and notify the parties of a date for the hearing.

Before the hearing, the medical member of the tribunal will examine the patient and take such other steps as he or she considers necessary to form an opinion of the patient's mental condition. The medical member may see the patient's medical records and examine the patient in private. The patient has the right to obtain an independent medical report to present at the hearing. This can be organised by the patient, a social worker, a lawyer, the nearest relative, or other interested person. The patient can be represented by a lawyer or other person. Legal aid is available for patients of limited means to obtain legal advice and representation at the tribunal. Legal representation can be organised by a solicitor.

Before the hearing, relevant documents will be disclosed by the tribunal to the parties, subject to the power of the tribunal to withhold documents from the patient or applicant on the grounds that their disclosure would adversely affect the health or welfare of the patient or others.

The tribunal hearing is held in private, unless the patient requests a public hearing and the tribunal is satisfied that a public hearing would not be contrary to the patient's interests. The tribunal may conduct the hearing in whatever manner it considers suitable, taking account of the health and interests of the patient. The tribunal may adjourn a hearing at any time to obtain further information or for such other reason as it thinks appropriate. At the beginning of the hearing the president of the tribunal should explain the procedure to be followed during the hearing. Unless excluded from the proceedings by the tribunal, the applicant, the patient (where he or she is not the applicant) and the responsible authority have the right to give evidence to the tribunal, to hear each other's evidence, to put questions to each other, to call witnesses, and to question any witness or other person appearing before the tribunal. The patient has an additional right to a private interview with the tribunal in the presence of his or her representative.

The approved social worker plays an important role in tribunal hearings. The relevant authority—in practice the approved social worker—is required by law (unless it is not reasonably practicable) to provide an up-to-date social circumstances report on (*a*) the patient's home and family circumstances, including the attitude of the patient's nearest relative or the person so acting, (*b*) the opportunities for employment or occupation and the housing facilities that would be available to the patient if discharged, (*c*) the availability of community support and relevant medical facilities, and (*d*) the financial circumstances of the patient. He or she must also give his or her views on the suitability of the patient for discharge. (See rule 6 of the Mental Health Review Tribunal (Northern Ireland) Rules 1986.)

The approved social worker attends the hearing and will answer questions on his or her report and other matters raised at the tribunal. The tribunal will be particularly interested in finding out whether the patient if discharged could be easily transferred into the community, if there is a suitable place of residence for the patient, and the nature of community care that would be available.

Once all the witnesses have been called and the evidence has been adduced, the applicant or his or her representative is given the opportunity to make a final submission to the tribunal. The tribunal's decision is reached by a majority vote, and it must be communicated to the parties within fourteen days of the hearing.

In 1993/94 the tribunal considered 41 applications and discharged patients in 8 of these cases. (See Report of the Mental Health Review Tribunal for the year ended 31 March 1994.)

7.10 Further Reading

Department of Health and Social Services, *Guide to the Mental Health (Northern Ireland) Order, 1986*.

Department of Health and Social Services, *Mental Health (Northern Ireland) Order, 1986: Code of Practice*.

Gostin, Larry, *Mental Health Services: Law and Practice*, London: Shaw and Sons (updated annually).

Gostin, Larry, and Fennell, Phil, *Mental Health Tribunal Procedure* (2nd edition), London: Longman Practitioner Series 1992.

Hoggett, Brenda, *Mental Health Law*, London: Sweet and Maxwell (3rd edition) 1995.

Jones, Richard, *Mental Health Act Manual*, London: Sweet and Maxwell 1994.

Northern Ireland Mental Health Commission, Biannual Reports, HMSO.

Northern Ireland Psychiatric Census Data, 1992.

Prior, P., *Mental Health and Politics in Nothern Ireland*, Avebury Press, 1993.

8

VULNERABLE PEOPLE

Brian Collins

8.1 *Introduction*

The purpose of this chapter is to examine the obligations imposed on the Health and Social Services Boards (and latterly on the Health and Social Services Trusts—see below) in respect of the client groups mentioned below. We have borrowed the collective term 'vulnerable people' from the authors of one of the main English textbooks, Brayne and Martin (*Law for Social Workers*, 3rd edition), to describe these groups. In particular we examine how such obligations should be discharged and the remedies that are available to clients who feel that they are not receiving the services to which they are entitled.

There are many groups of people that could be classified as 'vulnerable'. The common characteristic of all such groups is that their members are in need of particular types of assistance, more so than other members of the community. The vulnerable groups that we examine in this chapter are:

(1) chronically sick and disabled people;
(2) the elderly;
(3) people with learning difficulties;
(4) 'children in need'.

The extent of these groups is explained below (see 8.2), but it is necessary to make a few introductory remarks about the scope of this chapter before proceeding further. The law relating to child care and protection is dealt with in chapter 6. Here we outline the law relating to children who require the provision of services because of some special educational need or in order to improve their health or development. Also people suffering from long-term or short-term mental disability, disorder or illness fall within the definition of the chronically sick and disabled group, and what is said with respect to that group applies to them. However, the law relating to their assessment for treatment is dealt with in chapter 7.

The bodies responsible for the provision of services to vulnerable people, with the exception in certain instances of people with learning difficulties, are the four Health and Social Service Boards (set up under the Health and Personal Social Services (Northern Ireland) Order 1972). However, the management and delivery of health and personal social services in Northern Ireland underwent considerable change recently, in line with current government policy, and continues to undergo change. These changes have been brought about by the Health and Personal Social Services (Northern Ireland) Order 1991, and the Health and Personal Social Services (Northern Ireland) Order 1994, which created the 'purchaser-provider' split between the Boards and the Trusts. Boards are now responsible for assessing the health and social welfare needs of their resident populations and for commissioning services to meet those needs. The relationship between the Directly Managed Units (DMUs) formerly known as the local units of management, some of which have been established as Health and Social Services Trusts, and the Boards will be, henceforth, based on contracts.

The responsibilities of Trusts include the discharge of statutory functions delegated to them by the Boards. As each Trust is a legal entity separate from the Boards, it can be challenged in court where it is alleged that it is unsatisfactorily discharging functions delegated to it.

A number of functions have recently been delegated to Trusts. The important functions so far delegated are:

(1) the provision of personal social services to people in need (Health and Personal Social Services (Northern Ireland) Order 1972, article 15);
(2) the provision of accommodation and the protection of the property of people accommodated (Health and Personal Social Services (Northern Ireland) Order 1972, articles 37 and 38);
(3) disseminating information to and making social welfare services available to chronically sick and disabled people (Chronically Sick and Disabled Persons (Northern Ireland) Act 1978, sections 1 (2) and 2);
(4) the appointment and rights of authorised representatives of disabled people (Disabled Persons (Northern Ireland) Act 1989, sections 1 and 2*);
(5) assessment of the needs of and provision of services to disabled people and those leaving special education (Disabled Persons (Northern Ireland) Act 1989, sections 3, 4, and 5*);
(6) consideration of the ability of carers for disabled people (Disabled Persons (Northern Ireland) Act 1989, section 8*).

* Only sections 4 (except 4 (*b*)), 5 and 8 are in force at present.

For people with learning difficulties, additional responsibilities are owed by the relevant Education and Library Board.

The obligations imposed on Boards and Trusts by legislation can be classified as absolute, conditional, or discretionary. Where an obligation is absolute it must be carried out by the authority on whom it is imposed, irrespective of the difficulty in complying with it. If a Board or Trust fails to carry out an absolute duty it may be forced to do so by an aggrieved person applying to court for judicial review (see chapter 1).

If a duty is conditional, for example requiring the authority to do something 'so far as is reasonably practicable,' it need only be performed to the extent that the condition can be fulfilled. However, the authority will not be the sole arbiter of what is 'reasonably practicable': the High Court can, in a judicial review action, assess an authority's decision on this point, questioning whether the decision was unreasonable or made for the wrong purposes or whether all relevant considerations had been taken into account before the authority arrived at its decision.

Where a statutory provision confers a discretion on an authority, this is referred to as a 'power', and the authority to which it is granted decides whether it should be exercised. The usual form that powers take is a statement that a person 'may' perform a certain function. A failure to carry out a power can also be challenged in judicial review: it would of course be particularly difficult to successfully challenge such a failure, although should the authority to which the power is granted decide to carry it out, an action could be brought for damage, injury or loss resulting from its negligent discharge. Exactly what the Board or Trust is required to do depends on the wording of the legislative provision. It is wise, therefore, to be aware of the legislative requirements when offering advice to or advocating on behalf of clients.

One last introductory point: the law in Northern Ireland differs considerably from that applicable in Great Britain, both in its legislative basis and its substantive content. Northern Ireland residents do not have the same rights to community care that those in Great Britain have. The function of this chapter is to describe and explain the legislative basis for the provision of health and social services care in Northern Ireland rather than to be a comprehensive guide to the policy and practice in this area of social work.

8.2 *Statutory Framework for Provision of Services*

Here we briefly refer to the legislation governing these services and provide definitions of the groups. The key pieces of legislation relating to the provision of services for people suffering from physical impairments, such as blindness or deafness, or permanent or long-term substantial 'handicap' are the Health and Personal Social Services (Northern Ireland) Order 1972 (hereafter referred to as HPSS72), as amended by the Health and Personal Social Services (Northern Ireland) Order 1991 (hereafter

HPSS91), and the Chronically Sick and Disabled Persons (Northern Ireland) Act 1978 (hereafter CSDP78), as amended by the Disabled Persons (Northern Ireland) Act 1989 (hereafter DP89).

The 1972 and 1991 Orders do not deal solely with the chronically sick and disabled but with the provision of personal social services and the promotion of social welfare for the public in general. (Be aware that not all the provisions of HPSS91 or DP89 are yet in force. Where this is the case we will mention that fact.)

Unlike the law in Great Britain, there are no statutory provisions in Northern Ireland that relate exclusively to elderly people, although provisions of various pieces of legislation, such as HPSS72 (as amended), apply to them.

For people with learning difficulties the law is contained mainly in the Education and Libraries (Northern Ireland) Order 1986, as amended by the 1987 Order of the same name (hereafter EL86 and EL87, respectively). The Chronically Sick and Disabled legislation mentioned above can also be relevant for people with learning difficulties, because it also applies to children who are disabled.

In the case of 'children in need' the relevant provisions are contained in the Children (Northern Ireland) Order 1995. A degree of overlap between the various categories of people is also possible. Obviously some of the rights of disabled children are dealt with in the Chronically Sick and Disabled Persons legislation, and people with learning difficulties who are impaired in other ways may also be entitled to rights governed by that legislation.

The most important legislation relating to the accommodation of vulnerable people is HPSS72 and the Registered Homes (Northern Ireland) Order 1992. The 1972 Order deals with both voluntary and compulsory admissions to residential accommodation, while the 1992 Order deals with residential care homes and nursing homes.

8.2.1 *The Chronically Sick and Disabled*

Chronically sick and disabled people are defined by section 1 (1) of CSDP78, as amended, as people who are 'blind, deaf or dumb and others who are substantially handicapped due to illness, injury or congenital deformity and whose handicap is either permanent or lasting and those suffering from a mental disorder as defined in the Mental Health (Northern Ireland) Order 1986.'

8.2.2 *The Elderly*

Because there are no specific statutory provisions in Northern Ireland dealing exclusively with elderly people, there is no statutory definition of the term 'elderly'. Elderly people are, of course, entitled to the same welfare services as the chronically sick and disabled and/or the mentally ill if they satisfy one or more of the criteria specified in section 1 of CSDP78 or article 3 of the Mental Health (Northern Ireland) Order 1986. The only statutory reference to them is in the definition of 'persons in need' in the 1972 Order, which states that that expression includes persons in need of care and attention because of age.

8.2.3 *People with Learning Difficulties*

Article 29 of EL86 imposes a general duty on a Board to identify and assess children within its area who have special educational needs and children who the board thinks have, or probably have, special educational needs. 'Special educational needs', defined in article 33 of the Order, are needs that a child has when he or she has a learning difficulty as a result of which they require special educational provision to be made available. A child is deemed to have a learning difficulty if any of the three following conditions are satisfied:

(1) the child has a significantly greater difficulty in learning than the majority of children of the same age;
(2) the child has a disability that prevents or hinders him or her from using educational facilities of a kind generally provided for children of the same age at ordinary schools;
(3) the child is currently under five years of age and would, after reaching that age, be likely to fall within one of the above two categories if special educational provision was not made for him or her. (Special educational provision is defined as educational provision that is additional to, or different from, that provided in ordinary schools for children of the child's age.)

8.2.4 *Children in Need*

'Children in need' is a categorisation created by the Children (Northern Ireland) Order 1995, which has no counterpart in the Children and Young Persons Act (Northern Ireland) 1968. However, under section 103 of the 1968 Act a Board/Trust has a duty to care for children who have neither parent nor guardian, who have been lost or abandoned or whose parents or guardians are, for the time being or permanently, prevented 'by reason of mental or bodily disease or infirmity or other incapacity, or any other circumstances, from providing for his or her proper accommodation, maintenance and upbringing' (see chapter 6). When we discuss the law with respect to 'children in need' in this chapter we will deal in turn with children governed by the existing law, the 1968 Act, and the future law, the 1995 Order. For an explanation of the relationship of these two pieces of legislation, see 6.1.

A child in need is one who satisfies one of the following three criteria contained in article 17 of the Children (Northern Ireland) Order 1995:

(1) the child is unable to achieve or maintain a reasonable standard of health or development without being provided with personal social services;
(2) the child's health or development is likely to be significantly impaired if he or she is not provided with personal social services; or
(3) the child is disabled (within the definition of 'disabled' in section 1 of CSDP78).

8.3 Assessment

8.3.1 *The Chronically Sick and Disabled*

Assessment of the needs of the chronically sick and disabled is provided for in section 1 of CSDP78. It provides that when the department has informed itself of the number and identity of chronically sick and disabled people (as it has a duty to do), it must assess the needs of those people in order to be in a position to provide adequate services and thereby promote their social welfare. This means that Boards and Trusts are under a duty to collect and maintain confidential information relating to the name, address, age and types of impairment of people who are living within their area; the purpose of this is of course to formulate plans for the development of personal social services. The way in which the relevant information is collected and maintained is a matter for the Board or Trust to decide, and good social work practice should be to publicise as widely as possible, in places frequently used by the chronically sick and disabled, the definition of the criteria in section 1 of the Act. Places where this information could be usefully displayed include hospitals, health centres, and surgeries. Adequate publicity should also be given to the criteria for being registered with the Board/Trusts as chronically sick and disabled, although it should be remembered that there is no legal requirement for a person to be registered in order to qualify for a service. The process of collecting and maintaining the relevant information should be a continuing one, and boards and trusts should ensure that their records are updated regularly.

A Board/Trust is under a duty when requested to do so, either by a disabled person or by a person providing care for a disabled person who is living at home, to decide whether the needs of the disabled person are such that the services specified in section 2 of CSDP78 should be made available to him or her. (For details of these services see 8.4.1.) DP89 also allows for a request for assessment to be made by the disabled person's authorised representative, but so far the sections relating to the authorised representative have not been implemented. The position of disabled people is further weakened by the failure so far to implement section 3 of the 1989 Act, which deals with referrals for assessment and the rights of disabled people during the assessment process. If these sections were implemented, disabled people would enjoy a number of important rights, such as the right to make representations as disabled people concerning their needs, the right to be supplied at their request with a written assessment (or one in an otherwise accessible form) of their needs, and the right to question the decisions arrived at by a Board/Trust. There is no doubt that most, if not all, of these procedures are at present employed by Boards and Trusts when carrying out needs assessments, but it would be advantageous and correct for disabled people to be entitled to them as of right. Indeed the *Guide to Good Practice on the Disabled Persons (Northern Ireland) Act, 1989*, produced by the Health and Social Services Boards, sets out that Boards should abide by section 3 even though it is not in force.

While the nature of a needs assessment has not been defined in any of the relevant legislation, it is clear from section 2 of CSDP78 that all disabled people have a right to a comprehensive assessment, which must be carried out within a reasonable time of its being requested. Failure to do so can be remedied by the disabled person, or his or her carer, applying for judicial review to compel the board or trust to carry out its statutory functions. It is a matter for the Board or Trust to decide the factors that should be considered during an assessment procedure, but good practice would dictate that it include examination of such matters as the person's physical, mental and social abilities, the person's ability to provide for himself or herself, the person's own views, life style, risk factors involved, and the need for support for carers, if relevant. The disabled person and his or her carer should be invited to attend, and their views should be taken into account.

8.3.2 *The Elderly*

As mentioned above, the elderly are not treated as a distinct client group in the legislation, although article 15 (2) of HPSS72 is so broadly framed as to allow any elderly person to be assessed for need by a Board or Trust—although it should be mentioned that there is no specific legal obligation on a Board or Trust to do so. However, there is a general obligation on the department, under article 4 (*b*) of the 1972 Order, to provide personal social services to promote the social welfare of the general public, and in the provision of such social services, as mentioned above, assistance may be provided to people in need. On this general basis elderly people should be assessed for need.

Here again the form of the needs assessment and the considerations to be taken into account in such an assessment are matters for a Board or Trust. We remind you that if an elderly person satisfies any of the criteria of the definition of chronically sick and disabled people (see 8.2.1), that person thereby becomes entitled to a comprehensive needs assessment as of right under section 2 of the Act, and the comments made above obviously apply in that situation.

8.3.3 *People with Learning Difficulties*

Each Education and Library Board is under a duty to carry out an assessment of the children in its area who it believes have, or probably have, special educational needs (EL86, article 29). The detailed provisions relating to the form of the assessment and the rights and obligations of the participants are specified in part 1 of schedule 11 to the 1986 Order.

8.3.3.1 Where the Board Wishes to Assess

Where a Board is proposing to make an assessment of a person with learning difficulties, it is under a duty to notify a parent in writing (*a*) that it intends to make an assessment, (*b*) how the assessment will be carried out, (*c*) of the name of an officer of the board from whom further information may be obtained, and (*d*) of the right to make representations to the board.

A parent has twenty-nine days from receipt of the notification from the Board to make representations and submit any relevant evidence to the Board, which is then under a duty to consider all such matters in coming to its decision whether or not to assess the child. The Board's decision must be notified to the parent, and if it has decided to carry out the assessment the reasons for its decision must be given. A notice must then be served on the parent informing him or her of (*a*) the time and place at which the examination will be held, (*b*) the purpose of the examination, (*c*) the name of the officer of the Board from whom further information may be obtained, (*d*) the right to submit information to the Board, and (*e*) the right to be present at the examination.

In the assessment the Board must consider educational, medical and psychological advice from appropriate people and also any other relevant advice. This gives the parent the opportunity to ensure that the Board considers matters such as advice from any speech therapist, physiotherapist or other expert who may be working with the child. On the basis of all the advice available, the Board will decide whether to make a statement in respect of the child. If the Board has decided that it is not necessary to carry out an assessment, the parents must be notified in writing and also informed of their right to appeal against this decision to the department, which may direct the Board to reconsider its decision.

8.3.3.2 Where the Parent Wishes an Assessment to Be Made

Parents have the right, in certain cases, to request the Board to carry out an assessment of their child's needs. If such a request is made in respect of a child for whom no statement is already in existence, the Board must comply with it, except if it considers it to be unreasonable. In the case of a child in respect of whom a statement is currently maintained by the Board, the parents' request must be complied with, except where such an assessment has been carried out in the previous six months or where the Board thinks that an assessment would be 'inappropriate'. It is up to the Board to determine the unreasonableness or inappropriateness of the requested assessment. If the child is under the age of two, he or she must be assessed if the parents so request.

8.3.3.3 The Role of the Health and Social Services Boards

Health and Social Services Boards have a specific role to play in relation to those children under the age of two and those aged between three and five (EL86, article 36). If a Board that is exercising any functions on behalf of a child under five believes that the child has, or probably has, special educational needs, it is under a duty to inform the parents of its opinion; and, having given them an opportunity to discuss the matter with an officer of the Board, it must bring it to the attention of the appropriate Education and Library Board. There is also a duty on the Board to inform the parents of the existence and work of any voluntary organisation that it considers could be of assistance in dealing with the child's special educational needs.

The assessment procedure for children under the age of two is quite different from that used for older children. It can take whatever form the Board considers appropriate, and if the Board decides to make and maintain a statement for that child it can do so in whatever form it considers appropriate. An Education and Library Board can initiate the assessment procedure with regard to children over the age of two. The procedure is usually as described above.

There is also an obligation on the Education and Library Board to inform the relevant Health and Social Services Board of any person who is about to leave, or has just left, school and who, because of his or her physical, intellectual, emotional or social development, requires further care, treatment, or supervision. The Health Board can then request the Education Board to let it have all relevant information concerning that person, and the Health and Social Services Board or Trust then assumes responsibility for carrying out a needs assessment and deciding, on the results of that assessment, whether he or she should be provided with relevant social welfare services.

8.3.3.4 Disabled Children with Special Educational Needs

It is possible that a child who has special educational needs may also be disabled, and the needs assessment for the provision of social welfare for such children is dealt with by section 5 of DP89. This means that where an Education and Library Board has assessed a child under the age of fourteen as having special educational needs, it is under a duty to request an opinion from an 'appropriate officer' (who would usually be the Senior Clinical Medical Officer) as to whether or not the child is disabled. This assessment should be carried out during the child's fifteenth year. If the child is assessed as being disabled, the Education and Library Board must inform the appropriate Health and Social Services Board or Trust of this fact (at least eight months before the child is due to leave full-time education), together with details of the known disability, to enable the Board or Trust to arrange for an assessment of the child's needs. Arrangements for such assessment should be put in place before the child leaves school, and there should be full consultation with the child, the parents or members of the family, carers, and those with direct responsibility for the care of the child. Account should be taken of their views.

The assessment of the child's needs should be carried out within five months of receiving the notification from the Education and Library Board. This obligation does not apply in cases where it later transpires that the child is not leaving full-time education or if the child's parents, or the child, if over sixteen, request that an assessment not be made.

8.3.4 *Children in Need*

Though no formal system of assessment is provided for in order to deem a child to be 'in need', it will be necessary for the Health and Social Services authorities to conduct some sort of inquiry. Under the Children (Northern Ireland) Order 1995, there is no formal requirement for the needs of children to be assessed in the same way as, for example, people with learning difficulties.

Once it has been established that a child satisfies one of the three criteria of the definition of a child in need (see 8.2.4), that child becomes entitled to whatever services are necessary to safeguard and promote his or her welfare. (For information regarding services see 8.4.4.) As will be seen later, in certain cases it is not necessary to be 'in need' to be provided with some services. The assessment of disabled children aged fourteen who have special educational needs is explained in 8.3.3.4.

8.4 *Services*

8.4.1 *The Chronically Sick and Disabled*

Details of the services to which this client group are entitled are provided in article 15 of HPSS72. It provides that the department must make available to people in need 'advice, guidance and assistance' and that such provision must include facilities such as residential accommodation, home help, and laundry facilities. These services are to be provided 'to such extent as the Department considers necessary,' and the facilities to be provided are those that 'it considers suitable and adequate.' In practice it is the Board or Trust that will determine the facilities that should be provided, as those mentioned are only the minimum and indicative of the type to be provided, and in many situations different facilities will be required. The assistance that may be provided obviously depends on the person's needs and may include, for example, the provision of some form of assistance in, or adaptation of, the home. In an emergency the assistance can take the form of cash, but this is only available where no other adequate source of money is available to the person.

In addition to these general duties, further duties are imposed on the department, under section 2 of CSDP78, to provide specific social welfare facilities to those in need. These are:

(1) providing practical assistance for the person in his or her home;
(2) giving assistance in obtaining, or the actual provision of, radio, television, library or similar recreational facilities, or a telephone together with any necessary special equipment for its use by the person;
(3) providing lectures, games, outings or other recreational facilities outside the person's home or assisting him or her in taking advantage of educational facilities;
(4) providing or assisting in the provision of travelling facilities to enable the person to participate in social welfare services provided by the Board or similar services provided by other organisations;
(5) providing assistance to the person in carrying out suitable adaptation of the home or providing additional facilities in the home to ensure more safety, comfort, or convenience;

(6) providing meals, either in the home or elsewhere;
(7) facilitating the person in taking holidays;
(8) providing assistance in obtaining a telephone.

It is of course accepted and good social work practice for Boards and Trusts to make the listed services available to groups other than those strictly entitled to them, but they are not under an obligation to do so. The department is also required (under CSDP78, section 1 (2)) to publish general information about the services currently available for chronically sick and disabled people, and any person who uses such services must be informed about other appropriate services available from the department, other government departments, public bodies, and voluntary organisations.

8.4.2 *The Elderly*

Because there are no specific statutory provisions that deal with the entitlement of the elderly, as a group, to social welfare rights in Northern Ireland, their rights are not as comprehensive as those enjoyed by other vulnerable groups. The rights to which they are entitled are contained in articles 4 and 15 of HPSS72 if they qualify as people 'in need' and are exactly the same as those that apply to the chronically sick and disabled above, and therefore the comments made in 8.4.1 apply here also. The provisions of CSDP78 and DP89 do not apply to elderly people unless, once again, they satisfy one of the criteria in section 1 of the earlier Act.

8.4.3 *People with Learning Difficulties*

Where a Board has decided, having carried out a valid assessment, that a statement should be made in respect of the special educational needs of a child, it must comply with the procedure specified in part 2 of schedule 2 to EL86. Before making the statement the Board must deliver a copy of the proposed statement (usually by post or by sending an educational welfare officer to deliver it) to the child's parents, together with written information about their rights to make further representations to the Board and to object to the making or the contents of the proposed statement.

The parents have fifteen days to make representations to the Board about the contents of the statement, and they can insist on the Board arranging a meeting with an officer of the Board to discuss the matter. If they are still not satisfied they can, within another fifteen days, request the Board to arrange a further meeting or meetings with the person whose advice given during the assessment they disagree with. They are then entitled, within a further fifteen days, to make their final representations, after which the Board decides whether it is still going to make a statement, and if so what its contents are to be.

The parents must be notified of the Board's final decision in writing. Where a statement is being made, the Board must provide the parents with a copy of the statement, details of their right to appeal to the department against the statement, and the name of the person from whom they can get advice and information about their child's special educational needs. The form of the statement, as specified in the 1986 Order, should be as follows:

(1) introduction mentioning the child's name, address, and so forth;
(2) an explanation or description of the special educational needs of the child as found in the assessment;
(3) the details of the special provision the Board intends to make to meet those needs;
(4) the type, and if appropriate the name, of the school the child should attend;
(5) any additional non-educational provision, such as speech therapy and so forth.

A number of appendices are usually added to the statement, dealing with such matters as parental representations and evidence, educational and medical advice, and information provided by the Health and Social Services Board. It is important to emphasise that the statement represents the Board's acceptance of responsibility to meet the needs of the child as found in the assessment, and the Board is under a duty to make the provision specified in the statement.

The section of the statement dealing with the special provisions the Board intends to make should detail such matters as facilities and equipment to be made available, the curriculum to be followed—with emphasis on the areas of weakness, such as, for example, social and personal development—and any relevant staffing arrangements. Once a statement has been made, the services being provided under the statement must be reviewed annually by the Board, which is empowered to maintain or amend the statement or to cease its effect. If either of the latter two actions is taken the parents must be notified in writing and are once again entitled, within fifteen days, to make representations to the Board. The Board must take such representations into account and must inform the parents in writing of its decision.

A Board may of course decide as the result of an original assessment, or a review of one, not to make a statement, in which case it is declaring that the child has not got special educational needs. Should parents disagree with the Board's decision not to make, or maintain, a statement, they are entitled to appeal against the decision to the department, which has the power to direct the Board to reconsider its decision. If a Board refuses, without justification, to assess a child, or having so assessed a child refuses to make a statement when it is clear that a statement should be made, the parents may be entitled to apply for judicial review of such refusal.

8.4.4 *Children in Need*

A Board/Trust has a duty to children taken into its care under section 103 of the Children and Young Persons Act 1968, to use its powers to 'further the best interests of the child' and 'provide opportunities for the proper development of his character and abilities' (section 113). In other words, the Board/Trust has a duty to use all its powers to create the opportunity to allow the child to develop his or her character, potential and skills to the fullest possible extent. This duty requires it to provide information and assistance in relation to any available services outside the scope of the Board/Trust, for example social security benefits, job training, and schooling (section 113 (2)). Those under the age of eighteen who were in care must be advised and befriended by the Board/Trust, unless it is satisfied that their welfare does not require it. The Board/Trust has a discretion to assist a young person by providing him or her with hostel accommodation and financial assistance for upkeep and education, or to assist with employment training by acting as guarantors for apprenticeship deeds in 'articles of deedship' (section 124).

When examining the services to which children in need are entitled under the Children (Northern Ireland) Order 1995, one must be aware that the legislation divides such children into two categories: children who are being looked after by the Board or Trust and those who are not. (Any child who is in the care of a Board or Trust or who is being provided with accommodation by a Board or Trust for a continuous period of more than twenty-four hours is being 'looked after' (Children (Northern Ireland) Order, 1995, article 25).) For each category there are both general and specific duties imposed on the Boards and Trusts. However, it should be mentioned that while these duties are spelt out quite specifically in the legislation, the Boards and Trusts are given a very large degree of discretion and flexibility in relation to their discharge.

8.4.4.1 Children Not Being Looked After by a Board or Trust

There are two general duties and a number of specific duties imposed on a Board with regard to these children. The first general duty is to safeguard and promote the welfare of children in need in its area, while the second is that in so doing it must promote the upbringing of those children by their families by providing an appropriate range and level of services.

The second of these two distinct but related duties means that Boards and Trusts must provide not only an appropriate range of personal social services but must provide them at appropriate levels. Obviously the appropriate levels depend on the degree of need of each of the children involved, and this is likely to be different from case to case. It is also interesting to note that it is specifically stated that the latter duty is to promote the upbringing of the child by the family, and therefore services may be made directly available not only to children themselves but also to members of the family. Of course the provision of such services must be with a view to safeguarding and promoting the welfare of the child. The term 'family' has been given an extended meaning for the purposes of this legislation and includes any person who has parental responsibility (see chapter 6) for the child and any person with whom the child has been living.

To facilitate the Board or Trust in carrying out its general duties, schedule 2 to the Children (Northern Ireland) Order details the powers and duties that are available in this regard. Before we examine them, however, it should be pointed out that from the long list of powers and duties mentioned, only two are 'absolute' duties; the remainder are 'conditional' duties. (See 8.1 for an explanation of these terms.) The duties are couched in such terms that the only case in which a successful action against a Board or Trust would be guaranteed would be its complete failure to carry out these duties at all. Indeed it may be possible to argue that even in respect of those duties that are absolute, the whole tenor of the schedule is such that all its provisions should be regarded as being discretionary.

The duties that are owed under the schedule include the following:

(1) to take reasonable steps to identify the children in need within an area;
(2) to publish information about the services available to such children by the Boards and Trusts and, where it is considered appropriate, the provision of services by other bodies, including voluntary organisations;
(3) to take such steps as are reasonably practicable to ensure that those who might benefit from the services available receive information about them;
(4) to maintain a register of disabled children within an area and to provide services that will minimise the effect of their disablement on them and give them an opportunity to live as normal a life as possible;
(5) to assess the needs of children; such assessment may be carried out at the same time as the child is being assessed for another purpose, for example an assessment under the special educational needs procedure;
(6) to take reasonable steps to provide services to prevent children suffering ill-treatment or neglect;

(7) to provide services in support of children in need who are living with their own families, including, for example, advice, guidance, and counselling; occupational, social, cultural and recreational activities; and home help facilities and assistance to enable the child and his or her family to take a holiday;
(8) to take such steps as are reasonably practicable to promote contact between children and their families when they are living apart to enable them to rejoin their families.

Other duties relate to the provision of day care and accommodation. In respect of day care, Boards and Trusts must provide, as appropriate, day care for children in need up to the age of eight who are not yet attending school, and they have the power to provide the same for children who satisfy the age and school criteria but who are not in need.

It may also be significant that the article does not state that these services should be provided by the Board or Trust as it considers appropriate. Were this to be the case it seems reasonable to assume that the legislation would have said so. It may be that a Board or Trust may be challenged in respect of the level and scope of day care services provided by it or on its behalf. Boards also have the power, but not the duty, to provide training, guidance and similar facilities for those directly involved in providing day care facilities. As with day care, there is a duty to provide care and supervised activities for school-going children in need outside school hours and during school holidays, and a power to provide them for children not in need. It is worth noting that the wording here is the same as in relation to day care, and therefore perhaps a challenge could be brought on the same grounds.

Finally in relation to day care there is a duty on Boards and Trusts to review at periodic intervals the current provision of day care and child minding services.

8.4.4.2 Children Being Looked After by a Board or Trust

As mentioned above, there are both general and specific duties imposed on the Boards and Trusts when dealing with children who are being looked after by a Board or Trust.

Boards and Trusts are required to safeguard and promote the welfare of the children they are looking after. In doing so they are entitled to make use of the same services as those available to the category above (see 8.4.4.1). The Board/Trust is also under a duty before making any decision relating to a child, so far as is reasonably practicable, to ascertain the wishes and feelings of the child, the parents, any person having parental responsibility for the child, and any other person whose feelings and wishes the Board/Trust considers to be relevant. In coming to any such decision the Board/Trust is under an obligation to consider a number of factors, such as the wishes and feelings of the people mentioned above and also the child's religious persuasion, racial origin, and cultural and linguistic background. However, the Board/Trust may disregard all these duties if it believes it is necessary to do so to protect members of the public from serious injury. Indeed, if the department is of the view that it is necessary in order to protect members of the public against such serious injury, it may direct the Board/Trust as to how it should exercise its powers.

Contact between children and their families is beneficial for both parties, and the Children (Northern Ireland) Order 1995 recognises this by requiring the Boards to promote contact between children and their families by taking reasonable steps to inform the child's parents and any other person having parental responsibility for the child of the child's address. Parents and those having parental responsibility are required to keep the Board/Trust informed of their address (Children (Northern Ireland) Order 1995, article 29). Failure to do so is a criminal offence.

To ensure that children do not become isolated by parents who do not maintain contact, Boards may appoint an independent person to visit, advise and befriend any child who has not been visited by a parent or person having parental responsibility during the previous twelve months or who only receives infrequent visits (Children (Northern Ireland) Order, 1995, article 31). A child who is of 'sufficient understanding' to make an informed decision may object to any such appointment being made.

Finally, a Board or Trust's duties with respect to a child continue to some degree after the child's time in care. Boards/Trusts are required to advise, assist and befriend children to prepare them for the time when they cease to be looked after by the Board/Trust (Children (Northern Ireland) Order, 1995, article 35). (The department can make regulations governing reviews of cases of children being looked after by Boards and Trusts (Children (Northern Ireland) Order, 1995, article 45).)

8.5 *Accommodation*

8.5.1 *The Chronically Sick and Disabled*

As mentioned above, article 4 of HPSS72 specifies the general duties owed by a Board to members of the general public (see 8.3.2), while article 15 deals with the way in which those duties should be discharged. The latter article states that the Board or Trust must make available to people in need such facilities as they require, and specifically must provide for or arrange residential or other accommodation as the Board or Trust considers 'suitable and adequate'.

There is no doubt that to the extent that people who are chronically sick and/or disabled are entitled to be provided with personal social services they have the same rights to be provided with accommodation if they require it. However, there is no legislative explanation of the criteria that should be applied to identify the people who should be entitled to accommodation, and there is also a lack of clear statutory guidelines. Article 15 (2) of the Order provides that assistance may be given to people in need, and it seems reasonable to assume that such people should fall into the category of people possibly requiring accommodation. The definition of 'person in need' includes a person who is in need of care and attention because of infirmity or age, a person who is suffering from illness or is substantially handicapped by any deformity or disability, or a person who is homeless and in need of temporary accommodation. It is clear that people who are chronically sick and/or disabled (as defined in section 1 of CSDP78) come within the first two categories of this definition.

In the absence of statutory admission criteria, each Board or Trust has adopted its own, although the extent to which they vary from each other is slight. It would nevertheless be preferable if standard criteria were to be adopted by all the Boards. While acknowledging the difficulty of specifying precise conditions, the admission criteria of the Eastern Health and Social Services Board state that the factors that should be taken into consideration include an assessment of (*a*) the needs and wishes of the client, which should be of primary importance, (*b*) the range of service options available elsewhere, and (*c*) the capability of the residence to meet the needs of the client.

In addition there are a number of 'positive' and 'negative' indicators that are also taken into account in assessing suitability for admission. Examples of positive indicators are clients whose needs cannot be met in the community and for whom other forms of care are inappropriate; clients who are willing to accept the benefits and constraints of communal living; and clients who have the ability to attend to their personal hygiene, dress themselves, feed themselves and bath and use the toilet independently or with limited amounts of assistance and supervision. Examples of negative indicators are clients who are aggressive or display other antisocial behaviour to a level where it would be disruptive to others, clients who require a level of nursing or medical care that can be more appropriately provided elsewhere, and clients with problems of incontinence.

For the application to be considered by the residential accommodation panel, you must ensure that the appropriate documents (the social report, the medical report, and the 'declaration of means' forms) are completed. These are forwarded to the panel that will decide, on the basis of these forms and the above criteria, on admission. You, as the social worker involved, will be informed of the panel's decision. There is no statutory mechanism to be invoked if a person wishes to challenge a decision of the panel to refuse admission to accommodation, and as long as the admission criteria and factors to be considered are applied fairly and properly, the only possible way to challenge such a decision would be to apply for judicial review. It is possible that an applicant might, subject to the availability of places, be placed on a waiting list, and if such lists are operated by the Board they should be reviewed at least every six months.

8.5.1.1 Privately Provided Accommodation

Provision of accommodation for chronically sick and disabled people can be made other than by the Boards and Trusts. Boards and Trusts can make arrangements for accommodation to be provided by a voluntary organisation, a residential care home, a nursing home, or a private individual (HPSS72, article 36).

Residential care homes and nursing homes are defined in articles 3 and 16, respectively, of the Registered Homes (Northern Ireland) Order 1992, which legislation governs their operation. A residential care home is a place that provides residential accommodation with both board and personal care for people in need of them because of old age and infirmity, disablement, past or present dependence on alcohol or drugs, or past or present mental disorder. The term 'disablement' is also defined in the Order to cover people who are 'substantially and permanently handicapped by illness, injury, congenital deformity, sensory impairment or any other prescribed disability.'

Any person who wishes to run a residential care home must be registered (under article 6 of the 1992 Order), and failure to register is a criminal offence, for which the person concerned may be fined. Each Board is under a duty to keep a register of residential care homes within its area, and this must contain all relevant information. Applications for registration are made to the Board, which can refuse to register an applicant if it is satisfied that the applicant is not a fit person to carry on, or be employed at, the home, or if the premises are not fit to be used as a residential care home, or if the method of running the home does not enable the necessary services or facilities to be provided. The Board is entitled to issue the certificate of registration subject to whatever conditions it considers appropriate, for example conditions regulating the age, sex or category of people who may be received in the home; and the registration certificate will specify the number of people for whom accommodation, board and personal care may be provided in that home.

The Board may also cancel the registration of a person running such a home on a number of grounds, such as conviction for an offence in respect of this or any other residential or nursing home. A Board may apply for an urgent cancellation, or modifications of the conditions of a registration, by making an application to a justice of the peace. If it appears to the justice that there is a serious risk to the lives, health or well-being of the residents, he or she may make the order requested. If such an order is made the Board must serve on the person concerned a notice of the order, a copy of the Board's reasons for applying for the order, and information on the right of appeal by the person on whom the order has been served. An appeal lies against such a decision to the Registered Homes Tribunal but must be made within twenty-eight days.

A nursing home is defined as 'any premises which are used to receive and to provide nursing for persons who are suffering from any illness, injury or infirmity,' a maternity home, and premises that are used to provide certain services, namely 'the carrying out of surgical procedures under anaesthesia, endoscopy, haemodialysis or peritoneal dialysis or treatment by specially controlled techniques.' Certain premises where similar services can be provided, such as those used by a doctor for the purpose of treating his or her patients, do not come within the definition. There are similar provisions in relation to registration, refusal and cancellation (ordinary or urgent) of registration by the Boards and to appeals procedure as apply in the case of residential care homes. Also, detailed regulations relating to such matters as the conduct of homes, the facilities and services to be provided by them and inspection procedures have been made in the Residential Care Homes Regulations (Northern Ireland) 1993, and the Nursing Homes Regulations (Northern Ireland) 1993.

Finally, in relation to the chronically sick and disabled and the elderly, compulsory admission to residential care is possible (HPSS72, article 37 and schedule 6). In this case the social worker involved will start the process for admission. The social worker must ensure that any person who is to be compulsorily admitted is (*a*) suffering from a grave chronic disease or is aged, infirm or physically handicapped and (*b*) living in unsanitary conditions and unable to provide proper care and attention for himself or herself or to receive such care and attention from the person or persons with whom he or she is living or from persons living nearby.

Only if you are able to show that all the relevant conditions exist have you the power to compulsorily admit that person to appropriate accommodation. The procedure you must employ is clearly specified in schedule 6 to the Order. It provides that if you have reason to believe that it is necessary to remove a person from the premises in which he or she is residing, in their own best interests or in order to prevent injury to their health or to prevent a nuisance being caused to other people, you must consult the person's doctor and also a medical officer of the Board, who will provide you with a certificate that the removal of the person is necessary. The medical officer must inform the Board in writing of the fact that such a certificate has been issued, and the Board should provide that person's nearest known relative with three days' notice of its intention to apply to the magistrate's court for a removal order. The Board should also serve three days' clear notice of the intended application, together with notice of the time and place of the hearing, on the person who is managing the premises from which removal is proposed. The court may then order, if it is satisfied that the allegations in the certificate are valid, that the person concerned be removed to a hospital or other place to be detained. The period of detention can be for up to three months, although the court may extend that period by a further three months if it considers such extension to be appropriate. The person who has been removed, or someone acting on his or her behalf, may, six weeks after the order has been made, apply to the court to have the order revoked or varied, although he or she is required to give the social worker involved at least three days' notice of the intended application.

8.5.2 The Elderly

There are no significant differences in the legal provisions relating to the provision of accommodation for elderly people and those mentioned above relating to the chronically sick and disabled. Therefore what has been said in 8.5.1 above applies equally to elderly people.

8.5.3 Children in Need

Under section 114 of the 1968 Act a Board or Trust has a duty to provide accommodation and maintenance for children in its care, either by 'boarding them out' or by providing accommodation in a statutory or voluntary home (i.e. having them fostered). Young people in Board or Trust care who have reached the age of sixteen can be accommodated in hostel accommodation.

As regards the 1995 Order, as mentioned in 8.4.4, there are separate and distinct duties owed to children in need, depending on whether or not they are being looked after by a Board or Trust.

8.5.3.1 Children Not Being Looked After by a Board or Trust

Boards/Trusts have a duty to provide accommodation to any child who appears to require it if any one of three conditions is met: (1) there is no person who has parental responsibility for the child, (2) the child has been lost or abandoned, or (3) the person who has been caring for the child is no longer able to provide him or her with suitable accommodation and care.

There is also a duty to provide accommodation for any child who has reached the age of sixteen and whose welfare the Board/Trust considers likely to be seriously prejudiced if it does not provide him or her with accommodation.

In two further cases the Board/Trust has the power to provide accommodation. The first is where the Board/Trust considers that the provision of accommodation to a child would safeguard or promote the child's welfare, and this power still applies even if the person who has parental responsibility for him or her is able to provide accommodation. The second is where a Board/Trust considers that the provision of accommodation for a person between the ages of sixteen and twenty-one would safeguard or promote his or her welfare. In all the above cases the Board/Trust, before providing accommodation, must, as far as is reasonably practicable and consistent with the welfare of the child, ascertain the wishes of the child and, subject to the child's age and understanding, give due consideration to them.

That deals with the situation where no objection is raised to the Board providing the child with accommodation. What happens, however, where objections are raised to the provision of such accommodation?

If a person having parental responsibility is willing and able to provide or arrange accommodation for the child and objects to the Board providing accommodation, the wishes of the parent or carer take priority. Furthermore, if a child has been given accommodation by the Board, the parent or carer may remove the child at any time without having to comply with any formal procedure. There are, as would be expected, restrictions on the above rights of the parent or carer, and they apply in two cases. Firstly, if a residence order (see chapter 6) has been granted in favour of a person and that person agrees to the child being looked after in accommodation provided by the Board/Trust, the person's wishes take priority. Secondly, where a person has been entrusted with the care of a child as the result of a High Court order and that person agrees to the Board/Trust providing accommodation for the child, once again that person's wishes prevail.

Boards and Trusts are also under a strict duty to receive and provide accommodation for children who have been removed or kept away from their homes under an emergency protection order, for children who are being assessed away from home under a child assessment order, and for children who have been taken into police protection (see chapter 6).

Finally, in relation to children not being looked after by a Board/Trust, where the Board or Trust provides any of the services discussed above (other than providing advice, guidance, or counselling) it is entitled to charge the recipient an amount that it considers reasonable. If the child receiving the service is under the age of sixteen the charge must be paid by the parents;

if the child is sixteen or over the child must pay; and where the service is provided to a member of the child's family that person must pay. You should be aware that where the person liable for the charge cannot afford to pay it, he or she cannot be made to pay more than they can reasonably be expected to pay. Should the person who is liable for the payment consider that the charge for the service or services is not reasonable, he or she is clearly entitled to challenge it by way of judicial review.

8.5.3.2 Children Being Looked After by a Board or Trust

Children looked after by a Board/Trust must be accommodated by being fostered or maintained in a Board or voluntary home or a registered children's home. In fulfilling the duty to accommodate, the Board or Trust should attempt to place the child with relatives or friends or other suitable people, to ensure that the accommodation is near his or her home, to accommodate siblings together, and to ensure that the accommodation for a disabled person is not unsuitable to his or her needs. (Fostering will be subject to detailed regulations to be made in the future by the DHSS, which will deal with the welfare of the child, arrangements for the child's health and education, and ensuring that the religious persuasion of the foster-parents is the same as that of the child.) (For Boards' and Trusts' duty to maintain contact between a child and his or her parents see chapter 6.)

Boards and Trusts are under a duty (by virtue of article 72 of HPSS72) to provide homes for the care and accommodation of children they are looking after. Accommodation may also be provided by voluntary organisations or in children's homes. In these two cases there is a duty on a Board/Trust to satisfy itself that the welfare of all children so accommodated is being satisfactorily safeguarded and promoted. If a Board/Trust is not satisfied that a child's welfare is being properly safeguarded and promoted it is under a duty to take such steps as are reasonably practicable to remove him or her from the home and place them with their parents, with the person having parental responsibility, with a relative, or in a Board/Trust home. A Board/Trust is also under a duty to arrange that each child who is accommodated in a voluntary or children's home is visited, and people authorised by the Board/Trust may enter and inspect premises to ensure that the welfare of the children accommodated there is being satisfactorily safeguarded and promoted. Again detailed regulations dealing with the running of such homes will be issued at a later date.

Department inspectors can inspect premises where children are being accommodated (article 149). The powers of inspectors are comprehensive, entitling them to inspect any records, including information held on computer, relating to the premises, the children who are living there, and people who are living or employed there. They can also inspect the children themselves and may examine the management of the premises. An adverse report by an inspector could entitle the department to cancel the registration of the establishment concerned or take some other appropriate action. (The department can hold public or private inquiries into the exercise of the functions of Boards and Trusts and of voluntary organisations relating to children and any matters relating to accommodation for children in residential care homes, hospitals, nursing homes, schools, or other prescribed institutions.)

Where a child has been accommodated in a hospital administered by a Board/Trust, a private hospital, a residential care home or a nursing home for a consecutive period of at least three months, the authority must take such steps as are reasonably practical to ensure that his or her welfare is properly safeguarded and promoted during that period. It must also decide whether to exercise any of its powers under the Children (Northern Ireland) Order 1995 with regard to such children. It is a matter for the Board or Trust to decide whether to exercise any of its functions towards the child, and once it has properly exercised its judgment in the matter it would be quite difficult to challenge its decision unless it was, for example, clearly unreasonable. It is worth mentioning that if a child before being admitted to a hospital was ordinarily resident in the area of another Board or Trust, the duties mentioned above would be imposed on the latter Board or Trust.

Similarly, if an Education and Library Board is providing accommodation for a child for a consecutive period of three months or longer in a place other than a school, it must notify the relevant Health and Social Services Board or Trust, which is then under a duty to establish whether the child's welfare is being adequately safeguarded and promoted while he or she is being so accommodated. The board must then decide whether to exercise any of its functions under the Children (Northern Ireland) Order 1995 towards the child. The Education and Library Board must also notify the Board/Trust when it ceases to provide accommodation for the child.

A Board/Trust must ensure that the welfare of a child who is being accommodated at a school is being adequately safeguarded and promoted by the manager or managers of the school. An authorised person is entitled to inspect the relevant premises, the children, and any records, including those kept on computer, in order to enable the Board or Trust to discharge its welfare duty to those children. Any obstruction of an authorised person amounts to a criminal offence. If the Board or Trust is of the opinion that the manager of the school has failed to carry out his or her duty, it must notify both the DHSS and the Department of Education.

8.6 Representing Vulnerable People

8.6.1 Presenting their Views and Opinions

As has been mentioned in a number of instances above, the law considers it important that the views and opinions of vulnerable people be taken into consideration in relation to the provision of personal social services to them. These views and opinions may be put forward by the vulnerable person or by a representative on their behalf. All we examine here is the representation of the chronically sick and disabled and the elderly; the representation rights of people with learning difficulties and of children in need have already been dealt with in earlier parts of this chapter.

8.6.1.1 The Chronically Sick and Disabled

The statutory provisions relating to the representation of disabled people are contained in sections 1 and 2 of DP89. They are meant to give the same level of protection to the disabled in Northern Ireland as that given in Great Britain by the Disabled Persons (Services, Consultation and Representation) Act 1986. These two sections of the Act have not yet been implemented. However, given that all of the Act should (eventually) become operational, they are dealt with here.

Section 1 deals with the appointment of 'authorised representatives' of disabled people. The department is given the power to make regulations governing the procedure for the appointment and termination of authorised representatives. The function of a representative is to ensure that the disabled person's views and interests are fully and appropriately represented to those providing personal social services, and to enable them to do so they are granted a number of rights. The representative is entitled (provided that in each case the disabled person requests him or her to do so) to accompany the person to any meetings or interviews held by the Board or Trust, which must allow him or her access to information and relevant documents. The one circumstance in which the Board or Trust does not have to comply with these requirements is where it is satisfied that the presence of the authorised representative or the granting to him or her of access to information or documents would be likely to be harmful to the interests of the disabled person. However, in coming to this decision it should take the wishes of the disabled person into account.

Disabled people are not under any obligation to appoint a representative, and they are totally free to represent themselves if they so wish and are capable of so doing. However, a disabled person under the age of sixteen cannot appoint a representative himself or herself, and in such a situation that person's parent may appoint himself or herself or another person as the representative. The Board is entitled to appoint a representative in cases where the disabled person is a child who is in the care of the department or where the person is unable to appoint a representative because of mental or physical incapacity. There are no statutory provisions relating to who can be a representative, and therefore the disabled person can appoint a friend, carer, or relative, or someone from a voluntary organisation.

Even though the sections relating to the authorised representatives are not in force, you should consider using them to argue that a similar role might be played by someone acting on an extrastatutory basis.

There is another category of person who can act (albeit in an extremely restricted manner) in a similar capacity to an authorised representative. This is a carer who provides a substantial amount of care on a regular and informal basis to a disabled person who is living at home. As has already been mentioned, a carer is entitled, under section 4 of the 1989 Act, to request a Board or Trust to assess the needs of a disabled person who is living at home in order to ascertain whether that person is in need of being provided with personal welfare services. Under section 8 of the same Act the Board or Trust in coming to its decision must take into account the ability of the carer to continue providing care on a regular basis.

8.6.1.2 The Elderly

There are no specific legal provisions dealing with the representation rights of elderly people, although, as has been mentioned on other occasions, should an elderly person satisfy one (or more) of the definition criteria of the chronically sick or disabled, he or she is entitled to the same representation rights.

8.6.2 *Managing Property on their Behalf*

8.6.2.1 The Chronically Sick and Disabled and the Elderly

As the law in relation to the managing of the property of the above groups is the same, they are dealt with together here. The fact that a person suffers from a physical or slight mental impairment or has become slightly senile does not mean that they are incapable of managing their own affairs. However, if the impairment or senility is severe it becomes necessary for his or her affairs to be managed by another person on their behalf. Where a person is suffering from a mental impairment within the meaning of article 3 of the Mental Health (Northern Ireland) Order 1986, which would include a confused elderly or senile person, the Office of Care and Protection may take over the management and administration of that person's property and affairs (see chapter 7).

As has already been seen, under article 37 and schedule 6 to HPSS72 a person in need of care and attention may be compulsorily admitted to appropriate accommodation (see 8.5.1), and in this case there is a duty on the Board or Trust to protect that person's property. This applies to cases where, because of the person's absence, there is a risk of damage to or loss of any property belonging to the former resident. If, however, the person removed has made arrangements for his or her property to be dealt with during their absence, the Board or Trust does not have to discharge this responsibility.

Another method that can be used to manage or protect a person's property is for that person to grant someone an enduring power of attorney (see 7.7).

8.7 *Further Reading*

Collins, Brian (for Public Law Project), *Challenging Community Care Decisions in Northern Ireland*, London: Public Law Project 1995.

Department of Health and Social Services, *People First: Community Care in Northern Ireland for the 1990s*, Belfast: DHSS 1990.

Department of Health and Social Services, *Health and Personal Social Services: a Regional Strategy for Northern Ireland, 1987*, Belfast: DHSS 1992.

Lavery, Ruth, 'The Registered Homes (Northern Ireland) Order, 1992' in *Northern Ireland Legal Quarterly*, 1993 (44), 171–8.

Lavery, Ruth, *Law and the Elderly: Residential and Nursing Homes*, Belfast: SLS Legal Publications.

Northern Health and Social Services Board, *Disabled Persons (Northern Ireland) Act, 1989: Guide to Good Practice*, NHSSB 1992.

Southern Education and Library Board, *Special Educational Needs: Information for Parents*, SELB.

Western Health and Social Services Board, *Comprehensive Assessment and Care Management*, Derry: WHSSB 1994.

PART 3

The Law Affecting Clients

9

ANTI-DISCRIMINATION LAW

PATRICIA MAXWELL

9.1 *Introduction*

Discrimination based on sex, religion, political opinion, sexual orientation and poverty is a major issue of social justice today. The social worker has to deal with this discrimination on two levels: its relevance to personal attitudes, and its importance to clients in the form of laws, rules and practices that affect their everyday lives.

Your clients are all too often the victims of discrimination and prejudice. Members of minority groups find themselves disadvantaged in the employment field and in their access to goods and services, such as housing and education. If you understand the legal redress that might be available, the agencies that are there to assist, and the institutions that can be used, you will be in a good position to help.

Some forms of discrimination are now unlawful. The elimination of discrimination on grounds of sex or religion has been a concern of government for some twenty years, and it is this legislation that provides the main focus of the chapter. Discrimination against ex-offenders is also examined, as are the provisions relating to the employment of disabled people. The pressure for change is mounting in relation to the introduction of laws to protect racial minorities in Northern Ireland, and a section on race discrimination is also given.

One theme of the chapter is a look at how our laws have been influenced by the wider international community. International human rights obligations, the European Union and comparisons with the United States have all played a significant role in the development of anti-discrimination law. It is also important to appreciate that it is an area of law that is still developing. The movement towards proper anti-discrimination legislation on grounds of disability is growing apace. The notion of specific legislation to ban discrimination on grounds of sexual orientation is gaining acceptance. An industrial tribunal has ruled for the first time that an employer who used age as a reason for dismissing people acted unfairly (*Independent*, 7 May 1994). You should keep abreast of these issues, both as a matter of personal development and in the interests of the client.

Another significant influence has been the European Union. Even before the United Kingdom became a member, at the beginning of 1973, it was evident that action would be necessary to give effect to treaty obligations in domestic law. Article 119 of the EEC Treaty lays down the principle of equal pay for men and women. Thus in 1970, when membership was 'on the cards', domestic legislation on equal pay entered the statute book (though implementation was delayed for five years, to allow employers to gradually absorb the inflationary impact of the legislation). In addition to article 119 a number of important directives have been issued: on Equal Pay, Equal Treatment, Social Security, Occupational Pensions, the Protection of Self-Employed Women, and Pregnancy and Maternity.

EU law continues to play a crucial role in the development and interpretation of domestic legislation on sex discrimination and equal pay today. (For more on EU law see 1.2.10.)

The main aims of the domestic legislation are to prohibit the unequal treatment of the sexes in certain well-defined areas of the economy and in education. The White Paper *Equality for Women* stated the objectives: to deter prejudice, and behaviour that manifests that prejudice; to provide protection from prejudice and remedies for its victims; to adjust tensions and relieve grievances; and to support those who do not wish to discriminate. Above all, the law makes an unequivocal statement of public policy and official beliefs.

In Northern Ireland the principal legislation is the Equal Pay Act (Northern Ireland) 1970, and the Sex Discrimination (Northern Ireland) Order 1976. Both instruments came into force in July 1976, and both have been substantially amended. In theory they are to be read together, forming a 'harmonious code', though in practice this has proved difficult, as they are distinct measures with goals, mechanisms and enforcement procedures of their own. We shall examine each piece in detail.

9.2 *Sex Discrimination (Northern Ireland) Order 1976*

Although it is often assumed that the Sex Discrimination Order was designed to prevent unlawful discrimination against women, in fact the Order makes it equally unlawful to discriminate against men, or against any person on grounds of his or her marital status. The Order (as amended) provides a degree of protection against unequal treatment in the fields of employment, housing, education, and the provision of goods and services. Other areas are outside the scope of the legislation: social security, taxation, nationality, matrimonial and family law and other areas are not affected but are covered by separate legislation.

9.2.1 *The Equal Opportunities Commission*

In addition, the Order set up the Equal Opportunities Commission (EOC) for Northern Ireland, with the functions of working towards the elimination of discrimination, promoting equality of opportunity between men and women, and keeping under review the relevant legislation.

The EOC has power to assist individual complainants in bringing legal cases before industrial tribunals (a power it has used extensively since its establishment); it can undertake formal investigations where it believes that there is widespread discrimination; and it has power to keep the legislation under review and where necessary can draw up and submit proposals for amendments. In addition, the commission has powers to undertake research and carry out educational and promotional campaigns. To this end a considerable amount of very valuable written material has been produced and is readily available from the EOC.

9.2.2 *What Constitutes Discrimination?*

The test for determining whether or not an act amounted to discrimination is objective, not subjective. In other words, what is important is what was actually done rather than the reasons or motives behind what was done. This point was confirmed by the House of Lords in *James v. Eastleigh Borough Council* [1990] 2 AC 751. Mr and Mrs James were both sixty-one years of age. The local authority operated a policy whereby young children, the unwaged and anyone who had reached pensionable age were permitted free entry to the swimming pool, while everyone else had to pay an entrance fee of 75 pence. Mr James complained that he had been discriminated against because of his sex, as he was required to pay an entrance fee while his wife was not.

The House of Lords upheld his claim. Undoubtedly the subjective intention or motive of the local authority may have been impeccable, but that was not relevant. It did not alter the objective fact that men were treated less favourably than women. By adopting a criterion that of itself was inherently discriminatory (i.e. pensionable age), the local authority was acting unlawfully. The question to be asked is, would the complainant have received the same treatment but for his sex?

As far as discrimination in employment is concerned, there are three types of circumstance to consider: direct discrimination, indirect discrimination, and victimisation.

9.2.2.1 Direct Discrimination
This is the most obvious and blatant form of discrimination. It is defined in article 3 of the Order, and occurs when a person is treated less favourably

than a person of the opposite sex and when the sex of the person is the reason for the unfavourable treatment. To refuse to employ a woman because the employer considers that 'this is a man's job' is an example of direct discrimination. As we have seen, discrimination can take place even though the act is done for the best of motives. To establish direct discrimination an applicant will have to show that a comparator of the other sex has received better or more favourable treatment.

Employers must avoid generalised assumptions about men and women. For example, in *Hurley v. Mustoe* [1981] IRLR 208 it was held that an employer's policy of not employing women with young children (which was not applied to men with children) was direct discrimination. It is clear from the case that the employer made two generalised assumptions: firstly, that mothers have primary responsibility for children, and secondly, that this makes them unreliable employees.

Sexual stereotypes assume that the sexes are different. They perpetuate perceived differences and can become self-fulfilling prophecies. Stereotyping involves a denial of equality and ignores individual potential and autonomy. The courts will use anti-discrimination legislation to attack these assumptions. In *Horsey v. Dyfed CC* [1982] IRLR 395 the local authority refused to send the applicant on a social work course. The authority had learnt that the applicant's husband had obtained a new job a considerable distance away, and they thought that she would be leaving her own job in the near future in order to accompany him when he moved.

The decision was held to be unlawful. The Employment Appeal Tribunal stated that most discrimination flows from generalised assumptions: 'that people of a particular sex, marital status or race possess or lack certain characteristics... The purpose of the legislation is to secure equal opportunity for individuals regardless of their sex, married status, or race. This result would not be achieved if it were sufficient to escape liability to show that the reason for the discriminatory treatment was simply an assumption that women or coloured persons possessed or lacked particular characteristics and not that they were just women or coloured persons.'

In the case of *Wallace v. South-Eastern Education and Library Board* [1981] IRLR 193 the Northern Ireland Court of Appeal recognised that there is rarely nowadays clear evidence of direct sex discrimination. To ensure that the purpose of the legislation is not defeated, courts and tribunals must be able to draw inferences of unlawful discrimination from the facts and circumstances of the complaint.

9.2.2.2 Indirect Discrimination

In contrast to direct discrimination, indirect discrimination is a more detailed legal concept and one that is designed to have a wider impact. It is intended to deal with the situation where seemingly neutral conditions have a disproportionate impact on one sex or where such conditions are used to mask an intentional preference for one sex.

Indirect discrimination is defined in article 3 as occurring when a person applies a condition or requirement that appears to apply equally to men and women but that in reality is such that (a) the proportion of women who can comply with it is considerably smaller than the proportion of men, (b) it cannot be shown that the condition or requirement is justified irrespective of the sex of the person to whom it is applied, and (c) it is to that person's detriment because he or she cannot comply.

One obvious example would be a minimum height requirement of five feet six inches, which clearly excludes more women than men and would therefore amount to unlawful indirect discrimination unless the requirement could be justified. Similar examples include recruitment or selection criteria based on factors such as age, mobility, physical strength or educational requirement that are not essential to the job.

Other informal practices may amount to indirect discrimination, for example 'word of mouth' recruitment, extending overtime hours, imposing a requirement to work full time, and organising work schedules or training courses at times of the day difficult for workers with family responsibilities. All these practices could have an adverse impact on women and would have to be objectively justified.

In an indirect discrimination case the focus of attention is moved away from the individual to the wider perspective of looking at women as a class. The legal process must consider what the general characteristics of women are that prevent them from complying with what are apparently neutral conditions or requirements. In particular, such features as the biologically determined child-bearing role and the socially ascribed role of child rearing and responsibility for the family and home, as well as aspects such as social stereotyping in education and training, must be taken into account. These are the characteristics that have been ignored in the past and that significantly affect the participation of women in the labour market. By focusing on the effects of a particular discriminatory practice on an identifiable group within society, indirect discrimination appears to offer a more sophisticated response to redressing sex equalities.

However, proving indirect discrimination is difficult. The applicant must first establish that there is a requirement that constitutes a barrier. In general, courts and tribunals have interpreted this liberally and have accepted that requirements may be written or unwritten, formal rules or informal employment practices. Yet the process of definition is difficult. It is not altogether clear how much help the tribunal will give the applicant in the formulation of her complaint.

In *Home Office v. Holmes* [1984] 3 All ER 549 a single mother applied to return to work on a part-time basis after the birth of her child. It was Home Office policy not to employ part-time workers. The Employment Appeal Tribunal ruled that the words 'requirement or condition' were wide enough to include the obligation to work full time, which had not been justified by the Home Office. Ms Holmes had therefore been the victim of unlawful sex discrimination.

While the legislation does not stipulate specifically the need to prove statistically that the condition has an adverse impact on one sex, courts have generally required such evidence, which may be difficult to obtain. In one helpful decision the Northern Ireland Court of Appeal has ruled that a tribunal is entitled to conclude adverse impact, without the need for statistical evidence, from its own knowledge of the position of men and women generally in society (*North-Eastern Education and Library Board v. Briggs* [1990] IRLR 181).

There is one final point to note about indirect discrimination. If it is shown to be unintentional, no damages can be awarded. Recently, however, a Belfast industrial tribunal awarded compensation in a case of unintentional indirect discrimination, concerning the right to job-share (*Mulligan v. Eastern Health and Social Services Board* (1994) Case no. 1258/93). The tribunal reasoned that this was necessary to comply with the right to an effective remedy guaranteed by EU law. This has yet to be tested in the higher courts.

9.2.2.3 Victimisation

It is also unlawful to victimise a person because they have brought, or have been connected with, an action under this legislation or under equal pay legislation.

9.2.3 *The Extent of Protection*

The ambit of the legislation is wide, ranging from education and employment to the provision of goods, facilities, and services.

The 1976 Order (articles 24–29) makes it unlawful for schools and the Education and Library Boards to discriminate on grounds of sex, although there are special exemptions for single-sex schools. The most significant case in Northern Ireland on these provisions has been *In re EOC for Northern Ireland and Others* [1988] NI 223, in which the practice of awarding free grammar school places to the top 27 per cent of boys and the top 27 per cent of girls was held to be unlawful, because some girls who had higher marks than boys who were getting free places were being excluded.

Article 30 of the Order requires that women have equal access to goods, facilities and services 'in the same manner and on the same terms as are normal in relation to men.' While these are not specified, access to loan facilities, service in a public bar, insurance, housing and public facilities would seem to be covered. One exemption that limits the scope of article 30 is that governing private clubs, which can result in women being denied access to sporting facilities, such as golf clubs.

9.2.4 *Sex Discrimination in Employment*

The 1976 Order prohibits unlawful discrimination in employment, which is defined as 'employment under a contract of service or apprenticeship or a contract personally to execute any work or labour.' This is a wide definition, which can include people who are technically self-employed.

Article 8 sets out five types of unlawful discriminatory action: arrangements made for determining who shall be employed; the terms on which a person is offered employment; refusing to offer employment because of a person's sex; opportunities for promotion, transfer, training, or other benefits; and dismissing a woman or subjecting her to any other detriment.

9.2.4.1 Arrangements Made for Determining Who Shall Be Employed

The arrangements must ensure that job opportunities are open to all, irrespective of sex. Advertising (though treated separately in the Order) may be regarded as part of the 'arrangements'. Application forms, job descriptions, short-listing procedures and the conduct of interviews, as well as the ultimate decision about whom to employ, are covered by this provision, and all these procedures must be carried out fairly and without bias.

9.2.4.2 The Terms on Which a Person is Offered Employment

While pay itself is treated separately by the Equal Pay (Northern Ireland) Act 1970, the 1976 Order makes it unlawful to offer employment to a woman on terms that are less favourable than those offered to a man.

9.2.4.3 Refusing to Offer Employment Because of a Person's Sex

The Northern Ireland Court of Appeal has ruled that where a better-qualified or more experienced candidate is turned down in favour of a candidate of another sex, it is for the employer to show that sex discrimination did not take place (see *Wallace v. South-Eastern Education and Library Board* [1980] IRLR 193 and *Dornan v. Belfast City Council* [1990] IRLR 179). These rulings have made the situation easier for women in Northern Ireland (in contrast to other parts of the United Kingdom) when there is no direct evidence of discrimination.

9.2.4.4 Opportunities for Promotion, Transfer, Training, or Other Benefits

To deny a woman an opportunity for promotion (for example by refusing to send her on a development course) or to restrict her training opportunities is clearly discriminatory. However, employers and training bodies may be allowed to provide single-sex training in particular circumstances. This is where it is thought necessary in order to equip the under-represented group with skills necessary for work that they have not done traditionally, or to encourage people who have been out of the labour market because of domestic responsibilities. In addition, courses can be run in companies that are trying to encourage applications for particular posts where there have been few or no women (or men) in the previous twelve months (articles 17, 48, and 49).

9.2.4.5 Dismissing a Woman or Subjecting her to Any Other Detriment

Dismissal is a wide term, covering both the failure to renew a contract that expires and 'constructive dismissal', where the employer, by breaking a fundamental term of the contract, leaves the employee with little choice but to resign. Detriment is similarly wide. It may exist even though an employee is compensated for it, as in *Jeremiah v. Ministry of Defence* [1979] IRLR 436, where only men were forced to do 'dirty work', for which they received extra pay. An employer cannot buy the right to discriminate. To put someone on short-time working would be another example of a detriment.

9.2.5 *Sexual Harassment*

It is now generally accepted that sexual harassment can amount to a type of sex discrimination. Sexual harassment assumes many forms, from unwelcome sexual advances and sexually explicit comments and lewd suggestions to serious physical assaults.

The first successful claim in the United Kingdom was upheld by a Belfast industrial tribunal, in the case of *M. v. Crescent Garage Ltd* [1982] Case no. 24/83. Two years later the House of Lords put the matter beyond all doubt in *Porcelli v. Strathclyde Regional Council* [1986] IRLR 134. Ms Porcelli was a laboratory technician at a school. She alleged that two male technicians were sexually harassing her as part of a campaign to make her leave, by deliberately brushing against her and making suggestive remarks of a sexual nature. It was held that unlawful discrimination had occurred, as she had been subjected to unfavourable treatment of a sexual nature to which a man would not have been vulnerable.

In 1991 the European Commission adopted a Code of Practice on Measures to Combat Sexual Harassment. A number of tribunals have used this as a starting point when considering allegations of sexual harassment, and in particular its definition. This definition covers a wide range of behaviour and includes, for example, harassment on grounds of sexual orientation.

Compensation for sexual harassment must reflect the degree of detriment suffered by the woman, and may include a substantial sum for injury to her feelings. One problem that has arisen concerns the liability of employers for the actions of the harassers. They will only be liable for anything done 'in the course of employment'; they will not be liable if they can prove that they took such steps as were reasonably practicable to prevent the employee from doing the act.

9.2.6 *Pregnancy Discrimination*

The law on pregnancy is very complicated, involving EU law, unfair dismissal legislation, and social security law, as well as the law on sex discrimination. To dismiss a woman because she is pregnant may amount to sex discrimination.

As we have seen, the Sex Discrimination Order is centred on the notion of 'less favourable treatment'—of making a comparison between the treatment given to a similarly situated man and woman, or, to put it at its simplest, of comparing like with like. As a man cannot become pregnant, true comparisons are impossible, and this has given rise to difficulties in using the Sex Discrimination Order in pregnancy cases. Yet for many women who could not fulfil length-of-service requirements for unfair dismissal claims it was the only way to achieve compensation.

In Great Britain the approach adopted by tribunals and confirmed by the House of Lords in *Webb v. EMO Cargo (UK) Ltd* [1992] 4 All ER 929 has been to compare a pregnant woman with a man who needs time off work because he is sick. While this approach has helped many women, it clearly does not work where the employer would also have dismissed a sick man. In the *Webb* case the applicant was taken on as a temporary replacement for a clerk who was herself about to go on maternity leave. Shortly after starting work, and while she was still being trained, the applicant discovered that she too was pregnant, and informed her employer, who promptly dismissed her. The decision of the tribunal (and the appeal courts) was that this was not unlawful sex discrimination, because a man who had announced that he needed time off for a similar period would, in the circumstances, have been treated exactly the same.

The House of Lords, while upholding the decision, decided to refer the case to the European Court of Justice to see if there had been a breach of the Equal Treatment Directive. In July 1994 the ECJ ruled in favour of Ms

Webb, holding that it was contrary to the Equal Treatment Directive to dismiss a woman employed for an unlimited term who shortly after her recruitment was found to be pregnant. This was so even though the woman was appointed initially to replace another employee who was about to take maternity leave, and even though the employer would also have dismissed a male employee engaged for this purpose who required leave of absence at the relevant time for medical or other reasons.

This decision was very much in line with the approach to pregnancy discrimination taken by the ECJ in *Dekker v. Stichting Vormingscentrum voor Jong Wolvassenen (VJV-Centrum) Plus* C-177/88 (1990). In this case the applicant applied for a job as a training instructor. During her interview she informed the selection committee that she was pregnant. Although she was the most suitable candidate, she was turned down, because the employer knew that his insurers would not reimburse him for the sickness benefit he would have to pay Ms Dekker because she was pregnant at the time of her application. The ECJ ruled that the reason Ms Dekker was rejected was that she was pregnant. They reasoned that since only women can become pregnant, the refusal was based on her sex and was therefore unlawful. A reason that exclusively applied to one sex is a sex-based reason and amounts to unlawful direct discrimination.

In Northern Ireland, tribunals have applied this interpretation since the case of *Jordan v. NI Electricity Service* in 1984 Case no. 28/83. The tribunals have acknowledged the unsuitability of the Order in dealing with one of the most fundamental grounds for discriminating against women and have expressed the view that comparing pregnancy to sickness is clearly a most unsatisfactory situation. Unlike their counterparts in England, they have insisted that unfavourable treatment on grounds of pregnancy is unlawful direct discrimination, without the need for any comparison (see *Donley v. Gallagher Ltd* [1987] Case no. 66/86 and *McQuaide v. The Lobster Pot* [1989] Case no. 427/89). In 1992 the Northern Ireland Court of Appeal referred to the ECJ the question whether it was lawful to reduce the pay of a woman on maternity leave (*Gillespie and Others v. DHSS and Others* [1992] Case no. 309/89).

The importance of some of these issues has been diminished by the introduction of legislation to implement the EU Directive on the Protection of Pregnant Women at Work (no. 92/85). This legislation was introduced in Northern Ireland by the Industrial Relations (Northern Ireland) Order 1993. It amends earlier legislation to provide a right to maternity leave and protection against pregnancy-related dismissal for all women employees.

The provisions are complex and apply in addition to the existing rights for women who have completed two years' service, thus introducing a two-tier system of rights. The new legislation allows fourteen weeks' maternity leave to be taken by all women, regardless of length of service or hours of work. All existing terms and conditions of employment (except pay) must be maintained. It is automatically unfair to dismiss a woman on grounds relating to pregnancy, childbirth, or maternity leave. A woman who is dismissed while pregnant or on maternity leave is entitled to a written statement of the reason for her dismissal. Finally, anyone suspended from work while pregnant will have the right to be offered any available suitable alternative employment, or to be paid during the period of suspension. These new rights apply to anyone who gave birth to a baby on or after 16 October 1994.

9.2.7 *Permitted Discrimination*

Matters relating to death or retirement are said to fall outside the scope of the legislation. However, this has been challenged before the European Court on a number of occasions. In *Marshall v. Southampton and South-West Hampshire Area Health Authority* [1986] 2 All ER 584 it was held to be unlawful to operate different retirement ages for men and women. The implications of the case of *Barber v. Guardian Royal Exchange* [1990] 2 All ER 660 are still being fully explored, but it is clear that any form of compensation paid to an employee in connection with retirement must now be equalised and that pension benefits must be made available to both sexes at the same age.

Under article 52 of the Order it is permissible to discriminate against women in order to protect them against definable health risks that are specific to women, including risks associated with pregnancy and childbirth.

9.2.8 *Remedies in Sex Discrimination Cases*

Under the employment provisions of the 1976 Order, any person may complain to an industrial tribunal that another person has committed an act of discrimination. As noted above, the EOC can provide invaluable assistance in the preparation and conduct of a case. A person is free to represent herself at the tribunal, or to be accompanied by a 'next friend' such as a social worker or a union representative. Forms and explanatory information are available from the Office of the Industrial Tribunals and the Fair Employment Tribunal.

No legal aid is available for the hearing itself, although preliminary advice and assistance may be obtained through the 'green form scheme' (see chapter 1). A complaint of discrimination must be lodged within three months of the act complained of, unless it was not practicable to present it earlier. A conciliation officer from the Labour Relations Agency will try to promote a settlement between the parties, but if that fails the case will go to a hearing.

If the tribunal finds the complaint to be well founded it may

(*a*) make an order declaring the rights of the complainant;
(*b*) order the respondent to pay compensation; since the decision of the ECJ in *Marshall (No. 2)* [1993] IRLR 445 (ECJ) the victim's actual loss and damage must be made good in full: the fixed upper limit on compensation (of £11,000) is no longer effective, and full compensation (including interest) must be paid (legislation introducing this became effective in December 1993); or
(*c*) make a recommendation that the respondent take action to obviate or reduce the impact of the act of discrimination.

9.2.9 *Equal Pay*

The Equal Pay (Northern Ireland) Act 1970, is concerned with the establishment of equal terms and conditions of employment for men and women. The domestic legislation (which has been amended several times) must again be read in the light of relevant EU law, in particular article 119 of the Treaty and the Equal Pay Directive. Under EU law the term 'pay' is given a very wide meaning and covers 'the ordinary basic or minimum wage or salary and any other consideration, whether in cash or kind, which a worker receives, directly or indirectly, in respect of his employment from his employer.' Thus employers' pension contributions, free meals, paid holidays, company cars and other benefits would all come within the definition of pay.

Men and women who are in the same employment are entitled to equal pay in three circumstances: where they are employed on like work; where their work has been given the same rating under a job evaluation scheme; and where they are engaged on work of equal value.

9.2.9.1 Like Work

To be employed on 'like work' means, according to the Act, that the work must be the same or broadly similar and that any differences between the work done must not be of practical importance.

This does not mean that the work has to be exactly the same. There may be unsubstantial differences between the duties, or the responsibilities may vary slightly, or the work may be performed at different times (day or night shifts, for example), and the tribunal may still make a finding of 'like work'. Tribunals have agreed that it is wrong to take too pedantic an approach to this question.

9.2.9.2 Work Rated as Equivalent

A woman's work will be considered to have been rated as equivalent to that of a man if it has been given an equal rating under a properly designed and conducted job evaluation scheme. Such a scheme must be analytical in nature and must break the jobs down in terms of different demands made on employees, such as effort, skill, responsibility, and so on. It must be impartial and genuine.

9.2.9.3 Equal Value

The legislation on equal value was added to the Equal Pay (Northern Ireland) Act following the case of *Commission for the European Communities v. United Kingdom* [1982] ICR 578. The ECJ upheld the claim that the United Kingdom's equal pay law did not comply with the requirements of article 119 of the Treaty and the Equal Pay Directive. Although, as we have just seen, the Act provided for equal pay when an employer had instituted a job evaluation scheme voluntarily, there was no mechanism by which a woman could compel her employer to undertake such a scheme.

This mechanism was provided by the Equal Pay (Amendment) Regulations (Northern Ireland) 1984. The real importance of this legislation is that it allows a woman to compare her job to a completely different job done by a man. Thus in *Hayward v. Camell Laird* [1988] 2 All ER 257 a cook successfully claimed that her job was equal in value to that of a painter, a joiner, and an insulation engineer. Given the segregation of the labour market into jobs that are traditionally regarded as either 'men's jobs' or 'women's jobs', this measure has enormous potential for eliminating the differential between men's and women's wages that continues to persist.

However, progress has been slow. The special procedure for equal value claims is complex and lengthy, and only a handful of cases have been completed (although a number of important company and sectoral agreements to review complete pay structures have been achieved).

The procedure includes the referral of the case to an independent expert, who will prepare a report on whether the jobs compared are of equal value. The average time taken to prepare this report is just under two years, which adds considerably to the length of proceedings. Employers are given the opportunity to raise any matters that they consider might constitute a 'genuine material factor' defence to justify the difference in pay. The precise ambit of this defence is still being worked out by tribunals and the higher courts.

Given these difficulties, it is very unlikely that an equal value claim will succeed without expert advice and legal representation at every stage of the proceedings.

9.2.10 Remedies in Equal Pay Cases

A complaint should be referred to an industrial tribunal within six months of the person leaving the relevant employment. Under the terms of the Act the tribunal had power to order the inclusion of an equality clause in the woman's contract and to award arrears of up to two years' pay from the date proceedings were initiated. Since the decision in *Marshall (No. 2)*, noted earlier, the victim's actual loss and damage must be made good in full, and the validity of this two-year recovery limit must be in doubt. It is for the applicant—not the tribunal—to choose her comparator.

A woman is not precluded from seeking equal pay with a man receiving a higher rate because there happen to be some men who are receiving the same rate as hers (*Pickstone v. Freemans PLC* [1988] 2 All ER 803). It is also possible to use a former employee as a comparator (*Macarthys Ltd v. Smith* [1980] ICR 672).

9.3 Religious Discrimination

The need for greater equality between Catholics and Protestants has been recognised for a considerable time. A public commitment to preventing religious discrimination was given in section 5 (1) of the Government of Ireland Act 1920. This provided that the Northern Ireland Parliament could not 'give a preference, privilege or advantage, or impose any disability or disadvantage, on account of religious belief.' Despite the expression of such principles, it is clear that significant discrimination, particularly in housing and employment, existed in Northern Ireland. (See *Disturbances in Northern Ireland: Report of the Cameron Commission* (Cmd 352), London: HMSO 1962.)

During the 1960s the Northern Ireland civil rights campaign focused on the need to eliminate discrimination against Catholics. This movement led to some action by the British government; in 1973 the van Straubenzee Committee was set up to consider the question of discrimination in the private sector and produced an influential report (*Report and Recommendations of the Working Party on Discrimination in the Private Sector of Employment*, London: HMSO 1973). At the same time the Northern Ireland Constitution Act 1973, prohibited direct discrimination by public sector bodies. In 1976 the Fair Employment Act was passed, implementing in part the recommendations of the van Straubenzee Committee in the private and public sectors. In 1977 the Fair Employment Agency began operations.

However, the legislation had little impact on the problem. Research carried out in 1987 by the Policy Studies Institute showed that the great majority of employers believed that the Act had had little effect on their practices. (See D. Smith and G. Chambers, *Inequality in Northern Ireland*, Oxford: Clarendon Press 1991). Informal recruitment procedures were rife; the Fair Employment Agency appeared largely ineffective; and very few organisations carried out any form of monitoring or indeed any type of equal opportunity measure whatsoever. The research also confirmed the extent of the problem: for example, Catholic male unemployment (at 35 per cent) stood at two-and-a-half times that of Protestant male unemployment, and continued at this level despite over 100,000 job changes each year.

From the middle of the 1980s onwards, inequality between Catholics and Protestants became a live political issue, for a number of reasons. In the United States a campaign was started to persuade American corporations, state legislatures and municipal authorities with interests or investments in Northern Ireland to adopt a set of policies known as the MacBride Principles (modelled on the Sullivan Principles, which related to apartheid in South Africa). These principles called on employers to adopt affirmative action practices. The campaign gathered momentum despite the efforts of the American and British governments and amid concern that such practices were actually unlawful under Northern Ireland law (*New York City Employees' Retirement System v. American Brands Inc.* [1986] IRLR 239 (US Federal District Court)). A number of Bills have been introduced to accomplish similar goals at federal level, such as that sponsored by Congressman Kennedy, which applies US federal anti-discrimination requirements to defence contractors in Northern Ireland with which the American government does business. Pressure came too from the Irish Government through machinery established under the Anglo-Irish Agreement.

In September 1986 the local Department of Economic Development published a consultative document proposing new legislation. These proposals continued to place the emphasis on voluntary compliance and fell short of recommending effective affirmative action but prompted a considerable response. In particular the Standing Advisory Commission on Human Rights (a statutory committee that advises the Secretary of State for Northern Ireland) published a report in October 1987 (*Religious and Political Discrimination and Equality of Opportunity in Northern Ireland: Report on Fair Employment* (Cmd 237), London: HMSO 1987), which contained both a comprehensive analysis of the problem and a detailed set of proposals for legislation and other government action.

In December 1988 the government responded by publishing new legislation. After considerable amendment this was passed in July 1989 as the Fair Employment (Northern Ireland) Act 1989, and came into effect on 1 January 1990. An important feature of the Act is that it substantially amends (but falls short of repealing) the Fair Employment Act 1976. To understand how the legislation works it is necessary to read the two Acts together.

9.3.1 *The Fair Employment Commission*

The 1989 Act set up a new body with wide-ranging powers known as the Fair Employment Commission (FEC). The former Fair Employment Agency was absorbed into this new body, and the FEC took over many of the agency's functions and powers.

The FEC has an educational role, which will include activities such as the provision of training courses, the holding of conferences, the undertaking of research, and the dissemination of information and advice. It is also required to recommend affirmative action when appropriate, and to maintain a Code of Practice for the promotion of equality of opportunity. The current Code of Practice is that produced in December 1989 by the Department of Economic Development. This code can be taken into account in tribunal proceedings, though failure to observe its provisions does not of itself render anyone liable to civil or criminal proceedings (see 1.3).

The FEC can undertake investigations and review patterns and practices in employment and, where necessary, issue directions that are ultimately enforceable on employers (sections 11 to 18). Before beginning an investigation the FEC must serve a notice on those it intends to investigate, indicating the scope and purpose of the investigation. The investigation must take place in private, and an opportunity to respond must be given to those who are the subject of the investigation. The commission has extensive powers to compel the attendance of witnesses and the production of documents.

Any person complaining of unlawful discrimination is entitled to advice from the Commission, which is also empowered to give assistance, including legal representation, where the case raises a point of principle or where its complexity requires it (section 29). In addition, the FEC has a range of powers in respect of the affirmative action provisions in the Act. These are discussed below.

9.3.2 *The Fair Employment Tribunal*

The arrangements for handling individual complaints have been significantly altered from the system that operated under the 1976 Act. A person who feels that he or she has been the victim of religious discrimination should make a complaint to the Fair Employment Tribunal, a specialised wing of the industrial tribunals, within three months.

The Labour Relations Agency may attempt to achieve a settlement of the case, but if this is not possible the application will be heard by the Fair Employment Tribunal. This is organised along the same lines as an industrial tribunal: the applicant may represent himself or herself in person or may be legally represented. No legal aid is available. As noted above, the FEC may provide advice and representation in an appropriate case. Tribunal hearings normally take place in public but may be held in private where the interests of national security or public order require it, where confidential information will be disclosed in evidence, or where there is a risk of exposing a person to physical attack or sectarian harassment.

9.3.3 *What Constitutes Discrimination?*

The Fair Employment Acts make it unlawful to discriminate against a person on grounds of their religious belief or political opinion (section 16). As the names of the Acts suggest, employment is the field to which the legislation applies, and employers are the main bodies against whom claims of discrimination may be brought. At present the legislation (unlike the sex discrimination legislation) does not extend to the provision of goods, facilities, services, and premises, but this is under review (see *Race Relations in Northern Ireland*, London: HMSO 1992, paragraph 30). Employers are prohibited from discriminating against applicants for employment and against those whom they employ already, be they direct employees or 'contract workers' supplied by someone else.

In addition, a number of other organisations are covered by the legislation, including employment agencies, vocational organisations, people providing training services, people with statutory power to select employees for others, and people with power to confer qualifications that might facilitate employment.

As with sex discrimination legislation (see 9.2), the aim of the legislation is to cover the whole of the employment relationship, including the advertising of the post, the arrangements made for determining who shall be employed, the terms on which a person is offered employment, refusal to offer a post, access to promotion, transfer, training, and other benefits, and dismissal and redundancy arrangements.

Again, as with legislation on sex discrimination, the Act makes three types of conduct unlawful: direct discrimination, indirect discrimination, and victimisation.

9.3.3.1 Direct Discrimination

This is defined as less favourable treatment of a person on grounds of religious belief or political opinion. As noted above in the context of sex discrimination, this will include deliberate or malicious refusal to offer a job or a promotion, and also less favourable treatment that is committed out of a concern to protect the person involved or as a result of pressure applied by other people.

As we saw before, the test for discrimination is objective, not subjective: it focuses on what was actually done, not on the motives (see 9.2.2). In the case of *Neilly v. Mullaghboy Private Nursing Home* [1991] Case no. 31/90, the owner of a nursing home was found to have unlawfully discriminated against a cook whom she dismissed. The reason for the dismissal was the fact that residents of the home complained that they did not want a 'Catholic cook from the Irish Republic.' The employer herself had no such objections but was pressured into dismissing the cook.

The number of cases where religion or political opinion is given explicitly as the reason for a decision is likely to be small. In the case of *Department of the Environment v. Fair Employment Agency* [1989] NI 149, the Court of Appeal indicated that where a better-qualified or indeed an equally qualified person of a different religion is not short-listed, appointed, or promoted, the onus is on the employer to explain the reason for this and to show that it was not a discriminatory reason. Tribunals may well draw an inference of unlawful discrimination if no satisfactory reason can be produced.

Employers would be well advised to adhere to the Code of Practice and to use clearly demonstrable objective criteria for appointments, to ensure that those involved in the selection process are properly trained, to see that all interview notes are properly retained, and so on.

9.3.3.2 Indirect Discrimination

We have already studied the meaning of this type of discrimination in the context of sex discrimination (see 9.2.2.2). Its definition in the fair employment context is similar, and its inclusion in the 1989 Act was a significant development. Employers may now be liable for unlawful discrimination where their decisions are based on criteria that have the effect of reducing substantially the proportion of people from one religious group who can fulfil them. Examples of indirect discrimination in the fair employment field could include a requirement to hold a particular educational requirement, such as a GCSE in Irish, that was not relevant to the job; informal recruitment practices, such as word-of-mouth recruitment, where the existing work force is predominantly of one religion; the requirement to live in a particular locality; recruiting all employees from a particular school; or using length of service as the criterion for promotion or for redundancy selection where people from a particular religious group are unlikely to have that service.

As we have seen, the concept of indirect discrimination is not an easy one, and its application has given rise to difficulties for tribunals and courts. One issue that has been discussed is the question of the meaning of the term 'considerably smaller proportion'. In the case of *McCausland v. Dungannon District Council* [1992] Case no. 58/90, the question of the proportion of Protestants and Catholics eligible to be considered as a result of an internal trawl was at issue before the Court of Appeal. The question was whether 15 in 1,000 Catholics who can comply with a requirement or condition is a 'considerably smaller' proportion than 20 in 1,000 Protestants who can comply. The court ruled that these figures should be grossed up to be expressed as a success chance for Catholics that was 29 per cent less than the chance for Protestants.

9.3.3.3 Victimisation

This occurs where a person treats another less favourably because they have made a complaint of unlawful discrimination under the Fair Employment legislation or given evidence or information in connection with the Acts.

9.3.4 *Permitted Discrimination*

The 1989 Act (section 37) lists a number of specific employments to which the legislation does not apply. These include employment as a clergyman or minister of religion, employment in a private household, and employment as a teacher in a school. This last exception is to be kept under review by the FEC (section 38) and may in time be removed or limited by the Secretary of State (section 39). In addition, discrimination may be lawful where the essential nature of the job requires it to be done by a person holding (or not holding) a particular religious belief or political opinion (section 37).

A further exception is supplied by section 57 of the 1976 Act. This states that discrimination on the grounds of political opinion will not be unlawful where that opinion includes approval or acceptance of the use of violence for political ends connected with Northern Ireland.

Finally, section 42 of the 1976 Act allows the Secretary of State to issue a certificate indicating that an act was done for the purpose of safeguarding national security, public safety, or public order. Such an act will then be exempt from a challenge of unlawful discrimination.

9.3.5 *Remedies in Fair Employment Cases*

If a claim of unfair discrimination is successfully made out before the Fair Employment Tribunal, a number of remedies are available. These are similar to the remedies in sex discrimination cases noted earlier, except that there is a ceiling for compensation, at present fixed at £35,000.

The tribunal may (under section 26 of the 1976 Act):

(*a*) make an order declaring the rights of the complainant;
(*b*) order the respondent to pay compensation; awards may include sums in respect of injury to feelings; again, no compensation is payable in respect of unintentional indirect discrimination;

(c) make a recommendation that the respondent take action to obviate or reduce the adverse effect of the discrimination; if the respondent fails to comply with such a recommendation, the compensation may be increased.

Under section 27 of the 1976 Act there is a right for either party to appeal against the decision of the Fair Employment Tribunal. Such appeals must be based on a point of law, and will be heard by the Court of Appeal.

In the case of *Duffy v. Eastern Health and Social Services Board* [1991] Case no. 38/90—one of the first cases brought under the 1989 Act—the FET showed itself ready to use to the full the provisions on compensation. In this case, which involved discrimination against a Catholic worker in the laundry at Purdysburn Hospital, no financial loss was suffered by the complainant; nonetheless she was awarded £25,000. This was made up of £15,000 for injury to feelings, £5,000 aggravated damages for the way in which the respondents had conducted themselves during the hearings, and a further £5,000 by way of exemplary damages in view of the fact that the respondents were a public authority.

9.3.6 *The Affirmative Action Provisions*

So far we have been looking at ways in which employers are prohibited from discriminating against individual workers. These provisions, while important, are unlikely to bring about rapid changes in employment practices and patterns and are therefore supplemented by a range of measures designed to ensure equality of opportunity and fair participation in the work-place. These measures take the form of specific duties on employers, and include the requirement to register with the Fair Employment Commission, to monitor the religious composition of the work force, to periodically review the composition of the work force, and, where fair participation is not being enjoyed by members of each religious group, to take affirmative action. This may include measures such as the setting of goals and timetables, encouraging applications from the under-represented group by establishing links with minority schools or advertising in the hitherto neglected section of the press, or abandoning informal methods of recruitment.

In some circumstances the Fair Employment Commission may impose an affirmative action plan on an employer. It also has power to issue a notice that an employer is 'unqualified' to receive government grants or to be considered for public authority contracts. These provisions go far beyond what is required by any other piece of anti-discrimination legislation anywhere in Britain. Indeed, the Fair Employment legislation is the strongest anti-discrimination measure anywhere in western Europe. The two Acts are backed up by an array of regulations and a Code of Practice. A study of the detail of this is beyond the scope of this book.

9.4 *Discrimination Against Ex-Offenders*

Ex-offenders form a significant minority among today's work force, with recent figures suggesting that over 20 per cent of the working population have a criminal record. The Rehabilitation of Offenders (Northern Ireland) Order 1978, was passed to prevent discrimination against ex-offenders who are thought to have put their criminal past completely behind them. It reflects the tension between two interests: the interest of society and the social benefits of giving ex-offenders a chance to wipe the slate clean and start afresh, on the one hand, and on the other hand the need of employers to employ someone in whom they have full trust and confidence.

The Order, which is complex, operates by allowing some criminal convictions to become 'spent' after a certain period, known as the rehabilitation period. In other words, provided he or she does not commit another offence during that time, the ex-offender must be treated as though the offence had never happened. The conviction (at least with regard to employment law) is wiped from the record. It is unlawful for an employer to ask about spent convictions, or to let the fact that a job applicant has a spent conviction influence him or her in the decision whether to appoint or to continue to employ such a person. Similarly, the failure to disclose a spent conviction is not proper grounds for prejudicing a person as regards employment. A rehabilitated person may even have an action in defamation if someone later refers to the fact that he or she has been convicted of the offence.

The length of the rehabilitation period varies according to the type and severity of the original sentence (rather than the nature of the offence) and the age of the offender at the time. The period starts to run from the date of the conviction (not from the expiry of the sentence).

Sentence	*Rehabilitation period*
Absolute discharge Conditional discharge	Six months
Probation order Bind over/care order/ supervision order	One year, or until the order expires, whichever is the longer
Fine or community service order Imprisonment for 6 months or less Imprisonment for 6–30 months	Five years Seven years Ten years

(For an explanation of these sentences see 4.6.)

These periods of rehabilitation are reduced by half for offenders under the age of seventeen at the time of the offence, and there are special rehabilitation periods for some sentences confined to young offenders.

Prison sentences of more than thirty months are excluded altogether from the scheme. This means of course that for long-term offenders their convictions will never become spent, and they are unable to benefit at all from the provisions.

9.4.1 Excluded Occupations

The force of the legislation is further reduced because there is a wide range of specific jobs and professions excluded from its ambit by the Rehabilitation of Offenders (Exceptions) (Northern Ireland) Order 1978. These include several government appointments (generally concerned with the administration of justice) and a number of the professions, including social workers, doctors, lawyers, accountants, health service workers, chemists, and vets. This means that when applying for one of these excepted jobs the applicant is not protected by the Order, and a spent conviction will be legitimate grounds for refusing to employ someone. However, an applicant must be informed that the job for which he or she is applying is one to which the Order does not apply.

9.4.2 Remedies for Ex-Offenders

One of the main problems with the legislation is that of remedies. While the Order declares that it is unlawful for an employer to discriminate on the grounds of a spent conviction, the candidate who is the victim of such discrimination has no individual remedy if he or she is refused employment. On the other hand, an employee who is already in a post and who is dismissed when his or her employer discovers a spent conviction will almost certainly be able to claim unfair dismissal.

An example of this is provided by the case of *Property Guards Ltd v. Taylor and Kershaw* [1982] IRLR 175. The two applicants worked as security guards (which is not an excepted occupation). On starting employment they signed a statement to the effect that they had never been guilty of a criminal offence. When the employers discovered that they had both been convicted of minor offences of dishonesty some time previously, they were dismissed. The dismissals were held to be unfair. In both cases the convictions were already 'spent' at the time of signing the statement, and both men were entitled not to disclose their convictions.

A related problem arises where an employee tinkers with his or her curriculum vitae to disguise the fact of a 'spent' conviction, particularly where this has involved a spell in jail. In *Chuwen v. Debenhams Ltd COIT*

655/177 an employee stated on his application form that he was working in America at a time when he had in fact been in prison. He felt that the fact of his having been in prison would be prejudicial to his application, even though the conviction was 'spent'. When the employers found out they dismissed him, giving as their reason the fact that he had lied on his application form.

The tribunal did not accept this as the real reason for dismissal. They felt that if the employers had simply found out that the worker had been somewhere else, but not in prison, during the time he claimed to have been in America they would not have dismissed him. The real reason for his dismissal was the spent conviction, and accordingly the dismissal was unfair.

9.4.3 *'Unspent' Convictions*

Where an applicant has an 'unspent' conviction, the Order offers him or her no protection. An employer is free to ask about such convictions and to take them into account when deciding whether or not to employ the applicant. Candidates are, however, under no obligation to volunteer information about convictions.

If a candidate is asked about a criminal record and deliberately lies about an 'unspent' conviction, their subsequent dismissal will often be quite fair. In *Torr v. British Railways Board* [1977] IRLR 184 a guard was dismissed after working satisfactorily for sixteen months. He had obtained the job by concealing an 'unspent' conviction that had happened some fifteen years earlier. The Employment Appeal Tribunal ruled that the dismissal was fair, emphasising that an employment relationship must be based on trust. By lying at the recruitment stage, the worker had destroyed the foundation of trust and confidence on which his employment was based.

9.5 *Discrimination on Grounds of Disability*

Disabled people often face prejudice and discrimination in obtaining and retaining work. However, there is no specific prohibition of discrimination on grounds of disability. Employers have legal obligations regarding the employment of disabled people, but these are widely regarded as inadequate. Government policy on tackling discrimination against disabled workers reflects a belief that the interests of disabled people are best served by encouraging employers to adopt good practice voluntarily, rather than threatening them with prosecutions.

Recent years have seen some thirteen attempts to introduce disability discrimination legislation by the mechanism of the private member's Bill.

These have been influenced by the disability discrimination legislation of the United States, the Americans with Disabilities Act 1990, which imposes both anti-discrimination and affirmative action requirements on employers. The government has announced that it intends to introduce some form of disability discrimination legislation in the near future. At the time of writing it is not known precisely what form this legislation will take, but clearly this is an area of law that is likely to change significantly in the months ahead.

One problem is that the term 'disability' has a range of different meanings and raises questions of degrees of disability. It is thus unlike sex, religion, or race, which are generally predetermined and specific conditions. Disability is a generic term that covers a range of conditions, from invisible ones such as hearing impairment, epilepsy and mental illness to very visible ones such as paraplegia, spasticity, and blindness. A recent study in Northern Ireland found that 17.4 per cent of the adult population was disabled, a figure that is 20 per cent higher than the corresponding one for Great Britain.

People with disabilities face great disadvantage in the labour market. Unemployment is disproportionately high among disabled people, and disabled applicants are more likely to encounter discrimination. Fewer than 31 per cent of disabled people of working age are in paid employment, and on average they are paid considerably less than non-disabled people (Office of Population, Censuses and Surveys, *Disabled Adults: Services, Transport and Employment*, London: HMSO 1989).

9.5.1 *The Legal Framework*

The principal legislation is the Disabled Persons (Employment) Acts (Northern Ireland) 1945 and 1960. The original Act was passed in the wake of the Second World War in an attempt to secure employment for disabled ex-servicemen. The Acts aim to assist men and women who are handicapped by disablement to get employment that is suitable for them and makes the best use of their skills. They are based on the premise that the great majority of disabled people can take their place with others in ordinary work situations, provided that their occupation is carefully chosen. In brief, the Acts provide for the registration of disabled people; they lay an obligation on employers to employ a quota of such people and to reserve vacancies in certain occupations for those registered as disabled.

9.5.2 *The Register of Disabled Persons*

Registration is voluntary but can carry certain advantages. Those eligible to register are people who, on account of injury, disease, or congenital deformity, are substantially handicapped in getting or keeping suitable employment and whose disability is likely to last at least twelve months. A certificate is issued on registration, and an employer may ask for it to be produced.

Anyone wishing to register should contact the disablement employment adviser at any local office of the Training and Employment Agency. This adviser can also give information on the range of schemes and benefits that may be available. These include vocational training, the Fares to Work Scheme, the Special Aids to Employment Scheme, capital grants, and wages subsidy.

9.5.2.1 Vocational Training

Under the 1945 Act (section 2), the Department of Economic Development has the power to provide disabled people with vocational training and rehabilitation. The general policy on training is integrationist, so that young disabled people will generally be offered places on schemes such as Youth Training Programmes. Specialist training may be available where appropriate.

9.5.2.2 Fares to Work Scheme

Registered disabled people who cannot use public transport and who do not have their own car may receive grants to cover their travelling expenses under the Fares to Work scheme.

9.5.2.3 Special Aids to Employment Scheme

Technical aids for employment, such as special chairs and adapted word-processors, may be available free under this scheme.

9.5.2.4 Capital Grants

Where employers need to adapt premises or equipment in order to employ a disabled person, they may receive capital grants of up to £6,000.

9.5.2.5 Wages Subsidy

Under the 1945 Act (section 15), the Department of Economic Development has introduced a Sheltered Placement Scheme. This enables an employer to employ a severely disabled person at a reduced rate that corresponds to their capacity for employment (measured between 20 and 80 per cent). The remaining portion of the wage is subsidised by one of a number of sponsoring organisations and paid through the disablement employment adviser.

9.5.3 *The Quota Scheme*

The 1945 Act (section 9 (1)) places a statutory duty on employers who have a total of not less than twenty employees to employ a quota of registered disabled persons. The quota at present is 3 per cent.

Failure to employ the quota does not of itself constitute an offence but has two main consequences. Firstly, an employer in that position must not engage anyone other than a registered disabled person unless he or she obtains a permit to do so. Secondly, an employer must not discharge a registered disabled person without 'reasonable cause'. Failure to comply with these provisions is a criminal offence, carrying a maximum sentence of a fine of £400 or three months in prison or both. However, only the Department of Economic Development can institute proceedings, and then only with the consent of a Disablement Advisory Committee. So far no prosecutions have been brought in Northern Ireland. In Great Britain the last prosecution was brought in 1975, yet there is considerable evidence that few employers meet their quota. Figures for 1990 show that only 0.9 per cent of employees in the private sector and 0.8 per cent of employees in the public sector were registered disabled people (see *Equal Opportunities Review* no. 43 (May–June 1992), 1).

Under the Acts, a person has no right to enforce compliance with the duty. The only possible remedy may be an application for judicial review, where a person feels that he or she has been discriminated against by a public sector employer that is not fulfilling their quota obligations.

9.5.4 *Designated Employments Scheme*

The Department of Economic Development has power to designate an occupation so as to reserve further entry into it for registered disabled people (1945 Act, section 12). So far only two such employments have been so designated: car park attendant and lift attendant.

9.5.5 *Other Provisions*

Employers are obliged to maintain detailed records showing their compliance with their quota obligations and employment in designated occupations. Records must be kept for two years and made available for inspection to the Department of Economic Development. Failure to comply with these provisions is a separate offence.

Under the Companies (Directors' Report) (Employment of Disabled Persons) Regulations (Northern Ireland) 1982, any company that employs more than 250 people must present, as part of its directors' report, a statement describing the policy it has applied during the previous financial year towards the employment of disabled people.

In 1985 the Department of Economic Development produced a Code of Practice on the Employment of Disabled People, giving valuable practical advice.

9.5.6 *Unfair Dismissal*

A disabled person who has been dismissed from employment because the employer believes that the disability prevents proper performance of the job may have a claim for unfair dismissal. Employers who engage an employee in full knowledge of his or her disability will find it difficult to justify a dismissal on the grounds of inability to do the job. However, where the disability has worsened, or where a fit employee has become disabled while in employment, they may be able to do so. They must establish that the employee is no longer capable of doing the work, and also show that they acted reasonably in treating the incapacity as a sufficient reason for dismissal.

The failure by a job applicant to disclose to the employer full details of a disability that might affect their ability to do the job can have serious consequences. An employer might be entitled to dismiss such an employee on grounds of misconduct for having concealed a condition that the employer reasonably believes makes the employee unsuitable for the job to which they have been appointed.

The law on unfair dismissal is complex and cannot be discussed in detail here. Clearly an employer must act only after reasonable investigation of the medical situation, after reasonable consultation with the employee, and after due consideration of the availability of suitable alternative employment.

Further information on the law relating to unfair dismissal is available from the Labour Relations Agency.

9.6 *Racial Discrimination*

In Northern Ireland it is perfectly legal to discriminate on racial grounds, and there is no remedy for the victims of such discrimination. Legislation on race has been in force in Great Britain since 1965 but has never been extended to Northern Ireland.

This is a breach of the United Kingdom's obligations under the UN Convention on the Elimination of All Forms of Racial Discrimination but has been justified by the government on the grounds that there 'has been no race relations problem to date in Northern Ireland ... Where no problem exists legislation is not required' (*Tenth Periodic Report to the UN Committee on the Elimination of Racial Discrimination*). The absence of any EU provisions to combat racial discrimination in the work-place stands in marked contrast to the well-developed and long-standing body of EU law on sex equality.

The size and distribution of racial groups in Northern Ireland is not well documented; such information is not collected in the census. According to government estimates, racial minorities probably total around 10,000. It is possible that the number may be considerably greater than this.

There is growing evidence that racism is a problem in Northern Ireland. Instances of discrimination in the fields of employment, housing and education are well documented, as are cases of racial abuse and harassment. The Standing Advisory Commission on Human Rights has recommended that legislation parallel to that in Great Britain be introduced without delay (SACHR, *Religious and Political Discrimination and Equality of Opportunity in Northern Ireland: Second Report* (Cmd 1107), London: HMSO 1989).

It now seems likely that some action may be taken in the near future. In 1992 the Northern Ireland Office issued a consultative document on proposals for race legislation. These proposals seem to suggest the introduction of legislation to prohibit discrimination on the grounds of colour, race, nationality, or national origins. The legislation would extend not only to employment but also to the provision of goods, facilities, services, and premises. The model envisaged appears to be that provided by the British legislation, i.e. the Race Relations Act 1976, and the Sex Discrimination (Northern Ireland) Order 1976. One element that is unclear is whether the enforcement remit would be given to an existing agency (such as the FEC or EOC) or whether a separate enforcement authority would be created.

Any move towards the extension of anti-racism legislation to Northern Ireland is to be welcomed. No information on likely dates is available at present.

9.7 Further Reading

Bateson, P., and McKee, J., *Industrial Tribunals in Northern Ireland*, Belfast: SLS Legal Publications 1989.

Davies, C., and McLaughlin, P. (editors), *Women, Employment and Social Policy in Northern Ireland: a Problem Postponed*, Centre for Research on Women (CROW), PRI 1991.

Dickson, Brice, *The Legal System of Northern Ireland*, Belfast: SLS Legal Publications 1993.

Dickson, Brice (editor), *Civil Liberties in Northern Ireland: the CAJ Handbook* (2nd edition), Belfast: Committee on the Administration of Justice 1993.

Hayes, J., and O'Higgins, P. (editors), *Lessons from Northern Ireland*, Belfast: SLS Legal Publications 1990.

McCormack, V., and O'Hara, J., *Enduring Inequality: Religious Discrimination in Employment in Northern Ireland*, London: Liberty 1990.

McCrudden, C. (editor), *Fair Employment Handbook*, London: Eclipse Publications 1991.

10

THE BREAKDOWN OF RELATIONSHIPS

Ciaran White

10.1 *Introduction*

When a couple, whether they are married or unmarried, are experiencing the breakdown of a relationship, intervention by social workers may become necessary. On most occasions you will not be statutorily required to become involved. However, there will be occasions when clients will turn to you for advice as someone they trust, or perhaps because an emergency has arisen and they seek information on how the law may help them or where they can obtain advice. They may simply seek advice before consulting solicitors or other qualified people about whether any legal remedies are available to them.

However, there are a number of statutory functions that social workers can be asked to perform where a relationship is breaking down. For example, you can be required to produce a welfare report on the child or children of a couple who are in the process of divorcing, or where a care or supervision order or an article 8 order is being sought. (For an explanation of care or supervision orders and article 8 orders and the requirement to complete reports see chapter 6. Advice on how to compile reports is given in chapter 3.) Obviously you are also likely to become statutorily involved if the care and protection of the children of the relationship becomes an issue. (For a fuller discussion of child protection powers see chapter 6.)

This chapter outlines the law relating to the breakdown of relationships and provides some information on how it operates in practice to help you answer some of the many questions that may be asked. We consider firstly how the law can protect the victim of domestic abuse from further abuse, then we examine entitlements to housing and finance in situations of domestic violence. The formal termination of marriage and the resolution of financial and child custody issues, both for married and unmarried couples, are the focus of the remainder of the chapter.

10.2 Domestic Violence

Perpetrators of domestic violence can be subject to the criminal law and to the civil law for abusing others or to prevent further abuse from occurring. (For an explanation of criminal law and civil law see 1.3.2.).

10.2.1 Domestic Violence and the Criminal Law

No legal definition of 'domestic violence' exists, nor is there a specific crime of domestic violence. However, certain actions or behaviour that are common in domestic violence will amount to criminal offences. Thus, for example, rape, buggery, incest and indecent assault are all criminal offences that can be committed in the course of domestic violence, as are assault, assault occasioning grievous bodily harm, and wounding. (It may prove easier to prove the non-sexual rather than the 'sexual' offences.)

Prosecution for criminal offences is the task of the Director of Public Prosecutions and the police (see 1.3.5); individuals have almost no possibility of prosecuting abusers themselves. Victims of domestic violence can be compensated by the state for criminal injuries they may have suffered, though the scheme is not a criminal law one but a civil law one. In order to qualify the crime must be reported to the police within forty-eight hours and a notice of intention to apply for compensation made to the Secretary of State for Northern Ireland within twenty-eight days of the crime.

Should the matter come to court, the victim can be required to testify against the abuser, even if he or she doesn't want to, if the alleged crimes involved injury to the spouse or children or were sexual offences committed against members of the family (Police and Criminal Evidence (Northern Ireland) Order 1989, article 79). Spouses are then, in legal terminology, competent and compellable to give evidence in court relating to the prosecution of crimes of a domestic nature.

However, one should not be too optimistic about the benefits of the criminal law in tackling domestic violence. Many women subjected to abuse have not found the police very helpful, either before or after the introduction of new police guidelines on responding to domestic violence in 1991 (see McKiernan and McWilliams, *Bringing It Out Into the Open*, 92). Even if a conviction is secured, the failure to impose a prison sentence on the abuser, as often happens, means that the victim receives little satisfaction or indeed protection from the process.

10.2.2 Domestic Violence and the Civil Law

Victims of domestic abuse can obtain court orders preventing the abuser from engaging in the abusive conduct and/or excluding the abuser from the place of residence of the victim and children under the Domestic Proceedings (Northern Ireland) Order 1980 (hereafter referred to as DP80). These orders can be obtained by married people and cohabitants alike, provided that the cohabitation is 'marriage-like'. (The court determines whether cohabitation is marriage-like by reference to the time the parties have lived together and whether they have any children.)

There are three types of order: (*a*) a personal protection order, (*b*) an exclusion order, and (*c*) an emergency (interim) personal protection or exclusion order. All these orders are applied for by the victim and are granted by the magistrates' courts.

10.2.2.1 Personal Protection Order

The applicant (i.e. the victim) must satisfy the magistrate that the respondent (i.e. the alleged abuser) has used or threatened to use violence against the victim or the victim's children and that an order is necessary for the victim's protection or for the protection of any children. The order means that neither the victim nor the child or children can be 'molested' by the abuser. It should be borne in mind that molestation in this context is not confined to sexual or physical molestation but can include, for example, non-verbal intimidation. In this context it essentially means pestering or interfering. There were 2,500 personal protection orders issued in 1991/92.

10.2.2.2 Exclusion Order

Exclusion orders can be issued if the abuser has used or threatened to use violence against the victim or the children, or if the abuser is in breach of a personal protection order and the issuing of the exclusion order is necessary for the protection of the victim or the children. These orders can exclude the abuser from the family home, even if the abuser is the legal owner. An order can operate in other ways, however. It can, for example, prevent the abuser from selling the home or surrendering a lease on it, or it can prohibit him or her from interfering with any services in the home or destroying any goods in it. It can also be used to exclude the abuser from any premises in which the victims are residing. So, for example, an exclusion order could exclude the abuser from the refuge to which the victims have fled. There were 2,300 of these orders issued, on behalf of women, in 1991/92.

10.2.2.3 'Emergency' Orders

These are personal protection and/or exclusion orders that can be made by magistrates in an emergency. Their effect is usually temporary, lasting until a full hearing can be arranged or for a specified time but at any rate for not more than five weeks.

A police officer who reasonably suspects someone of breaching one of these orders can automatically arrest that person (i.e. no warrant is needed). It is a criminal offence to breach any of these orders, punishable by fine or imprisonment (Family Law (Northern Ireland) Order 1993, article 14). However, these orders have not proved as useful as was hoped in combating domestic violence. McKiernan and McWilliams have identified a number of reasons why this may be so:

(1) The police, it is alleged, do not treat domestic violence with enough gravity.
(2) The police are reluctant or unsuccessful in finding the abusers to serve them with orders.
(3) The orders are constantly broken by the abusers, with only a small fine or a reprimand the usual punishment.
(4) The orders often only apply to the matrimonial home, and therefore victims have been vulnerable while out shopping or bringing children to and from school, for example. The best protection was often for the victims to move to a secret address, but this does not remain a secret for long, as the order contains the address of the victims. Additionally, victims felt vulnerable in courtrooms and often found attending court to obtain an order a difficult experience (McKiernan and McWilliams, *Bringing It Out Into the Open*, 93–).

10.2.3 *Compensation from the Abuser*

As well as being able to obtain these orders, victims of domestic abuse may also use the civil law to obtain awards of damages, for example for assault and battery, from the abuser. The action is brought privately by the victim against the abuser. However, this option is only a realistic one where the abuser is financially well off. The possibility of obtaining damages under the Criminal Injuries Scheme has already been discussed (see 10.2.1).

10.2.4 *The Right to Remain in the Family Home*

Domestic circumstances can deteriorate to such an extent that one partner wishes to evict the other from the family home. 'Can this be done?' the vulnerable partner may ask.

Where the two partners in a relationship, whether married or not, jointly own the home in which they live, both have the right to reside in it. Even if only one partner owns the property, the other may have what is called an 'equitable title' by virtue of having contributed to the purchase of it—by providing the deposit, for example, or paying some mortgage instalments. If a partner has an equitable title then he or she has a right to live in the property. Determining whether a partner has made enough contributions to be entitled to a proportion of the home is a difficult legal matter, and your client should be referred to expert legal advice immediately if there is a possibility that this is the case.

However, if the couple are married there is a simpler way of ensuring that a spouse can remain in the family home. The non-owning spouse has a right to live in the matrimonial home by virtue of the Family Law (Miscellaneous Provisions) (Northern Ireland) Order 1984. However, the 'rights of occupation' created by this legislation must be registered to make them effective against others. By registering his or her rights of occupation a spouse is essentially informing any future purchasers or mortgagors of the property of those rights. Registration in the case of registered land can be made in the Land Registry and in the case of unregistered land in the Registry of Deeds. (Both registries are administered by the Department of the Environment, and they can tell you whether a property is registered or unregistered land. Both registries are at Lincoln Building, 27–45 Great Victoria Street, Belfast BT2 7SZ; telephone 251555.)

The effect of registration is that the non-owning spouse cannot be evicted or excluded from the family home by the other spouse, nor can the property be sold or mortgaged without leave of the court. A non-owning spouse should be encouraged to register his or her right of occupation as soon as possible, because those rights are not operable against a purchaser if they have not been registered before the purchaser makes the contract to buy the home. Conversely, if the non-owning spouse is not currently living in the matrimonial home this legislation allows him or her to apply to the court to be allowed to live in it. Therefore, for example, a wife who has been forced out of the house does not have to accept her eviction, and she can obtain a court order to allow her to return. Simultaneously she could consider obtaining an exclusion order to have the husband excluded from the home, thus affording herself and her children some protection (see 10.2.2).

The legislation also applies to married couples living in rented accommodation. Where the lease has been made between the landlord and one spouse only, the other spouse has a right to reside in the accommodation. This right is only enforceable against the spouse, however, not against the landlord, so that, for example, if the husband gives up the flat then his wife must also vacate it. These rights cease on termination of the marriage, whether by death or divorce.

It must be emphasised that these rights do not apply to unmarried cohabitants. Where a couple are cohabitants and the house is owned by only one of them, the non-owning partner has no right to reside there unless he or she can show an equitable title in the property. (For the law relating to the rehousing of victims of domestic violence see chapter 12.)

10.2.5 *Maintenance and Domestic Violence*

There are ways in which maintenance can be obtained even if the parties are not engaged in divorce proceedings. We are dealing here with situations where one spouse has failed to 'reasonably maintain' the other spouse or the children of the marriage. It should be emphasised that the marriage does not have to be broken down before maintenance can be applied for, nor do acts of domestic violence have to be carried out: the duty to 'reasonably maintain' exists independently of the issue of marital breakdown, although in practice maintenance for failing to reasonably maintain a spouse or children is usually only sought when the marriage is experiencing difficulties. (However, the courts must cede jurisdiction in the assessment of maintenance for the children to the Child Support Agency if the agency also has jurisdiction. For example, if the father is failing to maintain his children and was no longer living with and caring for them, it is the agency that will determine the amount of maintenance payable for the children. The courts can continue to decide the amount of maintenance payable to the wife and can also decide the amount of maintenance payable for the children if the father is still living with and caring for the children, i.e. if, in the language of the Child Support legislation, he is not an absent parent (see 10.4.3).)

A spouse or child who is not being 'reasonably maintained' may make an application for maintenance either (*a*) to a magistrate's court under DP80, article 4, or (*b*) to the High Court under the Matrimonial Causes (Northern Ireland) Order 1978 (hereafter MC78), article 29. The factors that the courts consider in deciding whether there has been a failure to reasonably maintain are the same in both the magistrate's court and the High Court. The decision is made with reference to all the circumstances of the case, including income, financial needs, standard of living enjoyed by the family before breakdown, age of each party, duration of the marriage, any physical or mental disabilities of either party, and contributions to the welfare of the family, including home-making. In making these orders, however, the court is required to give the welfare of the children first consideration, under the Matrimonial and Family Proceedings (Northern Ireland) Order 1989 (hereafter MFP89), article 7.

The difference between the two procedures is that the magistrate's court cannot award secured periodical payments, nor can it order a lump sum greater than £1,000 to be paid. (Secured payments are income from property that is put to one side, as it were, for example in a separate account, for the purposes of periodical payments being made to the applicant. It has the advantage that the payment is guaranteed and avoids problems associated with continuing enforcement.)

Under the procedure before the magistrate's court the court can adjourn the application if a reconciliation is possible and appoint a 'suitably qualified person' (acting under arrangements made by the Department of Health and Social Services) to attempt to effect a reconciliation between the parties. This person could, of course, be a social worker. That person must report in writing to the court whether the attempt has been successful or not 'but shall not include in that report any other information' (DP80, article 28 (3)). A similar provision is not made in respect of the High Court. The grounds on which the magistrate's court can make an order are that the respondent has committed adultery, engaged in 'unreasonable behaviour', deserted the applicant, or failed to provide reasonable maintenance for the spouse or children. The High Court can make an order for maintenance where the spouse has failed to provide 'reasonable maintenance' for the other spouse or children.

These provisions can only be used where the parents of children are married. Where the parties are unmarried, a partner cannot secure maintenance from the other partner on his or her own behalf; however, if the couple have children it will be possible to secure maintenance from the parent of the children by way of an affiliation order at present, or under the Children (Northern Ireland) Order, schedule 1, when it comes into force. This means that, for example, a woman who has a child by a man to whom she is not married may obtain maintenance for that child, though she cannot obtain maintenance for herself.

Affiliation orders are made by the magistrate's court on application by the parent looking after the child. However, with the advent of the Child Support legislation, where one of the partners is absent, leaving the other with the care of the children, it will probably be the Child Support Agency that will determine the maintenance payable (see 10.4.3).

10.3 *Ending the Relationship: Divorce and Judicial Separation*

A marriage can be brought to an end by one of the parties obtaining either a divorce decree or a decree of judicial separation. While divorce involves the dissolution of a marriage, so that the parties are no longer married to one another, judicial separation merely relieves the parties of the obligation to live together. With judicial separation the marriage remains in existence but the parties could be said to be 'officially separated'. This means, however, that neither party can remarry until the other party dies or until a divorce decree is obtained.

Where a spouse who has been judicially separated dies without having made a will, the surviving spouse is not treated as next of kin for the purposes of the law of succession (MC78, article 20 (2)). You should also be aware that a divorce decree will affect a will made by one of the divorced couple. Those parts of the will relating to the former spouse will in effect become void, because the former spouse is treated as if he or she were dead (Will and Administration Proceedings (Northern Ireland) Order 1994, article 13). If one of the parties remarries, that automatically renders the will void. Not surprisingly, when a couple has divorced, the surviving spouse cannot inherit the estate of the deceased if the deceased ex-spouse did not make a will!.

The fact that a judicial separation has been obtained first does not prevent either spouse securing a divorce later. Judicial separation is a useful option for those who have a religious or philosophical objection to divorce but wish for some formal separation from their spouse. Neither the option of divorce nor judicial separation is open to people who are unmarried cohabitants.

Annulment is another form of action that brings marriages to an end, though it is used very rarely nowadays. A decree of nullity means that in the eyes of the law a marriage never took place and that what at first glance appeared to be a valid marriage was in fact void all along. Some of the grounds on which an annulment may be available are that

- (*a*) one of the parties was under the age of sixteen;
- (*b*) one of the parties was already married (i.e. has committed bigamy);
- (*c*) the parties were not respectively male and female;
- (*d*) the parties were in a prohibited degree of relationship, for example son-in-law and mother-in-law;
- (*e*) one of the parties has an incapacity to consummate or wilfully refuses to consummate the marriage.

Given that this form of action is rarely used nowadays, little attention will be paid to it from now on. For completeness' sake we mention the fact that there are two types of annulment, a civil annulment and a church annulment. The church annulment has no effect in civil law, and therefore someone who obtains a church annulment must obtain a civil annulment before remarrying, otherwise they will be guilty of bigamy should they choose to remarry.

10.3.1 *Grounds*

The basis on which divorce and judicial separation are obtained is the same. Only one ground exists for securing a divorce decree, and that is that the marriage has irretrievably broken down. Irretrievable marital breakdown is proved by establishing that at least one of five factual situations has been arrived at. (To obtain a decree of judicial separation, irretrievable marital breakdown does not have to be proved, though one of the five factual situations must exist.) These five 'facts', as MC78 (article 3) calls them, are:

- (*a*) adultery;
- (*b*) 'unreasonable behaviour';
- (*c*) desertion;
- (*d*) separation for two years together with the consent of the spouse to divorce or separate;
- (*e*) separation for five years (consent of the spouse immaterial).

10.3.1.1 Adultery

Adultery, which occurs when the respondent engages in extramarital sex, cannot be pleaded if, after the aggrieved party has become aware of the adultery, the parties have lived together for a period or periods exceeding six months (MC78, article 4 (1)). (For an explanation of the terms 'respondent', 'petitioner' etc. see 10.3.2.) Northern Ireland law differs slightly from that in England and Wales in that in the latter jurisdiction it is necessary to prove not only that there has been adultery but that the adulterous spouse has been 'intolerable' to live with.

10.3.1.2 Unreasonable Behaviour

To succeed on these grounds the legislation requires that 'the respondent has behaved in such a way that the petitioner cannot be reasonably expected to live with the respondent'—what is often referred to for convenience as 'unreasonable behaviour'. (Examples of unreasonable behaviour from past cases include excessive sexual demands, financial irresponsibility, and frequent drunkenness.) The fact that the parties have continued to live together for a period or periods of up to six months after the date of the last incident complained of will not affect the court's decision and can be disregarded in deciding whether irretrievable marital breakdown is proved (MC78, article 4 (3)).

10.3.1.3 Desertion

Desertion by the respondent for a continuous period of two years before the petition is issued is necessary before these grounds can be successfully pleaded. It does not matter for the purposes of calculating the two years' desertion period that the parties resumed living together for any one period not exceeding six months or any two or more periods not exceeding six months in all, but obviously the parties cannot count the period living together as part of the necessary period. Desertion is a complicated legal concept, and it is advisable to obtain legal advice if it is unclear whether desertion has taken place.

10.3.1.4 Separation

The two grounds of separation for two years and separation for five years are similar. In each case the parties must have agreed to split up, and the relevant period of separation must be completed before the petition can be made. The difference between the two is that where the parties have lived apart for two years the consent of the respondent is required for a divorce, whereas if they have been apart for five years consent of the other spouse is not needed. It is possible, though it rarely occurs, for the court to refuse to grant a divorce decree where the petitioner relies on five years' separation if it is of the opinion that 'the dissolution of the marriage will result in grave financial or other hardship to [the other party] and that it would in all circumstances be wrong to dissolve the marriage' (MC78, article 7). If this article is invoked to oppose a petition, the court must consider all the circumstances, including the conduct of the parties and their interests as well as those of the children and any other people concerned.

The bulk of petitions for divorce in Northern Ireland cite separation of one of these types—what are referred to as the no-fault grounds—as proof of marital breakdown instead of the other facts, commonly called the fault grounds. Citing the no-fault grounds avoids the acrimony that results from establishing that the marriage has broken down as a result of the adultery, unreasonable behaviour or desertion of one spouse.

10.3.2 *Court Procedure*

A divorce or judicial separation is initiated by one of the spouses making a petition for divorce (who is therefore referred to as the petitioner, while the other party is referred to as the respondent), citing the relevant 'fact' or grounds and including information about the children. A petition for divorce cannot be made within the first two years of marriage (MFP89, article 3), though there is no time bar on making a petition for judicial separation. A 'decree *nisi*' is issued by the court, usually within six to twelve months of the petition being made, and this is almost always followed, not less than six weeks later, by the 'decree absolute'. The marriage is not dissolved until the decree absolute is issued, and therefore the parties cannot remarry before this.

The court cannot make a decree *nisi* absolute, nor indeed can a separation be granted, unless it is satisfied about the arrangements made for the care of children. Where the parties in the case have children, as soon as the petition is presented the court must appoint a 'suitably qualified person', who is likely to be a social worker of course, (*a*) to consider reconciling the parties and (*b*) for a report on the children and the suitability of any arrangements for their welfare (MC78, article 43). A report must be compiled even when the parties agree on the arrangements for the care of the children. The written report is presented to the court, and this is usually sufficient. However, should a dispute arise over 'residence and contact', the author of the report may be required to attend and testify. (For advice on acting as a witness see chapter 3.) The part of the report dealing with the arrangements for the care of the children will be repealed by the Children Order.

Unlike the situation in England and Wales, petitioners here must appear personally in court and give evidence. (There is a legislative provision exempting petitioners from this requirement if they are citing as a 'fact' two years' separation and consent or five years' separation. However, the court rules implementing this are not yet in place.) The court retains a discretion to relieve the parties from the obligation to attend in cases where any of the other 'facts' are cited.

Another slight though important difference between the procedure in Northern Ireland and that in England and Wales is that legal aid is available here for undefended divorces. Divorce hearings are not open to the public, and only the judge, court officials, the parties and others with divorce petitions before the court will be in attendance.

The majority of petitions for divorce, judicial separation and nullity are made by wives. Of the 2,716 divorce petitions filed in 1993, 846 were by husbands and 1,870 were by wives. Altogether 1,297 decrees of divorce, judicial separation and nullity were made. Of these, 1,289 were decrees *nisi* (of which 1,203 were made absolute), six were decrees of judicial separation, and only two were for nullity. You can see from these statistics that not every divorce petition ends in divorce, nor is every decree *nisi* made absolute. One of the reasons for this is that parties are reconciled after the petition is made or perhaps before the decree is made absolute.

Undefended divorces can be dealt with by the High Court or the county court, while defended divorces must be heard by the High Court. The great bulk of divorce petitions are undefended. The main reason for this is not that many respondent spouses do not care about their marriages but that there is little point in defending a petition, except perhaps to ensure that lies are not told. Defending a petition may involve the parties merely haggling over whose fault it really is that the marriage has broken down, and that serves no purpose in the long run.

The court may adjourn proceedings if there is a reasonable possibility of a reconciliation between the parties, to enable attempts to effect such a reconciliation (MC78, article 8). The court may refuse to make a decree *nisi* absolute where the 'fact' cited has been two years' separation or five years' separation if the respondent makes an application to the court regarding his or her financial position and the court is not satisfied with the financial provision made for the respondent.

10.4 *Property, Finance, and Care of the Children*

The least difficult part of the divorce or separation process is securing the decree. Making decisions about the matrimonial property, about maintenance and about custody of the children is far more difficult. These matters are referred to by lawyers as 'ancillary matters', and court orders regarding them are described as 'ancillary relief'.

10.4.1 *Care of the Children*

The law relating to the custody of and access to children will be significantly reformed by the Children (Northern Ireland) Order, and 'custody and access' will become known as 'residence and contact'. The Order provides for four new types of order a court may make with respect to children on divorce or judicial separation or indeed in any 'family proceedings' (article 8). (For more on family proceedings see chapter 6.) Indeed a court can make article 8 orders of its own volition without either of the parties having requested it to do so. The four types of order are:

(1) Residence order—outlining the child's living arrangements.
(2) Contact order—requiring the person with whom the child is to live to allow the child to visit or stay with another person having parental responsibility for the child.
(3) Prohibited steps order—providing that steps can be taken by a parent without the court's approval.
(4) Specific issues order—directing what is to be done in specific situations regarding the child.

(For more on article 8 orders see chapter 6.)

The Order will also create a number of other new orders that may also be made in 'family proceedings'—care orders and supervision orders, for example—and can therefore also be made in divorce or separation proceedings or indeed in any domestic violence proceedings (see chapter 6). Those, however, are the court orders that may be made in divorce or separation proceedings in the future.

Until the Children Order is fully enacted, what court orders can be made? Quite simply, the court may make any such custody or access order as it thinks fit, though you should be aware that in many cases the court is merely formalising the arrangements agreed between the parties for the care of the children. As mentioned above, a court cannot make a decree of judicial separation or make a divorce decree absolute until satisfactory arrangements have been made for the children.

10.4.2 *Financial Arrangements and Divorce*

There is no community property regime in our law, and therefore a wife, for example, is not automatically entitled to half her husband's wealth on divorce. Instead the law gives the courts a number of powers regarding the redistribution of the parties' finance and property. The parties apply to the court and ask it to use these powers, and the court considers whether to use these powers or not. This means that the redistribution of finance and property will depend very much on the circumstances of each case.

The orders the court can make are the following:

(1) Maintenance pending suit—payments from one spouse to the other pending the court's decision on the petition (MC78, article 24).
(2) Periodical or lump sum payments of maintenance (MC78, article 25).
(3) Redistribution of the parties' property (MC78, article 26).

Periodic payments are regular amounts paid by one party to the other. These can be 'secured' or 'unsecured'. Secured payments are explained above; the main disadvantage with unsecured payments is that they cease on the death of the person making the payments, whereas secured payments continue after the person's death. A lump sum payment is obviously a single payment is respect of all future maintenance. In most cases, however, the courts must relinquish their authority to make financial orders in favour of the children to the Child Support Agency (see 10.4.3). Redistribution of the parties' property involves the court in transferring ownership of property from one party to the other. The most usual example would involve the court transferring the ownership of the matrimonial home from the husband to the wife.

In making these orders, with the exception of 'maintenance pending suit', the court is required to pay attention to the criteria set out in MC78, article 25, as amended by MFP89, article 7. This means that all the parties' circumstances are to be taken into account—though the court must give first consideration to the welfare of any children—including

(a) income, earning capacity, property, and other financial resources;
(b) financial needs, obligations and responsibilities that each party has or is likely to have in the future;
(c) the standard of living enjoyed by the party before the breakdown of the marriage;
(d) the age of each party and the duration of the marriage; and
(e) the physical or mental disability of either party.

Maintenance paid to an ex-spouse comes to an automatic end should the party in whose favour the award is made remarry.

In exercising its financial distribution powers, the court must consider whether it would be appropriate for it to exercise its powers so that the financial obligation of each party towards the other comes to an end as soon after the grant of the decree as the court considers 'just and equitable'. This is referred to as the 'clean break' principle and is an attempt to ensure that divorcing couples do not carry forward any obligations towards each other after the divorce process has been completed: in other words, that in the divorce process all ties between them are severed. You can appreciate that this is a most difficult objective for the courts to achieve. Courts are also encouraged to impose time limits on orders for periodic payments, i.e. that they should cease on a particular date, rather than make orders that continue indefinitely (MC78, article 27A, as inserted by MFP89, article 6).

It is only where a couple is married that parties are entitled to maintenance—or 'alimony', as it is sometimes called—for themselves. Where a couple is cohabiting, one partner cannot be required to pay maintenance for the other partner. However, maintenance can be claimed in respect of any children of the relationship, irrespective of whether the parents of the children were married to each other. (Maintenance for children, including maintenance in the context of divorce and judicial separation, is dealt with in 10.4.3 below.)

10.4.3 *Maintenance of Children*

The decision on levels of maintenance for children on the divorce of their parents will increasingly be governed by the Child Support (Northern Ireland) Order 1991 (hereafter CS91), though the courts can continue making child maintenance orders where

(a) the child is in education and the maintenance is needed to pay for his or her education;
(b) the child is disabled;
(c) the child is not one governed by CS91 (i.e. he or she is a 'non-qualifying child'): an example would be where the absent parent was the child's step-parent, i.e. not the natural parent; or
(d) the maintenance is additional to that already set by the Child Support Agency (this will only apply where the divorcing couple are quite wealthy); the courts will also retain responsibility for setting levels of maintenance for children in some situations where there has been a 'failure to reasonably maintain' (see 10.2.5).

Essentially, wherever an application for maintenance for a child is made to a court where the Child Support Agency also has jurisdiction, the court must relinquish its jurisdiction to the agency. We outline below the circumstances in which the agency has jurisdiction.

The Child Support Agency will determine the levels of maintenance to be paid, and can ensure collection, wherever one parent is absent and the other is left caring for the child. An absent parent need not be one whose whereabouts are unknown or who shows scant regard for his or her children. It is payable not only where the couple is in the process of divorcing or separating but also where an unmarried couple have split up and one parent is left caring for the children. If the Department of Health and Social Services can obtain maintenance for children of single parents who are living on means-tested benefits, it is entitled to reduce the benefits paid by that exact amount.

Child maintenance assessments are made by child support officers, working under the supervision of the Chief Child Support Officer. Assessments can be made for a child already subject to a court order for child maintenance. Where such an assessment is made, the court order ceases to have effect. Lone parents caring for children and living on means-tested benefits can be forced to make applications (CS91, article 9). Benefits can be reduced for non-cooperation for up to eighteen months. However, parents cannot be forced to make applications if the agency reasonably considers that the parent or child would suffer 'harm or undue distress' as a result. All applicants, whether required by the agency to apply or not, must disclose enough information about the absent parent (a) to allow the absent parent to be traced, (b) to calculate the amount of child support maintenance payable, and (c) to enable the amount to be recovered from the absent parent (CS91, article 7).

The decision of a child support officer can be appealed to the Child Support Appeals Tribunal within twenty-eight days (see also 11.2.3.4), from the tribunal to the Child Support Commissioner (but only on a point of law), and from there to the Court of Appeal, though again only on a point of law.

The calculation of the child support maintenance is based on complex formulas outlined in the schedule to the 1991 Order. Any agreement that attempts to restrict the rights of any person to apply for a maintenance assessment is void (i.e. has no legal effect). Child support officers will make periodic reviews of the maintenance assessment.

Inspectors can be appointed to assist the child support officers in their statutory function. They are given wide powers, including the power to enter, at a reasonable time, the work-place of the absent parent and question any adult they find on the premises and make such examinations and inquiries as they consider appropriate. The inspector may require the occupier of the premises or any employee or employer there to provide documents. It is a criminal offence to obstruct an inspector.

10.5 *Further Reading*

Archbold, C., 'Family Law in Northern Ireland' in Hamilton, C., and Standley, K., (editors), *Family Law in Europe*, London: Butterworths (forthcoming).

Dewar, J., *Law and the Family*, London: Butterworths 1992.

Dickson, Brice, and Davison, M., 'Family Law and Sexual Matters' in Brice Dickson (editor), *Civil Liberties in Northern Ireland: the CAJ Handbook* (2nd edition), Belfast: Committee on the Administration of Justice 1993.

Dickson, Brice, and McBride, D., (editors), *Digest of Northern Ireland Law* (including update), Belfast: SLS Legal Publications 1995, chap. 2.

Law Commission, *The Ground for Divorce* (Law Com. no. 192), London: HMSO 1990.

McKiernan, J., and McWilliams, M., *Bringing It Out Into the Open: Domestic Violence in Northern Ireland*, Belfast: HMSO 1993.

Royal Ulster Constabulary, *Guidelines on Domestic Violence*, Belfast: RUC 1991.

11

SOCIAL SECURITY BENEFITS

Adrian McCullough

11.1 Introduction

Strictly speaking, social workers have no statutory obligations in this area, and so whether they should become involved or not has frequently been a topic of debate. Some take the view that with resources, as always, limited, this type of optional work should certainly not be a priority or even undertaken at all. Others put more emphasis on establishing relations with other agencies better qualified to assist, for example the Social Security Agency itself, through its network of local offices, citizens' advice bureaux, local advice centres, the Law Centre (Northern Ireland), etc. Others are inclined to the view that the social worker in dealing with a client should adopt a holistic approach, when the financial circumstances and possible benefit entitlement of the client are clearly an important factor, given that social workers frequently find themselves working with the most disadvantaged people in Northern Ireland, where levels of disablement and unemployment are high and well-recognised problems related to poverty and poor housing also occur.

If it is accepted that there should be some involvement by social workers in this area, the next issue is how great the involvement should be. If you have made inquiries into the client's financial situation, should mere information and advice be offered? Should help be given with pursuing a claim, for example accompanying clients to Social Security Agency offices, assisting with the completion of claim forms, writing letters, or making phone calls? If need be, should you assist with an appeal to a tribunal, whether simply as a friend, as a witness, or even as a representative? Certainly all the available evidence shows that people attending a tribunal hearing who are represented by someone, whether legally trained or not, stand a much better chance of success.

Clearly to some extent the degree of personal involvement in this area is a matter in the first instance for the social worker. Not everyone will have the time and the inclination for this type of work. Furthermore, colleagues would have to be consulted and a consensus arrived at before anyone began acting as an advice or representation unit or resource. Much will ultimately depend on the view taken of the role of the social worker and of the relationship between social worker and client.

However, assuming the decision is made to get involved in this area, the aim of this chapter is to familiarise the social worker with the basic rules relating to various benefits and also with the adjudication structure.

Entitlement to any social security benefit does not exist as of right. The claimant must usually first prove that he or she satisfies the conditions that have been laid down by Parliament for the receipt of that benefit. These conditions will be found either in the Social Security Contributions and Benefits (Northern Ireland) Act 1992, or in the large number of Regulations that have been made to fill in the detailed rules of entitlement for each benefit. Furthermore, it is a general rule that before entitlement can exist, a claim must have been made and pursued through the adjudication system, which is set out in the Social Security Administration (Northern Ireland) Act 1992, and various Regulations made under it.

For the non-lawyer there is probably little point in turning initially to the legislation, i.e. the Acts and Regulations, which are frequently complex and obscure. It probably makes more sense to begin by looking at one of the claimants' guides that are now available. The most appropriate of these would be *Social Security Benefits in Northern Ireland* by Eileen Evason (Belfast: SLS Legal Publications 1992) and also *The Work of Tribunals: a Guide to Practice and Procedure* by C. G. MacLynn and Adrian McCullough, due in 1995 from the same publisher. The role of this chapter is not to provide a definitive guide to entitlement but to allow you to be of practical help to your clients should the need arise.

11.2 *Social Security Law*

The law in this area can be divided into two distinct topics: (*a*) the adjudication and appeal system and (*b*) the detailed rules of entitlement for each benefit. We will deal with them in that order.

11.2.1 *The Adjudication Structure*

Here we examine the system by which decisions are made and by which they may be appealed. The adjudication structure is composed of three distinct elements—adjudication officers, appeal tribunals, and Social Security Commissioners—each of which is examined in turn.

Claims for benefit are made to the Social Security Agency, either at a local office or one of its branches, usually in Belfast. This is one of the newly created executive agencies, staffed by civil servants, with their own budgets and responsible for administering some particular area. For adjudication purposes the Social Security Agency is separate from and independent of the DHSS. The minister responsible for the DHSS is not answerable in Parliament for decisions taken by the Agency in individual cases.

11.2.2 Adjudication Officers

These are officers of the Social Security Agency who allow or disallow and review claims for benefit. In reaching their decisions they act independently of the DHSS. They must have regard to the law, as stated in legislation and in Commissioners' decisions, as well as to published departmental guidance interpreting these. They take most of the decisions in the social security field.

Any decision taken by an adjudication officer can be appealed to a tribunal. However, some decisions are taken by the DHSS and are called departmental decisions. Examples of departmental decisions are whether a claim was properly made, whether a person is an employed earner or self-employed, and whether a person satisfied the contribution conditions. The Act requires these decisions to be taken by the department, as it has access to the relevant records. These cannot be appealed to a tribunal but would have to be challenged in the courts by way of judicial review (see chapter 1).

11.2.3 Appeal Tribunals

Normally the tribunals hear appeals from decisions made by adjudication officers. Exceptionally, however, an adjudication officer, having investigated a claim and being undecided about it, can refer it directly to a tribunal. In addition, a claimant will frequently have to ask for a review by an adjudication officer of an unfavourable decision before he or she will be allowed to appeal to a tribunal.

There are six types of tribunal that operate in the social security field:

(*a*) Social Security Appeal Tribunal (SSAT)
(*b*) Medical Appeal Tribunal (MAT)
(*c*) Disability Appeal Tribunal (DAT)
(*d*) Child Support Appeal Tribunal (CSAT)
(*e*) Vaccine Damage Tribunals
(*f*) Housing Benefit Review Boards (HBRB)

The organisation of tribunal sessions (but not review boards) is carried out by the Independent Tribunal Service based in Omagh and Belfast.

11.2.3.1 Social Security Appeal Tribunal

This tribunal deals with all social security appeals unless they must go to an MAT or DAT. It is chaired by a barrister or solicitor of at least five years' standing, appointed for three years at a time by the Lord Chancellor.

The other members are appointed by the President of the Tribunals from a panel composed of people appearing to him or her to have knowledge or experience of conditions in the area and to be representative of people living or working there.

As far as possible, hearings are informal, the procedure being decided by the chairperson. The claimant will receive at least ten days' notice of the date, time and place of the hearing, along with the submission of the adjudication officer (AO), setting out the evidence, the facts as found by the AO, his or her decision, and the reasons for that decision, with reference as appropriate to legislation and case law. The claimant (or appellant) is entitled to speak, call witnesses, question the AO, and be represented. The AO will be represented by a presenting officer, who is there to assist the tribunal and should be ready to refer to points in the appellant's favour as well as against him or her.

11.2.3.2 Medical Appeal Tribunal

This tribunal deals only with disablement benefit and severe disablement allowance. As the questions for this tribunal are largely medical—for example the degree of a claimant's disablement—two of the members are doctors, usually of consultant status and usually a consultant surgeon and consultant physician, although this can vary depending on the type of case. For example, a consultant psychiatrist may sit if the appellant is complaining of depression or anxiety. The procedure normally includes a medical examination. The chairperson is always a lawyer.

11.2.3.3 Disability Appeal Tribunal

This tribunal deals normally with appeals related to disability living allowance. The chairperson is always a lawyer, and he or she sits with a general practitioner and someone experienced in dealing with the needs of disabled people, either in a professional or voluntary capacity or because he or she is disabled. The tribunal has no power to carry out a medical examination.

11.2.3.4 Child Support Appeal Tribunal

This tribunal deals exclusively with appeals relating to child support. Decisions are made by adjudication officers in the Child Support Agency, who must first be asked to review their decision before it can be appealed. There are relatively few appeals, because the amount of child support payable is fixed by an inflexible statutory formula, and the tribunal has no discretion to deviate from this. Furthermore, the tribunal cannot change a decision, only refer it back to the officer for further consideration.

11.2.3.5 Vaccine Damage Tribunal

This Tribunal deals exclusively with appeals relating to vaccine damage.

11.2.3.6 Housing Benefit Review Boards

The boards deal with decisions made by the Northern Ireland Housing Executive and the Rating Agency on rent and rates in the public and private sectors. They are not part of the Independent Tribunal Service but come within the remit of the Department of the Environment. The chairperson is not a lawyer, and the standard of adjudication in some cases has been disappointingly low. There is no right of appeal from a board decision, but it is possible to apply to the High Court for judicial review.

11.2.4 *Social Security Commissioners*

The Social Security Commissioners can hear appeals from the tribunals mentioned above but only on a point of law. This underlines the importance of appeals and the importance of properly preparing and organising evidence to be presented at them, as there will normally be no second opportunity to persuade a tribunal to accept the appellant's version of the facts.

The commissioners are appointed by the Queen from among barristers and solicitors of at least ten years' standing. Their job is to interpret the law and to set precedents in the form of reported and unreported commissioners' decisions, which are binding on the tribunal. Commissioners' decisions are kept in social security offices, some libraries, and the Law Centre (Northern Ireland), and copies can also be purchased from the Government Bookshop.

11.2.5 *The Courts*

Decisions of the Social Security Commissioners can be appealed on a point of law only to the Court of Appeal, from there to the House of Lords, and from there to the European Court of Justice in Luxembourg, but only if the case involves a point of EU law. It is also possible to challenge a decision of a tribunal chairperson or of a commissioner by way of judicial review in the High Court (see 1.3.4).

11.2.6 *Representing Clients before an Appeal Tribunal*

Legal aid is not available for representation at tribunals. This is unfortunate, because representation can make a difference to the outcome of a hearing. However, many of the appeals coming to tribunals are not so complex factually, evidentially or legally as to require legal representation. Often an unqualified representative who knows some social security law and procedures and is also familiar with the case can do just as well as a lawyer.

The basic rules, however, are the same for all representatives. Firstly, consider whether the client has any valid grounds for appeal. Tribunals have little discretion, and if the law clearly precludes a successful claim, appealing would be a waste of time. On the other hand, if there is a point to be made, even if it is not a strong one, a representative should hesitate to advise against appealing, bearing in mind that the tribunal's jurisdiction is inquisitorial and investigative and that it may itself identify a point, whether in the claimant's favour or not, that has not been spotted by the AO or the claimant (or representative). Secondly, if the decision is made to appeal, make sure this is done in writing and within the normal time limit (see 11.2.7). A form on which to appeal can be supplied by any social security office, but this does not have to be used. The Independent Tribunal Service does not supply this, nor will it help with completing it. The grounds of the appeal must be clearly set out; there is no point in holding things back until the appeal hearing.

Normally, once an appeal is received, the AO will review the decision, and if this is completely successful then the appeal will lapse. If the review does not give the claimant everything he or she could have got on appeal, the appeal proceeds.

Typically only two weeks' notice of the date, time and place of the hearing is given, along with the adjudication officer's submission. It will be necessary to go through this with the claimant to see whether the AO has overlooked any relevant facts and also to examine the law quoted to see whether the appellant has any case from a legal point of view. It is useful to bear in mind that an appeal can be withdrawn by the claimant at any stage if the AO consents, or even at the hearing with the consent of the tribunal.

It is important to have the claimant's evidence 'in shape' by the date of the hearing, as the tribunal may refuse to grant an adjournment to allow this. You should therefore carefully examine the case to see what evidence should be obtained, for example from a doctor or a landlord, what witnesses should be asked to attend, and what steps generally can be taken to strengthen the case and make it more persuasive to a tribunal.

It must be remembered also (*a*) that normally hearsay evidence (i.e. oral or written assertions of a person other than the witness giving evidence, which is inadmissible as evidence of the truth of what was asserted: see chapter 3) *is* admissible in tribunals (although such evidence will not be given as much weight as other evidence), and (*b*) that a representative usually cannot also be a witness and give evidence.

Any documentary evidence should preferably be sent to the tribunal in advance, but if this is not possible it can be handed in at the hearing (tribunals usually have photocopying facilities), although the tribunal may have to adjourn for a few minutes so that everyone has a chance to read it.

Representatives generally should adopt an objective and professional approach and should certainly never predict a successful outcome.

11.2.7 *Time Limits*

A claim should be submitted in writing as soon as a claimant thinks he or she is entitled. It is difficult to get benefits backdated for more than three months without showing good cause for the delay. In any event, entitlement cannot usually be established for more than twelve months before the date of the claim. It is important therefore to claim as quickly as possible.

If the claim is disallowed, the claimant usually has three months in which to appeal. It makes sense, however, to appeal as soon as possible, so that the appeal can be dealt with quickly. It is possible to appeal late for special reasons, when the tribunal chairperson can grant a late appeal.

11.3 *The Benefits*

Before dealing with the particular benefits it is worth noting some general characteristics of benefits, as these often affect the basis on which they are paid.

11.3.1 *Contributory and Non-Contributory Benefits*

This is the basic way in which social security benefits are categorised. Although much of the finance for benefits comes from general taxes, some of it is raised from employers, employees and the self-employed in the form of national insurance contributions. For contributory benefits, a claimant must have paid or been credited with a minimum contribution to the National Insurance Fund. Only if this condition is met can entitlement arise to, for example, unemployment benefit (or job seeker's allowance, as it is to become in April 1996), and widow's and retirement pensions.

Contributory benefits like these are not means-tested, so entitlement is not affected by savings, investments or other income. The non-contributory benefits, i.e. the benefits to which there is entitlement without a contribution record, such as income support and family credit, are, however, also the ones that tend to be means-tested.

11.3.2 *Means-tested and Non-means-tested Benefits*

In addition to any other condition that must be satisfied, anyone claiming a means-tested benefit will have to disclose information about, for example, their income, including earnings, savings, and other capital resources, so that a calculation can be made to ascertain whether the claimant is entitled or not. The most obvious examples are income support and family credit.

Some benefits, however, can be paid even to wealthy people, because there is no means test. Examples include unemployment benefit paid to a man whose wife is in paid employment, and child benefit, which is payable at the same rate to the single mother and the millionaire's wife.

11.3.3 *'Passport Benefits' and Overlapping Benefits*

'Passport benefits' is a colloquial, non-statutory term referring simply to the fact that someone entitled to one benefit will also be entitled to another. So, for example, a person on income support is also entitled to free school meals, dental treatment, and prescriptions. Similarly, someone receiving disability living allowance who claims income support can claim the disability or severe disability premium.

Bear in mind, however, the opposite of passport benefits, i.e. overlapping benefits. Regulations prescribe situations in which the receipt of one benefit precludes the payment of some other benefit. For example, where one benefit is contributory, the non-contributory benefit is only payable to the extent that it exceeds the contributory benefit, so that income support entitlement will be reduced by any receipt of unemployment benefit and invalidity benefit. Also, where the benefits are contributory and paid weekly, only the highest will be paid. The regulations are complex, and proper advice should be sought.

11.4 Particular Benefits

This section deals firstly with the non-means-tested benefits and then with means-tested benefits, and finally with benefits for people injured at work and disabled people.

11.4.1 *Non-means-tested Benefits*

11.4.1.1 Unemployment Benefit (Job Seeker's Allowance)

Unemployment benefit is a contributory benefit that is payable for the first fifty-two weeks of unemployment. Claimants must not only be unemployed but also fit for work, actively seeking employment, and available for work. Any claimant who has lost his or her employment because of misconduct or who has voluntarily left employment without just cause may be disqualified from receiving the benefit for a maximum of twenty-six weeks. (The actual period is a discretionary one for the AO or, on appeal, the SSAT, which can impose a longer or shorter disqualification.) As a general rule it is a criminal offence to work while claiming unemployment benefit.

In April and October 1996 unemployment benefit will be replaced by job seeker's allowance. This will place much more emphasis on finding new work. It will last for just twenty-six weeks, as opposed to the fifty-two weeks for which unemployment benefit lasts. There will, however, be financial incentives for employers to take on new staff.

11.4.1.2 Statutory Sick Pay

Statutory sick pay (SSP) is paid by the employer to an employee who is incapable of work because of illness. It is paid at one of two levels, depending on the level of the employee's pay. It is treated as income and is subject to deductions for income tax and national insurance. Employees can in addition receive sick pay under a scheme run by the employer. It is payable for a maximum of twenty-eight weeks.

11.4.1.3 Incapacity Benefit

This benefit replaced sickness and invalidity benefit from 13 April 1995. It is a contributory benefit, which is divided into short-term incapacity benefit for the first fifty-two weeks and thereafter long-term incapacity benefit.

For the first twenty-eight weeks, during which benefit is paid at the lower rate, a claimant must show incapacity for his or her own occupation. Thereafter claimants must satisfy the test of incapacity for all work. (This is done by scoring either fifteen points for physical disabilities relating to, for example, walking, climbing stairs, sitting, standing, hearing and manual dexterity, or ten points for mental disabilities relating to, for example, concentration, or by scoring fifteen points from a combination of physical and mental disabilities.) The benefit is taxable and is expected to generate many appeals to the SSAT.

11.4.1.4 Statutory Maternity Pay

Statutory maternity pay (SMP) is paid by employers to women during maternity leave for up to eighteen weeks. It is paid at two rates, depending on length of service. Like SSP, it is subject to income tax and national insurance contributions.

11.4.1.5 Maternity Allowance

This is payable to women who are not entitled to SMP but who have been employed for twenty-six out of the previous fifty-two weeks and have an appropriate contribution record. It is payable for eighteen weeks.

11.4.1.6 Child Benefit

It would be difficult to overstate the importance to families of this benefit. This is because it is non-contributory, non-means-tested, tax-free, and paid (usually to the mother) whenever there is a claimant looking after a child. It lasts until the child reaches the age of sixteen or finishes full-time secondary education. In addition, a single parent, i.e. a parent living alone, can claim one-parent benefit, an extra weekly payment for each child living with the claimant. If a person is caring for an orphan, guardian's allowance can be claimed in addition to child benefit.

11.4.1.7 Widow's Benefits

Entitlement to these benefits is dependent on the contribution conditions being satisfied by the widow's late husband. They are non-means-tested but are only available to a widow, i.e. a woman married to a man at the time of his death, and not to a cohabitant or divorced woman.

'Widow's payment' is a lump sum of £1,000 payable either when the widow is under the age of sixty when her husband dies or when she is sixty or over and her husband was not receiving a retirement pension.

Widowed mother's allowance is paid to widows who are entitled to child benefit and who have not remarried or begun cohabiting (i.e. living together as husband and wife without being married).

Widow's pension is paid to widows aged between forty-five and sixty-five when their husbands die or when they cease to be entitled to widowed mother's allowance while aged between forty-five and sixty-five.

11.4.1.8 Retirement Pensions

There are two main contributory retirement pensions. Category A pensions are paid on the claimant's own contribution record, while category B pensions are paid to married women, widows and some widowers based on the contribution record of the claimant's spouse. Retirement pensions are paid at present to women who have reached the age of sixty and to men at the age of sixty-five. However, these ages are being equalised at sixty-five, so that any woman now aged under thirty-nine will not qualify for retirement pension until she is sixty-five.

Category A pensions are paid to claimants on the basis of their own contribution records, and the exact amount will depend on these. In addition, some claimants will qualify for a graduated pension based on contributions paid between 1961 and 1975. Contributors since 1975 may get an addition based on their contributions to the state earnings-related pension scheme (SERPS). (Many employers, however, run their own pension schemes, and their employees contract out of SERPS.)

Category B pensions are paid on the basis of the claimant's spouse's contributions and are paid to a married woman, widow or widower over pensionable age. The additions available for category A pensions are also available for category B pensions.

Where the employer has not contracted out of the state earnings-related pension scheme (SERPS), this provides an earnings-related addition to the basic retirement pension. Where the employer has contracted out, the retired employee will be paid an occupational pension by the employer. Alternatively, employees can opt to join a personal pension scheme. Note that pensions can also be increased by deferring retirement to the age of seventy. The basic pension increases by 10 per cent for each year that retirement is deferred.

11.4.2 *Means-tested Benefits*

Means-tested benefits are non-contributory; qualifying for them depends essentially on the claimant's income and capital. So, as well as providing income they can be used to top up wages and other benefits.

11.4.2.1 Family Credit

This is a benefit paid to supplement the low income of some families. The reasons for the poor take-up of family credit are unclear, but it is unfortunate, because it could provide an important supplement to families trying to live on low wages. It is payable to couples or single parents with at least one child.

The amount of family credit is calculated by using a complicated formula that involves a comparison between the family's net income (i.e. after paying tax and national insurance) and the 'applicable amount'. This is an amount set by the government and increased each year (at present it is £73). If the family income is below the applicable amount, the family credit entitlement will be the maximum for the particular family calculated by reference to a scale of rates. If the family income is above the applicable amount, the family credit entitlement will be the maximum figure reduced by 70 per cent of the excess of income over the applicable amount. There are also complicated rules for calculating income, which is normally based on wages over the six weeks before the date of the claim; if earnings fluctuate it may sometimes make sense to delay claiming until the wages are lower.

Once awarded, family credit will normally be paid for twenty-six weeks, without taking account of any change of circumstances (for example an increase in income). To be entitled, the family must

(*a*) be resident in Northern Ireland;
(*b*) include an adult working for at least sixteen hours a week;
(*c*) include at least one child;
(*d*) have less than £8,000 capital; and
(*e*) have a weekly income below a certain level, which will depend on the number of children and their ages.

The best advice is that if the client is working at least sixteen hours a week, has one or more children, and is on a low income, a claim for family credit should be made. It is paid weekly by order book. Recent changes mean that recipients of family credit may also qualify for a new child care allowance.

11.4.2.2 Income Support

This is the benefit that is supposed to act as the safety net of the social security system. If a client appears to be entitled to no other benefit and has no or a low income and capital of less than £8,000, this benefit can be claimed. The basic conditions for entitlement are that the claimant must

(*a*) be in Northern Ireland;
(*b*) be aged eighteen or above;
(*c*) not be a student;
(*d*) not be working for sixteen hours a week or more;
(*e*) be available for work;
(*f*) be actively seeking work; and
(*g*) not have capital of more than £8,000.

Income support is the difference between the claimant's income and his or her 'applicable amount'. A claimant will be paid a personal allowance, depending on age and marital status. To this are added premiums for children, single parents, the elderly, the disabled, etc. If the claimant is paying a mortgage, income support will pay the interest on this.

As we have seen, claimants who have capital of £8,000 are not entitled to income support. You should be aware that when calculating income support, capital over £3,000 but under £8,000 is deemed to produce a weekly income of £1 for every £250 of capital. For claimants working part time, i.e. under sixteen hours a week, their income will be taken into account but the first £5 of income is normally disregarded (in some cases this increases to £15, for example for disabled claimants). 'Income' will also normally include income from other benefits, though some, for example disability living allowance, are ignored. Most maintenance payments are counted as income and taken fully into account.

For the purposes of calculating income support, the income and capital of a claimant are aggregated with the resources of his or her spouse or cohabitant. (There is a legal obligation on spouses to maintain each other and their children, but no such obligation exists between cohabitants: see chapter 10.) The consequence of this is that if a woman who is claiming income support begins to cohabit with a man, his resources will be taken into account, and if he is working full time her entitlement will cease, even though her new partner is not obliged to support her. (Any allegation of cohabiting by an AO can of course be appealed to an SSAT.)

Premiums increase a claimant's 'applicable amount'. The most usual ones are the family premium (where the claimant has a child), the lone parent premium, and the pensioner premium. Others are sometimes overlooked. These include the disability premium (for anyone receiving disability living allowance, incapacity benefit, or severe disablement allowance, and for anyone registered as blind). There is also a disabled child premium, a severe disability premium, an enhanced pensioner premium, a higher pensioner premium, and a carer premium. If you are working with elderly or disabled clients you should make sure with the Social Security Agency that they are receiving their full entitlement to these. Note, however, the general rule (to which there are exceptions) that normally only one premium—the most valuable—will be paid, even though there may be entitlement to more than one. However, the family premium can be paid in addition to any other, as can the disabled child premium and (sometimes) the severe disability premium.

11.4.2.3 The Social Fund

There are essentially two parts to the social fund. The first is concerned with maternity payments, funeral expenses, and cold weather payments. Claims are made to and decided by adjudication officers, and there is a right of appeal to the SSAT. Claims for cold weather payments, maternity payments and funeral payments are governed by regulations.

Maternity payments can be made where a woman is pregnant or has given birth and she or her partner is on income support, family credit, or disability working allowance. A funeral payment can be made where the claimant or his or her partner is on income support, family credit or disability working allowance or housing benefit and accepts responsibility for the costs of the funeral in the UK. Entitlement to cold weather payments depends on being in receipt of income support and being aged sixty or over or entitled to a disability premium or a disabled child premium or having a child aged under five in the household when the temperature conditions begin.

The rest of the fund is discretionary, and decisions are made by social fund officers. There is no right of appeal to the SSAT. However, there is a right to ask for a social fund decision to be reviewed by a different local fund officer, who will interview the claimant. If the review is unsuccessful, the claim is referred for decision to a senior social fund officer, and he or she will give a written decision. There is also a Social Fund Commissioner to keep a general eye on the standard of adjudication. This part of the fund is used for community care grants, budgeting loans, and crisis loans. Decisions are based on guidance from the DHSS, and payments can only be made as long as the local office of the Social Security Agency has not exhausted its social fund budget.

Community care grants are made to keep people in the community rather than in institutional care. They can also be used to assist someone coming out of institutional care or to help a family cope with exceptional pressure or stress. Claimants must be entitled to income support, and there is a capital limit of £500.

Budgeting loans are to help income support claimants meet extraordinary expenses that they are unable to meet from their normal weekly income. Income support must have been paid for twenty-six weeks, and there is a capital limit of £500. The maximum loan is £1,000, and all loans are repaid by deductions from income support payments.

Crisis loans are made to pay for costs arising from an emergency or disaster. Anyone (not just someone in receipt of income support) can apply, provided they have no savings and no other way of meeting the need and the loan is the only way of preventing serious risk to the health or safety of any member of the family.

Social workers dealing with the social fund should familiarise themselves with the many directions and the guidance given to social fund officers by the DHSS, which closely circumscribe the conditions in which help will be given.

11.4.2.4 Housing Benefit

This is a benefit paid to those on low income and renting their home or paying rates as owner-occupiers. In the former case it is paid by the NIHE and in the latter by the Rate Collection Agency (RCA). To be eligible, a claimant must

(a) not have capital of more than £16,000;
(b) be liable to pay rent: i.e. the claimant or his or her partner must be liable to pay rent or be in practice paying rent; and
(c) be living in the property for which the claim is made as the family home.

Those claiming income support obtain the appropriate forms from the local social security office, while those not on income support must apply directly to the NIHE district office (or the local RCA office if owner-occupiers). Housing benefit for NIHE tenants is paid in the form of a rent reduction, whereas for housing association and private tenants it is usually paid privately. Payment is direct to the landlord if a person is on income support, and the Social Security Agency pays part of the claimant's income support to cover rent arrears.

The method of calculating the benefit differs according to whether the claimant is on income support or not. People on income support are entitled to the maximum housing benefit, usually all rent and rates minus any deductions for non-dependent adults living at home. (The rationale for this is that adults living at home are expected to contribute towards the rent.) Housing benefit is calculated by comparing the claimant's applicable amount—essentially notional allowances given to claimants personally and for their children—with their income. If the applicable amount exceeds income, the maximum benefit is payable. If not, a percentage of the benefit may be payable.

If dissatisfied, a person can seek a review of an NIHE or RCA decision by making an application for a review within six weeks of receiving the decision. If a person remains dissatisfied, a second review can be sought before a Housing Benefit Review Board (see 11.2.3.6).

11.4.3 *Industrial Injuries Benefits and Industrial Preference*

These benefits are available to employees who have an accident at work or contract an industrial disease. 'Industrial preference' means that these benefits are normally paid at a higher rate than other benefits.

11.4.3.1 General Conditions

An industrial injury is a personal injury caused by an accident arising out of and in the course of an employed earner's employment. Employers and the self-employed are therefore excluded. An industrial disease is one that has been identified by law as having a clear occupational cause. An employee working in a prescribed occupation who contracts a prescribed disease will be entitled to benefit.

11.4.3.2 Disablement Benefit

This benefit is paid where the claimant, ninety days after the accident or onset of the disease, is suffering from a disability or from loss of mental or physical faculty that has been assessed at 14 per cent or more. The amount of benefit depends on the assessed degree of disablement.

11.4.3.3 Constant Attendance Allowance

Constant attendance allowance is an increase of disablement benefit and is paid to claimants who are 100 per cent disabled and require constant attendance because of their loss of faculty.

11.4.3.4 Exceptionally Severe Disablement Allowance

This addition to constant attendance allowance is only payable where there is 100 per cent disablement and where the need for constant attendance is likely to be permanent.

11.4.4 *Disability Benefits*

11.4.4.1 Disability Premiums in Income Support

The disability premium is paid to someone under the age of sixty if they satisfy the incapacity condition and if they or their partner satisfy the disability condition. (For those over the age of sixty the disability premium is replaced by the higher pensioner premium.) The incapacity condition requires the claimant to have been incapable of work for twenty-eight weeks. The disability condition is satisfied if the claimant or the claimant's partner is registered as blind or is receiving (*a*) attendance allowance, (*b*) constant attendance allowance, (*c*) disability living allowance, (*d*) disability working allowance, (*e*) incapacity benefit, or (*f*) severe disablement allowance.

The severe disability premium is paid in addition to the disability premium for a single claimant on income support who lives alone and receives attendance allowance, constant attendance allowance or the care component of disability living allowance at the middle or highest rate, on condition that no-one receives invalid care allowance for caring for the claimant. If the claimant is one of a couple, entitlement to the severe disability premium depends on both the claimant and partner receiving the benefits listed. They must not be receiving invalid care allowance.

11.4.4.2 Disability Living Allowance

This benefit, introduced in April 1992, is made up of two components, a 'care' component and a 'mobility' component.

The care component is payable at three rates. The lowest rate is paid where the claimant either requires attention in connection with bodily functions for a significant portion of the day or is unable to prepare a main cooked meal. The middle rate is paid for either day or night attention or supervision. The claimant must show a requirement either for frequent attention throughout the day in connection with bodily functions or for continual supervision throughout the day to avoid a substantial danger to the claimant or others. Alternatively, the claimant must provide evidence of frequent or repeated attention during the night in connection with bodily functions or a need for someone to be awake for a prolonged period or at frequent intervals to watch over the claimant during the night to avoid a substantial danger to the claimant or others. The highest rate is payable where the claimant satisfies both the day and night conditions listed above.

Important points to note are that

(*a*) children under sixteen cannot rely on the 'main meal' test (i.e. where the claimant is unable to prepare a main cooked meal, even if the ingredients are available);
(*b*) a claim for caring for a child under sixteen will only succeed if the child requires substantially more care than another child of the same age and sex;
(*c*) the conditions must be satisfied for three months before the benefit becomes payable and must be likely to be satisfied for six months thereafter;
(*d*) there are special rules for the terminally ill;
(*e*) the component must normally be claimed before the age of sixty-five.

To qualify for the mobility component at the higher rate, the claimant must show that he or she is unable or virtually unable to walk. The lower rate is available for claimants who require guidance or supervision most of the time when walking out of doors on unfamiliar routes. The qualifying periods of three months and six months for the care component also apply to the mobility component.

The mobility component cannot be paid for a child aged under five and cannot normally be claimed by people aged sixty-five or over. To qualify for the care and mobility components the claimant must show that he or she has satisfied the conditions for at least three months and that he or she will continue to do so for at least a further six months. In other words, the allowance is not for short-term incapacity.

11.4.4.3 Attendance Allowance 65+

People aged sixty-five or over cannot claim disability living allowance but they can claim attendance allowance 65+ instead. This allowance is payable at two rates. The lower rate is payable where either the day or night condition is satisfied; the higher rate is paid where a claimant satisfies both the day and night conditions.

The day conditions are that the claimant requires from another person either frequent attention throughout the day in connection with bodily functions or continual supervision throughout the day in order to avoid substantial danger to the claimant or others. The night conditions are that the claimant either requires from another person at night prolonged or repeated attention in connection with bodily functions or requires another person to be awake for a prolonged period or at frequent intervals to watch over the claimant in order to avoid a substantial danger to the claimant or others. Inability to perform household tasks, for example cooking, cannot be taken into account.

These conditions must be satisfied for six months before the allowance becomes payable, but there are special rules for the terminally ill.

11.4.4.4 Disability Working Allowance

The conditions for this allowance are that

(a) income support or family credit are not being received;
(b) attendance allowance, disability living allowance or constant attendance allowance is being received, or the claimant has an invalid carriage (i.e. equipment supplied by the DHSS up to 1976 to those who were unable to walk);
(c) invalidity benefit, severe disablement benefit, income support or housing benefit has been received for one or more days in the fifty-six days immediately preceding the date of claim;
(d) the claimant is engaged normally in remunerative work;
(e) the claimant has a physical or mental disability that puts him or her at a disadvantage in getting a job;
(f) the claimant's income does not exceed the applicable amount (at present £73 for couples and lone parents, £54.75 for single people) or does so but not greatly; and
(g) the claimant's capital is under £16,000.

The allowance is paid for twenty-six weeks and is not affected by any change of circumstances in that time.

11.5 *Further Reading*

Bonner, D., et al., *Non-Means-Tested Benefits: the Legislation* (8th edition), London: Sweet and Maxwell 1989.

Child Poverty Action Group, *National Welfare Benefits Handbook*, CPAG 1994.

Child Poverty Action Group, *Rights Guide to Non-Means-Tested Benefits* (9th edition), CPAG 1993–94.

Disability Alliance, *Disability Rights Handbook* (19th edition), ERA 1994.

Law Centre (Northern Ireland), *Frontline: the Social Welfare Law Quarterly.*

Law Centre (Northern Ireland), *Information Sheets (no. 2, Family Credit; no. 3, Income Support; no. 4, Electricity and the Law; no. 5, Social Fund; no. 7, Unemployment Benefit; no. 8, Statutory Sick Pay; no. 9, Disability Working Allowance; no. 12, Housing Benefit; no. 22, Disability Living Allowance)*, Belfast: Law Centre (Northern Ireland).

Ogus, A., and Barendt, E. M., *The Law of Social Security* (4th edition), London: Butterworths 1994.

Rowland, *Medical and Disability Appeal Tribunals: the Legislation* (2nd edition), London: Sweet and Maxwell 1994.

Income Support, the Social Fund and Family Credit: the Legislation, London: Sweet and Maxwell (annual editions and supplements).

12

HOUSING ISSUES

Angela Hegarty

12.1 Introduction

This chapter gives guidance on the law of housing in Northern Ireland in relation to particular issues or problems where social workers require some knowledge of legislation and practice. Social workers may frequently come into contact with clients who have problems with housing. Clients will often encounter difficulties in relation to repairs, disagreements with landlords, rent arrears, and lengthy waits on the public housing list. This is not an exhaustive guide to the law on housing in Northern Ireland, and further reading is suggested at the end of the chapter.

12.2 Some Terms Explained

The law distinguishes several types of relationship and different interests or 'estates' in land. People tend to think of an interest in land as indicating ownership, but in fact a tenant has an interest in land or property, just as an owner has.

In Northern Ireland the law distinguishes between the public rented sector and the private rented sector. As will become clear, the rights and obligations of an occupant are defined differently by statute law according to whether he or she is a public sector tenant or a private sector tenant. Indeed the law applies differently even within the private sector, where various kinds of tenancies are recognised. The law also governs the creation and operation of tenancy agreements or 'leases'.

In general, the law distinguishes between 'lessees' and 'licensees', i.e. between those who have a leasehold agreement with the landlord and those who have no such agreement but are on the property under the 'licence' of the landlord. It is important to determine whether someone is a licensee or a lessee, as their rights and duties often differ. In principle a lease creates an interest in the land that can be assigned to another—unlike a licence, which simply creates a personal permission to do something: the term 'licence' means no more than permission. There are many sorts of licence arrangements in law and in everyday practice: for example, a television licence allows you to use a television in your home; a dog licence allows you to own a dog; a liquor licence allows you to sell alcohol on your premises. In the context of housing law, it simply means that permission has been conferred to do something that would otherwise constitute trespass, for example the hire of a concert hall for several days or the grant of permission to occupy a room.

The fundamental difference between a tenant and a licensee is that a tenant, who has exclusive permission to occupy, has an 'estate' or legal interest in the lands, as opposed to personal permission to occupy.

The following is a guide to some of the common terms you may come across:

Landlord: the owner or holder of the land or property.
Tenant: the person to whom the land or property is let.
Lease: a written agreement creating a landlord-and-tenant relationship.
Lessor and lessee: landlord and tenant, respectively, where a lease has been signed.
Assignment: the transfer by a lessee of his or her interest in a property.
Covenants: terms or conditions of a lease, for example that the landlord will carry out certain repairs.

12.3 *The Public Rented Sector*

It was the building and allocation of public sector housing that sparked much of the controversy over civil rights in Northern Ireland in the 1960s. Much of the controversy centred around allegations that public housing—then the responsibility of local councils—was being built and allocated in a sectarian manner. The fledgling civil rights movement took housing allocation as one of its key campaign issues, and it became a matter of public concern at about the time that Austin Currie, then a Nationalist MP in the Stormont Parliament, squatted along with others in a house in Caledon that had been allocated to a single Protestant instead of a Catholic family.

Since then much of the debate around discrimination in housing has subsided. Responsibility for public sector housing is in the hands of the Northern Ireland Housing Executive (NIHE), which was established under the Housing Executive Act (Northern Ireland) 1971 (section 1), as an alternative to the English model of local authority responsibility. The Fair Employment Acts do not extend to the field of housing allocation, not least because the two religious groups in Northern Ireland live, for the most part, in separate areas.

The NIHE's functions and powers were laid down in that Act, which has since been substantially amended by the 1981 and 1983 Housing Orders. The functions of the NIHE are described in the 1981 Order (article 6):

(a) drawing up and implementing a programme to meet housing needs in Northern Ireland;
(b) providing housing information and advice services;
(c) the administering of grants (see below), redevelopment, and dealing with unfitness.

To carry out its functions, the NIHE is given a range of legal powers, including the power to provide housing accommodation and to acquire land for such purposes and the power to lend money—to housing associations, for example—for specific purposes.

12.3.1 *The Allocation of NIHE Tenancies*

Waiting lists are a perennial source of problems, and people frequently have queries about the manner in which public housing has been allocated. The NIHE allocates accommodation under the 'points scheme'. Applications for accommodation are categorised as either 'group A' (priority waiting list) or 'group B' (general waiting list). The scheme has become known as the points scheme because applicants are awarded points based on a range of criteria.

The waiting list is further divided into a number of categories.

A1 (emergency housing) applicants are given priority because of intimidation. Other A1 applicants (for example those made homeless) are allocated housing according to the date on which they are awarded priority status.

A2 (special health and social needs) applicants are placed in this category if they or a member of their family suffer from particular health problems or have specific social needs. Applicants may be classified as A2 if, in the opinion of the relevant Health and Social Services Board, their present housing is causing extreme hardship or may cause a breakdown in health. Elderly applicants are often placed in this category; so too are those who wish to move in order to be closer to elderly relatives with a view to looking after them.

A3 applicants are those who have been made homeless by vesting or redevelopment (where the NIHE or the Department of the Environment have compulsorily purchased the property).

A4 (key workers) are incoming workers in special or essential fields who hold 'key worker certificates'.

To qualify for the group B or general waiting list, an applicant must have been resident in Northern Ireland for seven years. Points are awarded on this list based on a number of criteria, including the length of time on the waiting list and the degree of overcrowding or unfitness of their present accommodation.

Certain other categories of people are also given points. These include hostel dwellers and ex-service personnel, for example. In addition the list has specific categories for the elderly and those over the age of sixty in need of sheltered accommodation.

12.3.2 *Complaints About Allocation*

When someone has a problem with the allocation decision there are a number of options available. Firstly, there is the internal NIHE complaints procedure. Secondly, a complaint may be made to the Ombudsman (see chapter 1). As a last resort, application may be made to the High Court in Belfast for judicial review of the decision.

12.3.3 *NIHE Tenancy Agreements*

All NIHE tenants are entitled to a copy of the standard form of tenancy agreement and to an explanation of its contents (Housing (Northern Ireland) Order 1983, article 38 (3)). Tenants should ensure that they have a copy. NIHE tenancies are 'secure' under article 25 of the same Order where a tenant occupies the NIHE dwelling as his or her only home (see 12.3.4). There are a number of exceptions to this, for example tenancies granted temporarily to incoming workers.

12.3.4 *Secure Tenancies*

Secure tenants have the right not to be evicted except by due process of law and after they have been served with a valid notice to quit giving four weeks' notice. Such tenants can only lose possession of the property if the landlord gets a court order (article 27). Such an order for possession will be made only if the court thinks that an order for possession is reasonable or where there is alternative accommodation available for the tenant, or both. The grounds for possession are laid down in article 29. Essentially a tenant can only be evicted—

   (*a*) if rent has not been paid, or there has been some other breach of a covenant in the tenancy agreement;
   (*b*) if the tenant has been causing an annoyance to neighbours, for example by having loud parties or keeping livestock;

(c) if the tenant has been using the premises for an illegal or immoral purpose;
(d) if furniture has been damaged, either by the tenant or by someone else in the house;
(e) if the tenant has lied about his or her circumstances in order to get the tenancy;
(f) if the landlord needs to carry out works to the property and the tenant refuses to give up the premises;
(g) if another secure tenant has paid a fee in respect of an exchange of homes and the tenant changes his or her mind and refuses to move;
(h) if a house designed for a disabled person is now occupied by someone who is not disabled and is required again for a disabled person;
(i) if the accommodation is for a person with special needs and the present occupant is a person who has not got those needs;
(j) if there is under-occupation of a house of which the tenancy was obtained through 'statutory succession' by a member of the previous tenant's family (other than the spouse).

If a secure tenant dies, the law provides for one succession by his or her nearest relative. ('Relative' is defined in the Housing (Northern Ireland) Order 1983, article 26.) The person with first claim on the tenancy is the spouse, so long as he or she occupied the property as the principal home at the time of the tenant's death. For any other relatives to succeed they must have lived in the property for at least twelve months before the tenant's death as the principal home. In practice the NIHE reduces the time requirement to six months.

Only one succession is allowed, and in cases of dispute the NIHE may nominate who that person is to be. It must be an uncle, aunt, nephew, niece, child or cohabitant of the deceased tenant.

12.3.5 *Transferring and Exchanging Tenancies*

The NIHE allows a tenant to apply for a transfer. This is not a legal right but ought nonetheless to be administered fairly and reasonably. To effect a transfer, the tenant applies to the NIHE's district office. Applications are then considered for priority, depending on whether the tenant has any rent arrears. Arrears are not always a barrier to a transfer, as the NIHE will look at any social and medical grounds, and the transfer can go ahead if an arrangement is made to repay the arrears. The allocation of priority is on grounds similar to those discussed in connection with homelessness (see 12.6).

Exchanges of houses are provided for by the Housing (Northern Ireland) Order 1983 (article 32 (*a*) (1)). This gives tenants the right to an exchange provided they have the NIHE's written permission, which can be withheld only on very specific grounds.

12.3.6 *Non-payment of Rent*

Where rent is not paid, the NIHE will take legal action in the county court to recover the amount outstanding or, eventually, to evict the tenant. Where there has been a mistake in calculating rent and a tenant has been overcharged, that amount is recoverable by the tenant. Any undercharging is, generally speaking, not recoverable by the NIHE.

When a tenant cannot pay because of financial pressures the NIHE in most circumstances will try to reach a voluntary arrangement with the tenant. When such a voluntary agreement is not possible the NIHE will sometimes apply informal pressures, such as refusing to carry out improvements, dragging their heels over repairs, and so forth.

Although the controversial Payments for Debt (Emergency Provisions) Act 1971, has been repealed, deductions may still be made from benefits for arrears of rent (as well as for mortgage, rates, and electricity arrears) under the Social Security (Claims and Payments) Regulations (Northern Ireland) 1987, the Social Security Contributions and Benefits Act (Northern Ireland) 1992, and the Social Security Administration Act (Northern Ireland) 1992. Deductions may usually be made only when a tenant is six weeks or more in arrears, or four weeks when a local benefit office agrees to the deductions.

Legal, formal schemes for recovery of debt are pursued through the courts. Amounts of less than £500 will generally be recoverable in the Small Claims Court, but more usually an action is taken in the local magistrate's court.

12.3.7 *Setting NIHE Rents*

NIHE rents are fixed annually by the Department of the Environment and vary according to the size, age and facilities of the property. Rent increases are notified to the tenant by the NIHE.

Quarrels about rent levels are remedied in a number of ways. Firstly, the tenant (or his or her representative) should write to the NIHE, outlining the complaint. If such representations fail, the tenant may then refer, via his or her MP, to the Ombudsman or to the High Court in Belfast for judicial review.

12.3.8 *The Tenant's Right to Buy*

Tenants have a right to buy the property in which they have been living by virtue of the house sales scheme operated by the NIHE under the Housing Order 1992 (article 96). This scheme will operate in much the same way as the previous arrangements: for example, tenants will generally have a right to buy after three years.

12.3.9 The 'Tenants' Charter'

This term is occasionally used by tenants' groups, and essentially encompasses the enactment into law (by the Housing (Northern Ireland) Order 1983) of certain basic rights, for example the right to security of tenure and the right to be consulted by the NIHE on certain matters relating to development. The 'Tenants' Charter', which originated with the 1977 English Housing Policy Review, applies only to tenants in the public sector.

12.4 The Private Rented Sector

Private tenants are those whose landlords are not the NIHE or a registered housing association. There are three types of private tenancies: 'restricted', 'regulated', and 'unprotected'. A tenant's rights depend, in many respects, on the nature of the tenancy.

Protected tenancies are governed by the Rent (Northern Ireland) Order 1978, and of these there are two types: restricted and regulated. Most privately rented tenancies are, however, not covered by the Order and are known as unprotected tenancies. Unprotected tenants have only a few legal rights outside those agreed with the landlord in any written or verbal tenancy agreement. Such agreements do not have to be in writing if they are for under one year or if they continue from year to year. They can be entirely oral or partly oral and partly written.

A tenancy will not be protected if any of the following conditions apply:

(a) the net annual value (NAV) is over £140; the NAV of any property can be checked at the local rates office;
(b) the property was built or converted after 6 November 1956;
(c) the landlord shares essential facilities (toilets, kitchen, etc.) with the tenant;
(d) the property has all reasonably necessary furniture, excluding cooking utensils and the like, unless a restricted rent certificate covers the dwelling or a public health notice has been served;
(e) the landlord provides food or services that are a substantial part of the rent, unless again a restricted rent certificate covers the dwelling or a public health notice has been served.

The easiest way to find out whether a tenancy is restricted or regulated is to telephone the Rent Officer at the Department of the Environment offices in Stormont: (01232) 520000.

A tenancy is a regulated tenancy unless it is subject to a restricted rent certificate issued by a district council or unless, immediately before the commencement of the Rent (Northern Ireland) Order 1978, the tenancy was controlled by the old Rent Restriction Acts and the NAV was under £60, in which case it is a restricted tenancy. A tenancy is also restricted if a statutory nuisance notice has been issued by a district council. If in doubt, check with the Environmental Health Office of the relevant council.

Regulated tenancies are protected tenancies other than those that are restricted, and these must meet certain standards. A dwelling will meet the regulated tenancy standards if it is fit for human habitation (these standards are laid down in the Housing (Northern Ireland) Order 1992). A landlord can apply to the local council to convert a restricted tenancy into a regulated one if it comes up to a certain standard. Unprotected tenancies cannot now be converted into protected ones.

12.4.1 Setting Rent

The mechanisms for setting the levels of rent are controlled differently for restricted, regulated and unprotected tenants.

12.4.1.1 Restricted Tenancies

The rents in restricted tenancies are fixed at what they were when the Rent (Northern Ireland) Order 1978, came into force, usually just a few pounds per week.

12.4.1.2 Regulated Tenants

The rent of regulated tenants is supposed to be approximately equal to what the NIHE would charge for similar property and is regulated by the 1978 Order (article 27 (2)). The rent is fixed by applying to the Rent Office to have it registered.

12.4.1.3 Unprotected Tenancies

The rent charged in these tenancies is generally the going rate for the type of property in the area, with the qualification that the NIHE can restrict the amount of rent that can be paid through housing benefit. This restriction may be appealed to an independent housing benefit review board (see chapter 11). A tenant is responsible for excess of rent over the amount of housing benefit received.

12.4.2 Rights of Private Tenants

12.4.2.1 Rent book

All private tenants are entitled to a rent book, and failure to provide one by a landlord is a criminal offence (Rent Order (Northern Ireland), 1978, article 38).

12.4.2.2 Freedom From Harassment

The tenant is entitled to be free from being harassed by any person who does so with the intention of forcing the tenant to give up his or her home, or any part of it, or the exercise of any right (for example a right of way) or remedy (for example rights to repair). Any such harassment can constitute the criminal offence of intimidation and should be reported to the authorities immediately.

Landlords are prohibited by law from depriving a tenant of his or her home, or any part of it. To do so is a criminal offence under the 1978 Order (article 54 (1)), unless it was reasonable to believe that the tenant did not live there any more.

12.4.2.3 Eviction

All private tenants are entitled to a notice to quit, which need not be in writing (though it normally is). It must be given at least four weeks in advance, unless the tenancy agreement specifies a longer period (1978 Order, article 62).

Even when a landlord is legally entitled to evict, he or she must follow the legal process of serving a notice to quit and a court action. Tenants who have a written agreement (or lease) can sue for damages if they are illegally evicted or harassed.

Both types of protected tenant enjoy this security. Those in unprotected tenancies generally enjoy only those rights that are conferred on them by the tenancy agreement (see below).

Schedule 3 of the Rent Order specifies the circumstances a landlord must show to the court (unless he or she proves that there is suitable alternative accommodation available for the tenant) in order to recover possession. The court must also be of the view that it is reasonable to make such an order. The circumstances in which a court is entitled to grant a possession order include:

(*a*) where a tenant owes rent;
(*b*) where a tenant has sub-let without the landlord's permission;
(*c*) where a tenant has been causing a nuisance;
(*d*) where a tenant has damaged or neglected premises or contents.

In certain other circumstances the court must grant possession, for example where the accommodation goes with a job that the tenant no longer holds.

If a landlord misrepresents any facts in order to get possession of the property, the tenant may be entitled to compensation for any resulting damage and loss (Rent (Northern Ireland) Order 1978, article 20).

The only other ways in which protected tenants can be evicted are if there is a closing or demolition order on the premises (Housing (Northern Ireland) Order 1981, article 45) or if the landlord applies to a county court on the basis that a tenancy was misclassified as protected (and in this case the landlord still has to initiate possession proceedings).

Unprotected tenants generally have little security. An unprotected tenant can remain in the property for any agreed period, but if he or she breaks the agreement (perhaps by non-payment of rent) the landlord need serve only a four-week notice to quit and then may take court proceedings, either in the High Court or the county court. A tenant can ask for a 'stay' (i.e. delay) on the operation of the court order for a few weeks or months. Legal aid is not available for court representation.

12.4.2.4 Succession to Protected Tenancies

Protected tenants can pass on their tenancies twice, after death, to successors. The first successor will be the tenant's spouse, if he or she is residing in the house. Other family members must be living with the tenant permanently for over six months before the death, and not as a nurse or caretaker. If there is a dispute about who should succeed, the Rent Order (schedule 1) provides a specific order of preference. There can be two or more joint statutory tenants, but the property will return to the landlord on the death of the second statutory tenant.

A statutory tenant occupies property on exactly the same terms as the original tenant, and the tenancy can be transferred during the lifetime of the statutory tenant as long as the landlord agrees and is a party to any agreement. The transfer must be voluntary, and no money should change hands, except to pay for the statutory tenant's outgoings or for any improvement he or she has made. If part of the premises is used for business purposes a sum can be paid for goodwill (1978 Order, article 18).

12.5 *Repairs*

The lease is the primary source of any legal obligation to repair. In the public sector this is the standard form of NIHE tenancy agreement. In the private rented sector this will be the lease. The duties of landlord and tenant in relation to repairs are usually contained here.

12.5.1 *Public Sector Tenants*

The tenancy agreement lays down that the NIHE agrees to keep in repair the structure and exterior, to maintain anything in the dwelling that is its responsibility, and to decorate the exterior every seven years. Anything that the tenant can remove is not the NIHE's responsibility.

The NIHE's view is that its duty to repair arises only when a district manager has received written and specific notice from or on behalf of a tenant and after a reasonable time has elapsed. The executive will usually respond to telephone calls in emergencies but maintains that it is not legally obliged to so do. Local offices will set priorities for repairs according to their urgency and set time limits within which the repairs will be done. The standard of repair should be consistent with the age, character and prospective life of the house. In other words, expensive major restoration work to property due for redevelopment is unlikely, while minor holding repairs may be carried out.

If a property is damaged by flood, fire, or other disaster, the NIHE is not obliged to repair or restore it but will normally do so unless the cost would be unreasonably high. The NIHE is entitled to enter the building to do repairs but will only do so between 9 a.m. and 6 p.m. and after giving twenty-four hours' notice, except in emergencies.

12.5.2 *Private Sector Tenants*

12.5.2.1 Restricted Tenancies

Restricted tenants rarely have any repairing rights in their tenancy agreement; usually the obligation to do repairs is on the tenant. Restricted tenants can normally only use the statutory nuisance and unfitness procedures described below to require the landlord to carry out repairs

12.5.2.2 Regulated Tenancies

The landlord's duties to repair are laid down in the Rent (Northern Ireland) Order 1978 (articles 41 and 43–45). He or she is responsible for the structure, the exterior (including paintwork), the supplies of electricity, gas, and water, and the interior, except for those obligations that are imposed by the Rent Order (article 42). These include responsibility for fireplaces, tiles, all glass, tap washers and seals, and any damage caused by the tenant or a lawful visitor. The tenant is also responsible for the interior decorative order.

If a landlord is in breach of his or her repairing duties by not carrying out the work, having been asked to do so, a regulated tenant has a number of options.

Firstly, they can apply to the rent assessment committee to have the rent reduced in accordance with the procedure laid down in article 31 of the Rent Order.

Secondly, they can make an application to the Environmental Health Department of the district council for an inspection of the property. If the landlord has broken his or her repairing duties, the council will issue a certificate of disrepair (COD), specifying the repairs required. If the landlord does not do the work, a case will ensue in the magistrate's court, and ultimately the landlord may be fined. The council can also carry out the work itself if the landlord has not done it, and recover the cost from the landlord. If the council refuses to issue a COD, a tenant can appeal to a county court within twenty-eight days.

Thirdly, the regulated tenant may ask the Environmental Health Department to inspect the premises to see if the disrepair is prejudicial to health or constitutes a nuisance (Public Health (Ireland) Act 1878, section 110). The council may issue a notice forcing the landlord to bring the nuisance to an end. If the council does not issue a formal notice it may use an informal 'seven days' notice' procedure. In urgent cases where there is default by the landlord, a 'nine days' notice' will be issued (Pollution Control and Local Government (Northern Ireland) Order 1978, article 65 (1)). Again the council can carry out the work and recover the costs. Lastly, the tenant can inform the NIHE that the house is unfit for habitation.

12.5.3 *Unfit for Habitation*

A new set of unfitness criteria was introduced by the Housing (Northern Ireland) Order, 1992, and they relate to:

(*a*) standard of repair;
(*b*) structural stability;
(*c*) freedom from damp;
(*d*) natural lighting;
(*e*) ventilation;
(*f*) water supply;
(*g*) drainage and sanitary facilities;
(*h*) food preparation facilities and disposal of waste water.

The following are the procedures a tenant should follow if a property is unfit for habitation.

12.5.3.1 Regulated Tenancies

If a house, or part of it, is deficient in one or more of the above matters so as to make it unsuitable for occupation, it is unfit. Regulation of unfitness is the responsibility of the NIHE, and it will first decide if the house can be made fit at reasonable expense. If it can, the NIHE will issue a repairs notice requiring the owner to do the work in a specified time. 'Reasonable expense' is based on whether the work can be carried out at a cost less than or equal to thirty-four times the NAV of the property.

If the house cannot be made fit at reasonable expense, a 'time and place meeting' is called by the NIHE. This meeting will involve the executive, the local council's Environmental Health Department, the owner, and any mortgagee (such as a bank or building society). The owner may offer an undertaking to make the house fit and not to use it for human habitation until it is made fit. If this is the outcome, a tenant cannot appeal. If no undertaking is accepted, the NIHE must issue a demolition order, unless this would affect adjacent buildings or the building is listed. If this is so, a closing order will be issued. The owner, or a tenant with more than one year to run on a lease, can appeal against a demolition order to a county court.

It is an offence to remain in the property beyond the date stipulated in a demolition order. Tenants should therefore try to ensure that they get 'emergency A1 status' (which permits them to be rehoused by the NIHE) and should apply for compensation for home loss, disturbance, and the like.

It is not open to a regulated tenant to withhold rent to do repairs if there is no repairing duty on the landlord contained in the written tenancy agreement. If taken to court for rent arrears, however, a regulated tenant may argue that any arrears should be set off against a failure by the landlord to do repairs. A tenant has no right simply to stop paying rent in protest at the lack of repair, although there are certain instances where, provided a particular procedure is followed, a tenant may be able to withhold rent in order to pay for repairs.

12.5.3.2 Unprotected Tenancies

While unprotected tenants, like restricted tenants, cannot use the certificate of disrepair procedure and cannot apply to the rent assessment committee for a rent reduction, it may be possible for them to get some relief. A tenant should first look at the express terms of the written agreement, if one exists. This will set out, to some extent, the repairing rights and duties. In addition, the law generally implies certain terms into most tenancy agreements, for example that the tenant has the right to quiet enjoyment, that a furnished property is fit for occupation at the beginning of the tenancy, and that the landlord is responsible for any common parts of which he or she retains control, such as stairways and halls.

If a landlord fails to carry out repairs, a tenant can take legal action for damages or a court order. Damages can include compensation for the reduction in value of the tenancy, inconvenience, annoyance, ill-health and distress, and damage to the tenant's goods. If the amount of damages is under £500 it can be claimed in the small claims court. If the amount is over £500 the matter will normally be dealt with by a county court. Legal aid is available in this court but not in the small claims court.

An unprotected tenant may also withhold rent in order to cover the cost of doing the repairs but should follow this specific procedure. Firstly, the landlord should be notified twice of the disrepair by recorded letter and given a reasonable time to deal with it. Copies of the letters should be kept by the tenant. If the landlord does not comply, three estimates should be sought and the job given to the lowest tender. Once the work has been done, an invoice should be sent to the landlord for payment. Lastly, rent should be withheld to cover the cost if the landlord refuses to pay; if the cost is high, rent may be accumulated in advance and put in a separate bank, post office or credit union account.

12.6 *Homelessness*

The law on homelessness has been altered in Northern Ireland in the past few years and has given rise to some controversy, not least because not everyone who is in fact homeless is deemed to be homeless under the law. As far as the law is concerned (Housing (Northern Ireland) Order 1988), 'homelessness' means that a person has no home in Northern Ireland that he or she can reasonably occupy, together with family or others who normally reside with that person.

There are two ways in which someone may apply to the NIHE for housing if homeless: under the non-statutory NIHE administrative scheme and in the category of statutory homelessness.

12.6.1 *Non-statutory NIHE Administrative Scheme*

This scheme, administered by the NIHE, does not result from any obligation or power under the law. A person is granted 'emergency A1 status' if they are homeless as a result of certain circumstances:

(*a*) fire, flood, or other circumstances beyond the applicant's control;
(*b*) marital breakdown;
(*c*) the ending of a tied tenancy;
(*d*) successful court action by a landlord for the possession of a dwelling needed for himself or herself;
(*e*) other circumstances, such as the move from the services to civilian life, the exceptional need to sell a home, or other circumstances regarded by the NIHE as unique.

12.6.2 *Statutory Homelessness*

Under the Housing (Northern Ireland) Order 1988, the NIHE is legally obliged to provide housing for those who meet the criteria it lays down. These are that one is

(*a*) in fact homeless, or deemed to be homeless, or threatened with homelessness, *and*
(*b*) in priority need, *and*
(*c*) not intentionally homeless.

12.6.2.1 Definition of 'Homeless'

Someone is homeless within the meaning of the Order if they have no place to live in Northern Ireland or if the accommodation they are at present occupying is such that no reasonable person should be expected to live in it.

The 'reasonableness' criterion has given rise to much litigation. The public authorities charged with housing those who meet the criterion, and thereafter the courts, have a difficult balancing exercise, weighing the circumstances, often poor, of the applicant against the resources available to the housing authority. The courts have been more willing to overturn the decision not to classify an applicant as homeless where the accommodation breaches the statutory standards on fitness or where there is excessive overcrowding. Courts have generally not been prepared to countenance severe overcrowding as anything other than unreasonable.

Issues other than accommodation can influence the consideration of reasonableness. Domestic harassment and violence are clearly issues the courts will take into account, but *threatened* violence or harassment from outside the family will have a lesser impact on the court's consideration. In Northern Ireland the problem of sectarian harassment and violence will certainly be a factor in such considerations.

12.6.2.2 Homelessness and Families

Even if an applicant has proper accommodation, he or she may be considered homeless within the meaning of the Order if family members, particularly children, cannot live there too. There must, however, be evidence that the members of the family have resided with the applicant at some period before the application. The Order does not define 'family', but the law has evolved a definition that includes blood relatives, cohabitants, adopted children and stepchildren, and those to whom the applicant acts in *loco parentis*. The legislation also covers 'persons who may reasonably be expected to reside with the applicant,' and this has been declared by the English courts to include carers residing with elderly or disabled people.

Children who are themselves in priority need can apply for housing in their own right. In a recent series of cases the matter has been considered at length, and the courts have concluded that while a 'healthy dependant living with his parents is owed no duty of any kind under the legislation' (*Garlick v. Oldham Metropolitan Borough Council* (1933) 2 All ER 65), children who are in priority need are entitled to be housed (*R. v. Northavon DC, ex parte Smith*) (*The Times*, 4 August 1993). This has arisen largely because the Children Act 1989, places an obligation on local authorities in England and Wales to safeguard the welfare of children in need and lays down a specific duty (section 20 (1)) to provide accommodation for such children. Even when the child's parents are found to be intentionally homeless, the child will be entitled to housing.

12.6.2.3 Homelessness and Temporary Accommodation

The question whether temporary or hostel-type accommodation constitutes accommodation within the meaning of the legislation has been refined by the courts. Temporary hostel-type accommodation (for example a refuge for battered women or a night shelter for the homeless) is not accommodation within the meaning of the Order, but bed and breakfast may be, depending on how 'reasonable' it is to occupy it.

12.6.2.4 'Deemed Homeless'

There are a number of circumstances in which the law declares someone homeless even though they may not be homeless in fact. In other words, the legislation provides for special cases. These include:

(*a*) where there is inability to secure entry—for example by an illegally evicted tenant, or someone whose accommodation has been taken over by squatters;
(*b*) where occupation of the property will in all probability lead to violence or threats of violence from some other resident; this is primarily intended to cover victims of domestic violence.

12.6.2.5 'Threatened Homelessness'

Where someone is likely to become homeless within twenty-eight days, they are classed as 'threatened with homelessness'.

12.6.2.6 'Priority Need'

Broadly speaking, this covers those who are pregnant, have dependent children, or are in situations of vulnerability and emergency. It includes those who are elderly or disabled, or anyone living with such a person. It also encompasses those who are subject to domestic violence or violence from outside the home (such as paramilitary or sectarian violence).

12.6.2.7 Intentionally Homeless

The legislation requires that a person not be 'intentionally homeless' but does not define what is meant by the term. That task has been left to the courts, which in a key case declared: 'A person becomes homeless intentionally if he deliberately has done or failed to do anything in consequence of which he has ceased to occupy accommodation which was available for his occupation and which it would have been reasonable for him to continue to occupy' (*Dyson v. Kerrier DC* [1980] 3 All ER 313 at p. 319). This has been one of the most controversial aspects of the legislation. It has been widely criticised by campaigning groups and has resulted in much litigation. It should be noted that it is up to the NIHE to establish 'intentionality'. Where there is doubt, the applicant should not be declared intentionally homeless.

The need to concentrate on the conduct of the applicant is important. The concept of intentionality applies solely to the applicant and not to other people who reside or who ought reasonably be expected to reside with him or her. This may well mean that in practice an intentionally homeless person can become accommodated as part of an unintentionally homeless person's family. In *R. v. West Dorset District Council ex parte Philips* (1984) 17 HLR 336, for example, Mr Philips had spent all the family's rent money on drink. The family were evicted for non-payment of rent, and Mrs Philips applied to West Dorset District Council as homeless. The council assessed her as intentionally homeless, because of her ejectment for non-payment of rent, but the court held that it was not Mrs Philips's actions that had rendered her homeless and that she could not therefore be described as intentionally homeless. The obligation on the housing authority, the court emphasised, was to look at the applicant and the applicant alone. Mrs Philips had neither agreed to nor colluded in her husband's behaviour, and so she could not be intentionally homeless. It is essential, therefore, to pick the right applicant when applying for public housing on the grounds of homelessness.

The notion of 'acquiescence' has become important and has been developed by the courts in a number of cases on the doctrine of 'infectious intentionality'. Essentially, this doctrine holds that if there is compelling evidence that the applicant has acceded to the behaviour of someone else (usually a family member) that has resulted in the loss of accommodation, that person may be said to be intentionally homeless. In Mrs Philips's case she had not agreed with what her husband had done, and therefore she was not intentionally homeless.

The following are examples of circumstances in which infectious intentionality arises:

(1) 'Where the individual deliberately has done or failed to do anything.' Clearly the act or omission must be deliberate, but it need not have the intention of creating homelessness: for example failing to pay the rent or mortgage because the money was gambled on a horse race.
(2) The act must be the cause of the homelessness: there must be a clear causal connection between the act concerned and the homelessness of the applicant.
(3) Loss of job-related accommodation. Where the loss of the job is through no fault of the applicant's, there is no intentionality.

12.6.2.8 Deciding Whether Someone is Homeless

The NIHE must make such inquiries as are necessary to satisfy itself whether the applicant is homeless or threatened with homelessness, whether or not they are in 'priority need', and then whether or not they are intentionally homeless.

It is up to the NIHE to make the inquiries, not for the applicant to produce evidence to satisfy the NIHE. The law stipulates that such inquiries should be made speedily and with due diligence. Under the Housing (Northern Ireland) Order 1988, the NIHE must make two suitable offers of temporary accommodation for up to twenty-eight days. They are also obliged, in any case, to provide advice and assistance. The NIHE can pay for the storage of property (1988 Order, article 13).

Article 9 of the 1988 order allows for an internal appeal process. Applicants lodge their appeal with the regional manager, and it then goes to the Director of Housing and Planning. An applicant is permitted to make representations. An alternative method is to challenge the decision in the courts by way of judicial review.

12.7 Squatting

A squatter is 'a trespasser who has intentionally occupied property belonging to another, without permission and who remains in occupation' (*McPhail v. Persons, names unknown* (1973) 3 All ER 393). When a squatter and his or her dependants first enter a house they are trespassers: they may be summarily evicted without a court order and are liable to criminal prosecution. Squatting in Northern Ireland is itself a criminal offence (Criminal Justice Order (Northern Ireland) 1986, article 10). This offence is committed when the squatter enters another person's property as a trespasser and fails to leave when asked to do so.

If dispossession by the squatters has involved force or threats of violence, an offence has been committed under the Protection of the Person and Property Act (Northern Ireland) 1969, punishable by a fine or imprisonment, or both. The law also makes it an offence to force entry to a property where that entry involves an actual or possible breach of the peace, even where the force has been used against property and not people. Barricading a building has been held to be sufficient to constitute an offence (*R. v. Robinson* (1970); *R. v. Mountford* (1971)).

12.7.1 *Squatting in NIHE Property*

The law makes a trespasser liable for compensating the owner of the property that he or she makes use of. This is called an action for 'mesne profits', and the amount of compensation is usually approximate to the rent that would be paid on the property. However, as the law makes clear, the payment of mesne profits is not the same as the payment of rent, nor does it create a landlord-tenant relationship. The most that an action for mesne profits creates is a licence for the squatter to remain on the property.

Whenever someone squats in NIHE property, the executive has a number of options available to it. It can take an action in the civil courts for possession of the premises, eviction of the squatter, and sometimes even compensation for the unauthorised occupation (mesne profits). It may also choose to prosecute the squatter under the Criminal Justice (Northern Ireland) Order 1986, article 10 (see above).

As soon as the NIHE is aware of an illegal occupation, its officials visit the property and encourage the squatters to leave. If they do not leave they will receive a warning letter giving them seven days to get out and threatening legal action if they remain beyond that time. If they still refuse to go, the matter is referred to the NIHE's solicitors to initiate a criminal prosecution or a civil action.

Immediately after the court proceedings a 'use and occupation' book is sent to the squatter, with a covering letter making it clear that the issuing of a book does not amount to the granting of a tenancy. Any amounts paid under such a payment book are to be seen simply as 'mesne profits', not as rent. Being a trespasser, the squatter has no right to have the property repaired by the NIHE, and, if injured, he or she may claim compensation only if the NIHE knew or should have known of the hazard involved. If the squatter continues to refuse to leave, the NIHE can proceed to enforce the court order through the Enforcement of Judgements Office.

The NIHE is entitled to enter the property so long as it does not use force. On occasion squatters have been 'evicted' by being asked to come for an appointment to the executive's local offices; the NIHE has then entered the premises in the squatters' absence and secured it against their return. This course of action is legal, if less than open.

Squatters are not protected by the illegal eviction and harassment provisions of the Rent (Northern Ireland) Order 1978 (articles 54–56); but a squatter who has been evicted may apply to the NIHE as someone who is homeless.

12.7.2 *Squatting in Privately Owned Property*

Private owners who become aware of squatters have, broadly speaking, the same options open to them as the NIHE to recover their property. If the owner manages to enter the premises and to change the locks, the squatter has no legal remedy. To force an entry would be a criminal offence. If the squatter has belongings inside, they should be removed by the owner and made available for collection; otherwise the owner may be guilty of theft. If, however, the owner leaves the belongings on the street outside the property and they are stolen, the squatter has no legal redress.

The law does afford some measure of protection to squatters by stipulating the extent to which an owner may go in evicting them. If the owner is physically evicting a squatter, only such force as is reasonable in the circumstances may be used. As the RUC have a duty to prevent breaches of the peace, they may well attend an eviction to ensure that peace is preserved and that no other offence is committed. The RUC themselves can arrest a squatter only if they reasonably suspect him or her of having committed a fairly serious criminal offence, such as forcing an entry or theft of the electricity supply.

12.7.3 *Squatters' Rights*

The rights of squatters, because they are trespassers, are minimal. The owner of the relevant property might in certain circumstances be liable for physical injury that was reasonably foreseeable, but owners are not necessarily required to carry out any repairs.

Once squatters have been explicitly, or tacitly, accepted by the NIHE as licensees, their position is improved a little. Anyone who is paying for 'use and occupation' may argue that the executive should maintain the premises in reasonable repair. It is the practice of the NIHE in such cases to accept responsibility to maintain the premises in a 'wind and weatherproof' condition. A licensee is not, however, entitled to the procedural protections from eviction that are enjoyed by tenants, notably the right to four weeks' notice and to a court hearing before possession is recovered by the landlord.

12.8 *Grants*

The regime in relation to grants is administered by the NIHE and was substantially altered by the Housing Order 1993, which revised existing private sector grant arrangements and introduced new mandatory grants in relation to unfitness.

The most important change to the grants regime is contained in article 47, which introduced a means test for owner-occupiers and tenants. The Order also lays down conditions that must be met before an application for a grant will be considered, for example that a property be at least ten years old (article 41).

Restrictions have been introduced by the 1993 Order governing when the NIHE may award a grant and include the means test condition as well as the exclusion of certain types of dwellings from grant aid (for example where the dwelling is unfit and the NIHE does not consider that the proposed renovations would remedy the unfitness). The Order also provides that applications for grants for disabled facilities will only be met by the NIHE when it is satisfied that the work is necessary and relevant as well as reasonable and practicable in relation to the age and condition of the property (article 52). The proposed work must also, of course, facilitate access.

The NIHE is given a discretion to award a grant, provided that certain criteria are met, among which is the stipulation that the renovations are for the purposes of putting the dwelling into 'reasonable repair' (article 53). The NIHE is also empowered to impose certain conditions when awarding grants (article 56). Restrictions on the letting of grant-aided premises are also imposed (articles 57–58).

The new categories of grants are as follows:

12.8.1 *Renovation Grant*

The main aim of this grant is to remove unfitness. It is available to owner-occupiers, landlords, and some tenants, and the dwelling concerned must be at least ten years old. There is an upper limit of £50,000 for 'mandatory work', and all work should be undertaken by a warranted builder where the work costs more than £5,000. All work must in any event be completed within twelve months of approval, and contractors must provide invoices before payment.

12.8.2 Replacement Grant

Replacement grants are available both to owner-occupiers and to landlords and are aimed at dwellings in isolated rural areas where a renovation grant is inappropriate. All applications are contingent on a cost/option analysis (i.e. that the replacement of the dwelling makes economic sense), and the existing dwelling must be demolished before the balance of the grant is paid.

12.8.3 Disabled Facilities Grant

The purpose of this grant is to assist with adaptations for facilitating access by disabled occupants to and around a property. There must be a recommendation from an occupational therapist if a grant is to be obtained, and the property must meet the normal fitness standard; and there is the facility to process a renovation grant simultaneously to remedy any unfitness.

12.8.4 Minor Works Assistance

This grant is available to specified groups in financial hardship for carrying out minor repairs, improvements, or adaptations. It is available to owner-occupiers and tenants who are elderly or disabled or live in redevelopment areas. The grant itself provides five types of assistance. However, grants are limited to £1,080 per application and must not exceed £3,240 over a three-year period. One very important factor that distinguishes this grant from the others is that applications are not subject to a means test.

12.8.5 'Common Parts' Grant

This grant was introduced with the purpose of improving or repairing the common parts of a building containing more than one flat. Such grants are available to owner-occupiers and groups of tenants.

12.8.6 Repairs Grant

This is available to landlords, agents and tenants where a property is the subject of a certificate of disrepair or a public health notice. Grants are subject to a maximum of £5,500 over a ten-year period, and a percentage system operates whereby grants are awarded on a sliding scale: (*a*) 100 per cent where the NAV is less than £60, (*b*) 90 per cent where there is financial hardship or where the property supports a regulated tenancy, and (*c*) 75 per cent in all other cases.

12.8.7 Grants for Houses in Multiple Occupation

These grants provide assistance in creating houses in multiple occupation (HMOs). They may be awarded to provide missing amenities and additional toilet, bathroom and kitchen facilities, fire precautions, and means of escape from fire. It should be noted that there is a different fitness standard for houses in multiple occupation.

12.9 Further Reading

Arden, A., and Hunter, C., *Manual of Housing Law* (5th edition), London: Sweet and Maxwell 1993.

Coyle, J., and Hegarty, A., 'Housing Rights' in Brice Dickson (editor), *Civil Liberties in Northern Ireland: the CAJ Handbook* (2nd edition), Belfast: Committee on the Administration of Justice 1993.

Hadden, T., and Trimble, D., *Northern Ireland Housing Law*, Belfast: SLS Legal Publications 1986.

Hoath, David, *Public Housing Law*, London, Sweet and Maxwell, 1989.

Housing Rights Service, *Housing Rights Manual* (loose-leaf), Belfast: Housing Rights Service 1994.

Law Centre (Northern Ireland), *Information Sheets (no. 6, Private Rented Sector Housing; no. 10, Public Rented Sector Housing: Access)*, Belfast: Law Centre (Northern Ireland) 1993.

Northern Ireland Housing Executive, *The Private Rented Sector*, Belfast: NIHE 1986.

Wylie, J., *Irish Land Law* (2nd edition), Oxford: Professional Books 1986.

INDEX

Abuse, duty to prevent, 123, 127–8, 138–9. see also Child protection
Abuse of children. see Child protection
Abuse register, 123–4, 125, 127, 136–7 see also Child protection
Abuser, 241, 242, 243. see also Domestic violence
ABWOR (Assistance by way of representation), 28
Access to reports
  Access to Health Records (Northern Ireland) Order 1993, 41
  Access to Personal Files and Medical Reports (Northern Ireland) Order 1991, 41
  Data Protection Act 1984, 40
  versus confidentiality, 40–41, 117
  see also Confidentiality
Accommodation
  admission procedures for, 199–201
  of children in need
    criteria for, 201
    looked after, 201–3
    not looked after, 203–4
  of chronically sick and disabled, 197–201
  of elderly, 197–201
  legislation regarding, 184
  and nursing homes, 199, 200
  privately provided, 199–201
  and residential care homes, 199
  see also Vulnerable people
Acts. see Statutes; names of specific statutes
Adjudication Officer (AO), 259, 261, 263, 268
Adultery, 247, 248
Advice see Legal aid scheme; Lawyers
Affiliation order, 246

Affirmative action, 225, 226, 230. see also Fair Employment Acts; Religious discrimination
Alimony, 253. see also Divorce
Ancillary relief, 251
Annulment, 247, 250. see also Divorce
Anti-discrimination. see Discrimination
Appeal
  grounds for, 118
  leave to, 18
  social enquiry reports (SERs) and, 110
  see also names of specific courts
Applicant, definition of, 55
Appropriate adult
  and confidentiality, 82
  definition of, 75
  duties of,
    during charging of detainees, 87–8
    during consents to search, 85–6
    during questioning of detainees, 83
    during review of detention of detainees, 85
  notification of, at time of arrest, 81, 82
  and relationship to lawyer, 82
  role of, 75–6, 80, 81, 82, 83, 85
Approved social workers (ASWs)
  duties of, 158–60
  and guardianships, 169–70, 178–80
  legal liability of, 160
Area child protection committees (ACPCs), 125–6. see also Child protection
Arrest and detention
  caution given during, 83
  definition of, 76–7
  at designated police stations, 77
  emergency powers of, 78

299

Index

Arrest and detention *(continued)*
  extending length of, 84–5
  force used for, 77
  informed of, 77
  length of, 77, 78, 84–5
  Northern Ireland (Emergency Provisions) Act 1991 (EPA), 73–74 passim
  Photographs taken during, 87
  Police and Criminal Evidence (Northern Ireland) Order 1989 (PACE), 73, 74, 77–78, 84
  Prevention of Terrorism (Temporary Provisions) Act 1989 (PTA), 73, 74, 78, 84
  purpose of, 77
  reasonable suspicion and, 77, 78
  rights after, 74, 77, 79, 80, 81, 82, 83, 84
  search at time of, 77–8, 80, 85–7
  treatment during, 78–9
  warrantless, 77 (without warrant)
  see also Detainees; *names of specific statutes*
Arson, 77
Article 8 orders, 135, 147, 148, 149, 150, 240, 251. *see also* Children (Northern Ireland) Order 1995; Child protection
Assignment, definition of, 276. *see also* Housing
Assistance by way of representation (ABWOR), 28
Attendance centre orders, 99–100
Attorney-General, 19–20

Bail, 9
Bail hostels, 106
Balance of probabilities, definition of, 57
Barristers. *see* Lawyers
Breach. *see* Court orders; Duty of care
Breakdown of domestic relations. *see* Divorce; Domestic violence
Budgetary loans, 269. *see also* Social security benefits

Burden of proof. *see* Standards of proof; Trials

Care orders, 143–4, 147, 148, 150, 240, 252. *see also* Child protection; Divorce
Case law. *see* Common law
Cautions
  formal, defined, 90
  informal, defined, 90
  issuing of, 88, 90
  versus arrest cautions, 90
Certificate of disrepair (COD), 286–7
  see also Private rented sector housing; Housing
Child. *see* Child protection; Children
Child abuse. *see* Child protection
Child assessment order (CAO)
  accommodation under, 201
  aims of, 141
  bases for, 141
  compared with emergency protection orders, 139
  duration of, 141
  see also child protection
Child benefit, 265. *see also* Social security benefits
Child care and protection. *see* Child protection
Child protection
  abuse, definitions of, 126–7
  assessment report of, 124
  care orders and, 143–4, 147, 148, 150
  case conferences on, 123–4
  case management of
    by area child protection committees (ACPCs), 125–6
    by child protection panels, 125–6
    by the Department of Health and Social Services Guide, 120
    by directly managed units (DMUs), 120, 125, 126, 138, 182
    by health and social service boards, 120, 126, 127, 128, 131, 132
    by National Society for the Prevention of Cruelty to Children (NSPCC), 121

Index

overview of, 121–6
  by police, 120–21
  reviews of, 125–6
  stages of, 123–6
  by trusts, 120, 125, 126, 127, 128, 131, 132, 138
Child Abuse and Rape Enquiry (CARE) Unit, 121
child assessment orders (CAOs), 139, 141–2
child protection plan, 123–4
child protection register, 123–4, 125, 127, 136–7
Children and Young Persons Act (Northern Ireland) 1968, 119, 127–33
Children (Northern Ireland) Order 1995, 119, 133–52
  court orders in cases, 124
  definitions in cases, 126–7
  education supervision orders, 144–5
  emergency intervention, 123, 129–30, 139–43
  emergency orders, 123, 129, 138, 139–41
  emergency protection orders (EPOs), 139–41, 141–2
  emotional abuse, 127
  family proceedings, 147–52
  fit person orders, 131, 133
  guardians *ad litem* (GALs), 150–151
  institutional framework for, 120–21
  investigations, 123–4, 127–9, 138–9
  legislation relating to, 199–20, 127–52
  need for care, protection or control, 127–8
  neglect, 126–7
  non-emergency options, 130–33, 143–6
  offenders, 115–16
  orders under family proceedings, 147–52
  parental involvement, 123–4, 145–6
  parental rights orders, 132–3
  physical abuse, 127
  places of safety, 129
  places of safety orders, 129–30
  and police, 120–21, 128, 129, 142–3, 154
  Police and Criminal Evidence (Northern Ireland) Order 1989 (PACE), 130
  police protection, 142–3
  prevention of abuse, 138
  principles regarding, 133–7
  private law and, 133
  probation officers and, 114
  programme of action, 124–5
  public law and, 133
  recognisance, 132
  recognising abuse, 123
  recovery orders, 142
  residence orders, 147, 148, 150
  secure accommodations and, 146, 152
  sexual abuse, 127
  significant harm, definition of, 140, 141
  supervision orders, 131, 133, 138, 143–4, 147, 149–50
  suspicion of abuse, 123
  training schools
    list of, 130
    orders to, 130, 133
  voluntary reception, 132
  warrants issued, 129, 154
  welfare principle, 134–5
Child protection panel, 125–6. *see also* Child protection
Child protection plan, 123–4. *see also* Child protection
Child protection register, 123–4, 125, 127, 136–7. *see also* Child protection
Child Support Agency, 253–5
Children
  age, defined, 120
  age of criminal responsibility, 75
  compensation orders imposed on, 94
  competency of, to testify, 61, 70
  and consent to search, 85

employment of, 152–4
fines imposed on, 94
as 'juveniles', 75
licensed, 153
non-imprisonment of, 98
oath-taking ability of, 69–70
as probationers, 96
public performances by, 153
unsworn evidence of, 69
versus 'young persons', 75
videotaped interview with, 70
as witnesses, 69–70
see also Child protection
Children in need
accommodation for, 201–204
assessment of, 190–91
category of, 181
Child and Young Persons Act (Northern Ireland) 1968, 185–6, 190, 194–7, 201–204
Children (Northern Ireland) Order 1995, 184, 186, 185, 190–91
criteria for, 186
duties owed to
looked after, 196–7
not looked after, 194–5
managing property for, 206–7
see also Vulnerable people; *names of specific statutes*
Children and Young Persons Act (Northern Ireland) 1968
children in need, 194–7
duties under
generalized, 123, 127
specific
emergency, 129–30
investigation, 127–9
non-emergency, 130–33
employment of children and, 152–4
status of, 119
Children (Northern Ireland) Order 1995
Article 8 orders, 147, 148, 149, 150
assessment, children in need, 190–91
Board/Trust duties under, 195–6, 197, 201–4

care orders under, 143–4, 150
child assessment orders (CAOs) under, 139, 141–2
children at risk, 142–3
children in need category, 184, 185, 186
contact maintenance, 145–6
contact orders, 147, 148
court proceedings under, 152–4
court structure under, 133–4
criteria for children in need, 186
education supervision order, 144–5
emergency intervention under, 139–43
emergency protection orders (EPOs), 139–41
employment of children, 152–4
family assistance orders (FAOs), 149–50, 256
family proceedings, 147–52
guardians *ad litem* (GALs), 150–51, 251–2
investigations, 123, 138–9
no delay principle, 135
no order to be issued principle, 135–6
non-emergency intervention, 143–6
overview of, 133–4
parental responsibility, 136–7, 142, 143, 148
prevention of child abuse, 138
principles under, 135–6
prohibited steps orders, 147, 148–9, 251–2
provisions of, generally, 184, 185
recovery orders, 142
residence orders, 147, 148, 150, 251–2
secure accommodations, 146, 152
specific issues orders, 147, 149, 251–2
status of, 119
supervision orders, 143–4, 149, 150
welfare principles, 134–5
welfare checklist, 134–5, 137
see also Child protection

Index

Chronically sick and disabled
  accommodation of, 197–201
  assessment of, 186–7
  Chronically Sick and Disabled Persons (Northern Ireland) Act 1978, 182, 184, 185, 186, 187, 191, 192
  defined, 184
  Health and Personal Social Services (Northern Ireland) Orders, 182, 183, 184
  managing property for, 206–7
  representation for, 205–6
  services provided to, 191–2
  see also Vulnerable people
Chronically Sick and Disabled Persons (Northern Ireland) Act 1978 (CSDP78)
  assessment under, 186–7
  definitions under, 184
  scope of, 182, 184
  services, 191–2
Civil cases
  appeals from, 16–17
  relating to child protection, 119–52
  relating to child employment, 152–4
  court hearings, 16
  parties in, 55, 242
  procedures for, 16–17
  see also Court orders; *names of specific courts*
Client's access to reports. *see* Confidentiality; Lawyers; Social Workers
Cohabitants. *see* Domestic violence
Cold weather payments, 268. *see also* Social security benefits
Commission of Human Rights, 12–13, 218
Committal proceedings, 91
Committal to remand home, 91, 100
Common law, 3, 11, 166, 167
Common parts grants, 296. *see also* Housing
Community care grants, 269. *see also* Social security benefits

Community service orders
  breaches of, 97, 113
  eligibility for, 96
  functioning of, 97
  social enquiry reports and, 108, 112
Compellability of witnesses, 62, 241
Compensation orders, 94
Compensation for victims, 94, 241, 243. *see also* Domestic violence
Competency
  related to confidentiality, 43
  of witness to testify, 61, 241
Confessions
  admissibility of, 83
  and right to remain still, 83
Confidentiality
  and appropriate adults, 92
  breach of, 40
  and children, 42–3
  and competency, 43
  and defamation, 43–4
  duty of, 39
  examples of, 39–40
  of informants, 41–2
  for patients, 158
  and probation officers, 117
  refusal to testify and, 64–5
  versus access acts, 40–41
  versus client's access to reports, 40, 41, 117
  versus public interest, 49, 42
Constant attendance allowance, 271. *see also* Disablement benefits; Exceptionally severe disablement allowance; Social security benefits
Constitution, absence of, 3, 4,
Contact orders, 147, 148. *see also* Child protection
Contributory negligence, 37
Convictions
  spent, 231
  unspent, 233
  see also Ex-offenders; Rehabilitation of Ex-offenders (Northern Ireland) Order 1978
Coroner's courts. *see* Inquests

Corroboration, definition of, 69
Council of Europe, 12
County courts
　cases heard by, 16
　hierarchical position of, 14
　qualifications for, 15
　records of, 15
　structure of, 15
　see also Court orders
Court of Appeal
　anti-discrimination decisions of, 214, 216, 217,220, 228, 229
　hierarchical position of, 9, 12, 13
　qualifications for, 15
　social security benefit appeals to, 260
　structure of, 15
　see also Court orders
Court of Criminal Appeal, 13
Court of First Instance, 12. see also European Union
Court of Human Rights, 12. see also European Union
Court of Justice, 12, 219–20, 223, 260. see also European Union
Court orders
　affiliation, 246
　Article 8, 147, 148, 149, 150, 240, 251
　breach of, 243
　care, 143–4, 147, 148, 150, 240, 252
　child assessment (CAO), 139, 141–2
　compensation, 94
　contact, 147, 148, 251
　education supervision, 144–5
　emergency protection (EPO), 123, 129, 138, 139–41, 242
　exclusion, 147, 242
　family assistance (FAO), 149–50
　fit person, 131
　parental rights, 132–3
　personal protection, 147, 242
　prohibited steps, 147, 148–9, 251
　recovery, 142
　residence, 147, 148, 150, 251
　specific issues, 147, 149, 251
　supervision, 131, 133, 138, 143–4, 147, 149, 150, 240, 252
　training school, 130–31
　see also names of specific courts
Courts
　cases. see Civil cases; criminal cases
　in child abuse cases, 124, 129
　hierarchical structure of, 9, 13, 14 (Figure 1)
　judicial qualifications for, 14–16
　in mental disorder cases, 155–80 passim
　precedentary rules of, 9
　unified structure of, 133–4
　see also names of specific courts
Covenants, 275. see also Housing
Criminal cases
　and age of responsibility, 75
　appeals from, 17
　appropriate adult in, 75
　bail in, 91
　breach of domestic violence orders, 243
　charging of detainees in, 87–8
　involving children, 75
　court hearings, 16
　definition of, 16
　inferences in, 83
　involving mentally disordered or impaired persons, 75–6
　involving juveniles, 75
　and non-scheduled offences, 73
　offences in, 90, 241
　parties in, 55, 241
　procedures for, 17, 90–91
　prosecution of, 88–91, 241
　remand in, 91
　and scheduled offences, 73
　sentencing options in, 93–102
　involving spouses, 241
　summons in, 88
　see also Arrest and detention; Prosecution; Sentencing options' Trials
Criminal offences
　committal proceedings for, 91
　court's trying of, 90
　and domestic violence, 241

indictable, 90
sentencing for, 93–102
summary, 90
see also Criminal cases; Sentencing options
Criminal procedure, 17, 90–91. *see also* Criminal cases; Detainees; Evidence; Trials
Crisis loans, 269. *see also* Social security benefits
Cross-examination of witnesses. *see* Witnesses; Testimony
Crown Court
  compensation ordered by, 94
  and indictable offences, 90
  use of pre-trial and post-trial reports by, 110
  use of social enquiry reports by, 110
Crown Solicitor for Northern Ireland, duties, 20
Custody officer
  decision to charge, 80, 87–8
  defined, 79
  duties of, 78, 79, 80, 81, 84, 85
  search authorizations, 80
  see also Arrest and detention; Custody record
Custody record
  contents of, 80–81, 82, 84, 86, 87
  detainee's right to, 74, 79
  defined, 79
  see also Arrest and detention; custody officer

Damages, in negligence
  causation of, 37
  compensation for, 37
  loss relating to, 37
  for nervous shock, 38
  proof of, 37
  reasonable foreseeability of, 37
  remoteness of, 37
  see also Negligence
Decree *nisi*, 249, 250
Defamation
  causes of action in, 44
  and confidentiality, 43–4
  defences against, 44
  proof of, 44
  types of
    libel, 44
    slander, 44
Defence, definition of, 55
Department of Economic Development, 235, 236–7
Department of Health and Social Services (DHSS), 120, 156, 165, 172, 175, 187, 258
  see also Social security benefits
Department of Health and Social Services Boards, 120–21
Designated employments scheme, 236. *see also* Disabled Persons (Employment) Acts (Northern Ireland); Disability
Detainees
  caution given to, 83
  charging of, with offence, 87–8
  confessions given by, 82–4
  delaying in granting of rights to, 79, 80–81, 82
  fingerprinting of, 87
  limits on length of detention of, 77, 78, 84–5
  photograph of, 87
  right of
    to copy of custody record, 74, 79, 80
    to explanation of rights, 74, 77, 81–2
    against ill-treatment, 78–9
    to be informed of arrest, 77
    to be informed of reason for arrest, 77
    to interpreter, 84
    to make telephone calls, 81
    to have someone informed, 74, 80, 81
    to medical treatment, 78–9
    to presence of appropriate adult, 74
    to remain silent, 83
    to removal to designated police station, 77

to safekeeping of belongings, 80
to separate cell, 78
to a solicitor, 74, 81–2
to specified conditions, 78
to sue for false imprisonment, 77
to writing material, 81
to written notice of rights, 74
samples from, 86–7
search of, 77–8, 85–7
see also Arrest and detention
Detention at the Secretary of State's Pleasure, 22, 100
DHSS. *see* Department of Health and Social Services; Social security benefits
Diplock Courts, 17
Directly managed units (DMUs), 120, 125, 126, 138, 182. *see also* Child protection; Vulnerable people
Director of Public Prosecutions (DPP), duties of, 20, 88, 241
Disability, discrimination based on
government policy against, 233–4
government schemes against, 235–7
laws against, 234–6
and unfair dismissals, 237
see also Disabled Persons (Employment) Acts (Northern Ireland)
Disability benefits
attendance allowance 65+, 272–3
living allowance, 271–2
premiums in income support, 271
working allowance, 273
Disabled facilities grants, 296. *see also* Housing
Disabled Persons (Northern Ireland) Act 1989 (DP89), 182, 184, 187, 205–6
Disabled Persons (Employment) Acts (Northern Ireland) 1945, 1960,
aim of, 234
capital grants under, 235
and designated employments scheme, 236
and fares to work scheme, 235
provisions of, 234, 236
and quota scheme, 236
register of disabled persons under, 234–5
and sheltered placement scheme, 235
and special aids to employment scheme, 235
and unfair dismissals, 237
Disablements, definition of, 199
Disablement benefits, 270. *see also* Constant attendance allowance; Social security benefits
Discharges from criminal offences
absolute, 93
conditional
versus absolute, 93
versus suspended sentence, 93
deferred, 93
see also Sentencing options
Discrimination
based on disability, 233–7
Equal Opportunities Commission (EOC) and, 213
Equal Pay Act (Northern Ireland) 1970, 212, 222
equal pay requirements, 222–4
based on ex-offender status, 231–3
Industrial Relations (Northern Ireland) Order 1993, 220
laws against, on basis of sex,
objectives of, 212
test for, 213, 219
based on race, 237–8
based on religion, 224–30
remedies for, 221–2, 224
based on sex
direct, 213–14
in employment, 217–18
and harassment, 218–19
indirect, 214–16
permitted, 221
victimisation, 216
Sex Discrimination (Northern Ireland) Order 1976, 212–24
sources of law on, 211–12, 216, 218, 219–20, 222
sexual stereotypes and, 214
Dismas House, 105

Divorce
  alimony, 253
  care of the children and, 250, 251–2
  decree of, 246
  financial arrangements and, 252–3
  grounds for
    adultery, 248
    desertion, 248–9
    irretrievable marital breakdown, 248
    separation, 249
    unreasonable behaviour, 248
  maintenance and, 252–5
  procedures to obtain, 249–50
  statistics on, 250
Domestic relationship, breakdown of. see Domestic violence; Divorce
Domestic violence
  civil law and, 241–2
  cohabitants and, 242, 243–5, 256
  criminal law and, 241
  criminal offences and, 241
  orders regarding
    emergency, 242–3
    exclusion, 242
    personal protection, 242
  prosecution of abusers for, 241
  and reconciliation, 246
  spousal testimony regarding, 241
  unmarried and, 240, 242, 243–5, 246
  victims of
    compensation for, 241, 243
    maintenance of, 245–6
    property rights of, 243–5
    rights of occupation of, 243–5
Duty of care
  breach of
    acts constituting, 33–6
    examples of, 33–6
    omissions as, 33–6
    proof of, 33
  standard of, 36

Education and Libraries (Northern Ireland) Order 1986 (EL86), 184, 185, 204

Education and Library Board, 144–5, 152, 153, 154, 188, 189, 216
Education and supervision orders, 144–5. see also Child protection
Elderly
  accommodation of, 206
  assessment of, 187–8
  category of, 181
  lack of statutory provisions on, 184–5
  managing property of, 206–7
  representation for, 206
  services provided to, 192
  see also Vulnerable people
Emergency arrest powers. see Arrest and detention; Prevention of Terrorism Act 1989
Emergency legislation. see Police and Criminal Evidence (Northern Ireland) Order 1989; Prevention of Terrorism Act 1989
Emergency orders in child abuse cases, 123–9. see also Child protection
Emergency protection orders (EPOs)
  accommodation under, 202
  duration of, 140
  evidence for, 141
  grounds for, 139–40
  provisions of, 140
  uses of, 139
  versus place of safety order, 139
  see also Child protection
Northern Ireland (Emergency Provisions) Act 1991 (EPA), 73, 74, 80, 81–2, 83, 84–5
Emotional abuse, definition of, 127. see also Child protection
Employment appeal tribunal, 214, 216
Employment for social workers
  contractual, 45
  and dismissals, 47
  duties of, 46
  rights of, 46–7
Enabling acts, 6
Equal Opportunities commission (EOC)
  aims of, 213
  powers of, 23, 213, 221

Equal pay
  equal value work
    defined, 223
    legal claims under, 223
  equivalent work, 223
  laws governing, 222
  like work, 222
  remedies, 224
  see also Discrimination; Equal Pay Act (Northern Ireland) 1970
Equal Pay Act (Northern Ireland) 1970
  anti-discrimination and, 212, 217
  equal value work
    defined, 223
    legal claims under, 223
  equivalent work under, 223
  and European Union laws, 222
  like work defined, 222
  see also Discrimination; Equal pay
Equivalent work 223
European Commission of Human Rights, 12–13, 218
European Community (EC). see European Union (EU)
European Court of First Instance, 12. see also European Union
European Court of Human Rights, 12
European Court of Justice, 12, 219–20, 223, 260
European Union
  Court of First Instance, 12
  Court of Human Rights, 12
  Court of Justice, 12, 219–20, 223, 260
  decisions, 11
  directives, 11
  laws of
    discrimination, 212, 237–8
  Francovich action enforcing, 12
  sources of, 3, 4, 11
  regulations, 11
Eviction, 283–4. see also Private rented sector housing; Housing
Evidence in trial
  admissibility of confessions, 83
  corroborating, 69
  detainee's silence, 83
  hearsay, 60, 66–9
  opinion as, 65–6
  relevance test for, 59
  types of
    circumstantial, 60
    direct, 60
    real, 61
  use of notes as, 65
  see also Trials; Hearsay; Witnesses
Examination of witnesses. see Witnesses; Testimony
Exceptionally severe disablement allowance, 271. see also Disablement benefits; Constant attendance allowance; Social security benefits
Ex-offenders
  convictions of
    spent, 231
    unspent, 233
  discrimination against, 231–3
  occupations excepted, 232
  Rehabilitation of Offenders (Northern Ireland) Order 1978, 231
  rehabilitation period for, 231–2
  remedies for, 232–3
Expert witness
  giving opinion, 60, 66
  qualification as, 66
  see also Witnesses; Testimony
Extern, definition of, 105

Fair employment Acts
  affirmative action, 225, 226, 230
  'considerably smaller portion' and, 228–9
  discrimination
    defined, 227, 228
    test for, 228
Fair Employment Agency, 224–5, 226
Fair Employment Commission (FEC), 23, 226, 230
Fair Employment Tribunal, 226–7, 229–30

impact of, 224–5
  1989 version, 225–6
  1976 version, 224
  remedies under, 229–30
  scope of, 227
  see also Discrimination; Religious discrimination
Fair Employment Commission (FEC), 23, 226, 230. see also Fair Employment Acts; Religious discrimination
Fair Employment Tribunal, 226–7, 229–30. see also Fair Employment Acts; Religious discrimination
Family, definition of, 195
Family assistance orders (FAOs), 149–50. see also Child protection
Family credit, 266–7. see also Social security benefits
Family Division. see High Court
Family proceedings
  definition of, 147
  orders under, 147–52
  see also Child protection
Family Proceedings Court, 147–52. see also Child protection
Fares to work scheme, 235. see also Disability' Disabled Persons (Employment) Acts
Financial aid for legal services
  Assistance by way of representation (ABWOR), 28
  civil legal aid scheme, 28
  eligibility for, 27, 28, 29
  fixed-fee interview scheme, 27
  legal advice and assistance scheme, 27
  and sex discrimination cases, 221
  see also Financial aid scheme
Fines, 94
Fingerprints. see Searches
Fit person, 100, 131
Fit person orders, 100, 131, 133
Funeral payments, 268. see also Social security benefits

Grants
  common parts, 296
  disabled facilities, 296
  for houses in multiple occupation, 297
  and Housing Order 1993, 295
  minor works assistance, 296
  renovation, 295
  repairs, 296
  replacement, 296
  see also Housing
Green form scheme. see Financial aid for legal services
Guardians ad litem (GALs), 150–51. see also Child protection
Guardianship
  mental disorders and, 169–70, 178
  orders of, 101

Handicapped persons. see Mentally ill and handicapped
Harassment, 218–19. see also Discrimination
Health and Personal Social Services (Northern Ireland) Orders
  1994 (HPSS94), 155, 182
  1991 (HPSS91), 182, 183, 184
  1972 (HPSS72), 182, 183, 184, 187, 191, 192, 197–8, 203
  see also Mental disorders; Vulnerable people
Health and Social Service Boards
  assessments done by, 186–91, 192–3
  child protection handbook, 120
  duties of, 120–81 passim, 182–3, 185–7, 189, 194–7, 200–207
  establishment of, 120, 181–2
  obligations on
    absolute, 182–3, 195–6
    conditional, 182–3, 195–6
    discretionary, 182–3
  powers of, 183
  see also Child protection; Mentally ill and handicapped

Health and Social Service Trusts
  assessments done by, 186–91
  duties of, 120–81 pasim, 182–3, 185–7, 194–8, 200–207
  establishment of, 120, 181–2
  functions of, 182
  liability of, 182
  obligations on
    absolute, 182–3
    conditional, 182–3
    discretionary, 182–3
  powers of, 183
  purchaser-provider split, 182
  see also child protection; Mentally ill and handicapped
Hearsay
  admissibility under Children Order 1995, 68
  compiled records exception to, 67–8
  examples of, 67–8
  exceptions for admissibility of, 60, 67–8, 141, 151, 261
  explained, 66–7
  inadmissibility of, 60
  and video-recorded interviews, 68
  in wardship hearings, 68
High Court
  appeals to, 18, 260
  cases heard by, 16, 245
  divisions of
    Chancery, 13–14
    Family, 13–14
    Queen's Bench, 13–14
  and domestic violence cases, 245–6
  hierarchical position of, 9, 13
  qualifications for, 15
  and social security benefit appeals, 260
  structure of, 15
Home circumstances report, 115
Homelessness
  acquiescence to, 291
  and children, 290
  deemed, 290
  definition of, 288, 289, 290
  and families, 289–90
  and housing schemes
    non-statutory, 288
    statutory, 289
  and infectious intentionality, 291–2
  intentional, 291–2
  NIHE determination of, 292
  and priority needs, 290–91
  and temporary accommodation, 290
  threatened with, 290
  see also Housing
Hospital admissions
  for assessment, 161–5
  compulsory, 160–69
  conveyance for, 162–3
  detention in, 163, 165–6
  grounds for, 161–2
  minors and, 164–5
  and treatment, 166–8
  see also Mental disorder
Hospital orders, 101. see also Interim hospital orders
Hostels
  bail, 106
  probation, 106
Hostile witness, 58. see also Witnesses; Testimony
House of Lords
  hierarchical position of, 9, 14
  qualifications for, 14
  and sexual harassment, 218, 219
  and social security benefits appeals, 260
Houses in multiple occupation grants, 297. see also Housing
Housing
  assignment, definition of, 276
  covenants, definition of, 276
  and homelessness, 288–92
  landlord, definition of, 275–6, 285–6
  laws on
    Housing Executive Act (Northern Ireland) 1971, 276
    Housing Orders
      1981, 277
      1983, 277, 278, 279
      1992, 280

lease, definition of, 275–6
lessee, definition of, 275–6
lessor, definition of, 275–6
licensee, definition of, 275–6, 294
Northern Ireland Housing Executive (NIHE), 276–95 passim
private rented sector, 281–4
private tenant, definition of, 281
public sector, 276–81
and repairs, 284–8, 296
tenant, definition of, 275–6
Housing benefits, 269–70. *see also* Social security benefits
Housing Executive Act (Northern Ireland) 1971, 276
Housing Order 1993, grants under, 295–7. *see also* Grants; Housing

Immunity, 64–5
Impairments. *see* Mentally ill and handicapped
Incapacity benefit, 264. *see also* Social security benefits
Income support, 267–8. *see also* Social security benefits
Indemnification of employer by employee, 36, 118
Independent Commission for Police Complaints, 24. *see also* Police
Industrial industry benefits, 270. *see also* Social security benefits
Industrial preference, 270. *see also* Social security benefits
Inquests, 18
Inquiries, 18
Intentional homelessness, 291–2. *see also* Homeless
Interim hospital orders, 102
International agreements, 10, 11, 12, 212
Interpreter
  appropriate adult's right to, 84
  detainee's right to, 84
  role of, 84
Involuntary hospital admissions. *see* Hospital admissions

Judges
  functions of, 3, 15
  laws made by, 3, 8
  legal interpretations by, 9, 10, 11
  precedents by, 9
  qualifications for, 14, 16
  as sources of law, 8–9
Judicial Committee of the Privy Council, 9
Judicial review. *see* Appeal
Judicial separation
  decree of, 246
  legal ramifications of, 246–7
  procedures to obtain, 249–51
  statistics on, 250
  see also Divorce
Juvenile Court
  child abuse cases and, 124, 128, 130–136 passim
  emergency protection orders and, 141
  social enquiry reports (SERs), acceptance of, 110
Juveniles
  appropriate adults and, 75, 80, 81
  attendance centers and, 99–100
  cautions given to, 90
  charging of, 87–8
  community service orders and, 96
  compensation orders imposed on, 94
  convicted of murder, 100
  definition of, 75
  fit person orders and, 100
  imprisonment of, 98
  interview of, 82
  length of detention of, 85
  places of safety for, 88
  presumption of status as, 76
  as probationers, 96
  recognisance as security for, 94–5
  remand of, 91
  remand homes and, 100
  searches of, 85–6
  social enquiry reports of, 108
  supervision of, 99

and suspended sentences, 97
training schools and, 98–9
treatment of, at arrest, 79, 81
versus 'young offenders', 75

Landlord, definition of, 275–6. see also Housing Law
anti-discrimination, 211–39
conflicts of, 3–4
  by European Union, 3–4, 11
  by judges, 3, 8
locating, 5–6, 8–9
non-laws, 8
  by Parliament, 3
precedents involving, 9
private, definition of, 133
public, definition of, 133
sources of, 4–6, 11
types of, 3, 4
Lawyers
complaints against, 26
duties of, 25–6
financial assistance with, 27–30
and relationship with appropriate adult, 82
service on social security tribunals, 358–9
suits against, 26
in trial, 62–3
see also Financial aid for legal services; Legal Aid scheme
Learning disabilities, people with
assessment of, 188–91
category of, 181
definition of, 185
Education and Libraries (Northern Ireland) Order 1986, 184, 185
managing property for, 206–7
special educational needs of, 185, 190, 192–3
see also Vulnerable people
Lease, definition of, 275–6. see also Housing
Legal advice and assistance scheme, 27. see also Financial aid for legal services; Legal aid scheme

Legal aid scheme
civil cases, 28–9
criminal cases, 29–30
divorce cases, 250
eligibility for, 28, 29
religious discrimination cases, 227
services available under, 29, 30
social security benefits appeal cases, 260
sex discrimination cases, 221
Legal duty of care. see Duty of care
Legal report writing. see Reports for court
Legal services
financial assistance with, 26–7
need for in equal pay cases, 224
types of, 24–5
see also Lawyers
Legislation
child abuse, 119–20
definition of, 3
emergency, 74
excepted matter, 4, 7
European Union, 11
orders in council procedure for, 4, 7
ordinary, 74
primary, 4, 5–6
reserved matter of, 7
secondary, 4, 6
transferred matter of, 4, 7
see also statutes
Lessees, definition of, 275–6. see also Housing
Lessor, definition of, 276. see also Housing
License to perform, 153. see also Children
Licensees
definitions of, 116, 275–6
supervision of, 116
see also Housing; Probation officers
Life Sentence Review Board (LSRB), 22, 100–101, 115
Like work, definition of 222. see also Discrimination
Lord Chancellor, duties of 19, 134

Lord Chief Judge, duties of, 15, 100, 173

MacBride principles, 225. *see also* Religious discrimination
McDermott Committee, 155, 163
Magistrate's Courts
    cases heard by, 16–17, 85, 245
    committal proceedings and, 90–91
    compensation orders by, 94
    domestic violence cases in, 245–6
    fines ordered by, 94
    hierarchical position of, 14
    justices of the peace (JPs) on, 15
    qualifications for, 15–16
    residential magistrates (RMs) on, 15, 17
    reviews of detention period by, 85
    social enquiry reports (SERs)
        use of, 108
        acceptance of, 110
    and summary offences, 90
Maintenance, 253–5. *see also* Divorce
Marriage, termination of
    by annulment, 247
    by divorce, 246
    by judicial separation, 246–7
    see also Divorce
Master and Office of Care and Protection, 172–3, 174–5
Masters, definition of, 19
Maternity allowance, 264. *see also* Statutory maternity pay; social security benefits
Maternity payments, 268. *see also* Social security benefits
Medical staff
    disclosure to patients by, 168
    hearings, 178–80
    as Part IV doctors, 157, 166, 177
    as Part II doctors, 157, 163, 165, 166
    as responsible medical officers (RMOs), 157, 163, 165, 166–7
Mental disorder
    approved social worker's role in, 158–60

Boards, 155, 156, 172, 175
    definition of, 157–8
Department of Health and Social Services, 156
disclosure, 168
discrimination based on, 163–4
duties of authorities as to, 156–7
guardianships and, 169–70, 178
hospital admission of
    for assessment, 161–5
    compulsory, 160–69
    conveyance for, 162–3
    grounds for, 161–2
    minors and, 164–5
hospital detention of, 163, 165–6
and mental handicap, 157
and mental impairment, 157
nearest relative hierarchy for, 159
Northern Ireland Mental Health Commission, 156, 175, 176–7
and patient's property and affairs, 172–6
police and, 171–2
social security claims and, 175–6
social workers's role and, 156–7, 158–61
statutes governing
    Health and Personal Social Services (Northern Ireland) Order 1994, 155
    Mental Health (Northern Ireland) Order 1986, 155
    Mental Health Regulations (Northern Ireland) 1986, 155
    Mental Health Review Tribunal, 177–80
    Order 109, 155
treatment of, 166–8
Trusts, 155, 156, 172, 175
visitors and, 173–4
warrants in cases of, 171

Parental responsibility, 136–7. *see also* Child protection; Children (Northern Ireland) Order 1995
Parental rights order, 132–3. *see also* Child protection

Parliament
  abolition of Northern Ireland's, 4
  devolved, 4
  enacting legislation, 4, 6
  European, 11
  intent of, 10
  law-making function of, 3, 4
  Stormont, 4
  Westminster, 4.
  see also Legislation; Statutes
Parliamentary laws, 3
Parliamentary sovereignty, 3, 4
Parties in lawsuits
  civil, 55, 242
  criminal, 55, 241
  defendant, 55, 241
  petitioner, 55, 242, 248, 249
  plaintiff, 55, 241
  respondent, 55, 242, 248, 249
  see also Civil cases; Criminal cases
Pay, definition of, 222
Penal establishments
  custody in, 97
  and juveniles, 98
  list of, 21
  and probation officers, 114–16
  regulation of, 21–2
  young offenders centre, 21
Peritus, definition of, 66
Perjury, 66
Person in need, definition of, 198
Personal injury *see* Negligence
Physical abuse, definition of, 127. *see also* Child protection
Places of safety
  compared with emergency protection orders, 139
  list of, 129
  orders, 129
  removal to, 172
  see also Child protection
Police
  cautions issued by, 88, 90
  Child Abuse and Rape Enquiry (CARE) Units, 121
  and child abuse cases, 120–21, 202
  and domestic violence cases, 241, 243
  duties of, 20
  and mentally disordered cases, 171–2
  offences charged by, 88, 241
  suits against, 21
  watchdog commission for, 24
Police and Criminal Evidence (Northern Ireland) Order 1989 (PACE)
  arrest under, 77
  arrestable offences under, 77
  child abuse cases under, 130
  detention, treatment and questioning by police under, 74, 78–9, 80, 81, 84, 87
  identifications by police under, 74, 85
  length of detention under, 77, 84–5
  non-arrest under, 77
  non-arrestable offences under, 77
  overview of, 73–4
  right of detainees under, 74–85
  see also Arrest and detention
Police Authority for Northern Ireland, 29
Political opinion, discrimination based on. *see* Religious discrimination
Post-sentence assessments, 115
Post-trial reports. *see* Social enquiry reports
Powers of attorney, 172–5, 207
Precedents, doctrine of
  definition of, 9
  obiter dicta in, 9
  ratio decidendi in, 9
Pregnancy discrimination, 219–21
Presumptions in trials
  irrebuttable, 57–8
  rebuttable, 57–8, 75
Pre-trial reports. *see* Social enquiry reports
Prevention of Terrorism (Temporary Provisions) Act 1989 (PTA)
  Detention, treatment, and arrest by police under, 74, 78–9, 80, 81, 84
  emergency arrest power under, 78

identification by police under, 74, 85
overview, 73–4
terrorism, definition under, 78
see also Arrest and detention
Primary legislation
definition of, 4
locating, 5–6
treaties as, 11
see also Legislation
Principles regarding child abuse, 134–7. *see also* Child protection
Prison Link, 105
Prisoners
parole of, 22
rehabilitation of, 22
sentencing of, 22
see also Sentencing options
Prisons. *see* Penal establishments
Private rented sector housing
breach of duty to repair, 285–8
certificate of disrepair (COD), 286–7
and rent setting, 282–3
repairs and, 285–6
squatters and, 294
tenancies under
regulated, 281–2, 285–6, 286–7
restricted, 281–2, 285
unprotected, 281–2, 287–8
tenant's rights under
eviction process, 283–4
freedom from harassment, 283
rent book, 282
succession, 284
unfit for habitation and, 286–8
see also Housing
Privilege
as a basis to not testify, 64–5
as a defence to defamation, 44
Probation Board for Northern Ireland (PBNI)
bail hostels maintained by, 106
and child abuse cases, 114
composition of, 104
guidelines on confidentiality, 117
liability of, for staff actions, 118
and licensees, 116
number of clients supervised by, 105
and prisons, 105
probation hostels maintained by, 106
and schedule I offenders, 115–16
scope of, 105
statutory basis for, 103, 104
and voluntary organizations, 105
see also Probation service; Probation officers
Probation hostels, 106. *see also* Probation Board for Northern Ireland
Probation officers
and child protection cases, 114
and community service orders, 97, 112–13
confidentiality of, 117
court attendance of, 111
disciplinary proceedings against, 118
duties of, 95–6, 103, 107, 110, 11, 113
hierarchy of, 104
and home circumstances reports, 115
and liability for injury or damage, 117–18
licensees and, 116
necessity for appearance at court hearings of, 113
as officers of the court, 106, 108
and perceived bias, 109
and post-sentence assessments, 115
and pre-release schemes, 116–17
prison-based, 114–16
and probation orders, 111–12
qualifications for, 106
and social enquiry reports, 107–11
social workers and, 113
as specialised social workers, 106
standards for, 103

statutory references to, 104, 107
and supervision order, 99, 113
as supervisors, 107, 111, 112, 116
welfare officers and, 113
Probation orders
and age of probationers, 96
breach of, 96
conditions of, 95, 111–12
definition of, 95
and social enquiry reports, 108
Probation service
hierarchy of, 104
for Northern Ireland compared with Great Britain, 103–4
preparation of social enquiry reports, by 107–11
Ramoan orders and, 106.
see also Probation Board for Northern Ireland; Probation officers
Professional responsibility
confidentiality and, 39–44
duties and obligations, 32–6
people to whom duties are owed, 33–6
Prohibited steps orders, 147, 148–9. see also Child protection
Proof beyond all reasonable doubt, defined, 57
Prosecution
bail in, 91
committal proceedings by, 91
definition of, 55
and domestic violence cases, 241
process in criminal cases, 89 (Figure 2)
remand in, 91
see also Criminal cases
Protection of children. see Child protection
Public interest immunity, 64–5
Public sector housing
allocation of, 277–8
exchanging tenancies and, 279
and non-payment of rent, 280
and Northern Ireland Housing Executive (NIHE), 276–81
repairs in, 284–5
secure tenancies and, 278–9
setting of rent in, 280
squatters and, 293–4
and tenant's charter, 281
and tenant's right to buy, 280
transferring tenancies in, 279

Questioning. see Testimony; Witnesses
Quota scheme, 236. see also Disability; Disabled Persons (Employment) Acts

Racial discrimination, 237–8. see also Discrimination
Rape, 77
Ratio decidendi (ratio), 9
Reasonable suspicion to arrest, 77, 78
Recognisance
in child abuse cases, 132
defined, 94
for juveniles, 94–5
and surety, 94
Reconciliation, 246. see also Domestic violence
Recorders. see County courts
Recovery orders, 142
Register of disabled persons, 234–5. see also Disability
Registration of rights of occupation, 244
Rehabilitation, 231–2. see also Ex-offenders
Rehabilitation of Offenders (Northern Ireland) Order 1978
convictions under
spent, 231
unspent, 233
occupations excepted under, 232
purpose of, 231
rehabilitation periods under, 231–2
remedies under, 232–3
Relationships, breakdown of, 240–55. see also Divorce; Domestic violence; Judicial separation

Religious discrimination
  affirmative action and, 225, 226, 230
  against Catholics, 224
  and 'considerably smaller portion', 228–9
  definition of, 227, 228
  Fair Employment Acts, 1976 and 1989, 224–30
  Fair Employment Tribunal, 226–7
  MacBride principles and, 225
  remedies for, 229–30
  test for, 228
  types of
    direct, 227–8
    indirect, 228–9
    permitted, 229
    victimisation, 229
  see also Discrimination
Remand
  homes, 91, 100
  procedure for, 91
Remand homes
  commitment to, 91, 100
  versus training school order, 100
Renovation grants, 295. see also Housing
Rent book, 282. see also Housing; Private rented sector housing
Repairs grant, 296. see also Housing
Replacement grants, 296. see also Housing
Report-writing for court
  conclusions in, 54
  due diligence in, 53–4
  form of, 52, 53, 54
  home circumstances reported in, 115
  information for
    accuracy of, 52
    completeness of, 52
    relevance of, 52
  length of, 53
  oral testimony and, 57, 64
  post-sentence assessment, 115
  post-trial, 110
  pre-trial, 110
  purpose of, 51
  and social enquiry reports, 107–11
  style of, 53
  at trial, 57, 64, 65
  versus witness statements, 55
Residence order, 147, 148, 150. see also Child protection
Resident magistrates. see Magistrate's courts
Residential care homes, 199. see also Accommodation; Vulnerable people
Residential medical officer, duties of, as to restriction orders, 102
Respondent, definition of, 44
Restriction orders, 101–2
retirement pensions
  category A, 265–6
  category B, 265–6
  state earnings related scheme, 265–6
Rule-making authorities, 6

Samples. see Searches
Schedule I offenders, 115–16
Scheduled offences, 73, 90
Searches
  authorization for, 80
  consent to, 85–6
  and fingerprints, 87
  intimate, definition of, 85–6
  non-intimate, definition of, 86
  and photographs, 87
  samples taken during
    intimate, 86
    non-intimate, 86–7
  strip-, 80
  at time of arrest, 77–8, 80
  see also Arrest and detention; Detainees
Secondary legislation
  enacting, 6
  by the European Union, 11
  locating, 4, 8
  statutory instruments, 6
  see also Legislation

Secretary of State for Northern Ireland
  duties of, 19, 85
  detention at the pleasure of, 22, 100–101
  and licensees, 116
  and mentally disordered people, 156
  and permitted discrimination, 229
  probation board and, 104
  restriction orders and, 101–2
  review of detention period by, 85
  review of juvenile's detention by, 98
Secure accommodations, 146, 152. *see also* Child protection
Self-incrimination, 64
Semi-official documents, 8
Sentencing options
  attendance centers, 99–100
  community service orders, 96–7
  community-based disposals, 95–7
  detention at the pleasure of the Secretary of State, 100–101
  discharges, 93
  fit person orders, 100
  guardianship orders, 101
  hospital orders, 101
  immediate custody, 97
  for juvenile offenders, 98–101
  monetary penalties, 93–4
  overview of, 92 (Figure 3)
  probation orders, 95–6
  remand homes, 100
  and social enquiry reports
    impact on, 109–10
    mandatory versus discretionary, 108
  supervision orders, 99
  suspended sentence, 97
  training schools, 98–9
Sex discrimination
  in employment, 217–18
  and Equal Opportunities Commission, 213
  as harassment, 218–19
  laws
    objectives of, 212
    test for, 213, 219
  and sexual stereotypes, 214
  types of
    direct, 213–14
    indirect, 214–16
    permitted, 221
    victimisation, 216
  see also Discrimination; Sex Discrimination (Northern Ireland) Order 1976
Sex Discrimination (Northern Ireland) Order 1976
  areas protected by, 212
  direct discrimination under, 213–14
  and employer's liability for, 219
  employment and, 217–18
  Equal Opportunities Commission (EOC), 213
  and Equal Pay Act (Northern Ireland) 1970, 212
  extent of protection under, 216–17
  group protected by, 212
  indirect discrimination under, 214–16
  permitted discrimination under, 221
  and pregnancy, 219–21
  remedies under, 221–22
  see also Discrimination; Sex discrimination
Sexual abuse, definition of, 127. *see also* Child protection
Sexual stereotypes, 214. *see also* sex discrimination
Sheltered placement scheme, 235. *see also* Disability; Disabled Persons (Employment) Acts (Northern Ireland)
Significant harm, definition of, 140, 141
Social enquiry reports
  acceptance of recommendations of, 110
  community service orders and, 108
  compared with pre-trial and post-trial reports, 110
  compulsory, for juveniles, 108
  compared with progress or response to supervision reports, 109

Index

consent to, 108–109
considerations used in preparing, 107–08
content of, 107
courts requesting, 110
defined, 107
and impact on sentencing options, 109–10
presented to court, 111
prepared by welfare authority, 109
and probation orders, 108
statistics on, 108, 109
see also Report-writing for courts
Social fund, 268–9. *see also* Social security benefits
Social Security Administration, 257
Social Security Agency
 adjudication officers of, 258–9
 appeal from a decision of, 258–62
 claims made to, 257–8
 hearing involving
  child support appeals (CSATs), 259
  disability appeals (DATs), 259
  housing benefit review boards (HBRBs), 260, 270
  medical appeals (MATs), 259
  social security appeals (SSATs), 258, 259, 264, 268
  see also Social security benefits
Social security benefits
 adjudication officers and, 257–8
 and appeal tribunals, 258–62
 appeals regarding, 258–62
 attendance allowance 65+, 272–3
 budgetary loans, 269
 categories of, 262–73
 child, 265
 claims made for, 257
 cold weather payments, 268
 community care grants, 269
 constant attendance allowance, 271
 contributory, 262–73
 crisis loans, 269
 disability, 271–3

disability living allowance, 271–2
disability premiums in income support, 271
disablement, 270
entitlement to, 259, 262
exceptionally severe disablement allowance, 271
family credit, 266
funeral payments, 268
housing, 269–70
incapacity, 264
income support, 267–8
industrial injuries, 270
industrial preference, 270
law pertaining to
 the adjudication system, 257–62
 the rules of entitlement, 262–73
maternity allowance, 264
maternity payments, 268
means-tested, 262–3, 266–70
non-contributory, 262–73
non-means-tested, 262–6
overlapping, 263
'passport', 263
retirement pensions, 265
social fund, 268–9
social worker's role in, 256–7
statutory maternity pay, 265
statutory sick pay (SSP), 265
unemployment (job seeker's allowance), 263–4
widow's, 265
working allowance, 273
see also Social Security Agency
Social security claims, 175–6. *see also* Social security benefits
Social Security commissioners, 257, 260. *see also* Social Security Agency
Social Security Contributions and Benefits (Northern Ireland) Act 1992, conditions for receipt of benefits under, 257. *see also* Social security benefits

Social workers
  as appropriate adult, 74–5
  approved, 158–60, 169–70, 178–80
  and the breakdown in relationships, 240
  confidentiality of, 39–44
  in conflict with agency, 66
  definition of, xv
  as employees, 45–7
  legal actions against
    breach of statutory duty, 34
    negligence, 32–8
  and the legal system, 49–70
  and professional morality, 47–8
  and professional responsibility, 31–48
  and report-writing for court, 51–4
  role of
    in discrimination cases, 211–38
    in guardianship orders, 101, 151
    in housing issues, 275
    in mental disorder cases, 156–7, 158–60
    in social security benefit cases, 256–7, 260–62
  standard of care of, 36
  as suitably qualified person, 151
  as witnesses, 55–8, 61–6
  see also Report-writing for court; *names of individual entries*
Solicitor-General, duties of, 20
Solicitors. *see* Lawyers
SOSPs. *see* Detention at the Secretary of State's Pleasure
Special aids to employment schemes, 235. *see also* Disability; Disabled Persons (Employment) Acts
Special educational needs, 185, 190, 192–3. *see also* Learning disabilities, people with
Specific issues orders, 147, 149. *see also* Child protection
Spent convictions, 231. *see also* Ex-offenders
Squatters
  definition of, 292
  eviction of, 293–4
  property occupied by
    Northern Ireland Housing Executive's, 293–4
    privately owned, 294
  rights of, 294–5
  versus trespassers, 292
Standards of proof
  in civil cases, 57
  in criminal cases, 57
  definition of, 57
State earnings-related pension scheme (SERPS), 265–6. *see also* Social security benefits
Statutes
  commencement of, 5
  definition of, 4
  enabling, 6
  geographical extent of, 4, 6
  indexes of, xxi–xxiii, 5–6
  interpretation of, 10
  locating, 5–6, 8
  passage of, 5
  precedentary rules for, 9
  private members' bill, 4
  public general acts, 4
  summary versus indictable offences, 90
  see also Legislation; Statutory instruments; Statutory rules
Statutory duty of social workers
  absolute, 182–3
  breach of, 34
  conditional, 182–3
  discretionary, 182–3
  examples of, 34
Statutory instruments (SIs), xxv–xxx, 6
Statutory interpretation, 10
Statutory maternity pay (SMP), 264. *see also* Maternity allowance; Social security benefits
Statutory officers
  Attorney-General, 19–20
  Crown Solicitor for Northern Ireland, 20
  Director of Public Prosecutions, 20

Lord Chancellor, 19
Masters, 19
Official Solicitor, 19
Ombudsperson, 23
Secretary of State for Northern Ireland, 19
Solicitor-General, 20
watchdogs, 23–4
Statutory rules (SRs), 7
Statutory sick pay (SSP), 264. *see also* Social security benefits
Suitably qualified person, 151, 246, 250. *see also* Divorce; Domestic violence; Report-writing for courts
Summons
 charged by, 88
 versus warrant, 77
Supervision orders
 in the breakdown of relations, 240
 court appearances necessitated by, 113
 probation officers and, 113
 as sentencing options, 99
 under Children and Young Persons Act (Northern Ireland) 1968, 131, 133, 138
 under Children (Northern Ireland) Order 1995, 143–4, 149, 150
Supreme Court of Judicature of Northern Ireland
 establishment of, 13
 Order 109 of the rules of, 155
 structure of, 15
Surety, 94
Suspended sentence, 97

Tenant, definition of, 275–6. *see also* Housing
Terrorism, defined under Prevention of Terrorism Act, 78
Testimony
 of children, 69–70
 and compellability of witnesses, 62
 and competency of witnesses, 61
 cross-examination, 56
 discrediting witnesses, 56
 examination-in-chief, 55
 and hearsay, 60, 66–7
 immunity from, 64–5
 leading questions and, 55–6
 oral, versus written statement, 57, 64
 perjury, 66
 re-examination, 57
 right to remain silent, 83
 and use of notes, 65
 of a witness, 63–4
 see also Evidence; Witnesses
Theft, 77
Training school order
 legislation regarding, 130–33
 specifications of, 98–9
 versus remand home, 100
 see also Child protection
Treaties. *see* International agreements
Trials
 adversarial procedure of, 50
 committal proceedings for, 91
 evidence in, 59–61, 66–7
 juries in, 90
 lawyer's role in, 62–3
 parties in, 55
 presumptions in, 57–8
 proceedings in order of, 55–8
 question-and-answer format of, 50, 55–7
 standards of proof in, 57
 testimony in, 50
 witness in, 63–6
 witness statement in, 55
 see also Report-writing for court; Testimony; Witnesses
Tribunals
 appeal from, 18, 258–62
 child support appeal (CSAT), 259
 composition of, 17
 definition of, 17
 disability appeal (DAT), 259
 distinction from inquiries, 18
 housing benefit review boards (HBRBs), 260
 medical appeal (MAT), 259

Tribunals *(continued)*
  procedures of, 17
  qualification of, 17
  social security appeal (SSAT), 258–9

Unemployment (job seeker's allowance) benefits, 263–4. *see also* Social security benefits
Unfit for habitation, 286–8. *see also* Housing; Private rented sector housing
Unspent convictions, 233. *see also* Ex-offenders; Rehabilitation of Ex-Offenders Order 1978

Vicarious liability
  definition of, 35
  indemnity against, 36, 118
  suits alleging, 36, 118
Victims
  compensation for, 94, 241, 243
  property rights of, 243–5
  rights of occupation of, 243–5
  see also Divorce
Video-taped interviews, use of, at trial, 68. *see also* Evidence; Trials
Visitors, 173–4
Vulnerable people
  accommodation of, 184, 197–204
  children in need, 181, 190–91
  chronically sick and disabled, 181, 182, 184, 186–7, 191–2, 197–201, 205–6
  as detainees, 87
  elderly, 181, 182, 184–5, 187–8, 192, 197–201, 206
  with learning disabilities, 181, 188–90, 192–3
  legislation relating to, 183–6
  managing the property of, 206–7
  representing, 205–7
  see also names of individual entries

Ward-ship hearings, use of hearsay in, 68
Warrants
  arrest without, 77
  in child abuse cases, 129
  in mental disorder cases, 171
  versus summons, 77
Welfare checklist, 135, 137. *see also* Child protection; Children (Northern Ireland) Order 1995
Welfare principle, 134–5. *see also* Child protection; Children (Northern Ireland) Order 1995
Widow's benefits, 265. *see also* Social security benefits
Widow's payment, 265. *see also* Social security benefits
Witnesses
  children as, 69–70
  compellability of, 62
  competency of, 61
  cross-examination of, 56
  demeanor of, 65
  discrediting of, 56
  examination of, 55
  expert, 60, 66
  and hearsay, 60, 66–7
  hostile, 58
  perjury, 66
  and recommendations for testifying, 63–4
  re-examination of, 57
  use of notes by, 65
  written statement of, 55
  see also Testimony; Trials

Young offenders
  and consent to search, 85
  and custodial sentences, 97
  definition of, 75
  versus 'juveniles', 75
Young persona
  compensation orders imposed on, 94
  definition of, 75
  fines imposed on, 94
  imprisonment of, 98
  remand of, 91
  versus 'children', 75
  versus 'juveniles', 75